HOMO SEXU ALITY

HOMO SEXU ALITY

Charles W. Socarides, M.D.

NEW YORK • JASON ARONSON • LONDON

I dedicate this book to
Richard, Daphne, Alexandra, and Charles

ACKNOWLEDGMENTS

It is impossible to thank individually all those who have contributed to this book. I owe a profound debt of gratitude to a large number of psychoanalysts whose work laid the foundations from which my own could evolve.

My patients must remain anonymous, but to them I owe special thanks for their persistence and endurance in attempting an alleviation of their condition, for their courage, and for their trust in the psychoanalytic process. The challenge and fulfillment have proven to be equal in measure for both analyst and patient. have proven to be equal measure for both analyst and patient.

Finally, and above all I must thank my wife, Barbara Bonner Socarides for her patient listening to endless drafts of this manuscript, for her invaluable suggestions and her keen editorial skills, as well as for her encouraging insistence on increasing the clarity of its contents. With her collaboration, the manuscript was brought to fruition.

CONTENTS

• Theoretical Features of Male Homosexuality During Adolescence 183 • Theoretical Features of Female Homosexuality During Adolescence 187)

Part II: Clinical

PREFACE

Ten years have passed since the publication of my original work on homosexuality, *The Overt Homosexual* (1968*). Now out of print, it still remains the only work under single authorship to present a comprehensive, systematized, and integrated psychoanalytic approach to both male and female homosexuality, reviewing the major psychoanalytic literature on the subject and covering the entire range of the disorder: etiology, theoretical considerations, psychoanalytic case studies, and therapy.

In a sense, however, that book proved only the beginning. During the intervening years further clarifications and distinctions have begun to take on their full meaning. This volume presents the evolution of my present views.

In the intervening years I have been privileged to treat psychoanalytically and see in consultation an increasing number of homosexual patients, as well as those with other sexual deviations. Refinement of my own theoretical and clinical understanding could take place only against a backdrop of advances in psychoanalytic knowledge, particularly in the areas of the ego-pathology of the narcissistic neuroses, the pathology of internalized object relations, and research into the earliest infant-mother relationship describing the nature of the earliest psychic functioning. Our understanding of homosexuality can only be enriched when viewed not only from the point of view of the psychology of the drives, their vicissitudes and defenses, but also from a more thorough application of concepts derived from the psychology of the ego and from the psychology of the self.

This present volume consists of (1) a complete revision of all the material in *The Overt Homosexual,* as well as corrections of any past errors, misstatements, or misunderstandings. In this connection I wish to express my appreciation to several scholarly reviews of the former volume which called attention to the areas which required further clarification and exposition, e.g., Wideman (1974), Friedman (1969), and Berliner (1971); (2) an expansion of all previous theoretical concepts and clinical material presented in the former volume, as well as an introduction and elucidation of new theoretical constructs; (3) a review of the major psychoanalytic literature published in the past decade, both that dealing directly with homosexuality and that which has been vital to my current understanding of it; (4) additional chapters dealing with crucial aspects of the problem, e.g., disturbances of gender role formation (sexual identity), the problem of aggression, schizo-homosexual acting out, and the issue of ego-syntonicity; (5) a systematized widely expanded, and vitally needed new section on the psychoanalytic therapy of homosexuality; and (6) a comprehensive chart of the homosexualities, their differentiating criteria and therapeutic implications.

chart of the homosexualities, their differentiating criteria and therapeutic implications.

* *The Overt Homosexual* was first published in 1968 by Grune and Stratton and in 1970 by Curtis Books and reissued in 1972 by Jason Aronson Inc. It was translated into French (Payot, 1970) and German (Suhrkamp Verlag, 1971).

Part I
THEORETICAL

Chapter 1
INTRODUCTION

This book evolved from the very beginning of my training in psychoanalysis. In the late 1940s and early 1950s homosexuality had still to be comprehended, and it was unusual for clinics to accept homosexual patients. They were "too difficult" and the prognosis too uncertain. Little information was offered the neophyte by his teachers, many practitioners being unwilling to take on homosexual patients for psychoanalysis because it was generally believed unrewarding to treat someone who was "satisfied" with his condition, albeit a perversion.

If little were known about the male homosexual, even less was known about the female. Several senior analysts informed me that they had seen only one or two female homosexual patients in their entire practice and then for only short periods of time. Except for the works of Helene Deutsch, Marjorie Brierley, Ernest Jones, Sandor Lorand, and Gustav Bychowski (plus a good deal of scattered data elsewhere in the literature), the presentation of detailed material was meager. Two of the most valuable papers on the subject were written before 1930: Hanns Sachs's "On the Genesis of Sexual Perversions" (1923) and Raymond de Saussure's

"Homosexual Fixations in Neurotic Women" (1929). I have arranged for their translation into English and have included them in the appendix to this volume.

I felt handicapped by the lack of information and the absence of detailed clinical case histories. The scattered psychoanalytic data I could track down were not sufficiently organized to be meaningful in my training. How could it be that a widespread emotional disorder of such striking dimension—a symptom picture which involves such a radical change in human relationships—had never been subjected to rigorous psychoanalytic investigation?

The first few homosexual patients I saw seemed to respond well to the psychoanalytic method, and I resolved to begin the collection and compilation of all available scientific findings on the subject of male and female homosexuality.

In 1958, at my suggestion, the American Psychoanalytic Association conducted its first panel on the clinical and therapeutic aspects of overt male homosexuality, for which I was appointed reporter. This report was published in 1959; the research activities and deliberations connected with it were surpassed only by those required for a companion panel on the overt female homosexual two years later. The conferences whetted my eagerness to pursue the answers to the problem of homosexuality—its origins, manifestations, and treatment methods.

As a young analyst I had become fully acquainted with the formal literature on homosexuality and was perplexed by the uncertainties of causation, treatment, and outcome. As my experience deepened and my private practice expanded, I began to focus on all aspects of this problem, as well as others in the realm of sexual development and its vicissitudes. More and more I began to observe recurrent patterns in homosexuality, however unique each patient's family background, personal endowment, and clinical picture seemed. Certain features became consistently evident and I began to formulate an etiology, developmental theory, and treatment techniques which proved effective in alleviating the major difficulties these patients suffered as a result of their sexual deviation. There is at present sufficient evidence that in a majority of cases homosexuality can be successfully treated by psychoanalysis, or at least that its symptoms and suffering can be greatly alleviated. Persuasion techniques, milieu therapy, and drug prescription cannot possibly eliminate a symptom so deeply embedded in the psyche; neither can homosexuality be successfully treated by suggestion and supportive measures. Since homosexuality is not organic in etiology, hormonal therapy and forms of surgical treatment are obviously contraindicated, as they would only make the situation worse.

This book is not only a compendium of the accumulated psychoanalytic knowledge on the problem as well as a presentation of the author's clinical experience and observations, but also presents a definitive theory as to the origin of homosexuality, the mechanisms involved in its development, and the procedures most effective in its treatment.

Homosexuality has been mislabeled as impulse neurosis, psychopathic personality, a form of addiction, a psychosis, a neurosis, a "transitional neurosis." In essence we are confronted by a condition which baffled clinical investigators attempting to determine its etiology. Of all the symptoms of emotional origin which serve simultaneously as defenses, homosexuality is unique in its capacity to use profound psychic conflicts and struggles to attain, for limited intervals, a pseudoadequate equilibrium and pleasure reward (orgasm), often permitting the individual to function, however marginally and erratically.

This neutralization of conflict allows the growth of certain ego-adaptive elements of the personality, and the homosexual may therefore have appeared not ill at all to others except for the masquerade in his sexual life. As a physician, as an individual sharing in the welfare and distress of mankind, and as a specialist in behavioral disorders, it is my hope that with publication of this book other psychoanalysts will undertake increasingly detailed studies of homosexuality so that in time this disturbance might be fully understood.

Over a hundred years ago, in 1844, the forerunner of the American Psychiatric Association, then known as the Association for Medical Superintendents of American Institutions for the Insane, was created. It undertook to explore nervous and mental disease on the basic premise that these were medical illnesses with a causation, clinical picture, and probable therapy which could be learned and taught by properly trained physicians. The prejudices, uncertainties, misinformation, and vested interests which have impeded our scientific understanding of homosexuality are similar to the problems once facing the first practitioners of psychiatry in this country and elsewhere.

The homosexual often asks if there is not some genetic or hormonal factor, innate or inborn, which accounts for his condition. Homosexuality, the choice of an object of the same sex for orgastic satisfaction, is not innate. There is not connection between sexual instinct and the choice of sexual object in man. Such an object choice is a learned, acquired behavior; there is no genetic or hormonal propensity toward the choice of one sex over the other. However, the *male-female design* is taught to the child from birth and is culturally ingrained through the marital order. This design is anatomically determined, as it derives from cells which evolved phylogenetically into organ systems and finally into two classes of individuals reciprocally adapted to each other. This is the the evolutionary development of human beings. The male-female design is perpetually maintained, and only overwhelming fear can disturb or divert it.

Homosexuals often express doubt about whether their condition can ever be reversed. The homosexual who attempts to extricate himself from a community of homosexuals is often tagged a "traitor," one who threatens to invalidate their claims of having been born that way and being "special." It is not uncommon for homosexuals to warn any individual attempting treatment that any change could at best prove only superficial.

A homosexual himself reported:

I've got to get this homosexual monkey off my back, I just frankly can't live with it. I must either extinguish it, if I can, or maybe by religion extinguish all sex. And the other thing is to be dead. To have anonymous sex with other sick men. I can't make a life out of that. The homosexuals I know think I'm copping out, and if it's not hereditary they feel at least that it's impossible to change. They say to me "Once homosexuality is established you can't get out or if you do try to get out you'll go nuts." They tell you that you will be turning against your own kind, that you're trying to do something and be something that you're not. They say you're self-indulgent and selfish, feeding your ego in a very selfish kind of way in that you're enjoying your neurosis in trying to get well.

The widespread incidence of homosexuality is due to the necessity for all human beings to undergo the separation-individuation phase of early childhood, a phase decisive for gender identification. A significant proportion fail to successfully complete this developmental process and therefore to form a healthy sexual identity in accordance with their anatomical and biological capacities.

While I can minimize neither the hard work and resoluteness required of the psychoanalyst in treating this serious disorder, nor the courage and endurance required of the patient; a successful resolution brings rewards fully commensurate with their labors.

Chapter 2
FREUD'S CONTRIBUTIONS

The Three Essays

The departure point for all theoretical and clinical research into the elucidation of the meaning, content, etiology, and therapy of homosexuality was Freud's "Three Essays on the Theory of Sexuality" (1905a).

In Part I, "The Sexual Aberrations," Freud first coined the term *invert* and designated the practice of homosexuality as *inversion*. He wrote that homosexuals are considerable in number but that there are many obstacles to establishing their number precisely. (Hirschfeld had attempted this in 1904.) His proposed classification of homosexuality was based largely on the motivational context of its occurrence.

He noted that many homosexuals feel their inversion is in the natural course of things; others rebel against it and feel it is pathological. It may persist throughout life, go into temporary remission, or be a detour on the path of normal development. It may appear late in life, after a long period of apparently normal sexual activity. There may be periodic oscillations between heterosexual and inverted sexual object choice. He remarked that of special interest are those individuals in whom the libido changes over to an inverted sexual object after a distressing experience with a normal one.

Freud clearly saw through the inverts' assertions that they could never remember any attachment to the opposite sex, realizing that in most instances they had only repressed their positive heterosexual feelings. He reviewed two misconceptions which had surrounded homosexuality for centuries: that it was innate, and that it was a form of degeneracy. Both he believed untrue and of no scientific value. Many homosexuals appear otherwise unimpaired and may distinguish themselves by especially high intellectual and cultural development. Were homosexuality innate (inborn), the "contingent" homosexual would be much more difficult to explain. Freud's assumption was that inversion is an acquired character of the sexual instinct, and he tested this hypothesis by removing inversion by hypnotic suggestion, an event he felt would be "astonishing" with innate characteristics. He hypothesized that some experience of early childhood had a determining effect upon the direction taken by the invert's libido.

He investigated inversion as the possible expression of a psychical hermaphroditism. All that was required to settle the question was that inversion be regularly accompanied by the mental and somatic signs of hermaphroditism; this expectation was not realized. It was impossible to demonstrate a connection between hypothetical psychical hermaphroditism and the established anatomical one. The truth, according to Freud, was that inversion and somatic hermaphroditism were, on the whole, independent of each other. Psychical hermaphroditism would gain substance, in his opinion, if the inversion of the sexual object were at least accompanied by a parallel change of the subject's other mental qualities, instincts, and character traits into those characterizing the opposite sex but it is only in invert women that character inversion of this kind can be found with any regularity.

In an addendum to "A Child is Being Beaten" (1919b), Freud stated that psychoanalysis had not yet produced a complete explanation of the origin of inversion. Nevertheless, it had discovered the psychical mechanism of its development and had made essential contributions to the statement of the problems involved. Foremost among these discoveries was his conclusion that in the earliest phase of their childhood, future inverts passed through a period of very intense but short-lived fixation to a woman, usually their mother. After leaving this behind they continue to identify themselves with the woman and take themselves as a sexual object. Proceeding from a narcissistic base they look for a man who resembles themselves and whom they may love as their mother loved them. In the 1910 edition of the "Three Essays" Freud underscored that the problem of inversion is highly complex. In the case of women it is less ambiguous because active inverts exhibit masculine characteristics, both physical and mental, with peculiar frequency and look for femininity in their sexual object. He remarked, however, that a closer knowledge of the facts might reveal great variety in female inverts.

In a 1915 note to the "Three Essays" he noted that psychoanalytic research decidedly opposes any attempt at segregating homosexuals from the rest of mankind as a group of special character. He noted that *all* human beings are capable of making a homosexual object choice and that many have, in fact, made one in

their unconscious. Libidinal attachments to persons of
the same sex play an important part in normal mental
life and, as a motive force for illness, an even greater
part than do similar attachments to the opposite sex.
Freud believed that object-choice independent of sex—
freedom to range equally among male and female
objects (as is found in childhood and in primitive
societies in the early phases of history)—is the basis for
a subsequent restriction in one direction or the other,
and from which both the normal and the inverted types
developed.

In the "Three Essays" the interconnections between
infantile sexuality, perversions, and neurosis were
made, and the conclusion was reached that the
neurosis represents the "negative" of a perversion. In
the next five years, Freud, along with Sadger (1914,
1915) and Ferenczi (1916, 1950, 1955) developed a
formulation of the essential developmental factors in
homosexuality:

1. In the earliest stages of development, homosexuals experience a very strong mother fixation. Upon
leaving this attachment they continue to identify with
the mother, taking themselves narcissistically as their
sexual object. Consequently, they search for a man
resembling themselves, whom they may love as their
mother loved them ("Three Essays").

2. The different types of narcissistic object choice
were outlined: one searches for a person he has loved;
what he himself is; what he himself was; what he
himself would like to be; someone reminiscent of
another who was once part of himself. Combinations
of these possibilities indicate the numerous varieties of
sexual object choice.

3. Clinical investigation of the genetic constellations

responsible for this developmental inhibition—an overstrong mother fixation with a resultant running away from the mother and a transfer of excitation from women to men in a narcissistic fashion—led to the discovery in these cases of an early positive oedipus complex of great intensity.

Contributions From Ego Psychology

By 1923 the problem of homosexuality was investigated from the points of view of ego development and the interaction of the ego, superego, and id. Freud (1905a) had remarked, long before the advent of ego psychology, that (1) (ego) functions of identification and repression play an important part in homosexuality, and (2) in homosexuals one finds a "predominance of archaic and primitive psychical mechanisms." The lack, however, of a systematic study of ego psychology and the absence of a concept of ego development comparable to the already established phases of libidinal development presented difficulties for many years in the application of structural concepts to homosexuality.

Freud (1921) saw that the late determinants of homosexuality came during adolescence, when a "revolution of the mental economy" takes place. The adolescent, in exchanging his mother for some other sexual object, may make a choice of an object of the same sex. In his work (1910) on Leonardo da Vinci, he pointed out that the absence of the father and growing up in a feminine environment or the presence of a weak father who is dominated by the mother furthers feminine identification and homosexuality. Similarly, the presence of a cruel father may lead to a disturbance in male identification.

He noted (1927) that fetishism and transvestism reflect different compromises between two simultaneous identifications: with the phallic mother and with the penisless mother. Furthermore, he observed that often in masochistic men a feminine identification may exist without homosexual object choice (1919b). In this way, a masochistic perversion may preserve the individual from overt homosexuality. Freud's "Wolf Man" (1918b) serves as a good example.

By 1910 Freud had recognized the defensive function of certain perversions. This was borne out in his study on da Vinci, in which he speaks of the fetish as constituting a substitute for the missed penis of the woman and male homosexuality as due to repression of the attachment to the mother. The latter attachment is colored by identification with her and the choice of sexual object is made on a narcissistic basis. He noted that some homosexuals are fleeing other women in order not to be unfaithful to their mother.

The complex psychic formations leading to homosexuality were further elaborated by Freud in "A Child Is Being Beaten" (1919b). The homosexual symptom represents both defense against and expression of id impulse. It is intimately related to the oedipus complex and to other perversions. Homosexual behavior is not a simple expression of pregenital component-instinct but rather may be compared to a light ray which, passing through a lens, is subjected to considerable distortion and refraction. The perversion itself is only a small conscious part of a large unconscious system, remaining simultaneously ego-syntonic and pleasurable.

In "A Child Is Being Beaten" Freud's emphasis was

on castration anxiety, and homosexuality was seen as a defense against the threat of losing one's penis. In 1922, new clinical material revealed that homosexuality may function as a means of defense against persecutory paranoia (Socarides 1963). Furthermore, the enactment of overt homosexual impulses could operate both as a repressive mechanism and as a technique whereby intense jealousy and hostility toward rival siblings is transformed into its opposite. In 1925 Freud further applied the theoretical framework of ego psychology to the consideration of perversions. The important mechanism of negation (1925a) was elucidated and shown to play an important part in homosexuality. Freud's formulations in this regard were compatible with views already expressed by Sachs in 1923 (see Appendix B). The overall importance of defensive processes in perversion formation was further explored in "Splitting of the Ego in the Process of Defence" (1938b) and in *An Outline of Psycho-Analysis* (1938a).

Perversions came to be understood by Freud as not simply the negative of neurosis or the persistence of the infantile components, but rather as complex formations involving defensive functions, expression of id drives, superego conflict, and ego adaptive moves. The role of the oedipus complex as described by Freud achieved tremendous popularity in an attempt to understand homosexuality. Freud himself, however, felt that to understand this condition would require a full understanding of its etiology—not merely an explanation of its structure or of how that structure came into being, but specification of the mechanisms responsible for it and an explanation of what determines this particular outcome rather than any other.

It became quite clear, however, that there was a great similarity between a neurotic symptom and homosexuality. They were not simply residues of the developmental process of infantile sexuality or the conscious representatives of unconscious instinct. Moreover, there appeared to be an alternation between phobia and perverse gratification (Gillespie 1956a, Sachs 1923). Furthermore, much study was needed on the relationship between perversion and the superego. Freud's work on the relationship of perversion to psychosis (1938) approached the matter from the point of view of the ego. In his paper "Negation" (1925a) he showed that the ego is capable of extending its boundaries to accept what would otherwise be repressed with the proviso that it be consciously denied. In *An Outline of Psycho-Analysis* (1938a) and in "Splitting of the Ego in the Process of Defence" (1938b), the splitting of the ego and of the object was brilliantly defined, as was their role in perversion formation.

The concept of a premature fixation of the libido playing a role in the genesis of homosexuality appeared in "Some Neurotic Mechanisms in Jealousy, Paranoia and Homosexuality" (1922). We must remember in all these matters to return to the "Three Essays" (1905a), in which Freud noted that even if "we had complete knowledge of the etiological factors we would know only their quality but not their relative strength (quantity) in determining the end result." In a reference to Freud, Wiedeman (1962) writes: "The qualitative factor, namely, the presence of certain neurotic or perverse formations, is less important than the quantitative factor, which is the amount of cathexis that these structures are able to attract to themselves."

As regards therapy, Freud stated that homosexuality could be altered by hypnotic suggestion (1905a, b), and that analysis could be applied to the treatment of perversions (1905a, 1921), although he was cautious regarding the possibility of curing homosexuality through analysis. "The goal of analytic treatment of homosexuality goes beyond the establishment of heterosexual potency, which frequently remains a pseudopotency as it has to be helped along by perverse fantasies. Analytically speaking, the criterion of a cure is the detachment of the cathexis from the homosexual object and the ability to cathect the opposite sex as well as the ability to love a woman." Freud (1935) mentioned that analytic treatment may certainly help the homosexual with his neurotic problems, even if there is no change in his object choice.

At various times Freud referred to homosexuality as inhibited development, arrested development, or developmental inhibition. He found difficulty in drawing a sharp line between normal and pathological behavior and stated that in cases where exclusiveness of fixation was present we are justified in calling homosexuality a pathological symptom. He maintianed that constitutional factors play a part in sexual perversions but that they play a similar role in all mental disorders. This was in no way a repudiation of the role of psychological factors in the predisposition to homosexuality. Freud was in fact emphasizing precisely these developmental factors, which remained to be elucidated. He was always of the opinion that the nature of inversion was explained neither by the hypothesis that it is innate nor by the alternative hypothesis that it is acquired. He was able to show that even in absolute inverts, for example, one can discover that very early in their lives a sexual impression left permanent aftereffects in the shape of a tendency toward homosexuality; in others it is possible to trace homosexuality to external influences, whether of a favorable or inhibiting character, which led sooner or later to a fixation of their inversion. Later factors included exclusive relationship with persons of their own sex, comradeship in war, and dangers of heterosexual intercourse (1905a).

Ultimately, Freud felt that homosexuality represents an inhibition and dissociation of psychosexual development, one of the pathological out-outcomes of the oedipal period. Analytic literature had not disclosed any single psychogenic or structural pattern that would apply to all or even a major part of the cases of inversion. It would be the task of future investigators, Freud wrote, to attempt to determine what psychogenetic factors are essential for the production of homosexuality, to eludicate a structural theory for the understanding of homosexuality, to examine therapeutic problems inherent in the treatment of homosexuals, and to shed light on the connection between the sexual instinct and the choice of object in homosexual behavior. To accomplish this, the psychical mechanisms used in the choice of a homosexual object for orgastic satisfaction, the purpose of such choice (beyond the orgastic purpose), and its infantile origin must finally be discovered.

Female Sexual Development

Freud (1933) characterized our knowledge of female sexuality as a "mysterious and dark continent." A girl's development is more complex and somewhat slower than a boy's. Because of the anatomical differences between the sexes, sexual energy does not find an outlet through the body of the girl as easily as it does through the body of the boy after the anal phase has receded. At this point diffuse narcissistic libido becomes directed toward the genital region. Freud held that the genitals of the female, with the exception of the clitoris, remain undiscovered and without sensation until puberty. Her interest and curiosity focus on the genitals of the opposite sex to which she compares her own unfavorably. Therefore her first affect as regards the genitals arises from the realization that she has no penis. Only later she discovers the clitoris as a substitute and a fateful comparison ensues. This crisis leads to a sense of inferiority which motivates the intense, biologically determined wish to acquire a penis. The belief that she is "lacking," mutilated, or damaged in the genital region may later become the basic fear in the female castration complex (Galenson 1976 a, b). (Revisions of Freud's basic tenets have been suggested by two recent panels held by the American Psychoanalytic Association in 1974 and 1975.)

Freud espoused a primary ambivalent motivation toward heterosexuality in girls. This arises from the fact that a girl's dependency needs are satisfied by the mother but her penis envy mobilizes the tendency to incorporate the penis, to hold on to it, and to possess it. In the normal course of maturation the feminine sexual anlage and its libido is directed toward the male sex, leading to an instinctual conflict: the girl has a desire for her father's love which is in direct conflict with the gratification of her dependency needs from her mother. This results both in a prolongation of the preoedipal phase in the girl and guilt feelings due to oedipal wishes. In this emotional upheaval she may resign herself to her dependency needs and regress to a dependent situation with her mother. The result is often a concurrent, diffuse erotization of the body and an increase in her pregenital autoerotic behavior. In turning to genital stimulation in masturbation new conflicts appear. Through such repetitive processes the girl ultimately enters the oedipal conflict.

The oedipus complex for the girl represents two conflicting instinctual tendencies: (a) the wish to be in mother's place and to be loved by the father; and (b) the wish to be the child and be loved by the mother. This is in direct contrast to the boy who wishes to be in the father's place and be loved by the mother. The girl's competition with the mother for the father produces both the fear of punishment and the fear of losing mother's love. If this anxiety is not overcome the girl regresses to the infantile but safe dependency relationship with the mother.

Regarding the second element in her conflict, the wish "to be the child," it is "safer" to be with the mother than against her. To accomplish this, the girl strives for an identification with the father or a brother, thereby safeguarding herself from her heterosexual wishes for the father and simultaneously remaining loveable to the mother as she assumes a father/brother role. Such a solution, however, produces an intensification of penis envy and a fixation of development on an infantile level.

The oedipus complex in the girl is repressed and resolved in various ways, including engaging in sexual activities and producing ego defenses against them.

What commonly occurs may be an increase in sexual curiosity; the invention of infantile sexual theories which help to deny the significance of the genitals; denial itself; and the production of a sadistic conception of sexuality. The latter, however, intensifies the girl's fear of her own sexual impulses and may produce massive inhibitions or an increase in identification with the opposite sex (Barahal 1953). This identification with the opposite sex intensifies the female castration complex which interferes with her further oedipal sexual development. The fear of the male (father's penis) tends to increase and intensify the girl's incorporative tendencies. Her fascination with the penis and her ensuing active curiosity have as their goal the possession of the penis. Thus her identification takes on qualities of being an identification with the aggressor, and her penis envy can be conceived of as a defense against her female sexual tendencies. This particular configuration of the oedipus complex extends into adult life.

Freud remarked (1933) that it takes the struggle of the oedipus phase to reveal the quantitative differences between male and female tendencies. At puberty, mounting sexual drives revive earlier castration fears, including fears of the envied male organ. As the sexual maturation process proceeds there is a further flight from the feminine sexual role. Ultimately the libido tension overcomes the fear of being hurt and the sexual act becomes possible. This outcome is possible only if the girl has proceeded in adolescence from an attachment to mother, to an identification with mother, to a wish to have a baby like mother. Raymond de Saussure once suggested to the author that it is important in the late oedipal phase for the father to present his daughter with a baby doll as a gift. Through symbolic efficacy this promotes an identification with the female supplanting the former infantile attachment to the mother.

Female Homosexuality

Freud believed that in the female, there are more severe early inhibitions or reaction-formations against sexuality such as shame, disgust, and pity, and there is greater passivity of the instinct components. Although the development of the two sexes can be outlined as moving in parallel fashion "since the guiding erotogenic zones are of an identical nature, either objectively or in the case of the genital (penis, clitoris) subjectively, at puberty the female face[s] the additional task of exchanging the infantile genital for the adult one whose stimulation in coitus will normally cause her to transfer the erotogeneity of the clitoris to the vagina."

The oedipus complex and castration fear became the focal point of Freud's discussion of both male and female inversion. They were frequently alluded to in the *Collected Papers* (1950) as the motivational force for potential or actual inversion. Freud published his first clinical study on female homosexuality in 1920. His patient was a beautiful and clever young woman of eighteen who adored a woman about ten years her senior. The precipitating events leading her into a homosexual relationship were the birth of a third brother when she was about sixteen and her mother's current pregnancy. Her object choice corresponded with both her feminine and her masculine ideal (a combined gratification of the homosexual tendency with that of the heterosexual one). She unconsciously wished to bear the father's child, as "it was not she who bore the child but the unconsciously hated rival (the mother)." This led to resentment, embitterment, and turning away from the father and from men altogether. She repudiated her wish for a child and her love of a man. The patient "changed into a man" and took a woman (the mother) in place of the father as a love object.

Freud carefully considered the implications inherent in the choice of object on the one hand, and of the sexual characteristics and sexual attitudes of the subject on the other. He stated that the answer to the former does not necessarily provide the answers to the latter. A man with predominantly male characteristics and masculine in his love life may still be inverted in respect to his object, loving only men instead of women. He added that the same is true of women, but here mental sexual characteristics and object choice do not necessarily coincide.

Freud (1917) developed the theme that all sexual perverts alter their sexual object. A female homosexual may dispense with the mutual union of the genital organs and substitute for the genitals in one of the partners another organ or part of the body, mouth, or anus in place of the vagina. He felt, in short, that perverted sexuality is representative of infantile sexuality, magnified into its component parts.

Freud also underscored our lack of understanding of the female regarding certain crucial developmental issues (1923a, 1924a). For example, psychoanalysis did not as yet possess an adequate insight into the little girl's incest wishes, the effect of the threat of castration, and the formation of her superego. By 1924 (Fliess 1950, Freud 1924a) he arrived at certain conclusions regarding castration anxiety and the fate of oedipal wishes in the female, in contrast to the male: (1) she accepts castration as an accomplished fact rather than fearing it as a threat; (2) consequently she lacks a powerful motive for the erection of a superego and for the relinquishing of her infantile sexuality; (3) she therefore gives up the oedipus complex more gradually than the boy, retaining a strong conscious wish for a penis and a child from the father.

Freud published the first of his studies on female sexuality (1925b) in 1925. In this essay he expanded his views of the castration complex of the girl and its effect upon infantile masturbation and the oedipus complex. He concluded that the second period of infantile masturbation was most likely disturbed by the inferiority of the clitoris. As a result the girl is forced to rebel against phallic masturbation. She develops penis envy in order to finally fully accept her castration. This introduces her to the oedipus complex. Her wish for the penis is then equated with the wish for a child; she thereby supercedes her previous attachment to the mother, the original love object of the infant of either sex. (A critique of Freud's changing concepts on female sexuality is not intended here and may be found in Robert Fliess's authoritative work on the subject [1954].)

Thus we see that the castration complex terminates the oedipus complex for the boy and initiates it for the girl. Freud believed that since the girl never completely relinquishes the oedipus complex, its heir, the superego, is never as inexorable in the normal female as in the male.

Six years later, Freud (1931) traced lines of development that resulted from the girl's acknowledging the fact of castration; her imagining the superiority of the male; and her rebelling, stemming from her sense of inferiority. The first developmental line would lead her to turn her back on sexuality altogether. "The budding woman frightened by the comparison of herself with boys becomes dissatisfied with her clitoris and gives up her phallic activity and therewith her sexuality in general and a considerable part of masculine proclivities in other fields." A second developmental line would lead her to cling in obstinate self-assertion to her masculinity. Thus what may be found clinically is her hope of acquiring a penis, a wish which is sometimes cherished to an incredibly late age, often becoming the aim of her life. Indeed, the fantasy of really being a man may dominate long periods of her life. Thus, she produces a "masculinity complex" which may result in a manifestly homosexual object choice. The third path is one which ultimately arrives at a normal feminine attitude in which the girl takes her father as love object (the oedipus complex in its feminine form). The oedipus complex in the woman represents the final result of a lengthy process of development whose motive force has been castration fear. The oedipus complex therefore escapes the strong hostile influences which, in men, tend to its destruction.

Freud postulated that women with strong father fixations have unusually long preoedipal periods. In this preoedipal phase the mother figure is the love object, though the relation to her is highly ambivalent. Hostility increases with each fresh experience of frustration until the girl's recognition of the absence of a penis, interpreted as a punishment by the mother for

masturbation, brings the girl's fear to such intensity
that she throws over the mother in favor of the father.
In other words, it is phallic frustration which is
decisive for femininity; the core of her complaint
against the mother is that she was born a girl rather
than a boy. Furthermore, a strong father fixation
implies a previously strong mother fixation. The
hostility to the mother is augmented by oedipal rivalry
but not initiated by it. Solutions to the feminine
predicament are therefore: (1) a general retreat from
sexuality; (2) a retention of masculinity which may
result in manifest homosexual object choice; (3) a
turning to the father with a consequent ushering in of
the positive oedipal attitude and subsequent feminine
development. In other words, the girl must choose
between sacrificing her erotic attachment to the father
or sacrificing her femininity. She must renounce either
the father or the vagina, including the pregenital
vagina. The bond with the father is retained through
identification.

Freud summarized his thinking on female sexuality
and homosexuality in a lecture entitled "The Psychology of Women" (1933). He reiterated his belief in an
exclusive mother attachment preceding the oedipus
complex of greater intensity and duration in the female
than in the male. The preoedipal phase in girls, he felt,
extended into the fourth or even fifth year of life and
included most of the phallic period. During this phase,
a girl's sexual aim toward the mother was first passive
and then active and corresponded to the partial
libidinal stages through which she had journeyed from
infancy, i.e., oral, anal, sadistic, and phallic. The girl's
giving up the mother and her acknowledgment of
castration, that is, change of object and change of

zone, occur in a complementary fashion. It is castration, conveived of as a denial of the male genital by the mother, which forms the nucleus of the girl's reproach and hostility toward the mother. A transition from the mother to the father follows. "This fulfills the biological necessity of transforming the masculine girl into the feminine woman by drawing on her passivity and her remaining positive sexual strivings....Thus the child-penis is also no longer craved from the mother but from the father" (Fleiss 1950).

Freud's important paper makes it apparent that female homosexuality is seldom, if ever, a direct continuation of infantile masculinity. It is characteristic of female homosexuals to take the father as love object for a while and become implicated in the oedipal situation. With the inevitable disappointments they experience from the father they regress to their earlier masculinity complex. These disappointments cannot be overestimated. Girls who eventually achieve femininity also experience them without the same results. The two phases of female homosexuality are reflected in the behavior of homosexuals who as frequently and as obviously play the parts of mother and child toward each other as those of man and wife.

Finally, Freud (1940) stated that if the girl persists in and adheres to her first wish to grow into a boy, in extreme cases she will end as a manifest homosexual or in any event will show markedly masculine traits in the conduct of her later life.

Chapter 3
CONTRIBUTIONS TO THE LITERATURE

Cultural Studies

Homosexuality, present throughout the ages, can be found in almost all cultures. It has been treated in ways ranging from acceptance to hostile rejection. Efforts to deal with it can be traced to some of the earliest writings: to the laws of Hammurabi (second century B.C.) in Babylon; to Egyptian papyri, in which it is referred to as an ancient custom of the gods; to the Old Testament, where it is described as a "sin and scourge," e.g., Sodom and Gomorrah. Under Roman law, many aspects of homosexuality were ignored, especially female homosexuality. Early Anglo-Saxon laws were not as lenient, but it is inaccurate to derive taboos against homosexuality entirely from the Judaeo-Christian code. During the Dark Ages, homosexuality was regarded as a form of heresy and those "afflicted" were burnt at the stake.

Fisher (1965) states that physical relations were definitely a part of the homosexuality of the Greeks (Athenians). "The evidence is strong that homosexuality in the form of pederasty came later and flourished in the historic period from the sixth century

B.C.) on, coinciding with the development of a monetary,
commericial, enslaved form of society."

In the Homeric period, the absence of pederasty
coincided with the more elevated status of women; in
the historic period, the presence of pederasty coincided
with the degraded status of women. According to
Fisher, "This pattern suggests that in approaching the
problem of homosexuality today, it is not enough to
deal with the so-called 'instinctual' and interpersonal
factors; social factors must be taken into account as
well."

W.K. Lacey (1968), the brilliant Cambridge classical
scholar, published a most comphrenensive examination of family life in ancient Greece. He writes:

We are sometimes told that the Greeks were fully bisexual,
enjoying both homosexual and heterosexual intercourse, and that
romantic love in Greece was associated with attachments to boys
and not to girls. Whatever the truth of the latter statement, there
can be no doubt that, while the Greeks had a deep admiration for
the physical beauty of the young male, in Athens the practice of
sodomy was strictly circumscribed by the law.

Boys still at school were protected against sexual assaults by a
law (said to go as far back as Dracon and Solon), and we hear of
strict regulations about schools with this in mind; schoolboys
always had a *paidagogos* escorting them; in art the *paidagogos* is
always depicted as carrying a long and heavy stick; what was this
for if not to protect their charges?

Sodomy was thought reprehensible for older men even when the
catamite was not a citizen, as is clear from the speech of Lysias,
but it was not illegal; it may be thought that the law in this field is
likely to have been similar to that about adultery; what was quite
legal with slaves and other noncitizens was illegal with citizens,
and the law took notice of the private morals of individuals, and
punished offenders [to the point of disenfranchisement].

Pederasty was expensive; whether this was because the youths' admirers wanted to compete in generosity for favors or the youths were able to use the law virtually to blackmail their admirers no doubt varied in individual cases, but the result of the expense was to make pederasty a habit of the upper class and of those who imitated them, and hence suspect to the common people and a means of arousing prejudice in legal cases. Plato's attack on sodomy, especially in the *Laws*, reveals that the practice was not unknown to him, and that it was more repugnant to his ideals than heterosexual intercourse outside marriage, since this latter (if secret) was tolerated in the *Laws* as a second-best to the ideal of virginity till marriage and sexual intercourse only within marriage for the purpose of breeding children.

Opler (1965) concludes from anthropological and cross-cultural studies that "actually, no society, save perhaps ancient Greece, pre-Meiji Japan, certain top echelons in Nazi Germany, and the scattered examples of such special status groups as the berdaches, Nata slaves, and one category of Chuckshee shamans, has lent sanction in any real sense to homosexuality. Regardless of what may be said concerning all the factors—social, legal and psychodynamic—entering into homosexual behavior, one thing is clear: in the absence of an organic or hormonal basis, homosexuality in practically all cultures is regarded as a deviation from the major values and norms of conduct." He points out that in nonliterate hunting and gathering societies homosexuality is generally rare and in some instances virtually nonexistent, e.g., the Mescalero and Chiricahua Apache.

Kardiner (1939), in a psychoanalytic study of anthropology, has shown that in the Comanche tribes of the midwestern United States there was no homosexuality; an occasional transvestite was treated like a foolish old woman. It was completely unadaptive for a young man to be homosexual in the Comanche tribe. The tribe was geared for warfare and for hunting. All children were bound physically close to the mother for the first year or two of life. Boys were thereafter turned over to the father and the other men to begin training and cultivating those attributes and skills necessary to become successful warriors and hunters.

Observers of kibbutz-reared children in Israel reported that there was no evidence of homosexuality in adulthood.

Biological Studies

There have been numerous chemical, genetic, and somatic studies over the past century in an effort to establish that homosexuality has an organic or nonpsychogenetic origin.

In 1896, Krafft-Ebing (1901, 1906, 1924) suggested that homosexuality is an inborn characteristic caused by large amounts of male and/or female substances in the hereditary composition of the brain. Havelock Ellis (1895, 1905) agreed with Krafft-Ebing's fallacy regarding the hereditary composition of male or female substances in the brain. Mantagazza (1932), in 1914, explained homosexuality as a genital malformation caused by the displacement of sensory nerves, normally originating in the penis, to the rectum; the erogenous zone is shifted correspondingly. Hirschfeld (1914, 1916-1921, 1938) stated that "Homosexuality is always an inborn state, conditioned by specific homosexual constitution of the brain." Glass et al. (1940) cited hormonal or endocrine factors. Contemporary scientific findings clearly establish that homosexuals can have endocrine dysfunctions just as can any other individuals but the androgen-estrogen ratio among male homosexuals usually falls within normal limits. Large doses of androgens or estrogens influence the overall sexual drive in homosexuals but cannot change the pattern.

Among more recent studies, Kolodny et al. (1971) reported that thirty-five exclusively homosexual subjects had a lower amount of testosterone in the bloodstream than would be found in heterosexual males. The authors' statement in the same paper is evidence of the inconclusiveness of this finding: "There is no suggestion that endocrine abnormalities will be found in the great majority of homosexuals, or that endocrine dysfunction is a major factor in the pathogenesis of male homosexuality."

Various objections were raised in connection with the Kolodny material. Barry and Barry (1972) wrote: "Their data showed that most of their subjects whose homosexuality had been rated as moderate to predominant had plasma testosterone levels within normal limits. Subjects with extreme degrees of homosexuality did have significant decreases in testosterone levels." The relation between decreased testosterone levels and decreased libido in heterosexual males is well known, the objection continues, so that it is not necessary to attribute any of these endocrine findings to homosexuality.

Commenting on Kolodny's alternative theory—that decreased testosterone levels could be a result of homosexuality rather than a cause and could be mediated through hypothalamic mechanisms—Barry and Barry point out that the life style of persons with obsessive-compulsive homosexual activity could also be involved. Many such subjects have said that while "cruising" and patronizing gay bars, they frequently averaged less than four hours of sleep. Testosterone levels normally decrease during the day by some 30 percent, and the high early morning levels are presumably restored during sleep. "Might not the result reported have been due to the cumulative effects of sleep deficits? Kolodny et al. did not mention any alcohol consumption...although an association between heavy alcohol consumption and homosexuality is not uncommon, and alcohol is believed to have adverse effects on the testes and male sexual activity. In view of the lability of testosterone levels and their wide variations owing to environmental factors, the reported decrease among adult males is more likely to be a result than a cause of homosexuality."

Neither can the concept set forth by Money and his co-workers (Money and Ehrhardt 1972), that a disturbance in prenatal circulating hormones effects sexual object choice, be of etiological significance.

In a 1973 report Birk et al. showed that the homosexual state could exist without a deficiency in serum testosterone. Examination of the serum testosterone levels in sixty-six male homosexual patients in psychotherapy for seven years proved that there was "no correlation between Kinsey number and serum testosterone level." Furthermore, Birk's homosexual subjects (mean Kinsey number 4.1) had normal testosterone levels.

As recently as 1975 Tourney et al. investigated hormonal metabolism in heterosexual and homosexual men and found no indication of disturbed endocrine functioning in the homosexual men.

Kallman's (1952) studies on the genetic predetermination of homosexuality in identical twins show "concordance as to the overt practices of homosexual behavior after adolescence." However, these statistical studies must always be viewed with considerable caution. The behavior may be due to the temperamental similarity of identical twins and their reacting similarly to environmental influences. More revealing would be studies of identical twins who have been separated at birth and brought up in divergent environments. Kallman, in the same paper, stated that the "project was extremely difficult.... It is fair to admit that the question of the possible significance of a genetic mechanism in the development of overt homosexuality may still be regarded as entirely unsettled."

Rainer and his co-workers (1960) described seven cases of monozygotic twins without concordance. Concordance does not prove a biogenetic etiology since the developmental history of monozygotic twins is uniquely different from that of other individuals. As Freud definitively set forth, there is no relationship between sexual drive and sexual object choice.

Ford and Beach (1951) have pointed out that the choice of sexual object is determined by learned experience. They prove that even in sub-human creatures psychological experience can determine the subsequent pattern: "Inexperienced males who suffer injury or are badly frightened during the first contact with a receptive female may never develop normal sexual aggression."

Assumptions as to the origin of human homosexuality cannot be based on the study of lower primates. In man the enormous evolutionary development of the cerebral cortex has made both conscious and unconscious motivation overwhelmingly significant in sexual patterning. Below the level of the chimpanzee, sexual arousal patterns are completely automatic and reflex. Beach (Karlen, 1971) disposes of the entire argument in a 1971 interview: "I don't know any authenticated instance of males or females in the animal world preferring a homosexual partner—if by homosexual you mean complete sexual relations, including climax.... It's questionable that mounting in itself can properly be called sexual."

In 1934, Henry (1934, 1937, 1941a, 1941b) studied 250 adult patients grouped according to the predominance of heterosexual or homosexual tendencies. He concluded that the sexual histories in the heterosexual and homosexual groups are conspicuously different. All patients in the heterosexual group were married and had from one to seven children. Only 25 percent of the homosexual patients were married; none of them had made a satisfactory heterosexual adjustment. Three fourths of these marriages were dissolved by separation, divorce, or annulment. Henry felt that when personality disorders occur, heterosexuals tend to develop benign psychoses while homosexuals are prone to have chronic paranoiac and schizophrenic illnesses. He found that while homosexual patients had considerably greater constitutional (physical) deviations on a general average than the heterosexually adjusted, this in no way indicated a physiological or organic basis for sexual object choice.

Albert Ellis (1945) studied forty-eight cases of hermaphroditism from the medical literature and it was shown that in the great majority of these the hermaphrodite assumes a heterosexual libido and sex role that accords primarily not with his or her internal and external somatic characteristics but rather with his or her masculine or feminine up-bringing. This applied to both pseudohermaphrodites and true hermaphrodites. The author concluded that heterosexuality or homosexuality in hermaphrodites is caused primarily by environmental rather than hormonal or physiological factors. Since, however, the hermaphrodite's environment conspicuously includes the somatic anomalies, it is also concluded that the problem of "normal" and "abnormal" sexual behavior among hermaphrodites is a psychosomatic one as is true of psychosexuality in normal human beings.

It can readily be seen from this review of the literature that homosexuality has undergone investigation of the most infinite variety. The issue appears to stand or fall on the following: "If a person of the opposite sex is available, why should a male choose another male or a female another female...or even, sometimes, a lock of hair or a piece of underclothing?" (Freud 1905a). The answer is to be found in the developmental history of the individual.

While Freud's contributions are dealt with comprehensively in chapter 2 certain brief references must be made in the context of this section. Seventy years ago he summarized the etiology of homosexuality thus: "The nature of inversion is explained neither by the hypothesis that it is innate nor by the alternative hypothesis that it is acquired. In the former case, we must ask in what respect it is innate, unless we are to accept the crude explanation that everyone is born with a sexual instinct attached to a particular sexual object. In the latter case it may be questioned whether the various accidental influences would be sufficient to explain the acquisition of inversion without the cooperation of something in the subject himself. The existence of this last factor is not to be denied" (1905a).

Freud felt that "it has been brought to our notice that we have been in the habit of regarding the connection between the sexual instinct and the sexual object as more intimate than it in fact is. Experience with the cases that are considered abnormal has shown us that in them the sexual instinct and the sexual object are merely soldered together...a fact which we have been in danger of overlooking in consequence of the uniformity of the normal picture where the object appears to form part and parcel of the instinct. We have thus wanted to loosen the bond that exists in our thoughts between instinct and object. It seems probable that the sexual instinct is in the first instance independent of its object; nor is its origin likely to be due to its object's attraction" (1905a).

Having introduced the idea of the importance of infantile experience, Freud stated that the libido, which at first was polymorphous perverse undergoes development and integration and passes through a *homosexual phase* before reaching the heterosexual level. Therefore, in homosexuals, the libido is fixed on the individual himself because of a congenital predisposition to fixation at that point as a result of psychic trauma which prevents the person from proceeding to heterosexual relationships (1905a).

For Freud, the etiology of homosexuality was intimately tied up with constitution. This was due to his belief, for a time, in the theory of constitutional bisexuality. Although embryological observation shows that sexual differentiation proceeds from an identical anlage in the developing fetus, the essential genital organs have homologues in each sex, i.e., penis and clitoris develop from the same embryonic structure, also uterus and uterus-masculina, a tiny cul-de-sac in the male urethra. This theory of bisexuality has received criticism as well as approval from various sources over the years. The theory itself came from Wilhelm Fliess: "The dominant sex of the person, that which is the more strongly developed, has repressed the mental representation of the subordinated sex in the unconscious. Therefore, the nucleus of the unconscious is, in each human being, that side of him which belongs to the opposite sex" (1954).

Freud changed Fliess's view to some extent but retained the concept of bisexuality and wrote of the constitution which included a homosexual component. In each person, he felt, there is a homosexual component which must be successfully repressed or handled to avoid conflict. This idea has been subjected to intense attack on the misleading grounds that the presence of a homosexual component in everyone would negate the concept of pathogenic psychodynamic factors in the causation of homosexuality. Nothing could be further from the truth. All of us inherit the constitutional strength of our sexual instinct. This is what Freud meant by the "constitutional factor."

The principal argument over the years against the psychogenic explanation of homosexuality often centers around the fact that many individuals exposed to a particular set of pressures become homosexual while others in similar circumstances do not. Actually, the important determinant in causation is that the sexual object may have a purely symbolic significance acquired at an extremely early age, usually during the period of the first three or four years of life.

The concept of bisexuality was generally agreed upon although not readily understood. Jones stated that although "the assumption of inborn bisexuality seems to me a very probable one, in favor of which many biological facts can be quoted...we should not take it for granted" (1912).

The suggestion that homosexuals are individuals suffering from a biological disturbance in which the soma is obviously male but the psyche is female is a variation on the misunderstanding of Freud's theory of bisexuality. As early as 1905 Freud stated, "The theory of bisexuality has been expressed in its crudest form by a spokesman of the male inverts: 'a feminine brain in a masculine body.'...There is neither need nor justification for replacing the psychological problem by the anatomical..." (1905a).

Bisexuality has erroneously been interpreted as the genetic (inborn) characteristic of attraction to persons of both sexes. This was not Freud's meaning. He did not believe that any specific genetic (chromosomal) factor was capable of directing the sexual drive into overt homosexuality. He always believed that there were a number of factors which determined sexual integration; of these the psychodynamic ones were the most important. The constitutional factors determine only the strength of the drive.

Those who stress a basic biological tendency toward heterosexuality commit the same error as advocates of the theory of constitutional bisexuality. Rado (1940) puts constitutional bisexuality in its proper place.

In both lines of experimental study, the available evidence points to the same conclusion: the human male and female do not inherit an organized neuro-hormonal machinery of courtship and mating. Nor do they inherit any organized component mechanism that would—or could—direct them to such goals as mating or choice of mate. In the light of this evidence, the psychoanalytic theory of sexual instincts evolved in the first decades of this century has become an historical expedient that has outlived its scientific usefulness. Each of the sexes has an innate capacity for learning, and is equipped with a specific power plant and tools. But in sharp contrast to the lower vertebrates, and as a consequence of the encephalization of certain functions first organized at lower evolutionary levels of the central nervous system, they inherit no organized information.

Major Contributions to a Dynamic Understanding of Homosexuality

Fenichel (1945) wrote that everyone is able to develop

sexual feelings indiscriminately, and the search for an object is less limited by the sex of the object than is commonly supposed....the fact that in a normal person the object choice later becomes more or less limited to the opposite sex is a problem in itself...since the homosexual, like any other human being, originally has the capacity to choose objects of either sex, but limits his capacity to objects of his own sex....Analysis of homosexual men regularly shows that they feared female genitals....the female genitals, through the connection of castration anxiety with all anxieties, they perceive as the castrating instrument capable of biting or tearing off their penis.

But how does homosexuality come about? In an article by Sherman and Sherman (1926) the attachment of the girl for the father accounts for the development of homosexual object choice in the female. Jung (1916) pointed out that "it frequently happens (in male homosexuality) that at the time of their first love, remarkable difficulties develop in the capacity for erotic expression which may be reduced analytically to disturbances through an aggressive attempt at resuscitation of the father image." In female homosexuality the type of sexual object that alone has the property of invigorating the female sexual functions is so highly specialized by parental attachment that no adequate image or substitute can be had; the individual tends to suffer from the horrors of incest. Passive homosexuality is usually the result of such conditioning.

Ferenczi (1914) divided male homosexuals into passive homosexuals or inverts and object-homoerotics; the latter remain masculine in their behavior and merely pursue another man as though he were a female. Thus, he differed from the observation that role reversal is more the rule than the exception. While he classifies homosexuals into active and passive types, female homosexuals very often are classfied either as masculine or feminine. Ferenczi defines the active male homosexual as one who in sexual relationships takes the active role toward making his partner adopt the female position in intercourse or to submit to, rather than perform, sodomy or other acts. The active physical role is usually accompanied by the social, emotional and psychic activities of seeking, courting and dominating. The same may be said for female homosexuals. The passive male and the active female homosexual are much more likely to show contrasexual traits of physique and mind and be irreversibly and solely homosexually inclined.

Fenichel (1945) maintained that "homosexual love is mixed with characteristics of identification and it is generally agreed that there is an element of identification with the object in all homosexual love." Homosexuality has proved to be the product of specific mechanisms of *defense* which facilitate the repression of both the oedipus and the castration complex. At the same time the aim of homosexual object choice is the avoidance of emotions around the castration complex which otherwise would disturb sexual pleasure or at least the attainment of real assurance against these anxieties. Also, a homosexual will reject a part of his personality; that part is externalized onto someone else who becomes a sexual object. The homosexual is seeking an image of himself in someone else. Therefore, the results are complementary relationships. Anna Freud expounded these views in considerable detail in the early 1950s (1951).

The idea that homosexuality is really a disguised form of psychosis has not been borne out. Homosexuality has frequently occurred during psychotic episodes when previously there had been no indication of its presence. In many others, however, homosexuality occurs without psychosis or disappears during a psychosis.

As early as 1926, Boehm (1926) established the importance of guilt feelings arising from hostility to the father as the genesis of homosexuality.

The Melanie Klein (1952) school holds that homosexuality is fundamentally concerned with the earliest phases of libidinal development. The chief factors, therefore, in the production of homosexuality are anxieties around the oral and anal phases. These anxieties produce insatiable need which binds the libido to oral and anal forms. Such binding leads to profound disturbances of the genital function.

One's happy experiences at the breast exert a

favorable influence in promoting genitality. Only when there is undue oral stimulation and frustration does the organism undergo an intense fixation to the oral phase and produce an undue degree of fear because of the rejection of its oral hunger. The object relationship of the genital phase becomes filled with a pattern acquired at the oral zone including the unconscious fantasies and feelings of desire and fear. In many men this may be interpreted as a fear of being devoured by the vagina. This is probably the most important factor responsible for psychosexual impotence in men. Similar unconscious fantasies may be responsible for fear of the penis and for frigidity in women and therefore for the development of homosexuality. The Kleinian theoretical framework emphasizes the preoedipal, oral cannibalistic fantasies as the basic psychological factors in the development of homosexuality. The oedipus complex is a later development and the emotional patterns elaborated in object relationships during this period enter into the defenses against both heterosexuality and homosexuality. However, the emotional nature and intensity of the oedipus fantasies are determined by the earlier repressed oral fantasies with their unconscious anxieties.

Sach's (1923) paper clearly demonstrates that we are not dealing simply with a fixation of a component sexual drive as the dictum about neurosis being the negative of a perversion would let us assume. Sachs's theory will be taken up in greater detail elsewhere as it directly pertains to the author's concept of the psychodynamics and therapy of homosexuality.

Alexander, in 1930, considered perversions in terms of partial failures of defense: disturbance of the process of desexualization of instinctual energy; and acceptance of aggressive impulses by the ego and their expression in relation to the sexual object. Nunberg (1938) formulated that the cannibalistic wish to bite off the partner's penis in an attempt to incorporate it and the partner is an effort to regain an endangered masculinity; destructive impulses make mature identification with the male impossible. The anal-sadistic impulses in homosexuality can be equated with stool=penis=baby=money. Sadger (1909) had earlier stated that the impulse to eat the father's testicles was the motivating force in homosexuality.

Bibring (1940) concluded that the homosexual tries to regain his endangered or lost masculinity by an oral attack on the partner's penis in order to acquire it.

Premature activation of libidinal zones may produce a precocious, but particularly vulnerable development according to Greenacre (1952). Excessive stimulation results in premature erotization long before the phallic phase. Traumatic stimulation in the first year or two of life increases narcissism and bisexual identification. She thereby emphasized the neurogenic-psychogenic aspects of homosexuality. Despite the intense interest in the anus in most homosexual activity, Loewenstein (1935) described a type of passive homosexuality expressed exclusively in the form of genital gratification in which no anal wish seems to be present.

Litton, Giffon, and Johnson (1956) highlighted the role of parental sanctioning of the homosexual. They described the mother's behavior as overseductive and frustrating, at the same time sanctioning the boy's homosexuality. In addition the parents' own unstable bisexual identification as well as their defective superego contributed to the development of homosexuality.

Bychowski (1954) delineated features of the ego in the homosexual which included such primitive defense mechanisms as splitting, introjection, denial, turning against the self and narcissistic withdrawal, considering them of paramount importance in the genesis of homosexuality. The ego is weakened in these cases because of the necessity of maintaining various identifications which have become not only unconscious but dissociated from each other, therefore allowing less of the libido to be available for object cathexis. Sudden releases of undifferentiated aggressive-libidinal impulses lead to brief attempts at establishing contact with objects because the poorly structured ego of the homosexual does not succeed in binding the instinctual energies of the primary process.

It was Edoardo Weiss's assertion (Socarides 1962, Weiss 1950, 1960) that most perversions center around the oedipus complex. Childhood misunderstandings and misinterpretations of the anatomy, the functions and the role of the other sex, and distorted attitudes toward family members, guilts and fears concerning the father's and mother's sexual activity and one's own were inevitably found in most of his patients. The ultimate choice of a homosexual partner may be due to a number of factors. Weiss emphasized that every individual is to a certain extent constitutionally bisexual. Bisexuality held a different connotation from the usual: he did not mean that in every individual there is an innate object choice of the same or the opposite sex. He meant that without elements within oneself of the opposite sex, a well integrated rapport based on understanding of the heterosexual love partner is impossible. In a majority of individuals the homosexual trends are sublimated, that is, desexualized, but individuals in whom the bisexual constitution is overaccentuated often fail to sublimate this component sufficiently. The reflexive form of narcissisms finds satisfaction by proxy where it cannot be directly gratified. In other words, one loves oneself in another person of the same sex in homosexuality. This is a "love choice" of the narcissistic type. In a strong bisexual constitution, homosexuality may be an outlet or an escape from a severe oedipal conflict. A girl may withdraw from oedipal competition with her mother through masculine identification. Homosexuality reveals more complex mechanisms, however. By projecting his femininity onto the loved woman the heterosexual man can thus vicariously enjoy his own femininity. Weiss adds that the male does not become the female; he simply enjoys the female's functioning in the loved woman, the loved object outside of himself. These comments are a significant contribution to understanding the love relationship between adult heterosexual pairs.

Bergler (1933, 1943, 1944, 1951, 1954, 1956, 1959) estimated that female homosexuality is nearly double that of male homosexuality (Kinsey 1948). Many female homosexuals live the lives of married women because they are driven to find social and economic security, permitting heterosexual intercourse without pleasure to themselves. He believed that female homosexuality was a pathological elaboration of the unsolved masochistic attachment to the preoedipal mother. So far as the congruity with male homosexuality exists there are in both male and female homosexuals identical childhood fears and the same defense measures. However, in the female it is primarily her unsolved preoedipal oral masochistic conflict with the mother which is involved. Therefore, in Bergler's opinion, the basic conflict in the female is not of a libidinal but of an aggressive content. Beneath female homosexuality lies a savage, defensive hatred for the mother which is warded off by a libidinous defense of denying hate and superimposing a feeling of love toward a woman. This defense is unconscious and these patients have great difficulty in admitting the aggression beneath their love for their woman partners. The female homosexual attempts to repeat the baby-mother relationship with occasional reversal of roles.

In male homosexual relationships, according to Bergler, the male is not aware that he is repeating an oedipal and incestuous tie with his mother. He does not have the slightest conception that he is substituting the penis of his partner for the breast of his mother.

Bergler's prolific contributions (1943, 1951, 1954, 1956, 1959) emphasized that the homosexual solution consists of a specific elaboration of psychic, masochistic vicissitudes stemming from the first months of life. During these earliest phases the aggression of the child recoils because of guilt; this guilt is secondarily libidinized. The masochism is further disguised and repressed through the illusion of aggression ("pseudoaggression"). The dynamically decisive masochistic substructure only becomes conscious through analysis. Homosexuality is a "way out" for one's imperious needs for masochistic suffering. Bergler pointed out that the oral-masochistic rather than the sadistic hate-filled basis of female homosexuality works on a multilayered structure.

In 1951, Karl Menninger believed that all formulations of the genesis of male homosexuality were too general and failed to elucidate the different kinds of homosexuality encountered clinically. He found it inconceivable that any one simplified formula could apply in all instances and maintained that aggressive hostile feelings toward the homosexual partner play a much more important role than indicated in the literature.

The difference between the pervert and neurotic, according to the American Psychoanalytic Association's 1951 panel on perversions (Arlow 1952), does not lie in the fact that one approves and the other rejects the component instinct. Difference resides, rather, in the different attitude of the ego toward the result of the defensive conflict and the defensive transformations and masking of the component impulse. Therefore, one must not be content with certain formulations such as: (1) the pathogenesis of perversions depends upon persons reacting to sexual frustration with regression toward infantile sexuality; (2) homosexuality is the result of castration anxiety solely related to the oedipal period; (3) fixation at a pregenital sexual level is the total etiology without including subsequent vicissitudes of development; (4) frustration and regression to previous levels of fixation are the entire explanation. Were this so, one could, by therapeutic techniques, simply bypass the systematic sexual development in infancy and concentrate mainly on the cause and effect of such frustration. The early classical theory which explains perversions as caused by early accidental fixating experiences, including seductions, followed by a traumatic oedipal period characterized by excessive anxiety, although important, according to the Panel, requires careful clinical validation in each case.

Freud's early theory that perversions were simply a breakthrough of id impulses unopposed by the ego or the superego has been disproven clinically. The introduction of the topographic approach (1923a, b, 1924) in psychoanalysis made it possible to clarify that both instinctual drives and the defenses against them are unconscious. Numerous analysts (Arlow 1952, 1954) observed that what appeared to be gratification of a perverse instinctual drive actually constituted the end product of a defensive compromise in which elements of inhibition as well as gratification were present. The patient's approval of a perverted action, however, is not equivalent to approval of the component instinct warded off in neurosis. In a perversion the component instinct must undergo extensive transformation and disguise in order to be gratified in the perverse action. This masking is conditioned by the defense of the homosexual's ego which resists the gratification of the component instinct as energetically as does the ego of a neurotic. Thus the perverted action, like the neurotic symptom, results from the conflicts between the ego and the id and represents a compromise formation which at the same time must be acceptable to the demands of the superego. In perversion, as in neurotic symptoms, the instinctual gratification takes place in a disguised form while its real content remains unconscious. Furthermore, the perverted action differs from the neurotic symptom by the form of gratification of the impulse: orgasm.

Benedek (1952) examined the psychodynamic motivations of each variety of homosexual perversion in the female. She found, after prolonged physiological and psychological studies, that correlations of psychodynamic constellations with bodily and hormonal indicators of the sexual aberrations are lacking.

In 1955 W. H. Gillespie presented his paper, "The General Theory of Sexual Perversion," at the International Psychoanalytic Congress in Geneva. His formulations represented the status of our theory and understanding of sexual perversion as of twenty years ago. His paper was remarkably comprehensive, taking into account infantile sexuality and affirming that the problem of sexual perversion lies in the defense against oedipal difficulties. It underscored the concept that in sexual perversion there is a regression of libido and aggression to preoedipal levels rather than a primary fixation at those levels. It stressed the importance of ego behavior and ego defense maneuvers as well as the importance of the Sachs mechanism. He delineated the characteristics of the ego which make it possible for the ego to adopt a certain aspect of infantile sexuality thereby enabling it to ward off the rest. The superego has a special relationship to the ego which makes the latter tolerant of this particular form of sexuality. A split in the ego often coexists with a split in the sexual object so that the object becomes idealized, "relatively anxiety free and relatively guilt free in part."

There were seven principal points in Gillespie's general theory applicable to homosexuality: (1) He believed that the raw materials of perversion are drawn from the constituent elements of infantile sexuality. (2) "A clinical perversion, however, is generally specialized in an elaborate way, leaving only one or two routes open for achieving sexual excitement, discharging sexual tension, and establishing a sexual relationship." (3) A perversion represents a defense

against the oedipus complex and castration anxiety.
(4) Defensive systems induce (a) a regression of libido
and aggression to pregenital levels with a resulting
increase in sadism and its associated anxiety, and (b)
guilt feelings and defenses against sadism and anxiety
"designed to protect both the self and the object." (5) A
special characteristic of perversion is the libidinization of anxiety, guilt and pain as a method of defense.
(6) No less important than the vicissitudes of instinct
are the ego's behavior and defensive maneuvers. (7) In
perversion the ego has adopted a certain piece of
infantile sexuality and is enabled in this way to ward
off the rest. Gillespie believed that the ego was able to
do this, first because the superego was especially
tolerant of this form of sexuality and, second, "because
of a split in the ego and in the object. . . an idealized
object and a relatively anxiety free and guilt free part-
ego are available for the purposes of a sexual
relationship, which takes place, so to say, in an area
where the writ of reality testing does not run."

Relationship to Other Perversions

Fetishism (Freud 1927, Lorand 1956, Socarides
1960), transvestism (Barahal 1953, Fenichel 1930,
1945, Freud 1927, Gillespie 1956a) and homosexuality
(Freud 1922, 1925b) reflect different compromises
between the simultaneous identification with the
phallic and castrated mother (Lorand 1956). In some
instances, the fetishist has both conscious and
unconscious homosexual wishes and desires, but may
never engage in overt homosexual practices. The use of
a fetish protects him against what he regards as more
catastrophic, that is, homosexual relations. In other

instances fetishism may be present along with overt homosexuality.

There is an interconnection and interrelationship between erotogenic masochism, sexual sadism, and homosexuality. Freud emphasized that in masochistic men a feminine identification may exist without homosexual object choice; the masochistic perversion can prevent the individual's overt homosexuality (Freud 1919b, Socarides 1958, Panel 1960). In the case of the Wolf Man (Freud 1918b) he described how a masochistic attitude toward the father, resulting in neurotic symptoms, serves a defensive function against assuming an overt passive homosexual attitude toward him.

Bychowski (1954) described the forms of homosexual object choice which can include a homosexual object in a masochistic or sadistic ego involvement. Individual factors determine whether the object represents one or both preoedipal or oedipal parents, but he qualifies this to mean that it is not the total parent represented, but rather the partial object: the maternal breast, the paternal phallus, or both. The rapidly shifting attitude of the homosexual ego makes it possible for the patient to combine the role of the aggressive father assaulting the oedipal mother with the role of a maternal substitute passively submitting to a homosexual object, the latter representing both his own phallic self and the aggressive father.

In sexual (erotogenic) masochists (Joseph 1965), men who seek physical injury, pain and suffering as an erotic requirement for orgastic satisfaction, one finds that a strong feminine identification may exist without overt homosexual object choice. Freud's Wolf Man (1918b) is a classic example of this. The masochistic perversion is often the alternative chosen by and acceptable to the ego in preference to overt homosexuality.

A number of female homosexuals show fetishistic and transvestite symptomatology. Barahal (1953) attributes the transvestism of his female patient to a wish for overt homosexual relations. However, it is often true that both male and female transvestites have no homosexual interest; they feel they embody both sexes simultaneously. They often respond to homosexual overtures with marked hostility and prefer autoerotic orgastic fulfillment. The pseudotransvestite is an overt homosexual who uses cross dressing solely for purposes of enticement. Fenichel (1930) felt that transvestism was particularly common in active masculine type women. The relationship of transvestism to homosexuality has been further explored by Sperling (1963), Orgel (1968), Segal (1965), and Ovesey and Person (1976), Scharfman (1976), and Jucovy (1976).

The homosexual content of sexual activities involving more than one heterosexual couple depends upon the motivational state of the participants. It may range from the overtly homosexual to unconscious homosexuality and may even appear as simply variational heterosexual experience. In an early paper Brill (1934) gives an example of ménage à trois, which he successfully analyzed as homosexuality. The case involved a male patient, his wife, and another male, the wife having intercourse with both men. The patient sought to defend himself against his passive homosexual desires, which corresponded to his earlier attitude to the father, by reacting to them with delusions of persecution. In the reported sexual acts the patient fulfilled both identifications: he enacted both the father and mother roles and felt, therefore, in control. The woman was "his woman," thereby bolstering his masculinity. He felt he loved both the wife and the other man (parents). He was gratified that his wife preferred him; she would say to him, "You are the one I really am attached to—I love your friends as long as you love them—my universe is your universe and what you want shall happen." In reality he was gratifying his passive feminine homosexual desires by identifying with the wife (mother) in sexual relations and was probably able to function sexually with his wife through identification with the other man's penis (father).

The trauma of viewing the female genital in childhood is overcome in certain cases, while in others it may lead to homosexuality or fetishism. For instance, the threat of separation from the mother is experienced as an equal if not greater danger than the loss of the penis. Fleeing to the fetish and all it represents serves a simultaneous means of defense against both castration and separation snxiety. Thus each of the triad—fetishism, homosexuality, and transvestism—illustrate different phases of the compromise between the biphasic identification with the mother (Lorand 1930, Jucovy 1976).

Freud (1919b) pointed out that "the beating fantasy has its origin in incestuous attachment to the father." Therefore, it is closely related to homosexuality. However, he stated that in the case of the boy the situation bears a greater resemblance to the original fantasy with its genital significance "since there is a difference of sex (at the conscious level) between the person beating and the person being beaten." By repressing and remodeling his unconscious fantasy, the boy produces a later conscious fantasy which has for its content a feminine attitude without an apparent homosexual object choice. The boy who had tried to escape from his homosexual object choice and "who has not changed his sex, nevertheless feels like a woman in his conscious fantasies and endows the women who are beating him with masculine attributes and characteristics." There is a prevalence of pregenital features in the sexuality of all erotogenic masochists.

In masochistic fantasies or in actual gratification men unconsciously identify themselves with the woman in her role in intercourse or in childbirth. In these cases "the pain or punishment which arouses them is a regressive expression of their passive genital desire…the punishing or cruel woman possesses phallic attributes which thus indirectly indicates that a woman here stands for a man (Loewenstein 1957). These phallic characteristics of the female partner point to another feature of great importance in the life of the masochist, namely, his insistence on denial of the absence of a penis in women and thus a denial of the castration danger. Loewenstein (1957) takes this to mean that the crucial problem which human sexuality has to deal with during its development is fear of the loss of the object and fear of the loss of its love together with castration fear and superego anxiety. Therefore, in both fantasy and actual acts of beating, passivity and helplessness have the aim of appealing to the mercy of the "threatening and protective parental figure."

In masochists strong homosexual tendencies are readily observed. All homosexuals suffer from a severe degree of psychic masochism. At its root this is an expression and fulfillment of the original masochistic relationship of the helpless child to the overwhelming, engulfing, overpowering, cruel mother to whom the child must submit in order to survive. This submission is perpetuated in the relationship with homosexual partners (Sherman and Sherman 1926). The sexual object has been changed but the sexual aim remains the same. Thus, his hope to escape from his masochistic enslavement to a woman (mother) by choosing a male partner is utterly defeated. The masochism of the homosexual often takes the form of, and is experienced as, the masochistic pleasure of social and moral censure and loss of personal dignity because of homosexual behavior.

Masochistic heterosexual and sadistic homosexual object choice may alternate. Both object choices represent one or both preoedipal or oedipal parents. The patient described in chapter 9 (Calvin) emphasizes the shifts which may occur from overt to latent homosexuality and the reverse. The psychopathology of this young patient clearly demonstrates shifting ego and libidinal constellations and the resultant alternation in types of object choice and clinical symptomatology. In his fantasy and activity he quite consciously denied the anatomical fact of his penis and thus the danger of castration. The pain or punishment which would arouse him was a regressive expression of his passive genital desires. His utilization of masochism and foot and toe fetishism as a defense passed within a short period from homosexual fantasy to overt homosexuality for approximately one year. At that time the overt homosexuality was repressed and the shift to an apparently heterosexual masochistic relationship began.

As already noted, Freud (1919) thought that the beating fantasy has its origin in an incestuous attachment to the father. In the case of the boy even though there is a difference in sex (at the conscious level) of the person being beaten, it is clear that he, too, was avoiding his overt homosexuality by repressing and remodeling his unconscious fantasy. The remarkable fact about Calvin's conscious fantasy—to be made to suffer at the hands of a female, to be nearly drowned, to be urinated upon—is that it has for its content a feminine attitude without overt homosexual object choice. The fear of castration is lessened by the substitution of a female figure for the father and the indignities, threats, and attacks which he contrives are a substitute for a passive genital penetration by the father.

In these outright perverse masochistic fantasies and practices what is actually taking place is a homosexual, albeit disguised, union. One could further predict that with a shift of forces involving drive, defense and ego-adaptive functions, one might expect the overt homosexual object choice to appear.

Views differ as to the relationship between transsexualism and homosexuality. Ovesey and Person (1974a, 1974b) classify transsexual individuals into two groups: those who suffer from primary transsexualism which is due to a core gender identity disturbance and those who become transsexual secondary to homosexuality or transvestism (homosexual transsexuals and transvestite transsexuals). Stoller (1975) believes that the term transsexual should be restricted to the most effeminate of boys who suffer from a severe core gender disturbance due to the continuation of a blissful symbiotic relationship with the mother, conflict-free in origin and due to a process similar to imprinting. In my opinion (Socarides 1970), transsexualism can arise from either transvestism or homosexuality. Transsexualism appears in the homosexual who, in attempting to resolve his emotional conflicts, fastens upon the idea of changing his sex through the mechanism of denial. He therefore abhors everything masculine about himself and develops an overwhelming desire to be a woman. It is well known that most homosexuals are content to keep their external genitalia intact. The homosexual activities of the transsexual serve the following functions: (a) To attempt to resolve the fact that he is suffering from homosexuality through this recasting of identity. (b) To alleviate guilt as to homosexual object choice. (c) To attempt to ward off paranoidal anxieties were he to engage in homosexuality in his true anatomical role. (d) To neutralize overwhelming destructive aggression through a negation of all masculine strivings. Volkan's opinions (1974) as to the origins of transsexualism are similar to my own.

Homosexuality and Psychosis

In the most severe form of homosexuality, Preoedipal form, Type II (see chapter 5), the predominance of archaic and primitive mental mechanisms, the severity of pathology of internalized object relations, and the disturbance in ego functions are of such an intense degree that the clinical picture may mislead the clinician to make the diagnosis of psychosis. Less severe forms, especially those of Preoedipal Type I and Oedipal, lack any psychotic coloration. In view of the homosexual's ability to form analyzable transferences and his ability to rebound from regressive episodes, one may conclude that he is suffering from a *transitional condition* lying somewhere between the neuroses and psychoses. This is in keeping with Glover's earlier assertion of 1933 that perversions (including homosexuality) may form a developmental series reflecting stages in the overcoming of anxiety concerning the individual's own body or external objects. They represent attempts at introjection and projection of anxieties by means of excessive libidinization. They are "the negative of psychotic formations" and "patch over flaws in the development of reality sense."

The homosexual behavior of some severely ill schizophrenic patients proves to be neither oedipal nor proedipal but rather an outcome of their confused, chaotic, and fragmented psychic organization. This form of homosexuality may be termed *schizohomosexuality* and is described in chapters 17 and 26. The desperate need to make human contact may involve all forms of perverse activities including homosexual acts, but, like other spasmodic attempts to experience relatedness, there is no consistent true structure of a perversion or sustained quality to these episodes. A large number of paranoid schizophrenics, paranoiacs, pseudoneurotic-schizophrenics-or-latent schizophrenics may have a concomitant homosexual conflict and may manifest homosexual behavior.

Freud (1911) first called attention to the possibility that certain psychotic symptoms were the manifestation of an underlying homosexual conflict. This hitherto unsuspected reason for the development of a psychosis demanded clinical investigation. Homosexual impulses and behavior in the psychotic have been studied mostly in cases of overt male homosexuality (Brill 1934, Freud 1922, Grauer 1955, Nunberg 1947). Freud's paper (1911) on Schreber first suggested a possible etiological connection between homosexuality and psychosis. He remarked, "It remains for the future to decide whether there is more delusion in my theory than I should like to admit or whether there is more truth in Schreber's delusion than other people...would like to believe." In the early years of psychoanalysis Brill considered paranoia to be the "first cousin of homosexuality" (Brill 1934). He concluded that homosexuality and paranoia are based on narcissistic fixation but where the homosexual reaches the goal of object choice, albeit on an inverted path, the paranoiac finds it impossible to attain and has to regress to ego libido.

Freud's early hypothesis that paranoid psychotic symptoms develop as a defense against emerging unconscious homosexual wishes was later subject to clinical investigation and statistical study in an attempt to determine its validity. Klaif and Davis (1960) obtained statistical data from the records of 150 paranoid schizophrenic female patients and from a control group of 150 nonpsychotics; all of them were examined in relation to this hypothesis. They believed that since "unconscious homosexual wishes are emerging during the acute illness," they should expect to find patients preoccupied with homosexual thoughts and wishes. They theorized that since a sexual problem is the basis of paranoia, delusions and hallucinations would have a predominantly sexual content. Freud (1911) had stated, "The person who is now hated and feared as a persecutor was at one time loved and honored." One could represent the principle forms of paranoia as contradictions of a single proposition: "I (a man) love him (a woman)."

Klaif and Davis found that the delusions and hallucinations of the paranoid group did not have predominantly sexual content, but comparison with the control group was impossible due to the absence of delusions in the controls. These investigators, therefore, could not verify the hypothesis that paranoid psychotic symptoms develop as a defense against emerging unconscious homosexual wishes.

In another study Klaif (1961) stated, "The data obtained from the study of the records of seventy-five female paranoid schiozphrenic patients and a control of one hundred female nonpsychotic patients was analyzed in relation to Freud's hypothesis concerning the development of paranoid symptoms." Klaif's data cast doubt on the application of Freud's hypothesis to female paranoid schizophrenia because 57.3 percent of the paranoid group had delusions and hallucinations of sexual content, but in 83.7 percent of these forty-three members, the delusions or hallucinations were of heterosexual content. This study suggested that a disturbance in previous heterosexual relations rather than unconscious homosexual wishes were important in paranoid schizophrenia in females. The findings on female patients by Klein and Horwitz (1949) basically agreed with those of Klaif.

In clinical experience, nevertheless, the connection between homosexuality and both paranoid schizophrenia and paranoia is striking in a great number of patients and it occurs with considerable regularity. Although this material may not be on the surface and therefore cannot be garnered by statistical methods, paranoid content may appear during the therapy of any homosexual. It is clear that the homosexual fears persecution and attack on many levels. Some of these, social censure, for example, seem realistic, but others involve threatened castration at the hands of either parent or both. He fears anal attack; he fears the use of feces as a destructive, powerful weapon against him; and he fears poisoning due to intense, oral-sadistic incorporative drives. The presence of archaic mechanisms suggest the primitive introjective-projective dilemmas which beset him.

It may be that the female paranoiac consciously makes the male the persecutor, although the unconscious homosexual conflict is equally present, because the fears she can admit—social sanction and censure of her environment—she attributes to men. Both women and men experience censure and punishment as coming from male authority figures.

It is obvious, however, to the psychoanalytic investigator that surface or manifest content of delusions, dreams, and hallucinations may serve as a disguise; beneath a woman's paranoid delusion of sexual attack by a male (the external symbol of authority, punishment, and degradation) may lie deeper homosexual dread and desire.

Chapter 4

THE THEORY OF
PREOEDIPAL ORIGIN

This chapter presents a theory of the origin of preoedipal homosexuality. It is based on intensive study, research, and individual analyses of homosexual patients over the past two decades. My findings are confined to the origin of overt homosexuality of the obligatory, preoedipal type.

This theory of the preoedipal origin of homosexuality rests on three pillars. The first is the presence of a fixation in the first three years of life. The homosexual has been unable to successfully traverse the separation-individuation phase of human development. The second is the utilization and application of the the Hanns Sachs mechanism of sexual perversion. The third is Spitz's (1959) theory of synchronicity which must exist between maturational compliance and its counterpart, developmental (psychological) compliance.

This theory contends that all preoedipal homosexuals have been unable to make the progression from the mother-child unity of earliest infancy to individuation. As a result, there exists in these individuals a fixation* on, with the concomitant tendency to

---

*I use the terms developmental fixation and ego developmental arrest synonymously. They both represent developmental disturbances and arrest of ego

regression to, the earliest mother-child relationship. This is manifested as a threat of personal annihilation, a loss of ego boundaries, a fear of engulfment, and a sense of fragmentation.

Pathological development toward homosexuality has been ascribed to all phases of development. Clinical studies have mainly considered homosexuality to be an outcome of oedipal conflict. The numerous references cited in chapter 2 are the background and the groundwork for new theoretical formulations.

Despite our knowledge of some of the psychical mechanisms involved, psychoanalysis "has not yet produced a complete explanation of the origin of inversion..." (Freud 1940). Whether the homosexual fixation belongs to the preoedipal or oedipal period has remained problematic as has the extent of the role of regression as a contributing factor.

Significant contributions concerning the psychical events of the preoedipal period have supplied information vital to the resolution of the problem of origin. In his study of adults, Bychowski (1945), noting the affinities between schizophrenic and homosexual groups, found in both related infantile libidinal organizations and primitive features of the ego and its introjects. He contended that the peculiar weakness of the homosexual ego is based on its narcissistic and prenarcissistic disposition. He concluded that this fixation is at a stage preceding the formation of a distinct ego (Socarides 1960).

functions. The latter term emphasizes the observation that early fixation points lead to developmental imblances, for if the ego is not established as "an organized psychic structure with a variety of systems, apparatuses and functions" (Spitz 1959, p. 96) the development of object relations is significantly affected, and fixation points are created which disrupt future adaptive patterns and defenses, and produce "developmental interferences" (Nagera 1966).

Melanie Klein (1952) and her co-workers (Heinmann 1955, Rosenfeld 1949) have demonstrated that perversions may be related to the earliest oral-sadistic impulses of forcing the self into another object. They set forth the importance of early, excessive aggression and libidinal impulses and their attempted relief through introjective and projective mechanisms.

The genesis of homosexuality may be the result of disturbances which occur earlier than has generally been assumed, taking place in the later stages of the separation-individuation phase. In these stages there are already manifestly important beginnings of structure formation (Arlow 1942, 1954, Hartmann, Kris, and Loewenstein 1964). Fixation to the mother and the characteristically narcissistic object choice of the homosexual may be traced back to these stages of differentiation from the mother-child unity. It may be assumed that relations which develop out of the original unity in the more differentiated stages are the forerunners of later object relations. Qualitative and quantitative factors, specifically the divergent tendencies in the separation processes beginning at birth— one leading toward separateness and differentiation and the other toward the primitive state of the original unity—leave their imprint on the developing modes of instinctual manifestations and on ego formation. They exercise a determining influence on the structuring of the introjects and their subsequent projection onto the external world. My theory contends that the preoedipal homosexual suffers from a failure in self-object differentiation.

The fantasies and latent dream thoughts of the adult about his earliest experiences are representative of what was once the earliest reality. Thus external situations become internalized in the stucture of the

ego. Introjection and projection are ego building
mechanisms of the infant, becoming, through change
of function, defensive devices of the child's developing
ego.

The normal child successfully establishes his own
identity as a prerequisite to the onset of both true object
relations and partial identifications with parents.
Jacobson (1964) notes, "The preoedipal child, vacillating between heterosexual and homosexual, between active and passive strivings, still enjoys the
freedom to assume, playfully, various roles: in fantasy,
in attitudes or actions, on a more or less primitive ego
level, he may alternately identify at one time with the
father, at another time with the mother, with an older
sibling, or with a rival baby. I have also remarked that
fantasies of merging with the mother are considered a
normal phenomenon up to the age of three; but the
child's discovery and establishment of his sexual
identity, which reflects his instinctual advnacement to
the genital level, considerably reduces the freedom to
play various roles."

During the homosexual's infancy, the mother has
been, on the one hand, dangerous and frightening,
forcing separation, threatening the infant with loss of
love and care; on the other hand, the mother's
conscious and unconscious tendencies were felt as
working against separation. Anxiety and frustration
press for withdrawal of libidinal cathexis from the
mother which results in a shift of libido economy
toward increased aggression. This image of the
introjected mother leads to a rupture (split) in the ego.
In his narcissistic object choice, the homosexual not
only loves his partner as he himself wished to be loved
by the mother, but reacts to him with the sadistic

aggression once experienced toward the hostile mother for forcing separation.

This unconscious hostility reinforces the denial of any loving and giving aspects of the mother. The homosexual seeks to rediscover in his object choice—in the most distorted ways—the primary reality of his narcissistic relationship with the different images of the mother (and later of the father) as they were first experienced. The first introjection of the mother image predisposes the pattern of later introjections.

Homosexuality, therefore, can be seen as a resolution of the separation from the mother by running away from all women. In fantasies and actions, in reality, and in the compulsive hunting for partners, the homosexual is unconsciously searching for lost objects, seeking to find the narcissistic relationships he once experienced in the mother-child unity. The homosexual is trying to undo the separation and also remain close to his mother in a substitutive way, by using the male. He is trying both to be one with her and to seek out the reduplication of himself as an object. He performs this through substitution, displacement, and repression. The mounting evidence of preoedipal conflicts as the causative factor in the formation of homosexuality required the pinpointing of a mechanism by which conflict could be transformed into homosexuality. In 1923 Sachs provided psychoanalysis with the first valid explanation of the mechanism of sexual perversion. This discovery, although noted by Gillespie (1956a), has not been widely applied to clinical material; the paper remained untranslated up to the present time (See appendix B).

The Sachs Mechanism:
The Repressive Compromise

Homosexuality preserves a particularly suitable
portion of infantile experience or fantasy in the
conscious mind through the vicissitudes of childhood
and puberty. The rest of the representatives of the
instinctual drives have succumbed to repression
instigated by their all too strong need for gratification
or stimulation. The pleasurable sensations of infantile
sexuality in general are now displaced onto the
conscious "suitable portion of infantile experience."
This conscious suitable portion is now supported and
endowed with a high pleasure reward—so high,
indeed, that it competes successfully with the primacy
of the genitals. Certain conditions make this fragment
particularly suitable. The pregenital stage of development upon which the homosexual is strongly fixated
must be included in it. The extremely powerful partial
drive must find its particular form of gratification in it.
This particular fragment must have some special
relationship to the ego which allows it to escape
repression.

One must keep in mind that in the ego unconscious
elements are present, e.g., guilt and resistance.
Instinctual drives are in a continual struggle throughout the developmental stages of life. The complete
subjugation of a drive which gives pleasure to the ego
is not possible. We have to resign ourselves to a
compromise, allowing pleasure to remain in a partial
complex, to be taken up into the ego and to be
sanctioned, while the remaining components are
detached and are repressed more easily. This separation or split "in which the one piece (of infantile
sexuality) enters into the service of repression and thus

carries over into the ego the pleasure of a preoedipal stage of development, while the rest falls victim to repression, appears to be the mechanism of perversion" (Sachs 1923).

We know that the most difficult work of repression is almost always to effect a detachment from the infantile object choice, the oedipus complex, and castration fear. Thus the partial drive does not continue directly into a perversion (homosexuality) but must pass through the permutations of the oedipal conflict. This alternation of the original drive eventually wipes out traces of the oedipus complex, eliminating both the important individuals involved and even one's own self-involvement. The product becomes the perverse fantasy which enters consciousness and yields pleasure.

It follows that fantasies which lie outside the circle of infantile sexual gratification present themselves as a "way out". For instance, male homosexuals cannot deal with their extremely strong fixation on the mother. They instead fixate on their own sex as a result of narcissism and in a retreat from later castration anxiety. This fixation is incorporated into the ego and is acceptable to it.

In essence, the ego has taken over a portion of what would otherwise be repressed. Nevertheless, the repressed portion may still remain strong enough to threaten a breakthrough and the homosexual may, at any time, develop neurotic symptoms.

In homosexuality the instinctual gratification takes place in a disguised form while its real content remains unconscious. It should be emphasized that we are not simply dealing with an aspect of infantile sexuality which was allowed into consciousness and which the ego could somehow tolerate. Furthermore, the homo-

sexual symptom does not come about simply because
the boy, disturbed in his sexuality by castration fear,
regressed to that component of his infantile sexuality
which in childhood gave him security or at least
reassurance against his fears. In actuality, the
overemphasis on the infantile expression of his
sexuality simultaneously serves to reassure him and to
maintain a repression of his oedipal conflicts and other
warded-off remnants of infantile sexuality. This is a
partial repression of infantile sexuality wherein other
sexual wishes are exaggerated. Repression is facilitated in homosexuality through the conscious stress of
some other aspects of infantile sexuality.

To recapitulate: homosexuality is a living relic of the
past testifying to the fact that there was once a conflict
involving an especially strongly developed component
instinct in which complete victory was impossible for
the ego and repression was only partially successful.
The ego had to be content with the compromise of
repressing the greater part of infantile libidinal
strivings (primary identification with the mother,
intense unneutralized aggression toward her, dread of
separation, and fear of fusion) at the expense of
sanctioning and taking into itself the smaller part. For
example, the wish to penetrate the mother's body or the
wish to suck and incorporate and injure the mother's
breast undergo repression. In these instances a piece of
the infantile libidinal strivings has entered the service
of repression through displacement and substitution.
Instead of the mother's body being penetrated, sucked,
injured or incorporated, it is the male partner's body
which undergoes this fate; instead of the mother's
breast, it is the penis with which the patient interacts.
Homosexuality thus becomes the choice of the lesser
evil.

Two defense mechanisms, identification and substitution, play a crucial role. The homosexual makes an identification with the masculinity of his partner in the sexual act. In order to defend himself against the positive oedipus complex, that is, his love for his mother and hatred for his father and punitive, aggressive, destructive drives toward the body of his mother, the homosexual substitutes the partner's body and penis for the mother's breast. Homosexuals desperately need and seek a sexual contact whenever they feel weakened, frightened, depleted, guilty, ashamed or in any way helpless or powerless. In the patients' words, they want their "shot" of masculinity. They then feel miraculously well and strengthened thereby avoiding any tendency to disintegrative phenomena (they thereby enhance their self-representation). They instantaneously feel reintegrated upon achieving orgasm with a male partner. Their pain, fear, and weakness disappear for the time being and they feel well and whole again.

The male partners whom they pursue are representatives of their own self in relation to an active phallic mother. There are two parts to this concept. The first is an identification with a partner of the same sex. In this way they achieve masculinity through identification with the partner's penis. The man chosen as a partner represents one's forfeited masculinity (and self-representation) regained. The second is a substitution of the penis of the male partner for the mother's breast. In every homosexual encounter there is a hidden continuation of the close tie to the mother through the breast-penis equation. The reassuring presence of the penis in place of the breast allows the homosexual to feel that he is maintaining the tie to the mother but at a safe distance from her. Furthermore he divests himself

of oedipal guilt by demonstrating to her that he could
have no possible interest in other females; he is
interested only in men. In addition, he is protecting the
mother against the onslaught of other men's penises,
allowing penetration into himself instead.

The homosexual comes to realize in later phases of
treatment that he is engaged in an act of major self-
deception, having been victimized into sexual activity
with individuals of the same sex by certain intricate
psychic transformations. He has not given up his
maleness at all; he urgently and desperately wants to
be a man but is able to do this only by identifying with
the masculinity, penis and body of his partner in the
sexual act.

Homosexuality serves to protect the personality
against regression. If homosexual behavior did not
take place the patient would regress to varying degrees
in which there may be, in the severest of instances, a
threat of loss of ego boundaries and a fear of
dissolution of the self. In the most severe forms of
preoedipal homosexuality overt homosexual acts are
crucial for the survival of the ego when it is faced with
the catastrophic situation of imminent merging with
the mother and the pull toward the earliest phases of
development.

The Preoedipal Nuclear Conflict

Child analysts (Mahler and Gosliner 1955) who
have studied the data of infant and early child
development by direct observation conclude that "in
the second year of life the infant gradually changes
from an almost completely vegetative being, sym-
biotically dependent on the mother, into a separate
individual....he becomes increasingly aware of his

own capacities as well as of his own separateness. This apperception is, however, still a very precarious one at twelve to thirteen months of age. During the second year of life it is the maturational growth of locomotion which exposes the infant to the important experience of deliberate and active bodily separation from and reunion with the mother...providing he feels his mother's encouragement and availability....This is that second eighteen month period of life in which pregenital libidinal phases progress in a rapid and overlapping procession. Yet this same period is no less fateful as far as the infant's ego development and object relationships are concerned." The period from between twelve to eighteen to thirty-six months is termed the "separation-individuation phase of personality development...the characteristic fear of which is separation anxiety. If the symbiotic and separation-individuation phases were normal, however, from three-and-a-half on, the child should increasingly be able to respond to the mother as a 'whole mother'...one who can both gratify and disturb him."

The homosexual repeatedly demonstrates that he was unable to make these advances. In a child so unsuccessful, "the fear of re-engulfment threatens a recently and barely started individual differentiation...beyond the 15 to 18 month mark, the primary stage of unity and identity with mother ceases to be constructive for the evolution of the ego in an object world." By this age the father has an advantage since "the inner image of the father has never drawn to itself since "the inner image of the father has never drawn to mother and therefore there is less discrepancy between the image of father and the real father....From the very beginning, the infant creates the world in his own

image, wherein the symbiotic partner is the indispen-
the world in his own image, wherein the symbiotic
partner is the indispensable catalyst and beacon of
orientation."

During the separation-individuation phase (eighteen to thirty-six months) the infant is attempting to
evolve and jealously guard his developing self-image
"from infringement by the mother and other important
figures...[and] a quasi-normal negativistic phase" can
be observed along with "the process of disengagement
from the mother-child symbiosis." Although the
fixation of the homosexual is likely to have occurred in
the rapprochement subphase of the separation-
individuation process, difficulties in earlier phases
have undoubtedly produced difficulties and
vulnerabilities relating to functions involving object
relations, affect formation, relationship to reality, and
so on. Thus the more parasitic the symbiotic phase
"the more prominent and exaggerated will be this
negativistic reaction." If there is severe negativism
there is severe fear of reengulfment "inasmuch as all
happenings in the symbiotic phase are dominated by
orality; the infant furthermore loses the neccessary
and normal delusional experience of incorporating
and thus having the good mother in himself, restoring
the blissful state of omnipotent fusion with the
mother.... Instead, he struggles in impotent rage and
panic, with the catastrophic fear of annihilation, by
introjected bad objects, without being able to
successfully invoke the good part object, the soothing
breast of the ministering mother."

Often, a "symbiotic parasitic mother cannot endure
the loss of her hitherto vegetative appendage...." This
type of mother-child relationship is often found in the
families of homosexual patients. The father did not

constitute an important support against the threat of maternal engulfment. One can see that in the homosexual act, the male partner is the father to whom the son looks for salvation from engulfment. The homosexual remains entirely faithful to the mother, but his object hunger drives him to seek the penis of other men as a substitute for the breast. In the most severe cases of preoedipal homosexuality where there is a complete lack of the needed support from either parent, there is a danger of a "reengulfment of the ego into the whirlpool of the primary undifferentiated symbiotic stage...."

Spitz's Theory of Synchronicity

Spitz (1959) has shown that "when a psychological development which is age adequate for a given critical period cannot take place, it will be difficult, if not impossible, for the individual to acquire it at a later stage...." This is because "at the appropriate critical period a given item of psychological development will find all the maturational conditions favorable for its establishment." He called this "maturational compliance"; its counterpart is "developmental (psychological) compliance." There must be "synchronicity of maturation and development...[as] an absolutely essential feature of normal development." Spitz showed that if a child does not have the wish to walk when the maturation of the innervation of the lower part of the body enables it to walk, the child may later be unable to stand or walk without support. Later, as a consequence of a trauma or affect deprivation, he may regress to the stage where he could neither walk nor stand nor sit. "If, during the critical period, the appropriate (psychological) developmental item is not forthcoming, then the maturational factors will seize on other (psychological) developmental items available. These developmental items will be modified and distorted until they comply with the maturational needs, an integration will be established which deviates from the norm....As a result when the bypassed (psychological) developmental item finally does become available at a later stage, it will find the maturational positions occupied by compensating, though deviant, structures and unavailable for normal integration." Deficiencies in adaptation are "pivotal points for pathological regression...and play a major role in the etiology of psychiatric disease."

Spitz's observations can be applied to the problem of the early development of the homosexual. He has failed to make the separation from the mother at the proper stage of development. As a result, there remains a chronic intrapsychic fixation point to which he remains fixed despite having passed through other developmental maturational phases with some success. In these maturational positions there have been compensating and deviant structures formed in an attempt to compensate for the infantile deficiency. These structures are intimately concerned with the problems of identity, faulty ego boundaries, introjective and projective anxieties, fears of invasion and engulfment, and disturbances in the capacity to form object relations.

Oedipal versus Preoedipal Factors in the Caustion of Homosexuality

Conclusive statements about the preoedipal origin of homosexuality must take into account the roles of oedipal versus preoedipal factors in perverse and neurotic formations.

A panel entitled "Some Theoretical Aspects of Early Psychic Functioning" (Rubinfine 1959) stated, "The validation, amplification and extension of psychoanalytic theories of earliest psychic functioning can be expected from meticulously observed and collected developmental data on the one hand, and from the reconstructive work of child and adult analysis on the other. The developmental data are used for the formation of developmental theories which converge with or diverge from the theories formed from the work of reconstruction, and they thus naturally correct, validate, and amplify each other."

In this volume I have attempted a clear differentiation between data and theory, utilizing direct infant observation by child analysts whose investigations delineated the early maturational failures and vicissitudes of child development (Mahler and Gosliner 1955, Spitz 1959, Mahler 1967, 1968, 1975, Stoller 1964, Galenson and Roiphe 1975, Galenson et al. 1975, McDevitt and Settlage 1971). In validating any hypothesis one must use all available sources of study: (1) reconstruction from the analysis of children; (2) direct observation; and (3) a longitudinal, long-range developmental study.

Manifest symptom formation has been assumed to be the result of oedipal conflict while mechanisms of character formation have been ascribed almost exclusively to results of fixation at pregenital libidinal organization (Rosen 1957). Studies of the earliest periods of life have yielded valuable germinal data as to ego states and ego development, for example, Lewin's dream screen; the Isakower phenomenon;

Rangell's work on poise and the snout or perioral region; Hoffer's findings on mouth and hand integration.

The oedipal phase retains its position as the "funnel through which pregenital influences must pass in order to leave their imprint upon both character and neurotic symptom formation in the adult" (Rosen 1957). The necessary condition for the development of "a neurosis is intrapsychic conflict and that intrapsychic conflict presupposes the existence of a psychic structure. It is during the preoedipal phase that decisive influences come to bear on psychic structuralization....Preoedipal factors in neurosogenesis must be assessed from the point of view of how they retard or advance the development of the structural elements of the psychic apparatus...and more detailed investigation of specific ego failures is necessary" (Rosen 1957). Symptom neurosis should not be considered as the result of early developmental arrest or ego deformity.

Berliner (1957) has noted that there is a great difference between preoedipal and oedipal parental figures. Characteristically, preoedipal conflicts produce a disturbance in the sense of one's own identity and constitute evidence of a severe ego disturbance. In all cases of preoedipal homosexuality the sense of identity is lost, floundering, or severely obscured.

"If any one point is to be underscored, it would be that in regard to the general problem of the preoedipal phase we have no such well-formulated concepts of childhood development as we have in the later phases" (Rosen, 1957). Investigating the preoedipal period as a probable source of homosexuality can lead to an expansion of our general knowledge of this period. It is necessary to consider whether or not there are two forms of homosexuality of the obligatory type: one arising from oedipal phase conflict alone, signifying that the phenomena observed in the acts, dreams, fantasies, and other symptoms, are due simply to a regression to a previous phase of development; and another, arising from a preoedipal fixation of prime importance, which constantly dominates the life of the individual in his search for identity. In the oedipal form it is implicit that the dangers of the oedipal phase so disrupt an already formed identity that a regression to early infantile periods occurs as an escape from the dangers of the oedipal phase. An alternative course is to handle such dangers by adopting a negative oedipal attitude.

Such a division is not indicated by my clinical experience in the treatment of homosexual patients. It is my opinion that the contribution of the preoedipal phase is basic to the problem of sexual identity, an issue central to the homosexual's difficulties. This issue will be dealt with at greater length in the chapter on classification.

Further refinements in our understanding of the types of homosexuality may lead us to conclude that the true perversion is a preoedipal disorder; although elements of oedipal conflict are present or apparently paramount in milder preoedipal forms, the well structured homosexual perversion does not arise from defending against oedipal conflict by a regression to earlier periods. Oedipal homosexuality is a different condition which may be treated like the neuroses. It occurs secondary to a temporary regression and does not represent a developmental arrest fixation or failure.

Handelsman (1965) is of the opinion that homosexuality may be explained by its relationship to the autistic and symbiotic modes of adaptation. "The fear of engulfment may lead to a partial regression to, or to a fixation at, the autistic phase in order to ward off the feeling of dissolution of the self representation....It is as if the male partner were the father to whom the son is looking for salvation from engulfment."

Should further validation prove my hypothesis correct, it would appear that preoedipal homosexuality is an intermediate condition somewhere between the psychoses, the borderline conditions, and the neuroses. Glover (1933) similarly places the homosexual symptom in our classificatory system.

There are certain findings which indicate that an individual is suffering from a fixation to a preoedipal conflict rather than a regression to it due to oedipal conflict and castration fear. The regression to a preoedipal conflict is, therefore, a secondary line of defense against deeper fears. Preoedipal fantasies serve as a defense against the emergence of oedipal material and vice versa. Hoffer (1954) has aptly described these phenomena under the heading of defense organization. Thus castration anxiety, the direct result of the oedipal conflict, may also be utilized as a defense against anxieties of the preoedipal phase. Likewise preoedipal drives may serve as a defense in warding off oedipal wishes and fears. There is always an interplay between the two.

Findings which indicate preoedipal fixation are:

1. A primary identification with the mother accompanied by severe gender confusion. It is well known that following the birth of the child the biological oneness with the mother is replaced by a primitive

identification with her. The child must proceed from the security of identification and oneness with the mother to active, competent separateness and male (phallic) striving. If this task proves too difficult, pathological defenses, especially an increased aggressiveness, may result. These developments have a great effect on the solution of conflicts appearing in the oedipal phase, under the pressure of castration fear, an additional type of identification with the mother in the form of passive feminine wishes for the father is likely to take place. However, beneath this feminine position in relation to the father one may ofter uncover the *original passive relation with the mother, that is, an active feminine preoedipal identification.*

2. These patients experience intense anxiety upon attempting separation from the mother, an affective state evident before the age of three, persisting unabatedly throughout life.

3. The patients' general behavior is markedly childish; acting out often replaces remembering. Preoedipal material is closely linked with particular traits characteristic of the object relations of that phase of development, for example oral and anal fantasies and practices.

4. There is moderate to severe disturbance in the sense of ego boundaries and body image.

5. The presence of oral incorporative, oral aggressive complexes largely dominate the patient's life and may internal persecuting objects, fears of poisoning, and fears of being swallowed.

Preoedipal homosexuality therefore constitutes early developmental arrest or ego deformity. In some patients the fixation is less than in others (quan-result in the semi-delusional oral anxieties, dreams of titative factor). Patients regress to those conflicts which have left a weak point or scar formation affecting the vicissitudes of later development, especially the oedipal period; the greater the oedipal weakness, the stronger the tendency to regression to the preoedipal period with the danger of borderline or psychotic-like manifestations, symptomatology and transference. The tendency toward regression also depends on the strength of the ego and superego formations. Some preoedipal homosexuals (depending on the degree of self-object differentiation achieved) may not portray the merging phenomenon —the threat of disintegration and the overwhelming anxiety—as vividly as others. However, the merging phenomenon may be seen in its derivative forms, for example, the fears of being surrounded by snakes, of being swept into whirlpools, and of being enclosed in caves.

Some patients may never approach the merging phenomenon with its danger of regression to the earliest stage of development, especially if they do not seriously attempt to interrupt their homosexual practices. Others, deeply afraid to face this overwhelming anxiety, will prematurely terminate psychoanalytic therapy in a period of resistance, with many rationalizations for their decision. Some of the latter will return to therapy for shorter or longer periods of time to relieve their suffering, only again to escape from facing the deepest conflicts. The failure to successfully resolve these conflicts is largely responsible for the inevitable continuance of homosexual practices.

Psychopathology in Preoedipal Homosexuality

Pathology, whether somatic or psychic, is defined as failure of function with concomitant pain and/or suffering. This failure, its significance, and manifold consequences, are striking in obligatory preoedipal homosexuality.

A number of items serve as indicators of psychic pathology in the preoedipal homosexual, the symptoms of which will be discussed in greater detail in the chapter of classification. The following may not appear in all cases, and vary in degree from patient to patient:

1. A lifelong persistence of the original primary feminine identification with the mother, and a consequent sense of deficiency in one's masculine identity. The end result is a pervasive feeling of femininity or a deficient sense of masculinity (Van der Leeuw 1958).

2. A fear of engulfment and consequent extreme anxiety whenever an obligatory homosexual attempts to establish any sexual relatedness to a woman (Handelsman 1965, Jacobson 1964).

3. A persistence of archaic and primitive psychic mechanisms, for example, the presence of incorporative and projective anxieties (Freud 1905a).

4. A deficit in the body ego boundaries, with fears of bodily disintegration (Socarides 1968) and unusual sensitivity to threats of bodily damage by external objects.

5. A fear of engulfment evidenced in the dream life of all preoedipal homosexuals. This is commonly symbolically represented by fears of encasement in caves, tunnels, or whirlpools; deep immersion into bodies of water; and so on, with a threat of personal annihilation

and loss of self (Fleischmann 1960). These symbols derive from the fear of engulfment by the body of the female.

6. Sexual acts carried out only with a person of the same sex or through the combined use of other perversions. In certain individuals heterosexual acts may be carried out with little or no pleasure.

7. Damaging, disruptive aggressive impulses which threaten to destroy both the relationship and the partner. This is particularly common in preoedipal homosexual relations in which the capacity to form object relations is severely impaired; the affects of love and affection are usually found to be surface rationalizations covering severe aggression.

8. Intense, insistent, homosexual acts carried out to lessen and neutralize projective anxieties which threaten the personality.

9. Homosexual acts whose effects are likened to those of the opium alkaloids in their magical restorative powers: the optimum "fix"—reinstating the body ego and sense of self against a threat of disruption, and, in severe cases, against regressive experiences which produce feelings and threats of imminent disintegration of the personality. Their urgency derives from the emergency need of survival for the ego of the homosexual.

10. A search for love from the father or father - surrogate and a concomitant wish to wreak vengeance upon him, which lies beneath the male homosexual's apparent devotion to men. The son's wish for masculine identification had been frustrated earlier by the father's absence, coldness, apathy, or disdain. Furthermore, the father fears his phallic, castrating wife and does not interfere with her domination of the

child. The son harbors deep distrust, rage and resentment toward men because the father failed to protect him from the engulfing mother.

11. A deep sense of inferiority, worthlessness, and guilt suffered consciously and/or unconsciously by all preoedipal homosexuals because of their inability to function in the appropriate anatomic role. These feelings are not caused by societal attitudes but are aggravated by them (Glover 1960).

12. A considerable degree of psychic masochism (Bergler 1951, Freud 1919b, Sherman and Sherman 1926). The aggressive assault toward the mother and secondarily toward the father is drained off into a psychic masochistic state. All homosexuals deeply fear the knowledge that their homosexual behavior constitutes an eroticized defense against this more threatening masochistic state (Freud 1918b). The masochism seeks discharge through homosexual activity.

13. Anxiety derived from preoedipal and oedipal conflicts which undergoes an eroticization or libidinization (Fenichel 1945).

14. A dramatic appearance of severe anxiety, tension, depression, and other symptomatology upon attempting interruption of homosexual activities, therefore underscoring a function of the homosexual symptom, namely, that it is a compromise formation against deep anxieties (Gillespie 1956a). This outcome upon interruption of activities is consistently seen in the course of treating homosexuals in depth.

15. Additional sexual deviations occurring simultaneously, or sometimes alternately, with homosexuality; the most common are fetishism (Freud 1927), transvestism (Barahal 1953), Feichel 1930b) and exhibitionism.

Recapitulation

The nuclear conflicts of homosexuals originate in the earliest period of life, forcing them into choosing partners of the same sex for ego survival. The homosexual has been unable to pass successfully through the later stages of the separation-individuation phases of early childhood, most likely the rapprochement sub-phase. Severe ego deficits and insufficient self-object differentiation result from this maturational (psychological) developmental failure. Homosexuality serves the repression of a pivotal fixation in which there is a desire for, and dread of, merging with mother in order to reinstate the primitive mother-child unity.

In the mother-child unity one can discern: (1) a wish for and fear of incorporation; (2) a threatened loss of personal identity and personal dissolution; (3) guilt feelings because of a desire to invade the body of the mother; (4) an intense desire to cling to the mother which later develops in the oedipal period into a wish for, and fear of, incestuous relations with her; and (5) intense aggression of a primitive nature toward the mother.

At a conscious level the patient attempts to compensate for his primary nuclear conflict by certain activities designed to enclose, ward off, and encyst the isolated affective state of the mother-child unity. He does not, therefore, approach any other woman, especially sexually; this will activate his fear of her. He does not attempt to leave mother because he fears provoking engulfing, incorporative tendencies on her part and on his own. Any attempt by him to separate produces an exacerbation of his unconscious ties. He instead attempts to keep the safest closeness to her, all the while remaining asexual regarding other females. All sexual satisfactions are carried out through substitution, displacement and other defense mechanisms. Having already made a feminine identification (a result of the continuance of the original primary feminine identification), he restores strength and reaffirms a sense of self through transitory male identification with his male partner. The homosexual is unconsciously enjoying sexual closeness to both mother and father simultaneously by substituting a man for sexual intercourse.

The homosexual is fixated on his wish for, and dread of, the mother-child unity. Consequently, he is prone to regression to earlier stages of development. He experiences a threat of ego destruction in union with the mother, an event to be avoided at all costs. The homosexual's life and development are designed to forestall and prevent the realization of this powerful affective state. Homosexual behavior is the solution to the intolerable anxiety connected with the pull to return to this earlier, less differentiated phase of ego development. The homosexual object choice, achieved through the Sachs mechanism, is crucial to the repression of the basic conflict: the fear and dread of the mother-child unity.

Chapter 5
CLASSIFICATION

Freud (1905a) referred to homosexuality as: inhibited development, arrested development, developmental inhibition, sexual infantilism, and dissociation of development. He concluded that the presence of exclusiveness and fixation are signposts of severe psychopathology. Valuable contributions toward clarifying the classification of types of homosexuality have been made by Alexander (1927, 1956), Gillespie (1952, 1956a, b), Bychowski (1956a, b), Glover (1933), Nunberg (1939, 1947), Ferenczi (1909, 1914), and Boehm (1926, 1930, 1933).

Over seventy years ago Freud (1905a) proposed the following classification based on both conscious and unconscious motivation:

1. Absolute inverts whose sexual objects are exclusively of their own sex and who are incapable of carrying out the sexual act with a person of the opposite sex or of deriving any enjoyment from it.

2. Amphigenic inverts whose sexual objects may be of their own sex or of the opposite sex because this type of inversion lacks exclusiveness.

3. Contingent inverts whose circumstances preclude accessibility to partners of the opposite sex, and who may take as their sexual objects those of their own sex.

The classification by Rado (1949) bears a striking similarity to Freud's earlier formulations; he divided homosexuality into reparative, situational, and variational types. Reparative homosexuality is "ushered in by the inhibition of standard performance through early fear"; it arises from processes of repair which are in the main unconscious and is marked by a high degree of inflexibility. The individual depends on homosexuality for full orgastic gratification in all circumstances. Though he may force himself to go through the motions of heterosexuality (the union of male and female genitals leading to sexual orgastic satisfaction and/or performance) he cannot, thereby, obtain satisfaction.

Situational homosexuality occurs where the lack of opportunity for heterosexual contact may push a healthy individual to seek homosexual orgastic outlet. Such expedient acts "are the products of conscious deliberation rather than of an unconscious process and as a rule are dropped as soon as the situation changes."

Variational patterns may occur in the individual who yields to the desire for an alteration of sexual excitation. In some cultures such surplus activity is a part of the established social order. In other cultures, it is entirely an individual departure contrary to the social order.

Reparative homosexuality initiated by early unconscious fears and characterized by inflexibility and stereotypy is the only type that can be considered true (obligatory) homosexuality.

Other attempts at classification depended on the type of overt behavior and the provocation for such behavior. But none, with the exception of Gillespie, clarified the nature of the original conflict, the level of development at which this conflict occurred (fixation point), and the relative importance of regression and/or fixation to the genetic development of the homosexual symptom.

The comprehensive classification system presented here derives from the psychoanalytic clinical research study of homosexual patients over a twenty-year period. Implicit in its presentation is the author's indebtedness to many earlier contributions in this direction. My research has prompted me to present five major forms of homosexuality. Classification is based on the following items: (1) the conscious and/or unconscious motivation; (2) the developmental stage from which the nuclear conflict arose; and (3) the degree of pathology of internalized object relations in the homosexual patient.

I will present the characteristics of each type in outline form. I emphasize at this point the general proposition that there are three major forms of clinical overt homosexuality derived from unconscious conflict and not due to situational or variational motivations. These are (1) preoedipal homosexuality, (2) oedipal homosexuality, and (3) schizo-homosexuality (the coexistence of homosexuality and schizophrenia). In the mildest preoedipal type (Type I), the clinical picture is largely one of oedipal conflict and regression does not involve severe impairment in object relations and other ego functions. In the more severe preoedipal type (Type II), preoedipal fixation is of prime importance, constantly dominating the psychic life of the individual in his search for identity and a cohesive self. Oedipal conflict and castration fear may defend against deeper fears, and preoedipal fantasies may defend against the emergence of oedipal material. There is always an interplay between the two.

Further refinements in our understanding of the forms of homosexuality may lead us to conclude that the true perversion is a preoedipal disorder and does not arise from an oedipal conflict with a regression to earlier phases (see Gillespie's views in this section, describing homosexuality as an oedipal disorder arising from regression). Oedipal homosexuality is a different form of homosexuality which may be treated similarly to the neuroses. The latter occurs secondary to a temporary regression and does not represent a developmental arrest.

The Preoedipal Form

1. The preoedipal form is due to a fixation to the preoedipal phase of development (from birth to three years).

2. It is unconsciously motivated and arises from anxiety. Because nonengagement in homosexual practices results in anxiety, and because the partner must be of the same sex, it may be termed *obligatory homosexuality*. This sexual pattern is inflexible and stereotyped.

3. Severe gender identity disturbance is present: in the male, there is a faulty and weak masculine identity; in the female, there is a faulty, distorted, and unacceptable feminine identity derived from the mother, who is felt to be hateful and hated.

4. The persistence of the primary feminine identification, as a result of the inability to traverse the separation-individuation phase (from one-and-a-half to three years) and develop a separate and independent identity from the mother, results in sexual identity disturbance. In the female, an identification with the hated mother persists which she must reject. It is

essential to note once again the difference between primary and secondary feminine identification (See chapter 4).

5. Homosexuals of the preoedipal type are beset by anxieties of an insistent and intractable nature, leading to an overriding; almost continual search for sexual partners.

6. Persistence of primitive and archaic mental mechanisms leads to an abundance of incorporation and projection anxieties.

7. The anxiety which develops is due to fears of engulfment, ego dissolution, and loss of self and ego boundaries. They need the homosexual act to insure ego survival and transiently stabilize the sense of self. Consequently, they must repeat the act frequently, out of an inner necessity to ward off intense anxiety. (The rare exceptions in this type who cannot consciously accept the homosexual act struggle mightily against it and, therefore, the symptom remains latent, as explained below in the section on the latent form.)

8. The homosexual symptom is ego-syntonic, as the nuclear conflicts, including fear of engulfment, loss of ego boundaries, and loss of self, have undergone a transformation through the mechanism of the repressive compromise, allowing the more acceptable part of infantile sexuality to remain in consciousness. (See the Sachs mechanism, chapter 5, the section on Developmental Factors..")

9. There is a predominance of pregenital characteristics of the ego: remembering is often replaced by acting out.

10. The aim of the homosexual act is ego survival and a reconstitution of a sense of sexual identity in accordance with anatomy. The male achieves "masculinity" through identification with the male sexual

partner; this lessens castration fear. The female achieves "resonance" identification with the woman partner; this lessens castration fear. She also creates the "good" mother-child relationship.

11. The subtypes of preoedipal homosexuality can be defined and differentiated by the degree of pathology of internalized object relations. The solution to this complex problem of separating the various types of preoedipal homosexuality has been facilitated by Kernberg's important work (1975) defining criteria for understanding borderline conditions and pathological narcissism. In utilizing this approach, the true nature and meaning of oedipal homosexuality is increasingly clarified as well.

The Oedipal Form

1. This oedipal form is caused by a failure to resolve the oedipus complex and to castration fears, leading to the adoption of a negative oedipal position and a partial regression to anal and oral conflicts (a partial preoedipal regression). The male assumes the role of the female with the father (other men); the female assumes the role of the male with the mother (other women).

2. In this oedipal form, homosexual wishes are unconsciously motivated and dreaded; engagement in homosexual practices is not obligatory. The sexual pattern is flexible in that heterosexuality is usually the conscious choice.

3. Gender identity disturbances of masculine sexual identity in the male (or deficient feminine sexual identity in the female) are due to a secondary identification with a person (parent) of the opposite

sex. (This is simply a reversal of normal sexual identification in the direction of the same-sex parent.)

4. The male develops anxiety due to fears of penetration by the more powerful male (father); the female fears rejection by the more powerful female (mother). Common to both are conscious and unconscious shame and guilt arising from superego and ego conflicts, attendant on engaging in homosexual acts in dreams and fantasies and, occasionally, in actuality, under special circumstances of stress. Homosexual acts in the oedipal form are attempts to insure dependency and to attain power through the seduction of the more powerful partner.

5. Primitive and archaic psychic mechanisms may appear due to regression. These are intermittent and do not indicate pregenital character of the individual, as they do in the preoedipal form.

6. The homosexual symptom is ego-alien. Although unconsciously determined, the anxieties which are held in repression through the Sachs mechanism are anxieties which are held in repression through the archaic conflicts and fixations. Sachs mechanism are not those concerned with primitive archaic conflicts and fixations. When the symptom threatens to break into awareness, anxiety develops. However, under certain conditions, for example, defiant rage overriding the restraining mechanism of conscience, or periods of intense depression secondary to loss with resultant needs for love, admiration, and strength from a person of the same sex, homosexual acts may take place. Such acts, however, do not achieve the magical symbolic restitution of the preoedipal form. They may exacerbate the situation through loss of pride and self-esteem.

7. The aim of the homosexual act is to experience dependency on and acquire security from "powerful" figures of the same sex. The sexual pattern of the negative oedipal form is not inflexible or stereotyped as in the preoedipal form. There are remissions in the sense of masculine identity in the male and in the sense of pride and achievement in feminine identity in the female, secondary to successful performance in other (nonsexual) areas of life. Feelings of success diminish any fantasied or actual need for sexual relations with persons of the same sex.

The differentiating criteria of the *clinical* forms of homosexuality and their implications for therapy are fully discussed in chapter 26 in the section on therapy.

The Situational Form

This form is characterized by: (1) environmental inaccessibility to partners of the opposite sex; (2) consciously motivated behavior; (3) homosexual acts which are not fear-induced but arise out of conscious deliberation and choice; (4) the ability to function with a partner of the opposite sex; and (5) a flexible sexual pattern which allows these individuals to return to opposite sex partners when they are available.

Bieber reported that with rare exception, men who had not been homosexual prior to military service did not engage in homosexual activity throughout their tour of duty, despite the absence of female partners. This finding suggests a possible revision of the concept of situational homosexuality in instances where the coercive factor is absent. Much of the so-called situational factor in prisons is an outcome of the struggle for dominance and is, in fact, rape. The infrequency of validated situations in which heterosexuals deprived of opposite sex partners engage in homosexual relations reaffirms the strength of the male-female design once it has been established in the human psyche.

The Variational Form

1. The motivations underlying the variational form of homosexual behavior are as varied as the motivations driving men and women to pursue power, gain protection, assure dependency, seek security, wreak vengeance, or experience specialized sensations. In some cultures, such surplus activity is a part of the established social order; in others, it is entirely a product of individual enterprise, contrary to the general social order. The homosexuality practiced in ancient Greece was probably variational in type. (see chapter 3, section on cultural studies.)

2. The behavior is consciously motivated.

3. Homosexual acts are not fear-induced, but arise out of conscious deliberation and choice.

4. The person is able to function with a partner of the opposite sex.

5. The sexual pattern is flexible, and these individuals do return to opposite sex partners when they so prefer.

Variational homosexuality may occur in individuals who seek to gratify the desire for an alternation of sexual excitation, often for reasons of impotence or near-impotence. Much of the heteroxexual group sex activity currently reported includes homosexual behavior between male and female participants and is variational in form. In some instances, individuals with unconsciously derived homosexual conflicts take part in such group activities in order to act out their homosexual wishes and to simultaneously deny their homosexual problem.

One may see variational homosexuality in the neurotic, the psychotic, and the sociopath. It frequently occurs in those suffering from alcoholism or depressive states.

The Latent Form

1. The latent form has the underlying psychic structure of either the preoedipal or oedipal form, without homosexual practices.

2. There is much confusion in the use of the term *latent homosexuality* due to the erroneous and outmoded concept of constitutional bisexuality, which implies that side-by-side with an innate desire for opposite-sex partners there exists an inborn or innate desire for same-sex partners. Latent homosexuality means the presence in an indivual of the underlying psychic structure of either the preoedipal or oedipal type, without overt orgastic activity with a person of the same sex.

3. The shift from latent to overt homosexuality and the reverse depends on several factors: (a) the strength of the fixation at the preoedipal level (quantitative factor), the severity of anxiety, and the intensity of regression from the later oedipal conflict; (b) the acceptability of the homosexuality of the ego, the superego (conscience mechanism), and the ego ideal; and (c) the strength of the instinctual drives, libido and aggression. These individuals may never or rarely engage in overt homosexual activities.

4. The latent homosexual may or may not have any conscious knowledge of his preference for individuals of the same sex for orgastic fulfillment. On the other

hand, there may be a high level of elaboration of unconscious homosexual fantasies and homosexual dream material, with or without conscious denial of its significance. They may live an entire lifetime without realizing their homosexual propensities, managing to function marginally on a heterosexual level, sometimes marrying and having children.

5. Another pattern is that of the individual who, fully aware of his homosexual preference, abstains from all homosexual acts. Others, as a result of severe stress, infrequently and transiently do engage in overt homosexual acts, living the major portion of their lives, however, as latent homosexuals. In the latent phase, they may maintain a limited heterosexual functioning, albeit unrewarding, meager, and usually based on homosexual fantasies. They may utilize homosexual fantasy for masturbatory practices or may abstain from sexual activity altogether. These individuals are homosexual at all times; the shift between latent and overt and the reverse constitutes an alternating form of latent homosexuality.

6. All forms of latent homosexuality are potentially overt. Social imbalance—where severe inequities exist between one's survival needs due to the failure of society to ensure their adequate satisfaction—has a precipitating effect in some borderline or latent cases of both preoedipal and oedipal homosexuality. Such imbalance also brings a flight from the female on the part of the male, a flight from all aspects of mature endeavor, and a retreat to a less demanding role. This is a possible explanation of the apparent rise in the incidence of male homosexuality during periods of social turbulence in which many traditional roles, privileges, and responsibilities are overturned. The

same factors may cause an increase in female homosexuality.

One can best explicate the concept of a latent form of
homosexuality by comparing it to latent forms of
organic or physical illness, for example, diabetes. This
condition has important effects on all body systems
even though it may not express itself as overt diabetes
mellitus. The patient may live without being aware of
this condition in its milder forms, being able, for many
years, to tolerate its various negative influences on his
general health. Only refined clinical tests can reveal
the presence of this condition and its ongoing consequences. Such a latent state can, of course, become
overt with its unmistakable clinical signs and symptoms.

It is misleading and incorrect to assume that because
an individual, due to regression, has dreams of
wishing to be admired, loved, and taken care of by
older, authoritative, and protective men, that he is
suffering from homosexuality in its latent form. This is
simply an infantile adaptation of extreme dependency
and has no connection with the complex of psychodynamic factors responsible for manifest or latent
homosexuality. Patients with an obsessional character neurosis in a decompensated phase of their neurosis
often have such regressive wishes.

The concept of sublimated homosexuality requires
clarification, as it is often equated with latent
homosexuality. The phrase, correctly used, refers to
activities and behaviors aimed at warding off the
expression of an actual underlying homosexual
conflict; such activities and behaviors fall within the
general concept of sublimation.

Ovesey, in the mid-1950s, first introduced the term
pseudohomosexuality. It should not be confused with

oedipal, preoedipal, or latent homosexuality since it is not a true form. Ovesey defines it as follows:

Pseudohomosexuality refers to anxieties in heterosexual men about being homosexual. Such anxieties may occur at times of failure in the masculine role in any area of behavior—sexual, social, or vocational. The failure may be unconsciously represented through symbolic equation: I am a failure as a man = I am castrated = I am a woman (I am effeminate) = I am a homosexual, causing anxiety about being homosexual. The terminal anxiety in this equation is not a true homosexual anxiety since it is not motivated by a homosexual wish, nor is it accompanied by homosexual arousal. It is simply the result of the masculine failure which has been symbolically misinterpreted as homosexuality; hence, the anxiety is a *psuedohomosexual anxiety* and the man experienceing it is said to be suffering from pseudohomosexuality. [Oversey 1976]

In this chapter I have described five forms of homosexuality. A sixth form, schizo-homosexuality, the coexistence of schizophrenia and homosexuality, is described in chapter 17 in order to more fully differentiate this form of homosexuality from both preoediapl and oedipal forms.

Chapter 6
BASIC CONCEPTS:
MALE HOMOSEXUALITY

In homosexuality, as in all perversions, the manifest activity represents the peak of a broadly based unconscious construction (Glover 1960). Reports have indicated that there exists a scatter of fixation points along the developmental line of the ego. This is of crucial significance for prognosis in therapy. Because psychical localization is difficult and unconscious content is variable, the origin of homosexuality remained uncertain. All theoretical information must therefore proceed from: investigation of fixation points; understanding of the unconscious construction; intimate knowledge of the developmental stages of the ego and the vicissitudes encountered at each stage; and study of the currently manifest activity.

Many of the developmental vicissitudes, their attempted solutions, and the resulting conflict are common to both male and female homosexuality. Therefore, where I do not specifically refer to the male, these factors pertain also to the female. Essential differences arising out of the more complex and intricate sexual development of the female will be noted separately.

The Role of Infantile Sexuality in the Production of Homosexuality

In 1905 Freud (1905a) penetrated the interconnections between infantile sexuality, perversions and neurosis. He concluded that in neurosis, infantile sexuality is repressed and represents the negative of a perversion. In a perversion, over-cathected infantile sexuality persists. The early theory that perversions were a breakthrough of impulses unopposed by the ego or superego underwent considerable modification. Introduction of the structural theory in psychoanalysis made it possible to clarify that not only the instinctual drives, but also the defenses against them, are unconscious. As a result, the gratification of a perverse instinctual drive actually constitutes the end product of a defensive compromise in which elements of inhibition as well as gratification are present.

In homosexuality the component instinct which seems to be approved has undergone excessive transformation and disguise in order to be gratified in the perverse act. The perverted action, like the neurotic symptom, results from the conflict between the ego and the id and represents a compromise formation which must also be acceptable to the demands of the superego (Freud 1923b). In both male and female homosexuality, as in the case of neurotic symptoms, the instinctual gratification takes place in disguised form while its real content remains unconscious. For this reason a perversion differs from a neurotic symptom, first by the form of gratification of the impulse, namely, orgasm; and second, in the fact that the ego's wishes for omnipotence are satisfied by the arbitrary ego-syntonic action. As a result, certain broader dynamic aspects of sexuality must always be considered. The defensive aspects of homosexuality and the warding off of guilt-laden fantasies are as crucial for the role of object relations as are family constellations and the specific opportunities to make adequate identifications. Freud's dual instinct theory is indispensable in the analysis of homosexuality. The fusion of aggressive and libidinal impulses, the presence of guilt and hostile aggressive drives, and the need for punishment, play important roles (Socarides 1960, 1962).

Freud (1905a) disclosed that the sexual aims of homosexuals were identical with those activities in children. Also, in homosexuality and other perversions, one component of infantile sexuality replaces genital sexuality. These perverse acts are distorted exaggerations and have a quality of uniqueness and stereotypy which does not appear in normal persons except as introductory activities prior to intercourse. Polymorphous perverse activity may be seen in most individuals at times, especially in foreplay. When there are severe obstacles in attaining genital satisfaction there tends to be a regression to earlier perverse formations. Although an individual seems ready to accept perversion as a way of life, his condition may prove to be only temporary, lacking the quality of stereotypy.

The tendency to perversion lies in the fact that all of us were once children. In the "Three Essays," Freud applied the formula that people are perverse who react to sexual frustrations with a regression to infantile sexuality secondary to arrested development. Indeed, perversions frequently make a sudden appearance after a severe sexual disappointment. This points to the meaningfulness of the regression hypothesis. But not all perversions represent regression to infantile sexuality. As Fenichel (1945) noted, "it is not easy to say where stimulation ends and where gratification begins," Most perverse acts are polymorphous; their main emphasis is simply displaced onto the forepleasure often without reaching actual orgastic pleasure (or, as in fetishism, displaced onto the fetish).

One must differentiate between the polymorphously perverse sexuality of children or infantile personality and the perverse sexuality of the true homosexual. The true homosexual has only one way of gaining pleasure and his energies are concentrated on one particular partial instinct. It was once thought that it was simply the hypertrophy of this instinct competing with genital primacy which constituted homosexuality and other perversions. These individuals do not simply "lack genital primacy" (Fenichel 1945). This capacity is blocked by some obstacle and is more or less overcome by the perverse act. Fenichel (1930a) provided important hints as to the direction of our investigations. He felt that the difference between neurosis and perversion lies in the fact that the symptom is desexualized in the neuroses, but is a component of infantile sexuality in the perversions; that its discharge is painful in the neuroses but brings genital orgasm in the perversions (Fenichel 1945).

What disturbs genital primacy? It is, of course, castration anxiety and guilt feelings directed against the oedipus complex. After genital enjoyment has become impossible because of castration anxiety and oedipal fears an individual regresses to that part of his infantile anxiety to which he is fixated.

In the first two decades of psychoanalysis castration fear was considered of paramount importance in the understanding of perversion, especially homosexuality. Castration fear resulted in a regression to that part of infantile sexuality to which one was apparently already fixated. It was not simply that some infantile component was substituted. Infantile sexuality was repressed but it was crucial to apprehend that there was a *hypertrophy* of one's sexual infantile component. This hypertrophy was then used for strengthening the repression of other aspects of infantile sexuality (Fenichel 1930a, 1945). Sachs (1923) utilized these findings for his important theory of the mechanism of perversion formation.

One must not oversimplify the concept of fixation. It is not merely that sexual excitement was experienced with an attendant accidental sexual circumstance and sexual response which then produced a fixation. These are merely screen memories which serve to disguise the real causes of the fixation which surround actual pregenital or preoedipal conflicts. Very often our patients will ascribe to these memories the reason for their fixation to a particular form of enjoyment. A fetishist will ascribe his interest in silk undergarments to the sexual excitement engendered by the rustling of his mother's nightgown as she put him to bed. A homosexual will attribute his condition to the excitement induced by the sound of his father urinating. The current interpretation of such experiences is that it is not the erotic experience per se which is fixated but the early *function* of the erotic experience which is regressively reanimated and reenacted in the perversion (Stolorow 1977).

The homosexual, disturbed in his genital sexuality by castration fear, regresses to that component of his infantile sexuality which once in childhood gave him security or at least reassurance against his many fears. At the same time he obtained some gratification in the regression. The overemphasis on the reassuring infantile expression of his sexuality simultaneously serves to maintain a repression of his oedipal difficulties and other warded-off remnants of infantile sexuality. This constitutes a partial repression of infantile sexuality wherein other parts are exaggerated.

The work of repression is apparently facilitated in homosexuality by the conscious stress of some other aspect of infantile sexuality. This guarantees, according to Sachs (1923), the repression of the oedipus and castration complexes. Fenichel (1945) wrote that the pleasure in perverse activities is not as intense as that in genital heterosexual activites. He felt that the former are possible only after hindrances and through distortions and therefore pleasure is necessarily incomplete.

Developmental Factors

In addition to the boy's negative relationship to the father and his identification with the mother, there is a renunciation of women in order to avoid all rivalry with the father (Freud 1922). Castration fear is of major importance in the development of homosexuality. However, this is a nonspecific factor present as well in normal, neurotic and any perverse psychosexual development. The male homosexual tranforms the hated rival into the love object in contrast, for instance, to the paranoiac whose male love object becomes the persecutor (Freud 1922).

By 1919, perversions were conceived of as precipitates or scars of the oedipus complex (Freud 1919b), not simply as manifestations of the sexual drive itself.

This was followed by other important contributions, especially that of Sachs in 1923, on the genesis of perversions in relation to the oedipal period (see appendix B).

Besides identifying the factors of narcissistic choice and castration fear of the oedipal period it was deduced that a pathological retention of the erotic significance of the anal zone provides a marked predisposition to homosexuality. The latter was first noted by Freud in the "Three Essays" and then reemphasized by him in 1913. In this connection, Nunberg (1938) made an important clinical observation on the anal-sadistic impulses in homosexuality. He referred to the importance of aggression when he wrote that the homosexual acquires strength by conquering a bigger and stronger man.

In "Some Neurotic Mechanisms in Jealousy, Paranoia and Homosexuality," Freud (1922) returned to his original concept that seduction may indeed be responsible for premature fixation of the libido and plays a significant role in the genesis of homosexuality far beyond what had been previously recognized. Jones (1933), in discussing his "protophallic phase," during which the child has no conflict over the possession or loss of the phallus, and "deuterophallic phase," during which a child becomes aware of the possibility of castration, felt that the largely heterosexual alloerotism of the early phallic phase is transmuted into a substitutive homosexual autoerotism. The latter stage represents a "phallic perversion" which led Jones to consider homosexuality as essentially a libidinized hostility to the rival parent. Loewenstein felt that passivity in the phallic phase produces potency difficulties and that a certain type of passive homosexuality, which is expressed exclusively in the form of genital gratification, may exist in which there is no anal wish. The fantasy of this type of homosexual consists in having his own small penis touched by the larger penis of the man he loves. There appeared to be a special affinity between phallic passivity and the negative oedipus complex.

It remained for Sachs (1923) to offer the crucial hypothesis that a perversion, the ego-syntonic remnant of infantile sexuality, becomes the ally of the ego in its repressive efforts directed against other component instincts as well as against the positive oedipus complex and castration fear. A small fragment of infantile sexuality survives puberty and becomes the precondition of sexual gratification all the other componets of sexuality become repressed.

Bychowski (Arlow 1952) and Bak (Arlow 1954) considered homosexuality largely from the point of view of the role of aggression and the inability of the ego of the homosexual to neutralize it. Homosexuality became a regressive adaptation through identification with the mother. This helped to resolve the destructive impulses originally directed toward the mother and at the same time libidinize the aggression against the rival of the same sex. Homosexuality thereby succeeded in defending against retaliation from both sexes. Other significant contributions were made by Freeman (1955); Nacht, Diatkine and Favrow (1956); Rosenfeld (1949); and Thorner (1949). All of them stressed the role of aggression and the presence of pregenital mechanisms and infantile primitive aggressive impulses as important factors which promote homosexuality.

In Anna Freud's opinion the crucial factor in homosexual behavior is the identification with the partner of the same sex through sexual contact. Bychowski (1945) devoted special study to the affinities between the schizophrenic and homosexual groups, finding analogies in psychic structure, especially "infantilisms in the libidinal organization and certain primitive features of the ego." The boundaries of the homosexual ego lack fixity which makes possible fleeting identifications. A peculiar weakness is based on its narcissistic and prenarcissistic disposition. It is fixated at a stage preceding the formation of a distinct ego. These dispositions produce clinging relationships to various persons which, in turn, are based either on infantile leaning or on narcissistic object choice. A clinging dependence is indicative of a feeling of weakness; a narcissistic object choice reveals the hypercathexis of the self. As a result of the overflow of primary narcissism with hypercathexis of the physical and mental self one sees tendencies toward hypochondriasis and an overevaluation of fantasy and of emotionally loaded object representations. This was seen to account for the low frustration tolerance in homosexuals. Due to the primitive character of the narcissism one frequently uncovers ideas of grandeur paradoxically existing along with a poor self-image.

Due to its archaic structure, the ego is extremely vulnerable to the impact of libidinal stimulation. Renunciation of primitive gratification with original objects becomes impossible. The homosexual's inability to bind the original instinctual energies and to transform them into a potential tonic energy available for secondary process had been cited by Freud. A primitive ego utilizes incorporation to a high degree;

the original objects, never really given up, and incorporated into the ego and remain the prototypes of future object choice. However, these objects become incorporated according to their original highly ambivalent cathexis. This contributes to a split and to the ego being filled with contradictory contents. To compound the situation, the weakness of the immature ego does not allow for its synthesis of the originally conflicting attitudes. Here according to Bychowski the analogy to the psychotic or prepsychotic ego is apparent. As a result of this split, the ego may function at times with one or another of its segments, that is, assume the role of one or another of the introjects. An example is the homosexual in whom the introject of a passive, submissive mother is paramount. This individual can be seen to enact this role in his homosexual activities.

Orality is intimately related to the mechanism of introjection. The homosexual changes easily from an active to a passive position because of his ambivalence and intense incorporative needs.

Pregenital elements constitute a decisive factor in fashioning the homosexual's object relations. The importance of the object lies in its ability to fulfill certain demands of pregenital partial drives in homosexuality including those of orality and anality. Homosexual object choice can be defined in shifting ego and libidinal constellations which may represent various object choices such as masochistic or sadistic homosexual object choice. In either case, masochistic or sadistic, the object can represent one or both preoedipal or oedipal parents; in many instances it is not the total individual but rather the partial object, the maternal breast, for instance, or the paternal phallus, which is sought. The preoedipal phallic mother as a sexual object may serve to protect the ego against the real incestuous mother and the oedipal castration threat. The homosexual, forced to deny his own phallus, is compelled to seek a substitute in other men whose genitals he desires. In all instances the image of the self, the narcissistic projection, is sought. The homosexual thus strives to become whole and complete.

He combines a number of roles in all his sexual activities. He may be the aggressor-father assaulting the oedipal-mother; at other times he may play the role of the maternal-substitute passively submitting to a homosexual object which may represent his own phallic self. He may play the role of a projected ego ideal. All these have one thing in common: the homosexual strives to fulfill his own masculinity, to identify with a strong male figure to reinvest his penis with male interest, to become whole, complete, satisfied and without fear of the castrating influences of both mother and father.

In normal heterosexual development the masculine needs of the male become to a great extent ego-invested, that is, the ego feels the need to discharge personally and directly this masculine tension (Socarides 1962). The feminine needs become object invested, that is, the ego feels a need for a feminine sexual partner whose feminine urges it cares to satisfy. The ego can thus obtain vicarious gratification of its own feminine needs. The more an ego "egotizes" the urges of its own sex and externalizes to a proper object representation the urges of the opposite sex, the more does such an ego feel complete. On the other hand, the more an ego egotizes the biological urges of the opposite sex, for the satisfaction of which it is not anatomically and physiologically equipped, and externalizes instead the urges of its own sex into an object representation, the more it feels mutilated (Socarides 1962), (Weiss, 1960).

Those homosexuals who do egotize masculine urges and externalize the feminine ones onto younger males substituted for females have a stronger ego. The most classic example of this type of masculine homosexuality was found in ancient Greece. Ego weakness, as described by Brchowski (Socarides 1960), is most frequently encountered in male homosexuals with a feminine ego. Weiss (1960) has stressed that children of both sexes identify in varying degrees with both father and mother. In normal sexual maturation, however, only the introject of the parent of the same sex is maintained while that of the parent of the opposite sex is externalized in a modified form (ego passage).

The answer to the question of narcissistic object love lies in the phenomenon of a boy's identification with his mother and "this identification can be effected only through the mobilization of the feminine urges in the boy's bisexual constitution. Every homosexual remains strongly fixated to his mother" (Socarides 1960). In other words, it is the mother's introject, to use Bychowski's term, "that pushes the original masculine ego outside into the object world." It is of crucial significance, according to Weiss, that a man's identification with a woman, the mother, must lead to many character traits of the ego different from those of a man who has an ego investment in the masculine part of his constitutional bisexuality while "the feminine part becomes object invested" (Socarides 1960).

Freud was the first to mention that homosexuals

may utilize masochistic, heterosexual, and, to some extent, homosexual perverse fantasies and fetishism as a defense against homosexuality. Often homosexuality may be disguised as a heterosexual masochistic perversion or fantasy in which the female (a phallic woman) is a substitute for a male, and what is actually practiced in disguised form is a homosexual union (Socarides 1960).

Other authors, notably Bacon (Socarides 1960), have emphasized the shift in quality of identification in homosexuals. Identification is needed in the hope of winning love and avoiding greater danger. An example of this is behaving like a passive homosexual son to a murderous or aggressive father.

Various aspects of pathological development toward homosexuality appear in all phases of development. The pathology in these phases is often a result of disturbances which occurred earlier than is generally assumed, in the later phases of the separation-individuation period just prior to the attainment of object constancy (Socarides 1967). The fixation to the mother and the characteristically narcissistic object choice of the homosexual may be traced back to these phases of unresolved mother-child unity. The theory of preoedipal origin of homosexuality is fully set forth in chapter 4.

Superego Factors

Pregenital and archaic superego formations, as well as oedipal ones, operate in all perversions in order to prevent destructive impulses toward the object which threaten both the self and the object. The superego of the preoedipal homosexual is primitive; it is characterized by splitting. Such splitting processes may involve not only the ego and the object but the superego as well. As Gillespie (1956a) has so well described it, the dynamics and economics of the situation cannot be understood without reference to the superego. That is to say, the choice by the ego of the particular piece of infantile sexuality is dictated to an important extent by the ego's judgment of what will please, or at least pass relatively unchallenged by parental imagos, eventually internalized, by superego formations. The attempt to please the superego is especially obvious in masochism, but it operates in other perversions also. This formulation must be understood to refer to pregenital archaic superego formations as well as to post-oedipal ones concerned with the supposed parental attitudes to genital sexuality...The perversion thus...avoids the unpleasure to anxiety and guilt feelings that would otherwise arise.

Parental sanctioning of homosexual behavior, studied by Litin et al. (1956) and by Kolb and Johnson (1955), indicates that the mother's behavior is overseductive and frustrating and sanctions the boy's homosexuality. The parents' own unstable bisexual identification as well as their own defective superego contribute in multiple ways to the development and reinforcement of homosexuality. These parents may consider pregenital sexuality as more permissible than genital sexuality due to their own superego difficulties.

In 1956 Otto Sperling described a special form of homosexuality which he termed *induced perversion,* in which there is a splitting of the superego by which a leader in group perverse activities replaces the patient's superego. This is a reactivation of a previously latent split in childhood.

A detailed clinical exposition of superego influences and the effect of guilt on the promotion and maintenance of a homosexual adaptation is presented in chapter 12, The Case of Campbell.

Chapter 7
BASIC CONCEPTS:
FEMALE HOMOSEXUALITY

Survey of Developmental Factors

While the literature on male homosexuality has been rather extensive, that on female homosexuality has been sparse.

In one of her several studies on the psychology of women, Deutsch (1925) observed that at the beginning of every new sexual function, for example, puberty, intercourse, pregnancy, and childbirth, phallic phase conflict is reanimated and has to be overcome each time before a feminine attitude can be attained once more. This complicates the development toward adult female sexual functioning and sets up a condition wherein female homosexuality may be activated at any of these periods in certain individuals.

Horney (1925) emphasized that oedipal fantasies and the ensuing dread of internal vaginal injury play an important part in the infantile genital organization of women. She thought it of causative importance that the little boy can inspect his genital to see whether any consequences of masturbation are taking place, whereas the little girl is literally in the dark on this point. An inner uncertainty so often met with in women results. Under the pressure of anxiety, guilt over clitoral masturbation may then take refuge in the production of a fictitious male role. The wish to be a man subserves the repression of feminine wishes and secures the subject against libidinal wishes in connection with the father.

In 1925 Jones simultaneously analyzed five cases of overt female homosexuality and reported on them at the Innsbruck Congress (jones 1927). He concluded that for the most part, female homosexuality could be traced back to two crucial factors: (1) an intense oral erotism, and (2) an unusually strong sadism. Together with Deutsch's and Freud's clinical studies, Jones's paper may constitute the most incisive theoretical and clinical point of view on this disorder as of that date. Jones wrote that in homosexual women the unconscious attitude toward both parents is always strongly ambivalent. There is evidence of an unusually strong infantile fixation to the mother, connected with the oral stage. This is always succeeded by a strong father fixation, whether temporary or permanent in consciousness. He postulated that castration anxiety is only a partial threat and coined the term *aphanisis* as the total threat, that is, threat of total extinction, including extinction of sexual capacity and enjoyment of life as a whole.

The deprivation experienced by the girl in not being allowed to share the penis in coitus with the father and thereby to obtain a baby is an unendurable situation, tantamount to the fundamental dread of aphanisis. There are only two ways in which the libido can flow for self-expression. The girl must choose between sacrificing her erotic attachment to her father and sacrificing her femininity; either the object must be exchanged for another or the wish must be given up. It is impossible to retain both; either the father or the vagina, including the pregenital vagina, must be renounced. A possible result of this conflict is that the father may be retained but the object relationship is converted into an identification. The girl develops a penis complex. Faced with aphanisis as a result of an inevitable deprivation, she must renounce either her sex or her incestuous wishes. What cannot be retained is an incestuous object relationship. A girl may choose the solution of homosexuality because it saves her from the dread of aphanisis.

It was Jones's belief that identification with the father is common to all forms of female homosexuality although it proceeds to a more complete degree in some than in others, where in a vicarious way some femininity is retained. There is little doubt that identification serves the function of keeping feminine wishes repressed by virtue of its assertion: "I cannot possibly desire a man's penis for my gratification, since I already possess one of my own, or at all events I want nothing else than one of my own" (Jones 1927). Jones remarked that this identification may be regarded as universal among young girls, so we have to seek motives which heighten this to an extraordinary extent in homosexual women. Those factors which appear decisive are an unusually strong oral erotism and sadism. Jones regarded this as the central characteristic of homosexual development in women.

Raymond de Saussure's work (1929), "Homosexual Fixations Among Neurotic Women" (see appendix C), was a major contribution on this subject. He concluded that at the root of homosexual fixations there is always a warped bisexuality arising from the fact that the woman has not been able to accept her femininity. This refusal derives from castration fear and consequent penis envy. In some of his patients an identification with the mother becomes impossible and the girl identifies herself with her father in order to give a child to the mother. He noted that homosexual fixations correspond to the patient's projections. Frequently the patient may project her femininity onto the mother and then onto other women who continue to represent the mother. Almost as often, the patient, thwarted at not being able to satisfy her own masculine tendencies, exaggerates her feminine qualities, becomes excessively narcissistic, and sees herself mirrored in some way in other women who have a high degree of feminine narcissism. In these cases, the woman projects her femininity onto others and enjoys an identification with herself. In other instances homosexual women refuse themselves to men, giving themselves only to other women who have learned how to make men suffer.

Deutsch's analyses of homosexual women (1932a) revealed an aggressive, murderous hate against the mother. Childhood memories (four to six years), which proved to be the nucleus of some of her patients' inversions, included the prohibition, by the mother, of masturbation and the inability of the father to come to the daughter's defense. These patients uniformly repressed reproaches against the father and experienced severe castration anxiety. She concluded that with puberty the final decision as to choice of sexual object takes place.

Brierley (1932) proposed that in homosexual women masochistic attitudes and fantasies concerning intercourse are a reflection of the fear of repetition of injury already experienced at the hands of the mother. These masochistic ideas are unconsciously connected to concepts of disembowelment according to the internal life injuries of the Kleinian type. "It is these masochistic ideas which make the heterosexual position untenable. In these cases, however, homosexuality is not a way out too often because it is too sadistic." Brierley firmly believes that most of these situations are not peculiar to women in the sense that there is no counterpart in male sexuality. Men have difficulties due to oral conflicts, failures in coordination of heterosexual and homosexual interests, and development of archaic superego formations. What seems to be specific in women is not any psychic drive as such but the balance which has to be achieved and maintained in order to produce an integrated feminine personality. This distribution of cathexis which might be normal in women would be abnormal in men and vice versa. "The only difference which we can register clinically seems to be differences in integration of drives common to both sexes. . . . If we ever achieve a psychological definition of femininity it looks as if it might have to be a definition in terms of types of integration."

By 1933 the preoedipal development and its significance for the girl's later life began to assume more importance. Deutsch emphasized the identification with the active mother, which as yet has no relation to the oedipus complex. In the analysis of homosexual women Deutsch found that the preoedipal libidinal components repeatedly appear. "The situation is independent of the man; and in libidinal relationships only the role of mother and child are taken into account without reference to men" (Deutsch 1933).

In her later research Brierley (1935) suggested that there is some evidence that female genital impulses do appear as early as the suckling period and these impulses must be regarded as primary because they arise in the genital system itself. If they are primary, they constitute a specific instinctual determinant in feminine development. This observation was the core around which Brierley evolved her own theory of the development of female homosexuality. The occurrence of true vaginal activity in early infancy could be associated with oral impulses. The relative weakness of the urovaginal system matters less than its establishment under pleasurable or painful conditions which determine the degree of sadism with which it is invested. While endorsing Jones's view (Jones 1927) concerning the role of oral sadism in the genesis of female homosexuality, Brierley believed that what is significant is not simply the oral sadism but a strong blend of oral and urethral sadism.

Over the years it became apparent that the psychic situation of female homosexuals is indeed more complex than that of their male counterparts, as was originally suggested by Freud (1905a). For example, homosexual attachment due to early sister rivalry was found to be quite prevalent. Glover (1939) noted that in all cases two complicating factors should be taken into account. First, the female passes through a negative mother attachment *before* reaching a positive father oedipus complex, not after, as is the case with males. Second, castration anxiety links up with deeper fantasies of bodily mutilation more frequently in the female than in the male, for the little girl believes that she had already suffered castration and that she is bound to suffer still further injury. To add to this burden, penis dread is reinforced by earlier breast dread, in turn provoked by oral hate of the breast. The sadistic reactions associated with breast hatred become elaborated into even stronger sadistic reactions directed against the mother's insides, her babies and her reproductive organs.

Lampl-de Groot (1933) was among the first to observe that in homosexual women fantasies of phallic coitus with the mother are quite frequent. This blow, aimed at the mother, gratifies the girl's own narcissistic conceit and vindictiveness but does not gratify her sensual love. Later, after puberty, this fantasy is endowed with sexuality and serves as a basis for a homosexual attitude.

Rado's (1933) masterful contribution traced female homosexuality back to its masochistic core. Since masochism arises from castration fear, the central source of danger for the masochistic woman became the man; the line of her defense in her neurosis would be toward him. There are three types of defensive means at her disposal: flight, combat, and the choice of the lesser evil. It is the mechanism of flight which, if extreme, leads to female homosexuality. However, Rado believed that the neurotic disturbance peculiar to female homosexuality is a sense of guilt, the avowed conscious source of which is the perversion itself with its attendant exclusion from the group. At unconscious levels, however, this guilt has at its root a tormenting sense of inferiority, an uneasiness that one will be found inadequate, and a fear of being exposed as ridiculous. The fear of exposure is both a derivative and expressive of the fear of castration.

Fenichel (1930a, 1934) emphasized the importance of the castration complex in the formation of female homosexuality. The turning away from heterosexuality originates in the castration complex although an early fixation on the mother is of vital importance. These factors supplement each other.

Female homosexuality and masculine identification in women serve as a protection against anxiety. Homosexuality accomplishes so much by its capacity to reduce triangular relationships to two-way relationships. In giving up the father attachment, the girl reverts to a two-way relationship with the mother (sister) figure in which "in fantasy all real love comes from the partner and all real giving goes to the partner. In spite of her dissapointments in her father the [homosexual] patient is unable to go to another man because of fear of retaliation on the *father's part*"(Bacon 1956).

Bergler (1951) proposed that the following unconscious psychic constellation produces female homosexuality: (1) an aggressive, dominating mother is the sole educator of the child while the father has a weak personality; (2) the child hates the mother and is incapable of splitting off this preoedipal ambivalent attitude toward her; (3) the oedipus complex therefore never reaches a normal intensity; and (4) self-damaging tendencies masked by a pseudoaggressive facade dominate the female homosexual's life. This individual reaches a decisive point when she is forced to deal with an overwhelming hatred of her mother, previously masked by her masochistic attachment to her. In this crisis, she may choose homosexuality.

The importance of Freud's dual instinct theory is indispensable in analyzing female homosexuality. The fusion of aggressive and libidinal impulses, the presence of guilt and hostile aggressive drives, and the consequent need for punishment all play important roles. In female as well as male homosexuality, the preoedipal period and its subsequent influence on psychic structure and ego functioning are decisive for sexual object choice. Lichtenstein (1961) clearly outlined the importance of early identifications and their influence on the later development of female homosexuality.

Female homosexuality is, to a large extent, analogous to male homosexuality, except for one factor which complicates the clinical picture. Women can achieve the exclusion of the penis by regression, since the first object of every human being is the mother. "All women, in contradistinction to men, have a primary homosexual attachment which may later be revived if normal heterosexuality is blocked" (Deutsch 1932a). A man in this situation, Deutsch continues, can regress only from object relationship to his mother to identification with her, while a woman can regress from object relationship to the father to object relationship to the mother.

Often a young girl will respond to disappointment over her oedipal wishes with an identification with the father and consequently assume an active sexual relation to women who represent mother substitutes. The attitude of these active, masculine homosexual women toward their mother-equivalent objects is frequently combined with all the features of a wish fulfillment type of female castration complex.

Klein (1954) states that the goal of masculine women is opposed to the pregenital aims of incorporation found in the feminine goal of men. In cases where frustration of the wishes for incorporation has led to a sadistic attack of taking by force what was not given, this force, originally often thought of as a penetration of the mother's body, may be remobilized into later masculinity.

Masculinity in women is not necessarily connected with homosexuality in Fenichel's view (1930a). The homosexual solution depends upon two circumstances: the intensity of the early fixation to the mother and a special configuration of the castration complex. Consequently, some active homosexual women, after having identified themselves with their father, choose young girls as love objects to serve as ideal representatives of themselves. They then behave toward these girls as they wished to have been treated by their father. Another configuration may be antagonism between sisters which becomes overcompensated, resulting in a mild homosexual love interwoven with a great deal of identification. Beneath the identification lies the original hatred. In such instances, the turning away from heterosexuality represents a regression which revives the memory of the earliest relationship to one's mother. In Fenichel's opinion (1934), therefore, female homosexuality might indicate a more archaic process than does male homosexuality. It brings back the behavior patterns, aims, and pleasures, as well as the fears and conflicts, belonging to the earliest years of life. Proof of this assertion lies in the observation that the usual activities of homosexual women consist mainly of the mutual playing of mother and child, and that oral erotism is in the foreground as compared to anal erotism in the male homosexual.

Bergler (1951), Glover (1939), and Jones (1927) all noted that the ubiquitous hatred of the mother found in homosexual women produces an intense sense of guilt which is transformed into a masochistic libidinal attitude. This attitude, expressed as "I do not hate you, I love you," originally directed toward the mother, is reflected not only in the form of direct oral satisfaction in homosexual intercourse with a young girl but also in the submissive passive attitude toward older love partners. The homosexual woman thus transforms the hate toward her mother into love, simultaneously giving the mother's breast to her partner.

Another source of aggression results from direct prohibitions of masturbation, including forceful interference with masturbatory activity. Deutsch (1932b) wrote that this may arouse a great deal of hostility against the disciplining mother, especially if, at the same time, discovery of the anatomic defect is made known, and the girl blames her mother for this deprivation. Thus, the sadistic impulses of the phallic phase become directed against the mother and become the impetus for the change of sexual object. The change in the direction of a sadistic attitude toward the mother facilitates a passive masochistic attitude toward the father. Deutsch called this "the thrust into passivity." Aggression is not entirely channeled into this passive attitude. Much of the aggressive impulse is turned against the disappointing father, and another portion of it remains attached to the mother, who is now regarded as a rival. The intensity of the aggression depends on the strength of the interfered-with phallic activity. The passive masochistic attitude, however, is full of danger; the patient harbors bloodthirsty and murderous revenge wishes toward the mother, especially the pregnant mother or the one who already has had another child. The girl's aggression leads to guilt. She turns to the mother to alleviate this feeling of guilt and to gain the security and protection offered by relieving the fear of the loss of object. "If my father won't have me and my self-respect is undermined, who will love me if not my mother?"

The element of identification plays a crucial role in the choice of object in female homosexuality. Thus, in

Jones's classification (1927), members of his first group, those interested in men, exchange their own sex but retain their first love object In this pseudo-object relationship, identification replaces true object relations; the aim of the libido is to procure recognition of this identification. Members of the second group, those interested in women, also identify themselves with the love object but then lose further interest in her. The external object relationship to another woman is very imperfect, for she merely represents the homosexual's own femininity through identification, the aim of which is to vicariously enjoy gratification at the hand of the unseen man (the father incorporated in themselves). In this connection it should be noted that identification with the father is common in all forms of female homosexuality. It is more severe in Jones's first group than in the second, in which some femininity is vicariously retained. In essence, identification with the father serves the function of keeping feminine wishes repressed and constitutes the most complete denial of guilty feminine wishes.

In protecting herself against the threat of aphanisis, the homosexual girl in late childhood and adolescence erects various barriers against her femininity, notably penis identification. These barriers are buttressed by a strong sense of guilt and a condemnation of her own unconscious feminine wishes. To reinforce this barrier of guilt she develops the idea that her father and other men are strongly opposed to feminine wishes; to ease her self-condemnation she actively believes that all men in their hearts disapprove of femininity (Jones 1927).

Bonaparte (1953) attempted a correlation between types of homosexual women and prognosis in therapy.

For example, some women refuse to abandon their masculinity and will give up neither their first love object nor the predominant phallic erotogenic zone. Others, despite their success in transferring considerable libidinal interest from the mother to the father, cannot conceive of a love object so contemptible as to lack a phallus, and cling tenaciously to a predominantly phallic position and will love and desire only female love objects that are seemingly masculine.

Some manifestly homosexual women continually reenact the primary scene of active-passive alternations of the mother's ministering to the baby. The most active among them superimpose their identification with the father onto a primary identification with the active mother and thereby become an intensely active type of homosexual female (Bonaparte 1953).

The Presenting Clinical Picture

The female homosexual usually does not seek psychoanalytic treatment in order to change her homosexuality. She may enter therapy because of family pressure, or due to a depression secondary to the loss of a love partner, or accompanying symptoms more often neurotic than psychotic (Socarides 1965). It is usually feelings of loss, loneliness, and severe anxiety arising out of rejection by another woman which impel her to seek help.

Although many overt female homosexuals experience little conscious guilt over their deviant sexual practices, many suffer intensely from a deep sense of inferiority often masked by the outward appearance of self-confidence and superiority. Indeed, inferiority feelings have been largely responsible for their covert homosexual activities, enabling them to lead double lives among their peers and associates. Some homosexual women engage only in companionate relationships and seem to have little orgastic desire, while others intensely seek orgastic and erotic pleasure.

Homosexual women may suffer from vaginismus or vaginal anesthesia. In some, orgastic desire with persons of the same sex may be so strongly repressed that there may be complete or almost total unawareness of homosexual desires and wishes.

The homosexual libidinal relationship is basically masochistic; it temporarily wards off severe anxiety and hostility only to give way at times to florid neurotic symptoms. The mother-substitute (homosexual partner) temporarily neutralizes infantile grievances by providing sexual satisfaction. Many overtly homosexual women acknowledge the mother-child relationship implicit in their choice of love object. Sexual satisfaction is usually obtained by a close embrace; mutual sucking of the nipples and genitals; anal practices; mutual cunnilingus; and vaginal penetration by the use of artificial devices. There is quadruple role casting for both partners: one now playing the male and the other the female; one the mother and the other the child. Female homosexuals are particularly engrossed in and satisfied by the sameness of their sexual responses.

In analysis it readily becomes apparent that in sexual experiences occurring between homosexual females the homosexual is able to transform the hate of the mother into love. At the same time, she is being given the mother's (partner's) breast and thus obtains what she once felt deprived and frightened of as a child. Invariably present is an intense conflict over masturbation which began in early childhood. In the homosexual act, the "mother" sanctions masturbation through sharing the guilt mechanism.

If she can overcome her reticence to confide in a man, she may display intense envy of the penis and hostility toward a male analyst from the very beginning of therapy. Often she suffers from suicidal ideas and murderous fantasies toward her mother (and partner), both arising from preoedipal unconscious wishes and dreads. The aggressive, murderous hatred occurs simultaneously with a desire to merge with the mother. As in the male, this is the nuclear conflict.

Sexual excitement in most homosexual women is bound up with maternal prohibition. On a conscious level there are extremely intense aggressive impulses toward the mother. These aggressive impulses are resisted and, in reaction to them, unconscious guilt toward the mother is generated. Hate impulses are then transformed into a masochistic libidinal attitude which disguises these feelings, diminishes guilt, and punishes through suffering. By punishing the mother, these patients are unconsciously dramatizing their self-defeat and reproaches against the mother.

Deprived of their love object, homosexual women very often become suicidal. They interpret this loss as a threat to survival and a total abandonment; they fear total extinction, that is, aphanisis (Jones 1927). Similarly, the male homosexual has a marked proclivity to become suicidal whenever he is rejected by a man who represents his ideal narcissistic image.

Psychodynamics

The homosexual woman is in flight from men. The source of this flight is her childhood feelings of rage, hate, and guilt toward her mother and a fear of merging with her. Accompanying this primary conflict are deep anxieties and aggression secondary to disappointments and rejections, both real and imagined, at the hands of the male (father). Any expectations of her father's fulfilling her infantile sexual wishes poses further masochistic danger. On the other hand, her conscious and unconscious conviction that her father would refuse her love, acceptance, and comfort produces a state of constant impending narcissistic injury and mortification. The result of this conflict is to turn to the earliest love object, the mother, with increasing ardor. What prevents her complete regression to this primitive unity is her unconscious fear of merging with and being engulfed by the mother. Deutsch comments, "The economic advantage of this new turning to the ersatz mother [the homosexual partner] lies in the release of the feeling of guilt, but it seems to me that its most important accomplishment lies in the protection from a threatened loss of object" (Deutsch 1932b).

Preoedipal fears of being poisoned and devoured by the mother lead to giving up in utter failure when confronted by the later conflicts of the oedipal period (Klein 1954). The homosexual woman resorts to flight to the mother in an attempt to gain her love and protection; to alleviate feelings of murderous aggression toward her; and to protect herself against the assumed murderous impulses of the mother. These fears of poisoning and being devoured relate to the earliest anxiety of the infant. Therefore, these patients, beset by primitive anxieties, demand the utmost effort and concentrated attention on the part of the analyst.

In homosexual women there are intense desires for revenge and uncontrollable aggressive feelings. The impulse to attack is associated with revenge ideas for betrayal by the father, especially in instances where another sibling has been born, replacing the patient during the preoedipal years. Strong penis envy components are mixed with intense oral wishes. The oedipus revenge ideas may exist in nonhomosexual women whose behavior stops short of the complete avoidance of men. These women get along fairly easily with less virile, presumably impotent men. This is due not simply to these men being less dangerous; they also offer less temptation to the women's sadism. Although oedipus revenge ideas may exist in nonhomosexual women, these revenge impulses reinforce violation anxiety and the two together produce a strong tendency to complete detachment from the father. It is a truism, however, that hate as well as love can bind, and the homosexual can find herself neurotically bound to the father, his life, and his activities.

Beneath the more obvious oedipal determinants of violation and revenge ideas there is a wealth of tangled fantasies of the primal scene leading back through all the pregenital phases apparently to the womb (Brierley 1932, 1935). At deeper levels, analysis reveals certain guiding threads. One set of masochistic thoughts expresses the fear that intercourse would prove a repetition of injury already experienced at the mother's hands. This injury has a vivid phallic version but equally definite fecal and nipple connotations. It harks back to the deprivation of weaning and castration and is in the latter instance a punishment for masturbation. Another set of masochistic ideas revolve around internal life injuries of the Kleinian type (Klein 1954): disembowelment and feminine impotence. *It is these masochistic ideas which make the heterosexual position untenable.* Homosexuality, however, is no complete solution because even sexual acts with a female partner arouse severe sadistic impulses (see chapter 19, The Case of Sarah).

Interwoven with masochistic fantasies are highly aggressive fantasies connected with the primal scene father, the penis, and the mother's body. "One often finds self-sufficient fantasies which are genital, fantasies of hermaphroditism, dreams of self-violation, dreams of babies and lovers...appearing as fecal characters. These are definitely archaic oral fantasies. There are fantasies also of oral intercourse and oral parturition....Genital ideas are not lacking...but the impression gains ground that in spite of evidence of regression we are here up against an original pregenital core which has a vital connection with the later genital failure and especially with the accentuation of aggression which bulks so largely in it. These fantasies center around introjected nipple-penis objects; there is a sense of oscillation between external and internal dangers" (Brierley 1935). This primal oral sadism does not always lead to homosexuality but sometimes results in a flight from homosexuality and indeed all sexuality (Brierley 1932).

All homosexual women markedly identify with the father since they must renounce any approach to femininity. A striking feature of these identifications is that they are all "maimed" (Jones 1927). The ego is always a castrated father or a barren, shattered mother, and the ego's conduct of life is correspondingly crippled. This nevertheless provides an economic advantage as it protects the homosexual woman from the dangers of gratification of her intense sadism, although at great expense to the ego.

Some prepubescent or adolescent girls may identify with the sexuality of an older female whom they know participates in sexual intercourse with men. (This form of identification may be termed *resonance identification*; see Socarides 1962.) In so doing, they attempt to bolster up a burgeoning femininity. By sharing the guilt in sexual encounters with these females they increase their own capacity for erotic feeling.

Those women who openly identify with males are in effect saying to the mother that she has nothing to fear from their sexual wishes toward the father, as they themselves wish only to be male. They thereby escape the fantasized retaliatory aggression of the mother toward them.

Other homosexual women, after identifying themselves with the father, choose young adolescent girls as love objects who are representatives of themselves (narcissistic object choices). They then love these girls as they wished their father had loved them.

In those homosexuals who assume a very masculine manner toward men there is an open wish to acquire traits of virility as their own. They believe they can be loved by the father only if they have a penis, convinced that the father once denigrated and demeaned them for this lack.

Certain women manifest their homosexuality only after marriage. There are common features in their reaction to marriage, in that they suffer from excessive guilt due not only to the incest and oedipal meaning which intercourse has for them but even more from the reawakening of their sadism when engaged in the sexual act. Violation-revenge impulses are frequently found. These patients are demanding revenge for childhood injuries but they often express disappointment if they are not hurt enough in heterosexual relations. This apparent contradiction is resolved when one realizes that actual sexual intercourse satisfies neither their primal scene expectations nor their need for punishment. Continuing to feel guilt-ridden, their superego threatens them with severe bodily punishment after marriage.

"The husband in these cases may often represent the tender, sexual father, safe enough to marry but not brutal or sensual enough to be satisfying" (Brierley 1932). Deutsch described a similar type of homosexual woman, in whom sexual sensation depends entirely upon the fulfillment of masochistic conditions. These women are accordingly faced with the necessity of choosing between finding "bliss in suffering or peace in renunciation."

Being married provokes already present masculine trends; penis envy takes the form of rivalry with the husband. The unconscious conviction that the penis ought to have been the wife's, based on the fantasy that the mother had deliberately given the infant's breast/penis to the father, is further augmented. The failure of the marriage transforms unconscious (latent) homosexual attitudes into overt homosexuality.

Homosexual women are exceedingly sensitive to being financially dependent because they regard this as a mark of inferiority. Beneath this resentment are deep feelings of guilt for their inordinate wishes to be completely sustained by the husband. These demands derive from their insatiable need for oral supplies from the mother. Prior to marriage they "may enjoy all the advantages of a man's life plus certain prerequisites belonging to womanhood without the disadvantages of either" (Brierley 1932). If such women are obliged to give up a career for marriage, this loss of outlet may play an important part in precipitating severe neurotic symptoms with or without overt homosexuality.

Clinical Groups

The clinician treating homosexual women encounters varied and multiple forms of this condition. For example, as noted above, in all homosexual women there is an intense unconscious aggressive and, in preoedipal types, murderous hatred against the mother and fear of her along with reproachful feelings toward the father. The fate of these conflicts, and the behavior and appearance of the patient, depend on the strength of repression, the capacity for sublimation, the defensive techniques of the ego and superego, and the ego-adaptive capacities of the individual. Thus, homosexual women show great variation regarding their external appearance and general behavior; their choice of homosexual love object; their sexual practices; and their unconscious dynamics. I have grouped these women below in line with Jones's (1927) and de Saussure's (1929) views.

Group One: These women may often retain their interest in men but are intent upon being accepted by men as one of them. They unfailingly complain of the unfairness of their position as women and their unjust and ill treatment by men.

Group Two: These women have little or no interest in men and their libido centers on women. In analysis one discovers that this interest in women is a vicarious way of enjoying other women's femininity (resonance identification). A corollary situation exists with male homosexuals who vicariously acquire the masculinity of their male partners in homosexual relations.

Group Three: This group obtains gratification of feminine sexual desires in sexual relations simulating heterosexual intercourse; the penis is replaced by the tongue or finger and the partner using this organ is a woman. Though clinically they may appear completely homosexual, they are nearer the normal than either of the previous two types as they insist upon a simulation of the male-female pattern. In Groups One through Three an identification with the father serves the function of keeping feminine wishes in repression. These types do not wish for an actual penis for gratification; they already "have one," and certainly desire no one else's.

Group Four: This type derives from a "warped bisexuality" (Jones 1927) conditioned by the ideas of castration and penis envy. A girl identifies with her father in order to give a child to her mother. In these cases, homosexual fixations correspond to the patient's projections. A woman may, therefore, project and thereby relinquish her femininity to the mother and displace it onto other women, who continue to represent the mother. She then sees herself mirrored in other women who must have a high degree of feminine narcissism. In effect, by projecting her femininity onto others, she enjoys an identification with herself. An additional factor in her choice of female sexual partner is that she projects her femininity only onto women who attract men sexually in order to make them suffer by refusing them satisfaction.

Group Five: This group identifies with the active mother and plays out a mother-child relationship in the conscious and unconscious context of excluding the intruding father. Thus, older homosexual women are often drawn to adolescent women.

Group Six: The younger member in the relationship mentioned in Group Five plays a passive role with their older maternal protective partner. Occasionally, both active and passive attitudes may alternate. The clitoris is their executive organ of pleasure and they abhor the presence of a penis or penis-like substitute. Similarly, neither individual wears masculine clothing at any time.

Group Seven: This group has a double identification: with the primary active mother who cares for the child and with the father. These women with this double identification—one identification superimposed upon the other—present more clitoral fantasies than the groups previously described. They wear masculine clothing, including ties, and strive to act the man in relation to a woman. Many find it extremely difficult to admit to any passive wishes to be caressed, fondled, genitally stimulated, or penetrated.

Group Eight: Another group of homosexual women cannot appreciate any love object which lacks a phallus. Although basically homosexual in their search for a loving female (the mother), they seek a father as their love object. Psychoanalytic examination reveals that unconsciously they cling tenaciously to the idea that they possess a phallus which they can put on or take off at will. Although they may engage in heterosexual intercourse, these relationships are extremely ambivalent. Their greatest pleasure is to be admired, sought after, and loved by women with whom actual sexual relations are infrequent and transitory. This group constitutes the most difficult of all homosexual women to treat psychoanalytically, as they have established what they consider to be fulfilling adaptations to both sexes.

Group Nine: The appearance of extreme femininity characterizes the final group. This is due to a special configuration of the castration complex: having identified herself with her father, she then chooses young girls as love objects to serve as ideal representatives of her own person. She thereby preserves her femininity. Feminine appearing homosexual women then behave toward masculine appearing homosexual women as they wished they had been treated by their fathers (Bonaparte 1953, Jones 1927, Socarides 1962).

Chapter 8
SPECIFIC MECHANISMS

Mechanism of Identification

In order to comprehend identification processes in the homosexual it is vital to delineate five important forms of identification: (1) primary feminine identification with the mother; (2) secondary identification with the male (male homosexuality) or the female (female homosexuality); (3) secondary identification with the mother; (4) identification with the aggressor (mother); and (5) secondary identification with the same sex sibling.

The continued *primary identification with the mother* arises from the inability to make the separation from her during the separation-individuation phase of development. The child persists beyond the preoedipal period in believing that the mother is all-powerful, all-controlling, and the only one to protect his interests and insure his survival. (This type of identification is more fully described in chapter 4, The Theory of Preoedipal Origin.) In the case of the boy, the absence of a strong father further predisposes the child to this primary identification and precludes a shift to identification with the father. The boy later becomes painfully aware of this deficient masculine identification and searches for it in his homosexual relations. He seeks partners who represent strong masculine figures and who would give him, almost by transfusion, the missing masculine attributes which diminish and deprive him, and make him feel empty, weak, and unmanly.

It is crucial to separate the primary identification with mother from the *secondary identification with the male* as achieved in the homosexual act. The latter identification is transitory and must be continually replenished by male sexual partners. In the female homosexual the identification is with the mother (primary feminine identification with the mother). A masculine identification is only secondarily established in order to avoid oedipal feelings and conflicts and to simultaneously escape deeper anxieties related to her conviction that the mother is sadistic, poisonous, and malevolent. The latter conflict may manifest itself in paranoid type anxieties or fears of merging with the mother.

Similar to the male, the female homosexual may identify with the "maleness" of her female partner and, through resonance identification (Socarides 1962), vicariously enjoy, seek, and demand incorporation of her partner's femininity. Both can occur simultaneoulsy, but usually one or the other identification is predominant in the course of any specific female homosexual contact.

Superimposed on his primary identification, the male homosexual develops a *secondary identification with the mother* (negative oedipal reaction) during the oedipal period because of castration anxiety and fears of retaliation by the father. At this juncture his passive negative oedipal wishes together with the continuation of an intense primary feminine identification lead to an anal fixation. Thus, wishes to enjoy a oneness with the mother and, later, sexual gratification with her become a wish to experience sexual intercourse with a man, just as his mother experienced sexual intercourse with a man, his father. He strives, therefore, in fantasy and in practice, to vaginalize his anus. He may attempt to turn his defeat into an assumed victory by behaving like a woman, assuming feminine characteristics, and "enjoying" sexual penetration into his anus. While passively submitting to anal intercourse he is unconsciously robbing the male partner of his masculinity through incorporation and identification with him. The homosexual male receiving the penis into his anus may frequently fantasy the gigantic growth of his own penis. In all acts of anal penetration and/or oral-genital activities, identification processes are effected and augmented through the incorporation of the partner or parts of his body, Thus, incorporative mechanisms play a crucial role in these identification processes.

Furthermore, in controlling another man through his apparent acquiescence, he is castrating him, exerting power over him through anal presentation, depriving him of his "masculine secrets," and extracting "love and affection." Analysis of these fantasies and actual encounter reveals that beneath the surface motivations for same sex partners lie unneutralized feelings of the need for mastery; extreme aggression; and impulses to hurt, castrate, and later cast aside his homosexual partner as he himself once felt rejected by his father. Through this pseudosubmissiveness the male homosexual is robbing the father of his potency, semen, and affection (see chapter 12, The Case of Campbell).

Another aspect of this secondary identification with the mother is that he can then behave lovingly toward men as he wishes his mother had behaved toward him. This reassures him against the depriving mother and affords gratification.

Secondary identification with the mother can be seen as an *identification with the aggressor*. In economic terms this means he need not fear attack from her as long as he remains identified with her. He also avoids oedipal feelings; he cannot be frustrated by her, as he and she share identification.

Secondary identification with the brother (Silber 1961), whether older or younger, may arise from envious and hostile feelings toward him in competition for the mother's favor. Very often hatred toward the brother may be a form of overcompensation, a reaction-formation against excessive libidinal feelings. A brother who seems by comparison more successful than oneself may produce feelings of disturbing hostility or hopeless anger, and a feeling that one cannot compete with the brother due to the danger of one's own murderous rage. Frequently, an older brother may escape becoming homosexual while the younger male sibling may become severely homosexual due to the mother's need to keep the younger child tied to her affectively, not permitting him to achieve autonomy in the separation-individuation phase. If the younger boy becomes homosexual and desires the brother sexually he will avoid all competition with him.

It cannot be sufficiently emphasized that the determinant of homosexuality is, in the last analysis, intimately related to the degree of primary identification with the mother. All other identifications are secondary and are accretions of this basic problem of identification. The simultaneous identification with the brother, for example, is completely secondary and does not exclude the primary identification with the mother. Subsequent identifications do not equal or exlude the primary one. The case of Claude (chapter 15) illustrates the identification with the brother superimposed on the primary feminine identification with the mother. The case includes a detailed exposition of superego influences and of the effect of guilt on the promotion and maintenance of homosexuality. The clinical section notes and explicates the interweaving and layering of the various forms of identification.

The Projective Mechanism

Overt homosexuals frequently show moderate to severe conscious and unconscious projective anxieties without evidence of clinical psychosis. While often present in the milder forms of homosexuality, they are invariably present in the preoedipal forms. The degree of severity and fixity of projective tendencies in homosexual patients may, in more extreme cases, produce complications in therapy regarding transference, resistence, and promotion of a working alliance. The projective tendencies must therefore be dealt with from the very beginning of treatment; they must be continually dissipated through early and unceasing interpretation. Clinically, paranoid attitudes and preoccupations begin to disappear only after the patient fully understands the early structure of the relationship to the mother and works this through in the transference. This working through considerably diminishes the need and desire to project.

The projective mechanism may take three principal forms: (1) projection as an expression of primitive aggressive destructive impulses; (2) projection leading to narcissistic object choice; (3) projection leading to idealization of the object.

The homosexual act may function as a defense against onslaughts of projective anxieties related to one's own fearful destructive and libidinal urges. These projective anxieties at times border on paranoid ideation. This ideation may be fleeting and lacking in intense conviction, psychotic elaboration, and delusion formation. It may be completely unconscious but is nevertheless often the central anxiety motivating the patient to a homosexual encounter, resulting in a temporary resolution of hateful impulses. It is vitally important that psychoanalytic investigation reveal to the patient the full meaning and content of this projective-paranoidal affective state which is neutralized by the homosexual act. A homosexual clergyman in therapy with me, while seated in a bus almost asleep, experienced a vivid fantasy of his throat being slit from ear to ear by a black man seated two rows behind him. This led to immediate sexual arousal and desire for a sexual encounter with a man, which he attempted to carry out. The hostility he impugned to his partner originated from his own anxieties, dreads, and aggression; he projected them onto his fellow passenger.

Through the mechanism of projection parts of the self, particularly the penis, may be projected onto another man. Freud (Rosenfeld 1949) commented that this projection may be one of the sources of the "narcissistic homosexual attraction." The patient is attracted to a man who represents the good parts of the patient himself; he may love this man as he wished to have been loved by his mother. In essence, he attempts to duplicate himself through searching and finding his narcissistic ideal image (A. Freud 1949, 1951).

In all instances of male homosexuality the patient attempts to deny the existence of a hostile, cold, and antagonistic father. The effect of this rejection in the unconscious of the patient may vary in harshness from rebuff to deprivation to persecution. Consequently, central to his attempt at any relationship with a man, he must idealize the good father figure. In the more severe cases he uses this idealization to deny the existence of the father persecutor; in milder cases, to deny the existence of the hostile, cold, and antagonistic father. In severe cases, therefore, homosexuality can be seen as a specific defense which appeases the "persecutor" with homosexual intercourse.

Utilizing a different frame of reference, Klein (1952) attributes "impulses of forcing the self into the mother" to the "paranoid position" and contends that this situation may be responsible for the frequent combination of paranoid symptoms and homosexuality.

The Erotization of Aggression and Anxiety

In all sexual perversions repressive efforts are directed against both libidinal and aggressive drives. The result of the repressive compromise (Sachs Mechanism) produces a remarkable transformation of aggression, hate, hostility, envy, and jealousy into their opposites and provides a high pleasure reward: orgastic satisfaction. Earlier psychoanalytic case studies discovered that aggression played an integral role in homosexual love relationships.

Freud (1922), for example, found that in certain instances homosexuals based desires and acts on a defense against earlier intense jealousy of and aggression toward rival brothers. Ferenczi (1914) noted during the analysis of a homosexual that the patient's alleged love for the male was essentially an act of violence and revenge. "Whenever this man felt himself offended by a man, especially by a superior, he immediately had to go hunt up a male prostitute. Only in this way was he in a position to avoid an outbreak of fury." Boehm (1926) discovered in his patient that "hostility toward the father induced guilt feelings, a fear of retaliation from men, and a wish to disguise the hate into love of men."

Nunberg's (1938) paper, "Homosexuality, Magic and Aggression," made evident the dynamic importance of aggression in homosexuality. He identified four "pure types" of homosexuality based on the predominance of libidinal or aggressive drives: (1) those which represent a flight from the woman due to the fear of incest; (2) those which represent an identification with the mother; (3) those which result from inhibition or restraint of aggression; and (4) those in which aggression is not avoided. Any individual betrays characteristics of differing types. The very prevalent disguised aggression type patient, through contact with a masculine man, believes he himself will become masculine. This is similar to Anna Freud's later concept (1949) that identification with the male partner is the basic mechanism in male homosexuality. Thus, a boy may become homosexual out of the inhibition or restraint of aggression against brothers or father. The contrasting type is one in which aggression is not avoided, but, on the contrary, makes up an integral part of the subject's homosexual life. In these cases Nunberg believed that the aim of the homosexual represents a compromise between aggressive and libidinal impulses.

In one of Nunberg's cases the mother of the patient actively encouraged him to seize love from the father through acts of aggression (homosexual seduction). It was as if the mother were saying, "Your father has deserted you. He doesn't support you any more so you are small and sickly. If you want to become a big, strong man go to your father and get money from him." Money here stood for food and nourishment and, as the patient conceived it, masculinity equaled virility. It was as if through sexual congress with men he himself became masculine.

Many of Nunberg's cases exhibited paranoid symptomatology. From the analysis of a paranoid homosexual he concluded that "anal homosexuality" is not only a gratification of the libido, but also a gratification of the impulses of aggression. He began to realize, however, that aggression plays an important part not only in the object choice of the paranoid psychotic but also in certain nonpsychotic homosexuals.

Rosenfeld's (1949) clinical material demonstrated that paranoid anxieties arising from intense aggression encouraged the development of strong manifest or latent homosexuality as a defense against aggression. When the homosexual defense fails, clinical paranoia may result. The homosexual uses the idealized good father figure to deny the existence of the persecutor, the hated aggressive figure.

Bychowski (1956b) and Bak (1956) describe the inability of the ego of the homosexual to neutralize aggression due to excessive early stimulation of aggression. Homosexuality becomes a regressive adaptation through identification with the mother, turning hate into love. This resolves the destructive impulses originally directed toward the mother and simultaneously libidinizes the aggression toward the rival of the same sex. Bak (1956) reported on a clinical example in which danger of destruction of the object led to a perverse defense against it.

The 1951 panel on perversions (Arlow 1952) held that the defense against retaliation from aggressive feelings was a central issue in all perverse formations. Important contributions in this direction have been made by Freeman (1955), Nacht et al. (1956), Rosenfeld (1949), Thorner (1949), and Payne (1939).

The nature and meaning of what Bychowski (1954) described as sudden releases of undifferentiated aggressive-libidinal impulses in homosexuals constitutes brief attempts at establishing contact with objects because the poorly structured ego of the homosexual has not succeeded in binding instinctual energies of the primary process. This facilitates chance encounters with pseudo-objects and leads the homosexual to attempt to incorporate the power of his partner through the homosexual act. However, the homosexual has never been able to separate his ego from the mother and the homosexual act becomes merely an attempt at a social experience on a regressive level (Bychowski 1945).

Melanie Klein (1954) emphasized the role of the earliest aggressive impulses with their associated anxieties and the defense mechanisms of introjection and projection in the development of homosexuality. Both Glover (1933) and Jones (1933) showed not only the importance of the aggressive impulse but also the close relationship which exists between perversion and psychosis. Perversions may be, to a large extent, the negative of certain psychotic formations: libidinization and idealization of the object being exploited as a defense against aggression and concomitant paranoid anxieties.

Miller (1956) underscored the vacillation between submission and hostility in homosexual acts. Homosexuals may express simultaneous aggression and submission in such acts because they lack a strong masculine identification and "have not worked out a submission-aggression pattern." When an aggressive urge is stimulated, their identification remains with the mother and strong aggression is expressed through the medium of female identification. Since the masculine identification with a virile father has been inhibited, the person's hostility and erotization seeks expression based on the identification with the female.

Building on earlier observations by Abraham (1920) and Glover (1925), Bergler and Eidelberg (1933) noted that behind the oral sadism and oral erotism in male homosexuality, lay a deep oral deprivation ("the breast had failed the child") and, as a result, there arose a quantitative increase in aggression. As a consequence, an intense hate for the mother and a need for her culminated in certain severe neurotic manifestations: (1) an excessive desire to eat, suck, bite, and drink from the breasts of the mother with a simultaneous reaction-formation against the breast, repressing interest in it; (2) an increase in oedipal hate for the father; (3) a rise in secondary narcissism; and (4) an intensified tendency toward female identification.

Jones (1927) has shown that in cases of female homosexuality in which oral erotism is more prominent than oral sadism, an individual will probably belong to a group in which she has an exclusive interest in women and is actually closer to the path of heterosexuality. If oral sadism is more prominent, the female homosexual is likely to show manifest interest in men and in masculine activities.

Female homosexuals dread being punished for their oral sadism. While punishment may stem from either parent, in the heterosexual female this dread relates primarily to the mother; in the homosexual female it relates primarily to the father. In the heterosexual this fear of punishment seems to be a simple retaliation for the death wishes against the mother who will punish the girl by coming between her and the father. The girl's response is to partly retain her femininity at the cost of renouncing the father and to partly obtain vicarious gratification of her incest wishes in fantasy through identification with the mother. In the female homosexual, when the dread of punishment arises from the father, it takes the obvious form of his withholding gratification of her wishes which she then transforms into the idea of his disapproval of them. Consciously she may express this as fears of his rebuff and desertion. If she is deprived on the oral plane, the result is resentment and castrating biting fantasies. If she is deprived on the later anal plane, the outcome is more favorable. In the latter instance the girl manages to combine her erotic wishes with the ideas of punishment in a single act resulting in fantasies of anal-vaginal rape. The familiar fantasies of being beaten are derivative of this. Thus, incest equated with castration and the fantasy of having a penis becomes a protection against both.

In comprehending the concept of the erotization of aggression one must bear in mind that destructive aggressive impulses threaten the existence of the object while the investment of the object with libido acts as its protection. As a consequence destructive aims invariably undergo some degree of modification because of the fusion of instinctual drives with libido prevailing over aggression. Destructive aggression (as well as nondestructive aggression) is modified by (1) displacement, (2) restriction of the aims, (3) sublimation, (4) fusion (the result of commingling of instinctual drives), and (5) neutralization (an activity of the ego) (Hartmann, Kris, and Loewenstein 1949). Neutralization itself is due to de-aggressivization and de-libidinization of the primitive drives. Thus, neutralization develops under the influence of secondary process activity and object constancy and is closely related to instinctual fusion and sublimation (Kris, 1955).

Similarly, the erotization of anxiety has produced a remarkable transformation of fear, apprehension, and anxiety into their opposite, libidinal pleasure and orgastic satisfaction. No doubt this is made possible by the multiple defense mechanisms of substitution and displacement inherent in the Sachs mechanism.

It is obvious that anxiety or mental pain can be neutralized or diminished through sexual stimulation and orgasm. Much is yet to be known about the exact mechanism involved in the erotization of anxiety. A fundamental observation is that when a homosexual's insufficient self- and object-representations are threatened he develops anxiety and is faced with the necessity to "shore up a precarious and imperiled representational world" (Stolorow 1977). To this end he uses his early psychosexual experiences. Stolorow psychosexual experiences. Stolorow makes the important point that it is not the fixated erotic experience per se, i.e. the instinct derivative that is then regressively reanimated in the perversion, but rather that it is the *early function* of the erotic experience that is retained and regressively relied upon. In this way, through erotization, the homosexual attempts to maintain the "structural cohesion and stability of crumbling, fragmentating, disintegrating self- and object-representations" (Stolorow, 1977). Ego survival is thereby insured.

The Hanns Sachs Mechanism

The intense attachment, fear, and guilt in the boy's relationship with his mother bring about certain major psychic transformations effected through the mechanism of the repressive compromise. Having developed infantile libidinal strivings of an intense nature toward his mother, with resultant guilt, anxiety, and savage hostility, the child must attempt to repress these strivings. Through repression, however, he is only partially successful in attaining relief. The ego then has to be content with the compromise of repressing the greater part of its strivings at the expense of sanctioning and taking into itself the smaller part. This solution by division, whereby one piece of infantile anxiety enters the service of repression (that is, is helpful in promoting repression through displacement, substitution, and other defense mechanisms) and so carries over pregenital pleasure into the ego while the rest undergo repression, is one of the major mechanisms in the development of the homosexual perversion (Sachs 1923). The repression of the wish to penetrate the mother's body or the wish to suck and incorporate the mother's breast undergoes repression; in either case a piece of infantile sexuality has entered the service of repression through displacement and substitution. Instead of the mother's body, it is the male body which is penetrated and instead of the mother's breast it is the penis which is sought after. Homosexuality then becomes the choice of the lesser evil. This is a basic mechanism in the production of homosexuality in both males and females.

The Breast-Penis Equation

In order to defend himself against the positive oedipus complex (his attachment to his mother and hatred for his father and punitive aggressive destructive drives toward the body of his mother), the homosexual substitutes the partner's penis for the mother's breast. The female similarly substitutes a fictive penis on her female partner in place of the abhorrent maternal breast. This can be in the form of a masculine attitude on the part of her female partner (or herself); the substitution and introduction of the finger and tongue in sexual contact; or the use of a penislike device. Simultaneously, she avoids her incestuous wishes toward the father. The breast-penis equation is a common observation during the psychoanalysis of homosexuals and has been well documented (Bergler and Eidelberg 1933, Fairbairn 1964, Fenichel 1945, Freud 1905a).

Psychic Masochism

The homosexual drains off into a psychic masochistic state the aggressive assaultiveness toward the mother and, secondarily, toward the father. All homosexuals deeply fear the knowledge that their homosexual acts constitute an erotized defense against a more threatening masochistic state. Libidinal and aggressive impulses against the mother and father lead to masochistic wishes whcih then seek effective discharge through the homosexual relationship.

Masochism is not only a method of neutralizing aggression but also of keeping the tie to the mother (Socarides 1958). The homosexual wishes to escape the all-powerful retaliative forces of the mother but he does not dare to cease being her masochistic, thinly disguised "slave" (Bergler 1951, 1956, 1959). In the masochistic state, guilt over incestuous feelings for the mother is continually bought off through self-punitive activies. However, the pain in masochism which is self-controlled and self-induced gives rise to a false sense of victory, elation, and omnipotence. He is in a state of masochistic invulnerability.

The presence of a masochistic element adds to the difficulty in treating homosexual patients. Masochism itself may constitute a central element in helping him maintain his precarious psychological equilibrium. The homosexual will state that he is not masochistic at all but that this is a conscious and deliberate way of life which he prefers. Nevertheless, in reality he is unconsciously committed to and captured by his need to avoid what he fears would be extinction due to the tremendous threat of maternal engulfment. To fortify himself and to make himself secure against this possibility he aggrandizes, elevates, and romanticizes his variant sexual activity. Masochism is not to be defeated; even in the course of his homosexual pleasure, masochism prevails.

Masochistic anxiety undergoes erotization in homosexual activity (Fenichel 1945, Freud 1919b, 1924b). Orgastic activity and pleasure partially and temporarily relieve the tendency toward regression and toward the powerful masochistic state which, were it to get out of hand, would threaten his psychic survival.

The Imperativeness of Impulse and Homosexual Acting out

Because the homosexual must forgo his striving for gratification of his intense attachment to the mother (and consequently to other women, as well as his closeness to the father because of the latter's abdication, he experiences severe feelings of loneliness throughout life.* Homosexuᵃˡⁱᵗy is an attempt to achieve human contact and to break through stark isolation. The homosexual claims that his motivation is to find love but in many instances this is merely a rationalization for the overriding and imperative need for neutralization of anxiety through homosexual orgastic contact.

Homosexuals have a weak ego structure based on narcissistic and prenarcissistic dispositions. The archaic, narcissistic ego structure makes the ego vulnerable to the impact of libidinal stimulation, and renunciation of primitive gratification becomes difficult if not impossible. In his repetition compulsion the homosexual dramatizes a repeatedly unsuccessful attempt by the ego to achieve mastery of libidinal and

---

* For an an exhaustive and detailed description of both theoretical and clinical aspects of acting out, including homosexual acting out, the reader is referred to the numerous papers in the Symposium on Acting Out presented at the International Psychoanalytic Congress in 1967.

aggressive impulses and of the archaically cathected objects. In place of object cathexis, the ego seeks gratification in a short circuit act between the self and pseudo-objects, for example, between various substitutes for the ego and for parental images (Bychowski 1954). The ego, when faced with the task of object cathexis, experiences a threat of further impoverishment. Concomitantly we find a lack of neutralized energy indispensable for control, postponement, and anticipation of gratification.

The homosexual's loneliness is in reality an acute, intense depression mixed with mounting anxiety which threatens his psychological equilibrium if sexual contact is not made quickly. He is unable to utilize sublimation or diversion, which so often forestall impulsive and self-damaging behavior in normal and many neurotic individuals.

The imperative need for sexual contact is a striking phenomenon in many male and female homosexuals. The homosexual is suffering from irresistible impulses in which the striving for security and the striving for instinctual gratification are intimately mingled. During psychoanalytic therapy he begins to perceive that this tension is like a dangerous trauma which he aims to get rid of, in addition to achieving sexual gratification. Gradually he becomes aware that these drives are not experienced in the way his other normal instinctual drives are. With therapy, he moves in the direction of first preferring homosexual fantasy instead of acting on his irresistible impulse, and then engaging in heterosexual fantasy and, ultimately, heterosexual activity. The imperativeness of impulse and its significance in therapy is further discussed in the section on therapy.

In the homosexual encounter itself, each partner is playing his part as if in isolation, with little cognizance of the complementariness of a sexual union. It is as if the act were consummated, with the other person serving as a device for the enactment of a unilateral emotional conflict. A rudimentary reciprocal affective situation exists in female homosexuality in which either may play mother or child, with alternate role designation.

The imagery accompanying the homosexual act between males is often total fantasy. It permits discharge and expression only of individual dynamic forces. There is often little reality awareness of the partner or of his feelings.

Multiple homosexual contacts with a variety of partners, either in a group or through one-to-one contacts, have as their aim the immediate gratification and alleviation of urgent destructive feelings threatening extinction of the self. Other individuals are the instruments through which the homosexual seeks expression of and release from oppressive and importunate anxiety, guilt, incestous feelings and aggression.

Most homosexual acts first disarm the partner through one's seductiveness, appeal, power, prestige, effeminacy, or "masculinity" and then take satisfaction from the vanquished. To disarm in order to defeat is a common motif, and, if one submits in defeat, gratification is nevertheless obtained by the victim vicariously, through identification with the victor.

The homosexual act is largely egocentric. Tender affective reciprocity may be entirely pretense except in the milder forms of preoedipal homosexuality and in the oedipal type where the capacity to maintain object relations is not completely lost. In such instances a love relationship may exist even though it is a highly neurotic one (Kernberg 1974, 1975). Some homosexuals prefer to achieve contact through the aperture in a toilet stall door and extend and/or grasp the penis without a face-to-face encounter. This enacts the fundamental nature of the object relations of many homosexuals, who relate to part objects, not whole objects.

Along with the narcissistic attitude of the homosexual there is often a supercasual air and a preoccupation with appearance and adornment which is meant to produce a show of perfection and imperturbability in order to conquer men and to deny a deep sense of inferiority. Ego boundaries must be carefully preserved through dress and studied action. The posturing of this self-presentation serves as a defense against deficient ego boundaries which cannot withstand stress or unexpected circumstances.

The imperativeness of impulse produces a florid and chronic acting out in perverts. Khan (1965), whose brilliant contributions to our understanding of sexual perversions have provided the most incisive observations on the meaning of certain aspects of the acting out process, notes that the perversions, including homosexuality, are a social acting out of the infantile neurosis. Through this technique the homosexual appeals to, involves, seduces, and coerces another object into sharing in the enactment of childhood conflict and its resolution. Khan calls this "the technique of intimacy"; acting out is its mechanism. It consists of a subtle balance between a defensive exploitation of regressive satisfactions of a pregenital instinctual nature and the mobilization of archaic psychic processes, in the hope of "freeing and enlarging the ego into an independent and coherent organization and achieving a sense of identity." The object in homosexuality occupies an intermediary position; it is not-self and yet "subjective." It is registered and accepted as separate and yet treated as subjectively created; it is needed as an "actual existent not-self being" and yet coerced into "complying with the exigent subjective need to invent it." With the narcissistic magical exploitation of the object, there is simultaneously an "intrinsic deficiency in the pervert's incapacity emotionally to focus and relate to an object externally and intrapsychically." This crucial lack, as noted by Anna Freud (1952), results in a deficiency in the pervert's object relations in terms of his incapacity to love and his dread of emotional surrender. This is due to the basic incapacity in the homosexual's ego to mobilize adequate, sustained cathexes of an external object or of its internal representations (internal object). In the "technique of intimacy" the homosexual tries to "press into another being something pertaining to his inmost nature, as well as to discharge his instinctual tension in a compulsive way. He engages in a temporary renunciation of separate identities and boundaries and attempts to create a heightened, maximal body intimacy of an orgastic nature. However, the pervert himself cannot surrender to the experience and retains a split-off, dissociated, manipulative ego-control of the situation." Khan (1965) believes that this is both the homosexual's achievement and his failure. It is the failure that supplies the compulsion to repeat the process again and again. The psychoanalysis of all obligatory homosexuals consistently reveals that while they arrange and motivate the idealization of instinct, "the technique of intimacy" fails because instead of instinctual gratification or object cathexis they remain deprived persons whose only satisfaction has been pleasureful discharge and intensified ego interests. They are, in Khan's phrase, "hommes manqués." Their sense of insatiability derives from the fact that every venture is a failure. The internal anxieties relating to the ego's "dread of surrender" (A. Freud 1952) never allow for gratification of the impulses involved. There is no "object relatedness, hence no nourishment"; it is a "dramatizing without affective or psychic internalization of the object" (Khan 1965).

Khan concludes that this failure to achieve any form of ego satisfaction leads to an idealization of instinctual discharge processes. This ultimately produces a sense of depletion and exhaustion and a paranoid turning away from or against the object. This vicious cycle gradually reduces the positive striving and expectancy of the personality. The patient comes in for treatment at the point when his autotherapeutic attempts have totally failed.

I agree with Khan when he notes that one of the greatest skills of all perverts is their "creative" ability to seduce, coerce, or involve others in the technique of "intimacy and acting out."

The following description of a homosexual encounter by a highly intelligent and articulate preoedipal type II patient, Willard, with concomitant narcissistic character pathology is a striking confirmation of the above observations.

"I am so driven by my homosexuality, but I am in the dark about these interests or drives. I just came from a homosexual experience last night which was almost divinely satisfactory. X, my friend, is very fine and friendly, and our whole raison d'etre has been our mutual sexual interests. I'm not really at all turned on by him, or he to me as a physical sex object, but he is turned on to me as a father figure, as an authority figure, an establishment figure, a reliable old friend. And I evidently have considerable emotional value to him in these ways—he is respectful of me, fond of me, respectful and sweet. I am almost not attracted to him but we do have sex together.

"I see myself as a cipher. I can't imagine anyone can see me in any other way. Together we later had sex with a young man and I was the catalyst that gave motion and impetus to the whole thing. The young man was highly experienced and X was very moved. There was sexual action for about three hours. X cried rather profusely at several times. It was caused mostly by me, by the fact I was adoring him, that I was expressing verbally my feelings about his beauty and perfection. While the other person was fucking him I was kissing him deeply and profoundly and this moved him to tears. And while the young man was appreciating X's beauty, I was the most important element I think. For example, with X the other night: there is nothing in this world—nothing—more beautiful to me than his anus. I don't know why that's true—I find it blindingly beautiful and I feel a state of being transformed into that mystical realm by staring at his beauty. I am sometimes responsive to X, but it didn't bother me at all that they were making love, but that I could *find identity* somehow there. I felt not only gratified and transformed, but I felt for these moments very integral to the emotional fabric that existed among us—but I still see myself as a cipher later.

"I spend a great deal of my time pursuing sexual gratification, and work therefore is only an interruption to it. Last week I had dozens of sexual partners. I came twelve, fourteen, sixteen times per week in the last two weeks. I can devote myself to endless hours in sexual circumstances—but then I begin to feel frustrated and empty after it's over and I get restless, and then I need it again. Any frustration, tension, the onus of being with my father, produces a desire to devote the rest of my life to X's anus. This may be somewhat hyperbolic but I do mean it. I would like to devote my whole life to the beauty of his anus."

Willard suffered from a pathologically disturbed relationship to his internalized objects in infancy and childhood and a loss of normal narcissistic self-esteem ("I feel I am a cipher"). He partially and transiently remedied this by inducing pleasure in an external object in an attempt to make up for his inadequacy and deficit ("It was caused mostly by me"). The great sense of isolation which a homosexual fears and endures for much of the time is temporarily assuaged through a rudimentary mode of communication with an external object in the homosexual act. The mutual intimacies of the threesome in sexual surrender to each other, and their mutual dependence, moves the patient to an eloquent description of an erotized flight from reality and the creation of pseudo–object-relatedness. For the moment, he diminishes the feeling that he is a cypher, in essence, empty, a "nothing," "zero," and he feels transformed into a feeling human being by the emotional fabric he weaves about him. But he cannot become truly involved, despite his almost lyrical description of the sexual act, for he cannot mobilize adequate, sustained cathexis of an external object or its internal representation (the internal object). He ultimately feels empty, a cypher once again after the sexual act. He strikingly revealed the inability to sustain the cathexis of the object with libido in many other sessions in which he chronically complained of an absence of emotional ties to any of his sexual partners, no matter how beautiful or how sexually engrossing the previous encounter had been.

Ego-Syntonicity

In homosexuality, as in other perversions, genital sexuality has been replaced by one component of infantile sexuality. The homosexual has only one way of gaining sexual pleasure and his energies are concentrated in this direction. Obstacles which block his capacity for other sexual pleasures are overcome, wholly or in part, by the perverse act. The gratification of the perverse instinctual drive constitutes the end product of a defensive compromise in which elements of inhibition as well as gratification are present. The component instinct itself undergoes excessive transformation and disguise in order for it to be gratified in the perverse act (Hanns Sachs mechanism).

The term *ego-syntonic* has long been used in psychoanalysis to denote behavior which is compatible with the integrity of the self. This concept requires further explanation, clarification, and refinement. In 1923 Freud described "in the roughest outline" the neurosis as "the expression of conflicts between the ego and such of the sexual impulses as seem to the ego incompatible with its integrity or with its sexual standards. Since these impulses are not *ego-syntonic,* the ego has *repressed* them; that is to say, it has withdrawn its interest from them and has shut them off from becoming conscious as well as from obtaining satisfaction by motor discharge" (1923c, p. 246). Such a patient is considered to be suffering from ego-alien formations or neurotic symptoms, for the dammed-up libido "finds other ways out from the unconscious" (p. 246); for example it regresses to earlier, weaker phases of development and earlier attitudes toward objects (points of fixation) and breaks through into consciousness, obtaining discharge in the form of symptoms. "Consequently symptoms are in the form of compromises between the repressed sexual isntincts and the repressing ego instincts; they represent a wish-fulfillment for both partners to the conflict simultaneously, but one which is incomplete for each of them" (p. 242).

A number of ego-syntonic phenomena can be successfuly analyzed at the present state of our knowledge. These include neurotic character traits, addiction, psychopathy, borderline conditions, psychotic characterology, and perversions. Some analysts believe that the choice between a symptom neurosis and a neurotic character trait or other ego-syntonic formation depends upon the libidinal type to which the patient belongs; for example, narcissistic types usually use ego-syntonic rather than ego-alien defenses. On the other hand, unconscious defenses will produce symptoms in patients who belong to the obsessional type.

When one speaks of the ego-syntonicity of homosexuality or any other perverse act, it is evident that we are dealing with two components: conscious acceptance and unconscious acceptance. The degree of conscious acceptance of a perverse act varies with the person's reactions to societal pressure and consciously desired goals and aspirations. The conscious part of ego-syntonicity can be more readily modified than its unconscious component. Analysis of homosexual patients reveals that ego-syntonic formations accepted by the patients are already the end result of unconscious defense mechanisms in which the ego plays a decisive part. In contrast, where superego or id plays the decisive role, the end result is often an ego-alien symptom. The splitting of the superego promotes ego-syntonicity. The superego is especially tolerant of this form of sexuality as it may represent the unconscious acceptable aspect of sexuality derived from the parental superego. The split in the ego and the split in the object lead to an idealized object relatively free of anxiety and guilt. The splitting in the ego leads also to an ego relatively free of anxiety, which is available for purposes of an incestuous relationship at the cost of the renunciation of a normal one.

The perverted homosexual act, like the neurotic symptom, results from conflict. It represents a compromise formation which at the same time must be acceptable to the demands of the superego. As in the case of neurotic symptoms, instinctual gratification takes place in disguised form while its real content remains unconscious. However, a perversion such as homosexuality differs from a neurotic symptom, first by the form of gratification of the impulse, namely, orgasm; second, by the fact that the ego's wishes for omnipotence are satisfied by the arbitrary ego-syntonic action. We can conclude that homosexuality differs from neurosis in that the symptom is desexualized in the latter; discharge is painful in the neurosis, while it brings genital orgasm in the perversion.

Chapter 9
THE DISTURBANCE OF GENDER ROLE FORMATION

Central to the etiology of preoedipal homosexuality is a disturbance in gender role identity. This disturbance while more apparent in some individuals than in others, emerged as a central finding in all my psychoanalyzed cases of homosexuality despite compensating structures and personality traits. For example, even a masculine-appearing homosexual man reveals deep feminine unconscious identification during analysis.

The term *gender role identity* is used synonomously with *sexual identity* and connotes the masculine-feminine polarity, a reflection of a psychological self-image. It is the individual's self-evaluation of maleness or femaleness as defined by Ovesey and Person (1976). Although its foundation is laid by age three or four, gender role identity is not a fixed entity but is subject to fluctuations and variations up until adulthood. I will use the terms *gender role identity* and *sexual identity* interchangeably to indicate an individual's awareness of being masculine or feminine in accordance with anatomy.

During the past decade psychoanalysts have conducted numerous direct observational studies on infants and young children; their aim was to discover the origins and development of self- and sexual identity. Their psychoanalytic formulations, which can be only briefly reported here, provide vital theoretical constructs which clarify and add depth to the clinical material reported in this volume.

In their most recent publication, Mahler, Pine, and Bergman (1975) note that the course of attaining enduring individuality consists of the attainment of two levels of the sense of identity: the awareness of being a separate and individual entity, and the beginning awareness of a gender defined self-identity. They observed that difficulties in gender identity development are revealed more by their failures than by normal variations. They noted that gender identity in the male develops with less conflict if the mother "respects and enjoys the boy's phallicity . . . especially in the second half of the third year." An identification with the father or possibly with an older brother facilitates the early beginning of the male's gender identity. The mother must not interfere with the boy's developing autonomy or his gender role identity will be threatened or disturbed. She must be able to relinquish her son's body and "ownership of his penis to him." Crushing activity or forcing passivity is extremely damaging to the development of gender identity. The rapprochement struggle unfortunately may take on the character of a more or less desperate biphasic struggle on the part of the boy to ward off the "dangerous mother after separation." They contend that the "fear of engulfment by the dangerous mother after the separation, the fear of merging that we sometimes see as a central resistence in our adult male patients, has its inception at this very early period of life" (p. 215).

While Mahler and her associates' major interest was to achieve an understanding of the development of the human infant and child in the course of normal separation and individuation processes leading to the establishment of object contancy, self constancy, and enduring individuality (the attainment of a separate and individual self), Galenson and Roiphe, in their psychoanalytic observational study of infants and young children over a ten-year period, directed their attention to illuminating those factors in the preoedipal phase which lead to the awareness of a gender defined self-identity (sexual identity). Their findings, especially as they pertain to symptomatology and the genesis of sexual perversions, can only be touched upon here.

In 1968 Roiphe made a definitive connection between the fear of object loss and early castration anxiety, noting that the major thrust of development during these early months is a concern with the differentiation of the self from the object and the internalization and solidification of the object representation. This early period of genital interest and activity takes place entirely during the preoedipal period. During these early phases of genital arousal, a primary genital schematization is taking place which gives shape to an emerging sexual current and a later primary genital schematization. "Early experiences that tend to challenge the child unduly with a threat of object loss or body dissolution result in a faulty and vacillating genital outline of the body at the time when a genital schematization normally undergoes a primary consolidation" (Roiphe 1968, p. 357).

From their work with healthy and disturbed children at the Albert Einstein College of Medicine, Department of Psychiatry, Roiphe, Galenson, and their associates concluded that there exists an early castration anxiety (a "nursery castration," if you will) which is later compounded by the castration anxiety of the phallic phase. In such children they found faulty, blurred or vacillating body ego outlines in addition to the beginnings of perverse formation (Galenson et al. 1975). By 1972 Roiphe and Galenson had firmly established that there is a normal period of genital interest occurring somewhere between fifteen and nineteen months of age involved with the consilidation of object representations in the body-self schematization and free from oedipal resonance.

While the mother plays an important role in allowing the child to separate and individuate, the father also serves a vital function. Abelan (1971) notes that it "might be impossible for either of the [mother or child] to master [intrapsychic separation] without having the father to turn to" (p. 248). The absent, domineering, hostile, detached father will not allow the male child to make an identification with him and thus become a bridge for the boy in achieving both an individual and a gender identity sense of self. This is later dramatized in a lifelong poor relationship between father and son. One may observe similar clinical phenomena in the adult analysis of female patients.

Greenson (1964) noted the central importance of substituting a normal identification with the father in place of the mother in his phrase "disidentifying with the mother." Stoller's important work (1968) during the past decade underscores the crucial importance of a father with whom a boy can identify in order to successfully traverse the separation-individuation phase.

Edgecumbe and Burgner (1975) of the Hampstead Child Therapy Clinic examined the development of object relatedness and drive development in preoedipal phallic phases and the oedipal phase proper. They traced the development of the body representation as an integral part of the developing self representation, and the processes of identification affecting these representations. They state: "This development of self and body representations and of identifications makes a crucial contribution to the establishment of differentiated sexual identity. . ." (p. 163). They conclude that "the process of acquiring a differentiated sexual identity rests largely on the child's capacity to identify with the parent of the same sex" (p. 165). They verify that acquiring a sense of sexual identity begins during the child's second year and continues through the anal phase, reaching its peak in the phallic phase. Although in agreement with Mahler's concepts, they differ with Mahler regarding timing and they attach greater importance to the phallic-narcissistic (preoedipal) phases as a time "in which the child may be expected to acquire and to shape his own sexual identity; having done this, the child is then better able to enter the oedipal phase of development" (p. 166).

Chapter 10
HOMOSEXUALITY DURING ADOLESCENCE

Psychosexual conflict is determined during the preoedipal and oedipal phases and occasionally in the latency period. These conflicts undergo subsequent alteration and the clinical form of their manifestation in the adult is usually not decisive prior to adolescence. The ultimate form of childhood conflict can appear as psychosis, neurosis, delinquency, character disturbance, and sexual deviation. Rarely does a clinical picture develop unchanged and with only minor alterations into adulthood.

Adolescence affords a "second chance" to overcome the anxieties and conflicts of childhood (Eissler 1958). Entrance into adulthood requires an increasing appreciation of reality and the development of inner control simultaneous with the appropriate expression of drives.

The psychopathology of adult years tends to assume its final form during the adolescent phase of development. This has enormous practical importance, as the sooner a fixed symptom complex is treated therapeutically, the more likelihood there is of therapeutic success and prevention of further maladaptive processes. Adolescence, therefore, is a highly favorable time to undertake psychotherapeutic measures to treat homosexual problems despite the serious technical difficulties which adolescence, with its violent shifts between the various structural components of the psychic apparatus, produces. At this period of life we can more readily undo recent overt homosexual behavior; redirect urges toward heterosexuality; reduce fear and guilt regarding heterosexual strivings; and begin to establish a firm basis for rewarding sexual maturity. During adolescence a healthy path toward instinctual gratification should be gradually cleared of any pathological obstacles; fears, impulses, and fantasies concerning heterosexual gratifications can be resolved. The ego is thereby strengthened and enabled to cope constructively with both the demands of the intrapsychic apparatus and the environment.

Freud (1905a) succinctly described the adolescent's position at the beginning of puberty:

With the arrival of puberty, changes set in which are destined to give infantile sexual life its final, normal shape. The sexual instinct has hitherto been predominately autoerotic; it now finds a sexual object. Its activity has hitherto been derived from a number of separate instincts and erotogenic zones, which independently of one another, have pursued a certain sort of pleasure as their sole sexual aim. Now, however, a new sexual aim appears, and all the component instincts combine to attain it, while the erotogenic zones become subordinated to the primacy of the genital zone. Since the next sexual aim assigns very different functions to the two sexes, their sexual development now diverges greatly. That of males is the more straightforward and the more understandable, while that of females actually enters upon a kind of involutional period. A normal sexual life is only assured by an exact convergence of the affectionate current and the sensual current, both being directed toward the sexual object and sexual aim.

An individual's final sexual attitude, according to Freud (1905a), is not decided until after puberty and is the result of a number of factors, some still unknown. He concluded that among these factors three are of particular importance in the production of homosexual individuals: (1) "a predominance of archaic constitutions and primitive psychical mechanisms"; (2) "a tendency toward narcissistic object choice"; and (3) a retention of the erotic significance of the anal zone. Accidental factors, a result of frustration, may influence object choice.

Major contributions to our knowledge on sexuality and adolescence have been provided by Deutsch (1944), Eissler (1958), Frieberg (1962), Blos (1961), Lorand and Schneer (1962), and Anna Freud (1958), to mention only a few.

Indicators for Therapeutic Intervention

Since adolescence is the pivotal time to treat homosexuality one should bear in mind the indications for psychotherapeutic intervention at this stage. By late adolescence some patients already demonstrate a rigid pattern for solving conflicts. The matter is further complicated by the exaggerated and fluctuating relationships between ego, superego, and id drives universally present in adolescence. Psychic swings are so swift that modifications of psychoanalytic technique must anticipate them (Eissler 1958, Geleerd 1957). Although all adolescents have difficulty stabilizing their appropriate sexual identity, there are several indicators which are of major significance in determining when therapy is needed:

1. In scrutinizing masturbatory practices of our adolescent patients we are concerned with the total absence, or late advent, of masturbation, and particularly with its fantasy content, whether or not heterosexual activity has occurred. Fantasies which are primarily or exclusively homosexual, especially with a sadomasochistic coloration, are of serious import. The total absence of masturbation or its late advent becomes meaningful when there is no manifestation of heterosexual interest whatsoever.

2. Homosexual behavior through adolescence in the absence of anxiety, guilt, or conflict together with perverted fantasies are an alarming sign. It is imperative to initiate therapy in order to create a conflict for the patient by driving a wedge between the id representatives and the ego. In many adolescent cases the homosexual symptom is acceptable to the ego without superimposed societal guilt.

3. When a beginning perverse form of activity takes place in adolescence, one often finds an apparent absence of true oedipal relationships. A typical clinical picture is that of a boy burdened with a primary identification with his mother and a weak or abdicating father, a boy who searches for his male identity by seeking the love of other boys and later of adult men. He may be filled with sadistic conceptions of heterosexual intercourse. The failure to successfully pass through previous maturational phases weakens the genital organization, and the boy retreats from oedipal desires and demonstrates little interest in forming a

heterosexual union as he approaches maturity. Preoedipal and oedipal patterns dominate rather than the structural organizations typical of adolescence. As an adolescent, the boy cannot cope with the heightened genital pressures of puberty, and soon develops a postpubertal full-scale perversion. Adolescence is a strategic time to begin the psychoanalysis of such a boy or girl; otherwise, a fixed progressive maladaptation may well occur.

4. Therapy is indicated when an adolescent engages in vivid homosexual fantasies, displays no interest in heterosexual socializing, relatively withdraws from social and interpersonal concerns, and lacks age-characteristic emotional fluctuation and lability.

By adolescence the healthy individual must have developed and come to grips with strong oedipal strivings. Otherwise he may be burdened throughout life with pregenital urges and feelings, and retreat into complete abstinence from sexuality or turn to perversion (Hartmann et al. 1964). In treating an adolescent homosexual, the analyst must assist him in all aspects of his struggle against infantile conflicts and ties and must prevent him from returning to an earlier psychic organization with its narrower, restricting patterns.

5. Adolescents sometimes suffer from such an intense degree of sexual fear that they never undo the repression of their sexual drives even in adulthood. They profess to and truly have no conscious awareness of any sexual interest whatsoever. Sexual release occurs only during sleep concomitant with sexual dreams. Conscious hostility toward desire may often supplant sexual yearning in some adolescents. Where hostility to one's libidinal urges is present and where conscious awareness of sexual feelings is absent,

analytic investigation is necessary to determine whether or not this is a result of homosexual conflict.

6. While not all overt homosexual experience during adolescence should be considered pathological, it should not be disregarded or overlooked without careful evaluation. It may be a temporary phenomenon of adaptation and may not connote a homosexual fixation. However, when there is some overt homosexual contact together with a resentment of anatomical "growing up" and a strong suppression and repression of instinctual demands, treatment should be instituted.

An adolescent should feel that he has begun to be "on good terms with his sexuality" (Fenichel 1945). Choosing a homosexual partner is not simply a manifestation of an infantile partial instinct. Although we know that to children the sex of the other person is of less importance than it is to adults, and that this attitude continues in some individuals into latency and into the earliest years of adolescence, beyond this point the analyst must view persistent sexual intimacy with persons of the same sex as a serious sign. My clinical material does not support the idea that a certain amount of more or less manifest homosexuality "appears regularly" in adolescence and is of no significance (Group for the Advancement of Psychiatry 1965).

7. A homosexual relationship with an adult constitutes for the adolescent "a dangerous regression to the original homosexual object" (Freiberg 1962). This dangerous regressive step toward the parent calls for immediate treatment, especially when, as so often happens, the relationship encompasses deep feelings of love on the part of the youngster. In such an instance

"the absence of conflict between the adolescent and his original love object can be an ominous sign" (Freiberg 1962).

8. Some adolescents verbalize their conviction that they are truly homosexual by stating that they have acquired this "homosexual identity" through "inner knowledge" (Freiberg 1962). They assert, "I know I am a homosexual; I just feel it," and admit to little distress regarding their discovery. In these instances therapy should be instituted immediately.

In summary, adolescence is a kind of lease permitting revisions of "solutions formed during latency which had been formed in direct reaction to the oedipal conflict. It behooves us to do everything in our power to allow this second chance for mental health and happiness in the future" (Eissler 1958). With this in mind, indications for therapeutic intervention as outlined above should require our most serious consideration.

Theoretical Features of Male Homosexuality During Adolescence

My first case to demonstrate certain hypotheses is that of a twenty-year-old male college student, Calvin, who started in treatment at the age of eighteen and had engaged in homosexual practices for one year. This immediately brings us to our first theoretical point.

FAMILY PATTERN

Certain preconditions of the family unit contribute to the problem of homosexuality. *The absence of the father or the presence of a weak father combined with a domineering, harsh, and phallic mother favor the development of homosexuality.* For example, the history of this boy revealed that the parents were cold and indifferent both to him and to each other. The father was almost entirely absent from the home and played no part in his upbringing except during later adolescence when he evinced some interest in his future academic pursuits. The mother was continually in the home and assumed complete control of the boy. Her cruelty is epitomized during his early childhood by her repeatedly "playing dead" in front of him, lying prostrate on the kitchen floor, breathing suspended, and not responding to his entreaties, whenever she felt he had not complied with all of her demands.

From the beginning of therapy it was apparent that the mother was a borderline psychotic. Parenthetically, the sister was accorded equally cruel treatment by the mother who, for instance, in order to insure good behavior in her absence from the home would consistently slap the girl before going out; were the daughter asleep the mother would awaken her in order to slap her.

FIXATION AND HOMOSEXUAL FEELINGS

By age six, there was strong evidence of a *fixation on the part of Calvin to an intense oral-sadistic relationship with the mother and passive homosexual feelings toward the father.* Both of these are fundamental theoretical postulates.

The oral-sadistic relationship to the mother and the passive feminine relationship to the father may best be illustrated by recounting some of the patient's fantasy life during late childhood. At the age of six he would continually fantasy kissing the toes of both parents.

By the time Calvin was eight, he developed the fantasy of sucking the father's or some other man's toes, a substitute for the penis. The smell of feet was important and this later became connected with the idea that feet were stepping on his face. By puberty, the following fantasy had developed:

Mother and I were captured by some sort of enemy, taken prisoner. I was tied down with her above me so that if she urinated it would be on my face. Sooner or later she would. She would not do it willingly but she could not control it any more and she would have to "go" and she would be trying to hold back and it would be coming out little by little—so I say to her not to hold back. She is only making it more uncomfortable, for soon it would come out. So then, with regrets and apologies, she would let go.

Despite the patient's attempt at levity in recounting this material, his fantasy portrays the intense sadism he attributes to his mother in the disguise that they have been "taken prisoner" and that she is *forced* to be cruel to him. There is a strong oral wish to be fed from her body (breast–fictive penis). Simultaneously, he attributes to her aggressive and destructive urges whose aim is to demolish his self-esteem and masculinity. These fantasies arise from a fixation but there are regressive elements which promote them.

PRIMITIVE PSYCHICAL MECHANISMS

In all homosexual patients there is a predominance of primitive psychical mechanisms. (1) Calvin is unable to form an appropriate identity consonant to his anatomic and physiological role in life; he is already beginning to engage in a wholesale *denial* of his penis and masculinity. (2) Through *incorporation,* the swallowing of body substances from the mother, he attempts to compensate for the deprivation in nourishment and love experienced in infancy and early childhood and simultaneously reinforces his identification with the mother. (3) He demonstrates a most commonly found primitive mechanism, *splitting of the ego,* with the result that sometimes he feels male and sometimes female. In the latter instance he assumes a feminine attitude toward his father, for example by sucking the father's toes, and later on undergoes masochistic punishment at the hands of the phallic mother.

ADOLESCENCE FORCES A DECISION

The genital pressures of adolescence force the individual to resolve his oedipal and preoedipal conflicts and to create an equilibrium in his life, at the same time allowing for orgastic satisfaction. If these conflicts remain unresolved, sexual expression seeks substitutive outlets such as heterosexual masochistic fantasies or behavior; homosexual fantasies or homosexual acts, either with or without masochistic features; or other perverse activities such as fetishism. Along with these distorted expressions of the sexual drive there may be psychotic or major neurotic symptoms. Homosexual conflict during adolescence may seek disguise and expression in delinquent behavior.

At seventeen, Calvin proceeded from homosexual fantasy to overt homosexual acts, particularly the practice of fellatio. Increasing anxiety, shame, and guilt forced him to suppress such acts. These shifts were due to the increasing strength of his sexual drive and to changes in the ego defenses. His first meaningful relationship with a girl enabled him to renounce overt homosexual behavior temporarily. However, sexual gratification with her could only take the form of sadomasochistic perverse activities, as he believed that "all women are at heart cruel." Sexual arousal and ejaculation occurred only in the context of sadistic acts practiced upon him by his girlfriend at his command. These ranged from her stepping on his face to burning his palm or chest with a cigarette. She ultimately fled when he requested to be put in the bathtub filled with water in order for her to step on his face as if to drown him. Upon entering college and being separated from his girlfriend, the one "loving" female in his life, he was suddenly overwhelmed by homosexual desire for adult men, producing severe anxiety, guilt, and panic. At this point he was unable to continue in school and sought psychoanalytic help.

HOMOSEXUAL SURRENDER

Some adolescents directly surrender to their passive homosexual desires for the father by establishing a sexual relationship with an adult male. This was not possible for Calvin. This form of homosexuality, in which the adolescent feels "fulfilled and in love" ("I know I am a homosexual and I have found my true self") indicates that he has established a serious, already rigid, and highly resistant form of homosexuality.

Theoretical Features of Female Homosexuality During Adolescence

FAMILY PATTERN

In the study of the female homosexual one uncovers a fear and dread of the mother and a fixation to her similar to that found in the male. The female, however, directs a more intense aggression toward the mother. In their early histories one commonly finds a dread of being hurt, devoured, and destroyed by a malevolent mother. This dread is aggravated by the girl's *secret wish to be loved exclusively by her father*—a wish which she renounces almost completely because of her conviction that her father not only refuses to love her but also rejects and hates her—especially for her phallic deficiency. If, in late childhood, the father does offer care and affection, she turns away in "revulsion," seeking the company, admiration, or love of other females. With the onset of homosexual behavior she displays to the mother her guiltlessness regarding unconscious sexual wishes toward her father. Through this apparent lack of any interest in the male organ, she thereby hopes to ensure maternal care and love.

The foregoing description aptly fits a professional woman in her mid-thirties whose first actual homosexual experience was in late adolescence, at age seventeen, but whose intense physical attraction toward girls began at approximately nine. The case of Sarah, presented in detail in chapter 19, is condensed here to illustrate specific theoretical formulations pertaining to adolescence.

ORAL-SADISTIC FEELINGS

As in the male, the potentially homosexual female almost always presents a history of *oral deprivation and intense sadistic feelings toward her mother.* Sarah had been told that although breast-fed, she never received enough milk and for the first two months of life lost weight and screamed continuously. As far back as she could remember she felt, "My mother did not love me and she really wanted to kill me." Her secret and persistent wish was that evenutally it would be discovered that she did not belong to her family at all. Her poisoning fantasies, which were most severe from the ages of three to thirteen, best exemplified her oral-sadism. "I often thought my mother would punish me so severely some day that she would kill me. Once she gave me sausages and I was frightened to death that they would be poisoned or something." The analysis later revealed that these semidelusional convictions were projections of her own sadism toward her mother.

PRIMITIVE PSYCHICAL MECHANISMS

In female homosexuality primitive psychical mechanisms are even more pronounced than in the male. They often take the form of outright denial of the anatomical differences between the sexes. For example, the girl often hallucinates a fictive penis, identifies her entire body with the male organ, or may substitute some characterological feature, such as intellectuality, for the penis. She may then continue to a protracted age to deny feelings of having been castrated and to cling to the idea of somehow acquiring a penis of her own.

She engages in a wholesale projection of her own fear and hatred onto the mother, whom she is convinced had denied her the male organ as a punishment, often for masturbatory practices in early childhood. The mother and subsequently all women are unconsciously perceived as malevolent or potentially malevolent beings who must be placated through a show of affectionate behavior. They thereby become good, safe, and loving. If this belief collapses as a result of personal slight or threat of infidelity, the homosexual woman may develop temporary or permanent delusional fears of poisoning or future mistreatment, at least from her homosexual partner. With the patching up of differences, what may remain is a chronic distrust of and suspiciousness of the partner.

By the age of eleven or twelve, Sarah actively felt repelled by her mother's body; she could not bear to look at it. She had a vague recollection of an attempt to swallow iodine at age fourteen. This occurred during a period in which she was intensely angry at her mother and represented a wholesale projection of her own murderous feelings and anxieties. She then developed suicidal thoughts for approximately six months, at which point obsessional ideas appeared which involved her touching the fenders of cars to prevent "something happening to my mother." At thirteen, with the onset of menstruation, she developed a horror and fear of death. She desired frantically to be a boy.

ADOLESCENCE FORCES A DECISION

The genital pressures of adolescence in the female are less directly expressed than in the boy. At adolescence the girl is forced to make a change of genital which the boy never has to make. If the girl feels, at the same time that she must shift from clitoris to vagina, a lack of interest from her father and hostility from her mother, she is likely to repudiate vaginal erotism and attempt to create a male role for herself. If she believes that nobody wants her in "this castrated, mutilated state"—not even her father—a prolonged and pathological extension of tomboy behavior into middle adolescence ensues. Such a renunciation of feminine strivings may create a temporary equilibrium. During this period she may engage in mutual masturbation or sexual investigation with girlfriends, but this is accompanied with considerable anxiety and guilt and is soon relinquished. The shifts between ego, id, and superego drives instituted by physiological sexual pressures do not usually produce in the female a multiplicity of overt sexual practices or disturbances (as described in Calvin's case), although some masochistic, masturbatory, heterosexual or homosexual fantasies may be entertained for brief periods. It is only upon reaching late adolescence and early adulthood, when she is confronted with society's and her own demands for appropriate role fulfillment and is forced to consider sexual intercourse, marriage, and children, that her previous conflict, apparently laid to rest in early adolescence, is reactivated in all its intensity.

HOMOSEXUAL "SURRENDER"

As with similar feelings in the boy, the girl's feeling of having "found" herself in pleasurable surrender to homosexuality is a serious sign. At fifteen, Sarah's friend told her that she was homosexual. Her immediate response was to feel relief and a "very close and loving" relationship to her friend for explaining some of the thoughts and attitudes which had upset her ever since she could remember. She greeted the friend's comment as a welcome relief—a bad prognostic sign indicating the need for therapy.

The adolescent girl in sexual conflict may appear rather fortunate in that she does not undergo the intense shifts that the boy undergoes. The absence of blatant and overt psychopathology during this period, however, only camouflages her need for help. The condition is no less acute in the girl but takes longer to manifest itself.

Part II
CLINICAL

Chapter 11
THE CASE OF PAUL
(PREOEDIPAL, TYPE I)

Paul entered psychoanalytic treatment at age twenty-seven, referred by a clergyman-uncle to whom he had confided that he was a homosexual. The patient was very pleased that his uncle took enough interest, for the first time in his life, to wish to help him. The patient was still a student preparing for one of the major professions.

At the initial interview he told the analyst he had been a homosexual since he was fourteen, and had led an active homosexual life from the age of eighteen. He was an attractive young man, vivacious, articulate, and generally personable. He sought relief from the futility he felt was ahead of him were his homosexuality to continue. He complained that such a course did not lead anywhere and that his only friends were homosexuals. He wished to enlarge his social life and to develop a heterosexual personal life. He had become increasingly fearful of exposure and the ensuing legal and social consequences. On one occasion he had been apprehended by the police and permitted to get off with a warning. He realized that his homosexuality could interfere with his future career were it to be discovered. He was extremely unhappy and suffered intensely because of his inability to desist from homosexual practices.

Developmental History

Paul came from a lower socioeconomic background; his parents had migrated from Europe without material resources or vocational skills. He felt it would be "pathetic to fail in the fundamental aspect of living—sexual fulfillment—when other things had turned out successfully" for him through his prodigious effort and persistent application to educational goals. In a somewhat defiant way he had announced to his parents, shortly before entering treatment, that he was a homosexual and requested their help in obtaining therapy. His uncle had demanded financial assistance for him from the parents and the mother consented to "help for a while." His father was alarmed and exclaimed that he could not understand how his son "could live in a sewer." The mother apparently accepted the pronouncements of both son and uncle but felt that the homosexuality was "only a passing stage."

Throughout childhood Paul was dominated by his tyrannical, overpowering, and often cruel mother. She was in complete charge of the family and responsible for all decisions. The husband was a passive and yielding individual, frightened of his moody, irascible, and uncontrollable wife. The mother controlled the social and academic life of the patient and his brother, concentrating mainly on the patient, the slightly younger of the two. Until his entrance into analysis every decision had first to be discussed with his mother; he submitted every concern, problem, and incident at school to her for approval. All friendships were to be discussed with her and no secrets were allowed.

His childhood was marked by endless parental bickering, violent argument, and open physical assault. The mother would harangue and finally provoke her husband into a physical attack, at which time she would seize a kitchen knife and threaten him. The patient constantly witnessed these scenes. The father was unable to offer any effective resistence to the mother's autocratic, domineering control of the patient, and assumed a submissive, completely passive role in the household. The father appeared to have been terrorized by his wife's psychotic-like behavior. She threatened the patient with abandonment and divorce of the father if he did not comply with all her requirements, wishes, and desires. The child could not handle the mother's aggression and soon began to identify with her, taunting his father at times, making fun of him, and siding with his mother on nearly all occasions. The father rarely prevented the mother from scratching the child deeply or otherwise abusing him physically and verbally. Paul learned that silence was his best recourse in protecting himself from his mother's vicious outbursts.

Paul's mother continually stimulated his aggression throughout early and late childhood. She teased, provoked, ridiculed, slapped, and clawed him. Whenever he would try to defend himself she would beat him to the ground by sitting or lying on top of him; scratching his arms and face; and hitting him in the stomach. Fighting back in self-defense only produced more physical damage.

During infancy he had difficulty eating and recalls that at three and four years of age he was often force-fed when he did not "clean up" his plate. On two or three occasions he vomited his food and was forced to "eat the vomit." Consequently, he vomited frequently upon becoming even slightly upset during adolescence and early adulthood.

Up to the age of thirteen Paul's mother often slept with him in the same bed. He would fold his arms around her from the back and feel as if he were merging with the mother and her body warmth. She frequently disrobed in front of him; at other times, half-dressed, she would walk around with her pendulous breasts exposed. In late childhood and early adolescence she continually asked his opinion of the shape and size of her breasts and her general physical attractiveness. There was no actual sexual fondling of the mother to the patient's best recollection. Occasionally she made fun of his penis, stating that he would never be able to function as a man with a woman in later years.

She criticized all his friends, especially girls, minimizing their good qualities and pointing out their weaknesses, failures, frailties and unworthiness in an attempt to isolate him. At the age of eight he was fond of a neighborhood girl; when her mother became psychotic his mother teased him relentlessly, saying his little girlfriend was "crazy like her mother."

Paul was allowed success only in intellectual and academic pursuits. During the patient's adolescence, his mother constantly jeered at him for failing to rival his brother academically. The brother successfully eluded the mother by staying in his room; her attention centered on her younger son. The father sided with the older brother and they both teased the patient for his attachment to the mother.

Although he surpassed his brother in college, Paul was not accepted at the graduate school of his choice. His brother was. The brother subsequently married, moved to a different city with his wife, and showed no signs of homosexuality.

The patient achieved remarkable success in the graduate school he attended. He was somewhat feared by his colleagues for his angry, aggressive verbal attacks upon those whom he felt were inferior to him or who tried in any way to take advantage of him, misused him, or misunderstood him. He took great delight in his verbal onslaughts (similar to his mother's) and took pleasure in revealing to people in authority their "falseness and weakness." This was due to the identification with the aggressor (his mother) and his wish to reveal to his father his weakness and inability to protect him and take care of him as a child.

Course of the Analysis

Paul determined to make a success of his psychoanalysis because he had no meaningful emotional activity in his life. He formed a strong working alliance; participated with vigor; attended to details, including dream material; and assiduously applied the analyst's interpretations. He voluntarily resolved to cease homosexual activities by the end of the first year of analysis and did so for approximately six months, only to revert to sporadic homosexual episodes. Within the first five months of analysis he had successfully engaged, for the first time in his life, in heterosexual intercourse with orgasm and considerable pleasure. He later complained, however, of the difficulty in finding suitable heterosexual partners. He spoke resentfully of the social pressures he felt were put upon a man, including any "suitable" woman's insistence upon marriage. He dwelt on the lack of available women as compared to the vast number of easily available homosexual contacts of every description. Nevertheless, he had several heterosexual relationships during the first two and a half years of analysis, feeling at times quite affectionate toward his female partners and elated because women did not reject him.

Paul's childhood recollections of his mother's asking him to help her dress or choose a brassiere were tremendously sexually stimulating. During analysis the emergence of sexual material concerning his mother induced marked fear and he realized that he wanted "to have her sexually." A favorite erotic fantasy was of his mother wearing only her brassiere and a skirt. "It was a strapless bra, low-cut and she had an attractive face, made up just right." He was afraid to speak of childhood erotic incidents and of the fantasies they later gave rise to, but he began to realize that when he had "sex with a man perhaps I am having sex with Mother. It's fantastic but it's what I want to feel. It's my sexual interest. It has to do with the fact that I want her, to be a part of her, and that she wants me. She's always wanted me to see her that way, as a sexual interest. I guess I've always wanted her body. That sounds stupid when I say it. When I used to sleep next to her that's what I wanted and I would put my arms around her and sort of enfold myself right into her and that was terrible. I'd forgotten that since I was a little child. I didn't get an erection but it seemed to me I always went too far. I recall that I used to have fantasies around age twelve and thirteen, about putting my penis into my mother's vagina with my arms around her. It wasn't like a lover but like mother and son and I'm getting pleasure out of it. It's a terrible sick picture that I get of myself. And she's gloating at me, she's enjoying it, too, and she has control and power over me."

It was important for the patient to relive this memory and affect because he was able to engage in heterosexual relations only when he could see that he had been fearful of domination and the woman's (mother's) great power over him. He discovered that he had to dictate the terms of sexual intercourse if he were to function properly. He had to be more powerful than the woman and therefore not be controlled by his mother, as he was in his fantasies of sexual intercourse with her. These recollections brought up further incestuous feelings and memories, including those of the primal scene. On occasion he had seen his mother having intercourse with his father when he entered their bedroom. He always felt that his mother controlled his father as she controlled the patient.

For a brief period, when the patient was age seven or eight, he was not permitted to get into bed with his mother and instead "she took my brother." Within a few weeks he was again permitted to sleep with his mother frequently. Sometimes he would hear the noises of sexual intercourse from the parental bedroom, especially his father's grunting and groaning. He would then "stick my head under the pillow—I didn't want to hear it. I remember his climbing on top of her at times. I can picture her submitting to the whole thing." He was obviously confused as to which parent was the aggressor in the sexual act. His mother had told him over the years that she was completely uninterested in sexual relations with his father and was truly not interested in any sexual matters. "I would picture my father's penis going into my mother who was lying there very innocent-like and mother not being very instrumental in the whole thing."

When, during the course of analysis, the patient began to enjoy heterosexual relationships, he felt that "bond between my mother and myself—that crappy bond—was being broken. But it's like I'm losing something when I tell you about my interest in women and when I begin to think of having sexual intercourse." His first intercourse with a woman was preceded by an identification with his analyst, as revealed in a dream in which the analyst was on top of him. There was no penetration but he felt the power and penis of the analyst. He reported the dream as follows: "You being on top of me. We are not having intercourse but you're telling me, forget my real father and you're my father and not to tell my mother about it. We were clothed. And then you got up and left. It was very nice. But you didn't really leave. You just got up." This dream preceded heterosexual intercourse by a few hours. He stated in his associations that he was beginning to have a good relationship with his father. He felt more confident of his masculinity. It was like the analyst's telling him to be a man.

After intercourse he had the following dream: "My mother is sitting in a car and my father is with her and I'm coming toward her carrying two pieces of luggage and she leans over so that I can see her face which looks very twisted, a very twisted, distorted face. She keeps calling me a bastard. 'Move yourself, bastard, Hurry up, bastard.' I put down the luggage and just look and she keeps saying, 'Hurry up, bastard.' My father has a very relaxed, pleasant false-pleasant look.

He's trying to get me to do what my mother wants by his facial and hand expression. He's trying to get me into the car. Instead I push the two bags up. I go off to the right. And the last thing I see is the expression on my mother's face. She is bewildered and shocked like a stupid error of some kind has been committed."

Immediate associations were his protest against his mother's attempt to deprive him of the analysis. She continually plagued him with the financial burdens of analytic therapy and attempted to attack the analyst at every turn. He was very angry with his father in the dream. He is trying to push the two of them out of his life and obviously wants a strong male figure. It is apparent that Paul feels his father has threatened him with his mother in order to "get off the hook himself." There is no protection or love offered by his father, and Paul bears considerable hatred and aggression toward him for delivering him both now and as a child into the hands of his mother.

Paul is protected only by his confidence and trust in the analyst. As a result, he can muster enough strength through identification with the analyst to consummate his first heterosexual experience, which he feels is a triumph.

He reported the following dream at his next session: "It's about burying my father, and my mother's being her usual bastard self and stating how he was going to be buried. We are both very angry with each other." His associations concerned his wish to get rid of his father. He was burying him with a shovel. He wanted to do it right. Prior to this dream his father had argued with him about not working in the family business, saying that his mother wanted him to work part-time. Paul was angry that his father did not protect him. It was as if his father were threatening him with his mother. "I got a little fear in me at that point. I became angry that my mother could control everything. She said, 'All that we have given up for you!' " He said to his father, "You know something. I don't know who's worse, you or your fucking wife."

Both dreams represent: (1) the patient's fear of his mother and of her retaliation for any sexual activity on his part with a female; (2) his feeling that he has been duped by a weak father who failed to make him secure against both his incestuous and murderous aggressive feelings toward his mother and his fears of her abandonment of him; and (3) his ability, despite these fears, to defy them both and to initiate heterosexual activity despite their condemnation, indignation, irritation, and destructive verbal assaults.

The dream material further shows that for him to have heterosexual intercourse he must give up the quasi-friendly contacts with men (his father) that he experiences in homosexual relationships. He feels he has to "bury" his father and forget him. It was apparent that in heterosexual intercourse he felt fear and guilt, and he believed that he would somehow lose the attention and affection of his mother, the attraction to her, and the unity with her. "A lonely type of feeling would come over me after every time I had intercourse with a girl." Paul realized that his mother's dismissal of his homosexuality as unimportant actually sanctioned it. If he were interested only in men he would never leave her for another woman. The mother accepted homosexual activities in her son as a "necessary outlet" for his instinctual needs.

Paul's homosexual relationships began in early adolescence. In the beginning they consisted of mutual masturbation with boys his own age, occasionally mutual fellatio, and, rarely, anal penetration of the partner. Twice he had brief masochistic relationships with an adult male who pinched and slapped him on the buttocks, but Paul rebelled when subjected to a mild beating with a leather strap. He had since discontinued these practices.

Paul was exclusively homosexual until a few months after beginning psychoanalytic therapy, picking up casual partners in public restrooms and sometimes having intercourse with fellow students. There had been no "love" relationships and no prolonged affectionate contacts with one particular man. It was only later in the analysis that he could perceive the aggressive and sadistic nature of his homosexual relationships. His homosexual activities constituted a severe sadistic assault upon men (his father) and were highly overdetermined. For example, by having intercourse with a male he was forcing his father to give him the affection and love which he could not acquire passively or actively in childhood. In addition, he was substituting the penis of the male for the female breast (mother) and was enjoying disguised sexual intercourse with her (Sachs mechanism). He dissipated feelings of weakness by acting out his own destructive, powerful urges. Anxiety, which always preceded homosexual arousal, was libidinized and neutralized through homosexual orgastic contact.

Desire for and actual homosexual relations occurred whenever he felt frustrated by life's disappointments or fearful of abandonment by his mother. The act quieted fears of loss of mother and gratified sexual wishes toward both his mother and father. Thus, he felt assured of their love and warded off fears of castration by acquiring a potent and strong penis from his partner. His homosexual desires progressively diminished in both frequency and intensity throughout the analysis. They were revived when he: (1) "felt abandoned by Mother" and frightened regarding his dependency and security needs; (2) felt frightened by the omnipotent powerfulness and aggressiveness of other men who might threaten him socially and professionally; (3) felt tense and anxious depressive loneliness, a state which demanded he search for and gain possession of another male; or (4) experienced an overwhelming aggressive drive due to unsatisfied love needs.

In several instances, following his first successful heterosexual experiences after starting analysis, he would dream of his mother attempting to pull his testicles or his penis away from his body or of wanting to run back to homosexuality to escape her retaliation. "I should be screwing my mother and not other women. She always wanted to mold me into being a girl and as a result I've always wondered about how I look. I think I look too effeminate. My chest is not big enough." On such occasions he would feel depressed over the loss of his mother and experience fear that she "would somehow pay me back" for his interest in girls.

Paul discovered that his homosexual feelings were filled with violent impulses. "When I get a sexual feeling the man must become extremely submissive and as I say this I get a dizzy feeling as though I'd like to punch these men or strangle them or strangle their genitals rather than do anything else with them. I'd like to remove their genitals by pulling them off, tearing them off, and to cause them pain and enjoying their pain. I'd like to strangle them with my legs

around them and I'd like to see the pain on their faces. I
get a real charge out of this. I have a lot of angry
feelings within me and all this facade of being nice to
people, it's all an act.... And I hate my mother so. I hate
her for all that she did to me, her selfishness and
everything being for her. I feel like crying and I feel
awful and the hate is getting more and more about all
the things that have happened to me and I guess I've
wanted to kill her for a long time."

These feelings toward his mother had been both
repressed and suppressed. As he began to recognize
and verbalize the murderous hatred he had felt for his
mother over the years, he had the feeling that the
analyst was creating a "magnificent monster." With
this verbalization and the emerging ability to tolerate
his aggressive feelings, he began to feel liberated from
his hatred for his mother. "It's not a nice feeling to hate
somebody but what was there is there still. She was a
very sick woman and still is and this is what she did to
me. I called my father after I felt these things last time
and I told him I was all right. When I spoke to him he
suggested I not come home as often as I have in the
past because of getting my mother upset."

When Paul's girlfriends became demanding, his
homosexual feelings would reappear. He reacted to
these demands as if they were attacks by his mother.
Verbal onslaughts by his mother about his lack of
appreciation of "all we have done for you," any
feelings of disapproval (imagined or real) on the part of
the analyst, or fears of the failure of his father's health
could arouse homosexual feelings. The mother constantly told the patient she hated his father, pouring
invective on him because of his poor health. On other
occasions she deviously attempted to foster in Paul a

feeling of trust due to her "great interest" in his welfare. The analyst continually had to point out to the patient his mother's unending manipulations and machinations in the service of making him into "her masochistic slave" since Paul was still vulnerable to her despite his growing insight. On numerous occasions his mother teased him by saying, "I'm going to see your doctor and from what I tell him he's going to throw you out." She repeatedly threatened to stop the analysis by withholding funds.

Body-Ego Disturbances

Paul presented a severely distorted body-image. "You know, I don't feel I have my own body. I want somebody else's body. My body is flat, I guess because the penis is flat or never gets erect with girls. I keep looking for a body in another man and that's one of the reasons for choosing a man, especially if he's clothed so he looks masculine. It seems I'm reaching for that when I want a man. It has to do with the muscles. I want more muscles. I was never allowed to do anything that would make muscles for me, such as sports. My mother would laugh at me and say to me, 'What are you trying to be? A killer?'" Paul's mother would continually make fun of his penis. "I used to think at moments I wouldn't be able to have children. My mother used to say something like that. She'd look at me and say, 'You'll hurt yourself if you ever have sex.' She said if I ever exercised strenuously or lifted heavy things that I might hurt my penis. She'd stop me and have my father or brother do it for me. My brother used to be a fat little boy. She once made me eat the vomit I had vomited up. I'm nauseated now. She made me eat it as she fed me and I'd gag and she'd say, 'If you vomit you'll have to eat it again.' I don't feel I have a chest, I'm very narrow, no contour, more of a V-shape. It's like my arms are very thin, like an image of an emaciated person. I'm startled sometimes when I look in the mirror to see that I have muscles and I am a man and other times when I've felt down and out and frightened I see no muscles. It was only after several months of analysis that I began to see that I had these muscles."

The patient's body-image changed gradually over the course of treatment; he felt attractive, that his chest size had increased, and that he suffered from no physical abnormality. In reality he had always looked attractive and masculine. As an adolescent he put his penis and testicles between his legs in order to make them disappear. He saw only "a lot of hair," reproducing the image of the mother's pubic region which he had seen quite frequently in childhood when she appeared nude before him. This was a self-castration and an expression of a desire to be a female, thereby avoiding incestuous feelings toward his mother.

Identification With the Analyst

Paul consciously feared and hated both parents. His identification with the good male figure, the psychoanalyst, allowed him to take steps toward heterosexuality. However, even his identification with the analyst was not strong enough at times to withstand fierce interventions by the mother, who threatened him with loss of funds and abandonment, and continually belittled and demeaned him.

The analyst showed Paul by diagrams of the external female genital system there was nothing to fear and that he certainly could have heterosexual intercourse. He constantly exposed the ruthless, irresponsible, fearful, totally negative, and destructive behavior of the mother. The patient gained courage through facing this reality, accepting the analyst's objective appraisal of his mother's behavior and lifting himself out of his unconscious, masochistic, sexual submission to her. On numerous occasions he requested advice, helpful criticism, and insightful knowledge concerning current life problems and interactions in his professional and social life. This constituted in essence a "new" education by a "new" good father who would protect him against his crushing mother and inept, inadequate, and weak real father. He thus became a man. As his functioning improved at work he opened his own office. This development increased his sense of independence and his conviction that he could exist without his mother and be strong enough to stand any of her onslaughts, no matter how manipulative or vicious. He no longer needed to be ashamed of himself. He had a good body with a penis that could function; he could earn money and become self-sufficient; and he could feel kind and compassionate toward others. In time he would be confident enough to not feel threatened by women and to be able to control any "vicious woman," epitomized by his image of his mother, were he to be confronted with this type of person in reality.

He no longer needed the defensive gratifications of the homosexual act to survive. He could now relate comfortably to women; their affectionate feelings gradually freed him from the anxiety of being rejected, "sat upon," and crushed by the female. Occasionally he cried because of the trust he felt for the analyst, wishing that his father had somehow shown him feelings of love, affection, care and protection.

Precipitating Factors in Homosexual Acting Out

Paul's homosexual inclinations recurred when he felt lonely after quarrelling with his girlfriend or after feeling abandoned by the analyst, especially if the latter were on vacation. "I wanted to screw somebody. I wanted to be with somebody. I felt angry at the thought of being alone, the thought of your not being in your office, and I was alone. This frightened the hell out of me. It made me feel very unhappy and the anger gets me all annoyed now. My father said when I was two years old he thought of divorcing my mother and this was after my brother was born. He had the two of us. He thought of it and he was going to leave my mother. The reason he didn't was because of us children. The fact that he could think of leaving us, when I recall it, makes me feel lonely now." Loneliness led to massive anxiety. The anxiety became libidinized in the homosexual act. Before engaging in homosexual activity he frequently dreamt of his mother punishing him or calling him insulting names. In certain dreams he felt that she was about to suddenly jump on him from behind the curtain. She would usually be dressed only in a skirt and a brassiere. On one occasion he had a fantasy that his mother walked in with a lighted cigarette, dressed in her brassiere and half-slip. "She bends her head down and presses the lit cigarette down on my penis and I feel a great pain." On other occasions it became clear to him that he engaged in homosexual experiences in order to exasperate and upset his mother. He hoped she would feel guilty for his homosexuality.

He developed homosexual feelings if the analyst did not answer a question in the session. "If I feel I love you, and you don't answer, I get scared and I have a lonely feeling. If you don't participate the way I want you to it makes me feel alone and maybe later on I'll have a homosexual desire." On several occasions the patient developed guilt feelings after heterosexual relations. He felt guilty about doing something against the best interest of his mother, which he verbalized as giving his body to another woman. His sexual feelings for a man were often preceded by severe masochistic attacks of loneliness. He would almost invariably develop a severe rash on both arms which he scratched until they bled. These masochistic dermatological manifestations were part of his homosexuality and were relieved in the homosexual act through the discharge of unconscious sadomasochistic fantasies. Deep masochistic loneliness ensued from his desire to be caressed, fondled, and touched by his mother. At times his masochism found direct expression in homosexual episodes under conditions where he might be apprehended by the police as had occurred twice before.

In the seventh month of the analysis the patient voluntarily attempted to desist from all homosexual contact, saying he "felt strong enough" to resist it. "I can take a guy or leave a guy now. I have that strength. This has been built up because of my relationships with girls, and that I now have the ability to go to bed with a girl, and the fact that I realize now how sick my mother is. She's very sick, and she doesn't have the big hold on me, and she can't frighten me as much. I think it also has to do with not wanting her breast and that the breast is the penis that I wanted in men. I remember that I never used to look at a guy's genital area because I guess I was afraid that I was looking at a breast." Following this point in treatment the patient discontinued homosexual relations completely for two months without much difficulty. This improvement was only short-lived, however, and on other occasions, whenever lonely, depressed, rejected by a girl, frightened by his mother, or lacking strong masculine figures with which to identify, homosexual episodes would occur. It was only in the third year of the analysis that he successfully eliminated homosexual contacts for intervals lasting several months. He began to develop affection and object love toward a particular girl. Although he occasionally experienced homosexual fantasies of mutual masturbation, during the last year of analysis, his fourth, he was nearly free of all homosexual fantasies and homosexual episodes. Even though the patient achieved heterosexual functioning with full orgastic satisfaction early in treatment, he characteristically developed homosexual wishes when he felt "imprisoned" and constrained by his girlfriend. This reaction clearly stemmed from his fear of the overpowering female, his mother, and the consequence of this fear: turning to men for orgastic satisfaction and acquiring a penis and male identity through homosexual fantasies and experiences. By turning to men he continued his masochistic relationship with his mother, utilizing a substitute figure, the male, who evoked less conscious conflict. He felt that women only weakened him if they came "too close,"

became too possessive, invaded his life, demanded
services from him, or attempted to control him in any
way.

Masochism and Aggression

The patient's omnipresent conscious and unconscious masochistic suffering at times became vivid
during homosexual intercourse. He cried and whim-
pered during acts of mutual fellatio. "I relate it to my
mother. I feel like I don't trust her and I am leaving
myself open to a blast by calling her or doing anything
for her and I feel dizzy as I am talking about it. If I do
call her I am giving in to her and I have a guilty feeling
when my father tells me about how she was ill the other
day and my not calling her. I'm still not calling her and
I'm a terrible son as she is so ill. Everyone says she's ill
and that I'm being terrible. My father tells me the same
thing, too. He wants me to go all out and give myself to
my mother in order to protect him. He also took the
promise of money away from me that he was going to
give me."

Homosexual intercourse also afforded discharge for
his murderous aggression toward his mother. His
mother's continual provocation of him in childhood
leading to severe aggressive outbursts and temper
tantrums is described earlier in this chapter. She would
scratch him with her fingernails and he would hit at
her hands violently up to the age of thirteen. He would
also strike her on the arms and enjoy seeing her cry. At
times she so enraged and provoked him that he
attempted to choke her. On many occasions she
mockingly offered her throat, inviting him to choke her
to death. "I became frightened that I would kill her and

then suddenly I would be overwhelmed with an awful sense of guilt and then I would stop." He was the guilty captive of his mother through her provocation.

During analysis he realized, "I want to choke my partner with my legs around him or my hands around his neck just the way I wanted to choke my mother. However, I guess I substitute a man for a woman. I want to choke her by shoving my penis so far down the man's throat that he is choking and gasping for breath. I get pleasure out of that."

After having homosexual relations the patient usually felt an increased strength as reflected in the following dream. "My cousin and myself going to the basement of the house and we crept into a peculiar kind of position with our legs wrapped around each other and leaning backwards as if we were pulling something out of each other and we hear somebody coming and we stop it." His associations were to a cousin with whom he first had homosexual relations when he was very young. "There is a certain strength in the position. I wanted to pull away and still keep contact. I was pulling something out of him. He is my penis and that's why I feel so strong."

As treatment progressed the patient became aware that when he was attracted to men he would concentrate on parts of the body, especially the genitals or the buttocks. With women it was quite different and he began to notice for the first time that when he became attracted to them it was to a "pleasant overall picture—their total appearance, dress, manner, and gestures. In homosexual feelings there are always lonely feelings and also the wish to be a man. At the same time there is an angry component. I'm angry with myself and angry with all these guys, angry with wanting homosexual sex and angry with my parents. This has come through quite clearly recently to the point where I grit my teeth hard. When I can turn off the homosexual feelings I feel pleasant and thankful toward you and determined not to do it again. I'm thinking about you at the same time and have a determination to be a person, a good person, and I realize that heterosexuality is there. It's there to be taken and it means being a good person, not being an angry, destructive one."

Whenever the patient's mother hurt him through her verbal attacks he became weakened, frightened, and masochistic. Following one such incident, which was brought up in the analytic session immediately thereafter, he went to the subway toilet and engaged in mutual masturbation with a casual pick-up. Simultaneously he observed two other men. "This one guy went over to the other one, went down on his knees and started sucking him. The second guy was dirty looking, a positively dirty guy. It showed extreme masochism. It looked so terrible. This first guy dressed splendidly in a business suit, clean-cut and good-looking. I've seen guys suck other guys but it was never like this. He was on his knees on the dirty subway floor and he was feeling this guy, running his hand up and down his arms and legs and taking him all in and with his other hand he was masturbating himself. I was watching. I know why I was. I was punishing and hurting myself, too. I *was* the guy on his knees and I wanted the disgust to go all over me. I was watching his degradation and enjoying it. Every time I engage in homosexuality I'm sure that I am enjoying a degradation with men. Also I feel that I only degrade myself in front of my mother and I really want to eat her up, eat her breasts, eat her, eat all of her. Other girls are out. Her breasts are to be eaten and they are substituted for by the penis of men."

This incident was followed by a dream that night. "My mother and I walk into a place like a restaurant and we see a girl sitting there and she is a pleasant girl. I keep saying that my mother is crazy, that I don't want to hurt her. My mother doesn't hear. She is with me and, of course, she hears what she wants to hear, you know that. Somehow or other this girl is involved, perhaps the girl I am having intercourse with now but getting involved with her further will hurt my mother. I yell over to this girl, 'I know my mother is crazy but I don't want to hurt her.'"

His associations were that if he becomes progressively involved with a girl it will hurt his mother because he will eventually wish to marry the girl. He retreats from heterosexuality, submitting himself to a "crazy mother" who will only hurt him. He feels that his mother "probably is crazy," but this further ties him to her because then she needs him even more. "I feel sorry for her. I remember her cold, hard self and how she used to treat me but it seemed at least she loved me. In my homosexuality I think I'm giving in to her, too. I do not take another woman; I take a man. I subject myself to such humiliation and torture in these subway things."

Beneath the veneer of affection and friendliness, Paul's motivational state during sexual intercourse with a man was severe aggression. For example, while having anal intercourse he realizes that, "I have my fist clenched and I have a killing fantasy, like I wrap my arms around the guy and strangle him by grabbing him around the waist or around the neck with my feet or my hands. I want to get a better grip on him to jab harder into his rectum with all my might, a lot of force behind it. I become angry even as I describe this. I'd like to punch and kick him at the same time

and maybe even kill him." Whenever a homosexual
partner-to-be became gentle and began to talk plea-
santly and like him, the patient could easily lose his
sexual interest.

"I often have fantasies about hitting a man, hurting
him. I thought about this guy the other night, screwing
him in his office, and sometimes it even changes from
sexual to pure aggression, like just jabbing him. After I
talk of these feelings I feel somewhat kindlier toward
men. When I started my homosexuality with the boy
across the street it used to start out as a fight and it
always starts with people who appear aggressive. Or I
start fights with women, not sex, with women who are
aggressive and might hurt me, just like my mother.
And even though I know it's my aggression there's
suffering involved in it. In my search for my partner
with whom to be aggressive I can stay up all night and
not get enough sleep and not establish any relationship with anyone, either male or female. And in case
the man is stronger than I it goes the other way, too, a
wish on my part that the guy become more aggressive
than I and do all these things to me. There's my
masochism."

In the above session the patient expresses the
sadomasochism underlying his homosexual relations.
The homosexual, while behaving as a sadist to his
partner, can at any moment switch into masochistic
behavior if the strength of the partner overwhelms
him. He plays a dual role, vicariously enjoying the
partner's role. There is a continuous oscillation,
therefore, in the actual act or in the fantasy, between
sadism and masochism. The aggression serves multiple functions: (1) to protect the breasts of the mother by
venting the aggression on the substituted penis; (2) to

have intercourse with the father and force his love and affection; and (3) to punish the father for denying the son's masculinity and for his failure to protect him against the crushing mother. These constitute lost vital requirements for separation and individuation from the mother.

Nuclear Preoedipal Conflicts and Superimposed Oedipal Conflicts

The patient's conviction that he would hurt his mother by going with girls and having intercourse with them had a double meaning. If he had intercourse with girls he felt he was much more directly having intercourse with his mother than when he substituted men. If he penetrated another woman he felt he was penetrating his mother, a dire event to be avoided at all costs. The importance and meaning of penetrating the mother and its deep implications regarding Paul's basic conflict became apparent a few months later. He reported a dream of central importance, demonstrating the basic conflict of all preoedipal homosexuals. The understanding of this dream, its associative material, and its affective discharge became a major turning point of the analysis. Paul reported the dream as follows: "It's only a short dream. It's of my mother bleeding right down the middle and I'm rolling over on top of her." His associations were, "I am hurting mother by talking against her, by going out with girls. You recall the last dream I had of importance, it seems to me, was the dream that I was hurting my mother when I approached other girls. Every time I feel I've hurt my mother I then begin to have homosexual desires. In the dream the blood was all over me. It strikes me as odd that I'm telling this all to you, that I have to force myself to talk. Last night I tried to masturbate with this girl's image in mind but I couldn't. I could only masturbate with a man's penis in my thoughts. I find I look at certain guys depending on what I feel I'm missing or needing at the time. If I feel loneliness I need a gentle guy. If I need strength I get a fierce-looking, wise type, hate-look-in-the-eyes kind of man. In the dream my mother was bleeding from the heart but it was in the midline and it was a slash, a long cut, deepest at the heart and some sort of conflict in the dream. She deserved it but I didn't want her to have it. She deserved to die. I was almost choking in the dream myself, like almost it was my death, like Siamese twins together, the blood. I got almost vicious in the dream, pushing away and yet not pushing away, holding tight to her, the way I hold tight to homosexuals. It makes me feel very nauseous, very upset, and my heart is going very rapidly and I'm frightened like I wish it was over and I didn't have to keep going back to it. Suddenly, I feel shame about wanting to have intercourse with my mother. I know I've wanted to for years (oedipal conflict clearly revealed, superimposed on preoedipal conflict). It brings tears to my eyes when I say that and I'm crying now. I'm loving her all over that way but I wish my mother could have my father and my father her and that I could just let it go at that, the two of them."

Paul felt shame and guilt for his incestuous feelings and deep anxiety for his desire to unite with the mother. He substitutes a man in homosexual intercourse to alleviate both oedipal and preoediapl anxieties. The analyst asked if Paul could now see why he had not tried intercourse with women instead of

men. He responded with intense emotion that he
wanted to be a child with his mother; in approaching
other women he would not rid himself of his incestuous
wishes and his guilt of joining with her. Furthermore,
he felt unable to control his aggression, vividly
depicted by the slashing of her body in the dream. By
not approaching a woman, he shows he has no interest
in his mother and thereby denies his aggressive,
murderous, and libidinal wishes toward her. "In the
dream I am loving her all over and she is holding me,
even though she's bleeding, and it's mostly her holding
me and my clinging, and all those things make me feel
ashamed. I hated myself and my feelings and my
mother, but more I felt ashamed and now I feel relief as
I tell you and it brings tears to my eyes...relief from
guilt. I didn't feel I did anything wrong as a child but I
see now that in loving her I'm killing her and
destroying her. The killing of her and below that is the
intercourse with her; but I feel there is a good reason to
kill her, to kill our relationship, to get her out of my life,
to let my father have her. There is an expression, 'Go in
health and peace'; if it could happen that way my
mother could have my father and my father her."

In this session the patient expressed great affective
release by tears, grief, sorrow, thrashing on the couch,
and despair. He telephoned the analyst a few hours
after this session saying that he "never felt so happy"
in his life.

In this last session the nuclear conflict of the
preoedipal homosexual is apparent. What he attempts
to ward off is the isolated affective state associated
with mother-child unity, a threat to self-differen-
tiation. He therefore experiences: (1) a wish for and fear
of incorporation; (2) a threatened loss of personal

identity and resulting personal dissolution; (3) guilt
over any attempt to heal the wound through invasion
of the mother; (4) intense desire to cling to the mother
expressed at oedipal levels as a wish for and fear of
incestuous relations with her; and (5) intense aggression of a primitive nature toward the mother.

Paul experienced his nuclear fear at this point in the
analysis because he was engaging in heterosexual
relationships (casting off the defensive function of
homosexual relations) and he was able to tolerate and
experience his unconscious aggression aimed at the
mother. He recognized that alongside destructive aims
toward her were wishes to merge with her, to cling
together "like Siamese twins" in everlasting union.

Out of the nuclear conflict of such patients certain
secondary conflicts develop in childhood: (1) aggression against the father and other men who do not
protect him from the female; (2) a sense of inferiority;
(3) increased confusion as to body-image; and (4) an
avoidance of anxiety producing situations, especially
being left alone without the mother.

Almost invariably in preoedipal homosexual men,
as in Paul's case, there is a history of protracted
screaming, lasting for hours, whenever they were
separated from the mother. This occurs even in the
presence of the father or of a satisfactory maternal
surrogate should the mother not be available. Screaming will stop abruptly with the mother's return. This
phenomenon probably starts at around two years of
age and may last up to age seven. This screaming is
probably tantamount to a scream for survival as the
child fears for his life when the mother is not present
due to feelings of being threatened with ego dissolution
and of being unable to achieve a sense of individual
separateness.

The screaming is intense and prolonged. Often it cannot be remembered by the patient but is confirmed by relatives who observed it.

In the normal child screaming is usually a reaction to frustration and is not protracted; the child's attention and interest can be diverted and he can accept a mother substitute. The normal child can invest other objects with interest and can allow them to substitute their care and affection for that of the mother. The child who develops into a homosexual is not interested in acquiring care and affection but in the survival of his ego.

Viewed schematically, one can designate Paul's nuclear conflict as the centrum or nidus around which secondary conflicts and a tertiary layer of action and behavior were formed. These tertiary patterns and attitudes are designed to enclose and ward off the isolated affective state of the mother-child unity. The following result: (1) He does not approach any other woman, especially sexually, as this will touch off the isolated affective state of the fearful mother-child unity. (2) He does not attempt to leave his mother or else she would, by her actions, provoke the isolated affective state. He attempts to maintain the "status quo" by being asexual toward other females. (3) He unconsciously carries out sexual activities with the mother through substitution, displacement, and other defense mechanisms. He therefore gratifies his sexual desires through a masquerade. (4) He reinforces his identification with mother, but to gain strength must seek a transitory male identification through the penis of his partner. (5) He substitutes a man for his mother in sexual intercourse but is in essence enjoying sexual intercourse and closeness with the mother in a disguised state. This helps him overcome his loneliness and fear of abandonment.

To summarize, the homosexual is fixated on the wish for mother-child unity. This connotes, however, a threat of total destruction of the self, which is to be avoided at any cost. All further activities of his life are designed to ward off the realization of this unity. Homosexual behavior appears to be the solution for forestalling a powerful affective state which threatens to destroy the individual both by anxiety and by the loss of personal identity with a return to less differentiated stages of the ego. The homosexual chooses a partner of the same sex to aid repression of the basic conflict: the wish for the mother-child unity accompanied by the dire fear of loss of self. This is in accordance with the Sachs mechanism of sexual perversion.

Guilt

During the course of treatment Paul discovered a number of sources of his guilt feelings. They arose from his wish to penetrate his mother, to destroy her, and at the same time to join with her in the mother-child unity. This aggressive, destructive, murderous urge increased his guilt (preoedipal guilt). He also felt guilty for his incestuous wishes toward his mother and his desire to replace the father in intercourse with her (oedipal guilt). Whenever he attempted to break the mother-child bond and become a mature and independent man he felt guilty because he felt beholden to his mother for his very life and security. Thus anxiety and guilt were associated with the failure of development in the phase of self-object differentiation—the result of an object-relations conflict.

Paul remembers since childhood both his fear of the mother's breast and his fear of looking at the breasts of other women. "When I think of breasts I get a little nervous. It has to do with my mother's breasts and how she would walk around and show them to me. I can remember seeing a scar on one breast of my mother." She blamed the breast operation on breast-feeding, although he does not believe his mother's assertion that he was the cause of a scar.

Erotization of Anxiety

The patient became increasingly aware during analysis that many of his fears, whether having to do with work or social engagements, had been libidinized into homosexual activity (erotization of anxiety). "At several points I stop thinking of what causes my fear, it takes over. Even if I think at work I'm not doing enough of what I'm supposed to be doing I develop a quick fear and this is immediately replaced by homosexual desire and then when I do this I feel well again." Homosexual activity is here generalized from its initial and primary use in warding off fears of the mother-child unity.

When the mother threatens to engulf him, the patient develops fears which lead to sensations of "weakness." These sensations develop into homosexual desire and terminate in the homosexual act. "It's like an automatic response, first caused by my mother in childhood, and she does it now, too. If I show her in any way I have a problem or bring it to her, instead of showing her I could handle it, the only thing I can do is have her handle it for me. To get away from my mother I then look for a man to protect me from her, to help me,

to guide me, to show me how I can work without my
feeling weak. To help me develop, to teach me. I didn't
just want that only. I wanted somebody continually
there, as my mother is so strong and so overwhelming I
need a full-time man. My homosexuality defends me
against these fears, the problems and anxieties of life,
the reality of life. On another level it's a defense
against being able to help myself, against the thoughts
about my lack of ability to help myself—my very
helplessness with my mother. But when I act homosexually I strengthen myself with masculine strength to
do all the things I have to in everyday life. I sneak in a
shot of masculinity between encounters with my
mother. It's also a way of postponing the challenging
things of life until the last moment." It is not the erotic
infantile experience per se which is sought in the
perversion but the reassuring and reaffirming *function* of the erotic experience which is reanimated in
the homosexual act.

On the Path to Heterosexuality

As treatment progressed the patient commented on
certain difficulties in turning to heterosexuality.
Homosexuality was "much easier. Homosexuality
itself has a wildness about it, an urgency and a
mystery. It's true you can have that with a female but
in heterosexuality there's a slowness about things and
no wildness. You can't just go and lay a girl on the
street. Everything that I noticed in heterosexuality is
in moderation; there are no extremes. If it were, of
course, I guess it would be so sick. So to become
heterosexual in a way means a much more boring
existence. I was also wishing this weekend that it

would be different if I had been stopped before expressing my homosexual life so completely." In his sexual intercourse with men not only is there a wildness but he also does whatever he wants to do to the man. He claims he is "truly free" as he cannot be with a woman. "Fucked him and he did everything I wanted him to do. I had temptations to hit him and I was very rough. I don't like talking about this aggressive side as it is one step removed from my mother and the way she was so sadistic to me. It makes me feel that I'm acting the way she does. I never got a good feeling from being beaten once or twice but I do get a wild feeling from subjugating other men and making them love me and think highly of me the way my father did not."

It was not until an advanced phase of treatment that the patient remembered his first homosexual feelings, long repressed. They occurred at about seven or eight years of age. "The children used to take a nap in the afternoon in an after-school group where my mother left me and there was something about a bigger boy....I wished to have him as a substitute for my father and for a friend and he'd do something in bed with me. He was twelve years old and he'd lay on top of me and I liked that. Before that time I was a sexless kind of kid. I don't remember any sexual feelings. All the other boys in the group seemed weak except for that one."

He recalled that at the age of fifteen "We used to play with each other's penis and I remember I had an ejaculation but didn't know what was happening." Paul could now remember that in the earliest years of life "my father always loved me a lot" and "that he loved me most and that's why my mother took it out on me." He granted that his father did try, for a short

while in his mid-childhood years, to fight against the
mother's undue attentions and torture of the patient,
but the mother turned on the father in rage and the
father left Paul at her mercy. This memory was
especially meaningful in that the patient now realized
that his father did love him during an early period of
his life. His father was not completely helpless and
weak and did indeed care for him, but eventually "sold
out" to the overwhelming mother. Maternal domination intimidated not only the child but the father.
Yielding to the female was a means of survival for
father as well as son. Paul began very early, however,
to show an identification with the aggressor. "I began
to make my father feel like shit. He was a skunk and a
shit and I would hurt him and embarrass him and
it would give me satisfaction and my mother satisfaction. I would gang up with her on him. If I couldn't
fight my mother it seems to me I would join with her. I
would fight and hurt my father and this would please
her. I feel terrible and ashamed in realizing what I
did."

Paul's comprehension of a crucial factor, that he
should be "in control" of the sexual situation, improved his heterosexual performance. Whenever he
lost an erection it was "because the girl was trying to
control things and I feared her the way I feared my
mother when she would control me." He also feared
that the woman's sadism would take over and
therefore stimulate his own sadistic assault against
her (his mother). Gradually, however, he began to
allow a more active sexual participation on the part of
the female and to enjoy her sexual excitement. His
heterosexual desires became progressively more intense and some feelings of warmth and affection began

to appear. Occasionally the glance of a girl passing him on the street could produce erotic arousal and genital sensations. He saw the difference between relationships with men and with women partners and that you could "have a good feeling" in heterosexual relations. However, he was always upset by the fact that homosexual desire was an extremely powerful force while heterosexual desire had to be slowly built up. He recognized, however, that the latter was better "as it led up to something" while all homosexual activities were "transitory, vicious, and aggressive," lasting only for the moment and yielding no ultimate satisfaction comparable to that possible in the relationship between a man and a woman. Furthermore, Paul realized that the power of homosexual desire and acts was due to his need for discharge of primitive tensions and anxieties within himself and not due to the attraction of the object.

He was much more able to control homosexual desires when he felt it inopportune to act on them. The analyst never asked him in the sessions to desist from homosexual activities; the patient himself first suggested this course. On numerous occasions near the end of treatment, upon having initiated a homosexual contact, he would, on the slightest pretext, end it without proceeding to any sexual activity. These momentary lapses were attempts to be reassured that he could capture the affection of men; at the same time he would punish them by abruptly leaving them. He found he no longer desperately needed his "shot of masculinity." He found homosexual relations uninteresting and even boring in direct contrast to his earlier estimation of their being "wild and exciting." His deep feeling of loneliness could be alleviated by calling a girl and spending the evening with her. Above all he came

to recognize the truth of the analyst's position that
there was no innate desire for sexual intercourse with
men. He contrasted his sexual feelings toward women
with that toward men. "There's a relaxed pressure in
my sexual feelings with girls. Toward homosexuals
there is an angry feeling, a big force behind the genital
feelings and a pushing forward. It's not a pleasant
relaxed genital feeling and I would rather have that
with a girl."

He saw that sex with men arose from aggression,
while with women aggression does not create desire.
He began to comprehend that sexual intercourse with
men was really a repetition of the incident in childhood
(ages seven to eight) which he had transformed into a
childhood fantasy. After having been threatened,
subdued, and harrassed by his mother and not
protected by his father, he would lie on his bed face
down, move his body, and say, "Fuck you, Father." He
added, "I had similar things happen to me with my
mother, and when I was younger and angry at her I
might lie down on the bed face down and I'd get a
genital feeling and I'd say, 'Fuck you, too, shit-ass
Mother.' It was always translated into sex, this angry
feeling, and finally I would masturbate and it would
take out some of the hate and I'd have a feeling of
relaxation" (erotization of aggression). The substitution of the man for the mother with the resultant
relaxation, dissolution of anxiety, and quieting of hate
was an essential factor in retaining his mental
equilibrium.

Whenever he had intercourse with a girl his dreams
revealed that he felt "unfaithful to my mother. There's
a big conflict between my interest in girls and my
relationship with my mother, which has been so

satisfying in so many ways all these years and on a certain level I want to keep this mother relationship. I want to keep it subconsciously and therefore when I dream that I spray a girl with my ejaculation I send her away angrily. Even after I was with this girl and had intercourse and left her apartment I felt alone; there was no continuity. Like I'm sometimes glad it's all over. I don't have a feeling I want to talk to these girls or get a good feeling out of telling them any of my problems or the good things that happen to me. I don't get that certain feeling that I get with my mother, that secure feeling. Why is that? Why is it so strong with my mother that it can't be with other girls? I derive a *strength* from my mother. This contrasts so much with the way she treated my father. She was just so destructive it frightened me. It was no help just swearing at him. If he ever had a problem she made him feel very bad. I even have the feeling most of the time that she wants him to die." These associations aptly demonstrate the mother-child bond. He wants her close. The loneliness he sometimes experiences when he has been with a girl comes from jeopardizing the close mother-child relationship.

Following his remark about deriving "strength" from his mother he commented on her destructiveness. It induced such fear in him that he could not separate. He also felt that if he attempted to go against his mother her full destructiveness, now in part visited upon his father, would be turned against him.

When the patient did not engage in homosexual intercourse he would occasionally have homosexual impulses which abated through masturbation with a homosexual image in mind. "I would be able to get my shot of masculinity this way in the morning on waking up and also before I went to sleep occasionally." This homosexual image would be "somebody that I knew, that they want me and that they would be close to me, touching my penis, masturbating me, putting their penis in my anus or vice versa. All of this would *strengthen me,* combining with another guy." Part of the meaning of the homosexual behavior is again emphasized by the patient himself, that is, gaining strength through identification and incorporation with the potent penis of his partner, thus overcoming feelings of weakness due to separation from the mother.

Following an episode when his mother again threatened to stop paying for the analysis, he sobbed in the session, "My lousy mother and my lousy father, too." He got angry at his mother and felt terribly weakened. Between bursts of anger he experienced intense homosexual desire. At the same time "I hated the whole mess and then I wanted to hit her." Mixed with these desires he rebelled against having homosexual feelings and frantically attempted to deny them and to rise above them. That night he dreamt, "A woman in a fur coat with her breasts hanging out. She is holding her coat open so that the breasts can hang out to be seen. There are four or five fellows nearby and she's walking away from them and these fellows are happy, as if they had had intercourse with her. She's looking back as if she's pulled a sneaky one and holding her coat out as if showing the breasts to me. The guys are happy and have a pleasurable look. As a matter of fact, they begin to imitate the liltlike walk, a bounce, as she starts running from them when halfway down the block. She is no longer holding her coat open. She has pulled a fast one and she's getting away and one of the fellows is now looking as if something has been stolen from him. Some of the others discover that something has been stolen from them and they get a hate look on them. They are very angry and they make a motion as if to chase the woman and maybe kill her. I then awaken."

The patient's associations to this dream had to do with his quarrel with his mother on that day. "I think I am the boys and this is the kind of, sort of, helpless feeling I have. I guess I have intercourse with my mother and then I want to kill her. I guess they feel helpless as I do. When I went to our store and helped my mother this equals looking for my mother's breast then realizing that you have your own masculinity taken away from you by her, your own identity. These men are not themselves either. They have a bounce but they are not really feeling themselves. The bounce is a phony, a fake, they are not really themselves. It's like all those guys who walk around with a bounce and pretend they are masculine. It's not normal to walk around that way. Then they realize they've been robbed and she looks like a dirty woman. The breasts hang like a blob, like an old woman's breasts. These young men, they just had the old woman. Yesterday my father wanted to get mother off his back and on to me. The breasts upset me. In describing these breasts I feel terribly anxious. I can't appreciate the breasts with women. My mother's breast, it is always threatening, it was always a threat. I get now a very angry feeling thinking about her breast, a hateful feeling, like I'd like to hit the breast and pound at it. Why? Because I don't like my mother. If my mother's breast represents her bad treatment of me, too, it's like I must have taken poison milk in me. I remember once I ate anchovies and one day I got a terrible taste from them and it took a long time before I could enjoy anchovies again. My mother's breasts are like this. I can't enjoy women's breasts because of this. It had to do with the controlling factor, like doing something for a woman is giving in to her the way my mother wanted me to give in to her. It's why I feel uncomfortable when I touch or lick these breasts, always the same feeling of loss of control. I feel the same way about the vagina, that is, when I try to suck the vagina. It means being passive and commanded by my mother. She is offering herself to me, teasing me and stopping me from going with other women by saying that I don't need other women. Other women are just like her. This is it. Big deal! Nothing more to it. Don't get aroused by women. Not making it pleasant and she makes it something not to be aroused by."

The dream further clarifies certain issues: (1) Paul's feeling that the mother is very powerful: she can command men, control them, and rob them of their masculinity through sexual intercourse. (2) His severe aggression toward his mother. (3) His sexual interest in her and jealously of other men. (4) Paul's sense of defeat at her hands and fear of castration. (5) The mother's interdiction against sexual interest through her showing of herself to the patient (heterosexuality-incest). (6) His strong emphasis placed on the breasts of the mother, which were tremendously stimulating to the patient when he was a child, resulting in an aversion to all women's breasts in later life.

Paul struggled mightily to rid himself of all traces of homosexual urges. There were certain characteristics of homosexual stimulation which seemed to him stronger than those of heterosexual urges, although he experienced both. With homosexual stimulation, he had an instantaneous reaction, involving primitive desires. This continually surprised him, and at times its strength disappointed and depressed him. He clearly saw, however, that the sexual reaction to a man was due to a number of forces, not the least of which was the discharge of aggression which accelerated and augmented his excitement and orgasm. The "visual thing" in homosexuality was important, although he acknowledged that it also occurred with the female. "The acceptance that the look is saying, the immediate acceptance of wanting me (narcissistic component) and you don't get that with a girl. The look of the homosexual goes immediately to the genitals compared to a girl where it would go to the face or to the body in general. (The homosexual deals in part objects.) It was like having a mouthful of penises—that goes along with the look at the genitals and the nauseous feeling that comes after it. I get slightly nauseated now when I look at a guy's genitals."

His response to a homosexual was so immediate that Paul experienced considerable difficulty in dampening it even with his knowledge of the multiple functions that homosexual intercourse and homosexual "acceptance" signified. "There is a childish desire, it's like becoming a child and wanting a father, wanting a man. You become small. Your facial expression becomes sort of simple. It's really like you want to look for a daddy. Maybe it's what we have said, that the man is substituting for a girl. In actuality I don't really like the feel of a beard and the man has to be soft and have some feminine qualities, it seems. I seem to have both my mother and my father in a love relationship and it's true happiness, like I'm reunited with both of them in my homosexual relations." At other times he related the great pleasure of the homosexual urge to the release of these primitive feelings without concern for the demands of reality.

He became aware, as the analysis progressed, that sexual intercourse with a girl involved more sublimation and less aggressive "output." The homosexual "look" itself satisfied his desire to be wanted, but he thought he could get that satisfaction from a woman who wanted him if he was not frightened by her. But he also suspected and mistrusted a woman who might readily give him friendship and love. He would feel closed-in and trapped as if by his mother. "With a woman you have to cater to her, that's because she's the all-powerful woman like my mother. I might just become a complete masochistic slave and then become engulfed and lose my identity, become a girl or become like my cruel mother."

In the late phases of analysis he again commented, "In homosexuality it's a wild-type, groping thing. In heterosexuality I'm left with nice feelings, there's something intangible there, an overall feeling of warmth; sometimes some of the girls I find I become dependent on and I'm not frightened. It doesn't leave me guilty and dissatisfied and cold. I have something that I want. I'm left 'me'; I don't feel torn apart."

The patient became increasingly clear on the connections between breast and penis. "The realization right along that this had something to do with my becoming homosexual is very important and has helped me a great deal. My mother's breast and the penis of these men is quite the same. I don't have the same kind of homosexual feelings now. I realize they're wrong for me and when I think of sucking a man's penis or his sucking mine my homosexual feelings vanish. The penis is the breast. This is the feeling that

I've had since I discovered that penis and breast are the same. It has something to do with talking about it to you. *It gives me a masculine feeling rather than a homosexual one to realize this.* It's very sick. This is not really a part of my life and should not be. The attraction of the penis seems to be fading away like the homosexuality is fading away. But as I say this I'm frightened and I begin to feel a terrible lonely feeling so I give up the penis and breast. It has something to do with feeling alone, a lonely feeling. What is it due to? It's leaving the security of the home which to me *represents my mother.* As long as I know that the breasts of women are not my mother's breasts I can approach them and enjoy them. I realize to give up my homosexuality seems to be to give up my mother. It is sex with my mother's breast, that is what I do when I have homosexual intercourse."

Patients often strenuously resist the insight that masochism is an integral part of homosexuality until late in the analysis. This was the case with Paul. While masturbating to ejaculation he would fantasy that he was being jabbed in the "rear end" and "it hurt like hell. I jumped up and I was shouting, I remember, when this really happened. I associate maturbation with homosexual fantasies, with hurting myself, and it's pleasurable. This is my masochism that you have been talking about. I do this and I think all the time that it will basically hurt me. I was angry with my mother today and I had a sudden homosexual feeling. It was obvious to me that I do not have a father to stand between me and my mother and the only way I can get one is through homosexuality and the only way I can enjoy her is through homosexuality. My homosexual thoughts have to do with my need for my father, too,

wanting the father and hating the father and hating
the mother and loving the mother. Why do I have to
contend with these things? In actuality I no longer
need a mother and a father. I'm an adult, I no longer
need them to take care of me."

During the course of analytic treatment the patient
became aware of and had to deal successfully with
several major issues:

1. His basic problem of his inability to separate from
his mother. Whenever he tried, he developed anxiety
despite his understanding that she was false, malevolent, and inimical to him in every way.

2. His unconscious incestuous desires for his mother
which he first became aware of in dreams.

3. His incorporation of the mother.

4. The necessity to ultimately detach himself from
his mother to become truly heterosexual.

Approaching the end of analysis he commented,
"The worst thing that my mother can say to me and the
worst   thing   she   can   do—which   makes   me
homosexual—is when she tells me, 'You are just like
your father.' First she tears him down and then by
saying this with a terrible smile on her face she makes
me feel awful."

Paul had just finished reading the story of a
homosexual boy who, realizing he cannot escape his
mother, wants to travel to a distant city. The mother,
first desiring him not to go away, allows him to travel
to this city in order to separate him from and destroy
his interest in a local girl. Her terrible malevolence and
destructiveness was similar to Paul's mother's. Paul
wished to finally and ultimately "get rid of her," to
purge himself of this terrible need for her. He then
developed anxiety and nausea. He could not go to sleep

that night and did not want to. He was afraid he might "think or dream something terrible."

Finally, upon falling asleep, he had the following dream: "I was with a woman and we had intercourse twice. During the process of these two times I was sucking and kissing her ears. I've found women's ears to be very sensitive and I've used this with women when I have intercourse now. It gets them excited. I was screwing her very well. The third time instead of this woman it was my mother and she lets me do it a little bit and then she says, 'Oh, no, you don't!' She prevents me so that she won't let me fuck her. This is what she does to me in real life, of course. She stimulates me just enough and then stops with everything she does. I pretend I have an ejaculation anyway to hurt her and I pretend that my ejaculum comes on my pajama pants...my pajama pants...often I have laid down in my pajama pants and had homosexual fantasies and ejaculated on these pants. I usually had a penis fantasy in the past and I masturbated....To return to the dream, I pretend I come on my pajama pants and I pant as if I had obviously come. She is very much annoyed at what I've done. It's as if I had said to her 'Screw you, Mother, I am going to have my fun anyway. I am going to be a man.' She goes out to buy the newspaper. When she came back another woman is in the room and she throws my things at me and she says I should get out and take my things with me and she says 'Don't take the paper.'

"In actuality this is what she has been doing now. She threatens to make out another will and all the money she has will no longer go to me because I'm changing. She's threatening me with taking all the

money in the bank that she has in my name. She is
going to leave nothing for me and this has upset me but
this is a pain in the ass and that's all. I smile at this
now. Let her do it. What is more important—my life or
this money? To be a man or this money? Then she
chases me around the room in the dream and we are
both deriving pleasure from it. It is a pleasure but it is
mostly sadistic now in my mind as I'm going to *leave
anyway,* no matter what she says or does, and in a way
I'm torturing her for the first time because she has to
chase me. She always says no money for analysis and
no seeing her. Well, all right, we'll put up with that.
That's what we'll do. One of the reasons she's chasing
me is that she really wants to see if I've come. I think
maybe I can spit on myself but I don't have a chance to
do it. She comes into a small room and just before she's
going to look at me I wake up."

In his associations to this dream he recalls that the
analyst stated at the last session that an older woman
who paid some attention to him was not necessarily
someone with whom he could not have a personal
relationship. He was annoyed at the analyst. He was
also very upset about the short story of the homosexual
boy and his mother. "This was so true, a typical
engulfing, dominating, castrating mother who had no
concern for her child but simply to use him in her way
and no other woman should ever get him. Only for her
own benefit. When I read that story was when I
developed the nausea and confusion and after that
came my dream which means I'm going to get away."

This session clearly indicates the patient's further
stabilization toward heterosexuality. He no longer
fears the mother in the same sense as he had in the
past. He wants a heterosexual life and he will defy his

mother to have it. He is able to express himself heterosexually; he can even tolerate the ideas of incest and make peace with his infantile wishes and impulses without being frightened by them. He realizes that his mother has had a tremendous effect in promoting this incestuous conflict by her provocative behavior and possessive, seductive attitude. He feels unsure of himself at times and experiences loneliness and fear when confronted with the necessity to finally separate himself from the mother, but he fully realizes this must be done and he will do it.

A period of mourning for her loss followed Paul's full venting of feelings of aggression toward his mother. He reported the following dream: "I was talking to a girl, telling her I had to give up my mother. She kept asking why and I started to cry and I opened the door."

He associated that talking to a girl meant leaving the mother or having intercourse with her. He was losing his mother. He felt sad over the weekend and felt he had no friends. "Also, it's not simply that I am sad. I knew I was frightened. It's stupid to be frightened. Talking to you of not seeing my parents again. This is a childish approach. It isn't that I don't ever have to see them again. I don't have to be part of my mother. That's the real matter. An emptiness that I shall lose her. I can clearly see now that as soon as I've had desire for girls, and especially for Anne, it's taken away when I'm afraid of losing my mother."

As he became heterosexual he experienced a stabilization of his body-ego. "What I don't like now is when I go on the street and if I want a man to look at me, to like me, I don't like that feeling. I don't know myself when I do that anymore. I can't feel my body or my face when I do that. It takes me a while to get over it." He did not

want to experience these feelings because he had
started to feel full-bodied, having reconstituted his
body-ego; he felt pride in himself, in his movements,
and in his new identity. "There's a lot more independence in me now. I don't even try to force my
heterosexual feelings any more. They just happen. I
don't have to convince myself they're happening or try
to induce them."

It was through repeated intercourse with his
girlfriend that he began to attain complete orgastic
response and finally deep feelings of tenderness and
affection for her. "I admit that I am giving up my
mother." He also clearly saw that the conscious and
unconscious needs of both parents were served by his
remaining homosexual.

Paul was not to be dissuaded from his newfound
freedom despite the increased interfering machinations of his mother. He felt exultant and happy. "It's
more exciting this way. A whole big new world ahead
of me." He began to feel more powerful than his mother
and that he did not have to be like her. He began to
report spontaneous arousal, erections, and further
investment of libido in his female love object. At first
this cathexis was not without anxiety but this
gradually diminished. Finally, during the fourth year
of treatment, these feelings were uninhibited and he no
longer doubted their qualities of genuineness, depth,
and strength, a consideration which had previously
concerned him. "The first time it happened, this
natural feeling, it was like a cascade of water coming
out under high pressure."

In the latter part of the fifth year of his analysis Paul
proposed marriage to Anne. "I never felt so good. It's
quite a thing to give yourself completely to a person, to

just let go. We have the best sex life. I touch her differently and I say things to her that I've never said before. I never thought I would be able to have something like this."

A seven year follow-up interview with this successfully treated patient is found in appendix A.

Chapter 12
THE CASE OF CAMPBELL

At the age of twenty-six Campbell dropped out of
graduate school because he experienced periods of
"confusion" and depression, and a progressive build-
up of homosexual desire which produced intense
anxiety. He greatly feared the imminent return of his
mother from abroad. Concurrently he was troubled by
a relationship with a girl, intended by him to remain
quite superficial; she was now insisting on sexual
intimacy, the idea of which he dreaded.

The pressure on him was so intense that he would
fall into fits of crying and despondency, and would
"roll on the floor in agony." These attacks culminated
in his first homosexual relationship on the evening
before his mother's return. The partner, an older man,
was a street corner pickup. Since that time, two years
prior to the beginning of treatment, he had engaged in
several isolated episodes of homosexuality with older
partners, most of these while he was in Europe the
summer before entering treatment.

Developmental History

Campbell was an attractive, personable, extremely
intelligent, cultured, and charming young man, with

a winning manner. He was born and raised in a
large metropolitan area where he lived for most of
his life. He attended private schools during childhood, entered preparatory school, graduated from
a large university and received a Master's degree. He
was employed at a professional level in an organization dealing with social and economic issues. Campbell was an only child. His parents were of mixed West
European extraction, the mother highly cultivated and
intellectual, the father a rugged explorer, contemptu-
ous of what he deemed his wife's ultrarefined tastes.
The father became an alcoholic and was at times
openly abusive and hostile. He left the home without
legal separation but continued to reside nearby. He
contributed intermittently to the support of his wife
and son. The mother, an attractive woman, worked in
an important sales position for many years, supple-
menting the father's reluctant and unwilling financial
contributions. She instigated the separation after
years of dissension. She constantly rejected her
husband's sexual advances. Her attitude toward him
was one of condescension mixed with convictions of
her social, esthetic, and moral superiority. The
husband, resentful and defensive, exaggerated his
objectionable traits in order to provoke his wife to futile
retaliation. In effect, the mother's depreciation of the
father forced his withdrawal from the family. He
became an insubstantial and weak figure to his son in
every way. The father habitually demeaned his son for
his lack of athletic proficiency, openly referring to him
as a "sissy."

In the chaotic year prior to entering therapy,
Campbell became increasingly caught up in and
deeply troubled by his homosexuality. He decided to

send a letter "of explanation and self-exposure" to his
mother, whom, he felt, he dearly loved. Although he did
not send the letter, the patient brought it to the analyst
early in treatment:

The fact that I write this letter at all is a tribute to the utter
closeness of our relationship. As you read it I ask only that you
think about what I say calmly and soberly. Don't let maternal
pride cloud the facts and offer some easy solution, for, believe me,
there is none...Not all of what I have to say is pleasant but I think
it should be told if only in deference to the frankness which has
been a unique and noble part of our friendship.

As you know, my personality has grown and developed over the
years. I feel honestly that I have progressed in more senses than
just growing up. For this progress I hold you chiefly responsible
and for it I will always be deeply grateful. But along with this
progress, constantly coexistent with it, has grown the "flaw" in
my nature. Now, the pure question of my sexual orientation is
compounded of biological and psychological factors in great part
beyond my control. Unfortunately, the ramifications of any
deviation extend into every phase of my life and development. No
one knows better than you how the "sissy" problem hurt and
tortured my childhood. It was always with me, and although it
didn't keep me from a happy youth it was the ever present problem
and bogeyman.

As I have grown older the direct brutality of childhood has worn
off and the luck of having a personable face and personality has
aided me. Too, the greater sophistication and enducation of the
environment in which I live has all kept the problem from the
brutal urgency of childhood. Nevertheless it is still with me. I've
known since childhood that there was something confused in my
"boy-girl" balance, i.e., dressing up as a girl, etc. As I came into
adolescence the "divergencies" in my reactions startled me.
Instead of the one fairly directed urge, mine was diffuse and

confused. My own solution to the problem was a tremendous repression of it. So long as the other avenues of life were free and clear I could keep under full sail.

The navy experience broke into the problem. I was thrown with rough people, the screen of breeding and education was off. I was back in the "jungle" of early childhood. The fact that I nearly died that winter can, I'm sure, be traced to the mind as well as the body....The problem still torments me. The full blast of college learning in the social sciences also only increased my fears by showing for facts what I had hoped were fears but at the same time it freed me from the sense of a unique affliction.

Last December came the great struggle which nearly snapped me....As far as men go I haven't had any contact at all. I do know that I have always wanted a man to love me. I think because I always felt Daddy didn't. I've had crushes on boys just as I have had on girls. I always desperately want them to like me....Nothing seems more horrible to me than the "fairy" life, flitting from one affair to another in a world where all values are changed, no love permanent.

I think I would kill myself rather than partake of it....How it will work out I can't venture to say. I only ask for your help and patience. I cannot marry under false colors. As sad and terrible as it is, I am not looking at it with a hopeless attitude. If it can be worked out, it will be. If not I will do whatever is most graceful. It is a pity that with so much talent and real worth I should be afflicted with something that Conrad said "is really a terrible cross." In any case I'm sure I will have to go away for about a year to work it out by myself. By its very nature it must be done away from home, away from any environment where it might prove fatal. In many ways this is the deciding year of my life and it will cast the frame in which my future will be set.

Ever since late childhood Campbell had daydreams in which he planned to "eradicate" his father. These occurred frequently, as it always seemed his father was a "nuisance." One form the daydream took was to find his father drunk with an unlit gas jet turned on, which he, the patient, would leave on. He might daydream of dropping a "potion" in his father's drink. Equally "attractive" was the daydream of saying, when his father telephoned, "I really don't need you any more, so go to hell." Alongside his aggression against the father was a great need to be loved by him. The father upset the patient by frequently talking provocatively about his wish "to go out and punch some fairies." At other times the father would become salacious in the course of a telephone conversation, attempting to shock his son by crude and obscene language.

For years after the father moved away from the mother he took Campbell out one morning a week, from ten-thirty to noon. He sent the boy home punctually, in a taxi, and the patient would feel depressed. "I would be sure he had promised to stay together longer so we could go to a movie." He had an early homosexual fantasy of someone older than himself being proud of him, "Give me a job and then say 'You did that so well.' I want an older man to love me, put his arm around me, be interested in me. But he would have to be a person and a real man." He felt throughout his childhood that boys didn't like him but after his experiences in the Navy he felt better, realizing that young men his own age did "care" about him.

Early in treatment the patient felt that his homosexual problem must be tied up with his mother and his feelings toward her. "There's a big 'voltage' toward my mother but not so much with father. There's a strong resentment against her and a tremendous dependency." As a small boy he hated sports and felt awkward. His mother pushed him into going to dances, told him where to stand, and with whom to dance. He did everything he could to stay away from girls.

In late childhood he and his mother enjoyed uninterrupted "closeness." She undressed in front of him, nearly to complete nudity. As an adult he found it "terribly irritating whenever she is in a state of undress in front of me. I kid with her about it and say, 'Mother, aren't you the provocative one." He tried to make it a rule that she not walk into the bathroom when he was there. He could not imagine "that I would ever want to go to bed with my own mother." He felt she "got a bad deal, an alcoholic husband to whom she had to act the mother. Always the mother to her younger sisters and brothers. Then she became engaged first to someone who was brutal to her. Then she married my father, which proved to be a disaster."

Campbell was born within ten months of the marriage. It was a difficult birth which required extensive surgery for his mother in order to repair a severe perineal tear. She had a long convalescence, suffering a series of complications, while at the same time taking care of her infant son.

"Father was a very powerful man physically who gave Mother a raw deal. I feel that the homosexual business may be my mother's fault, something she didn't do consciously." He screamed a great deal (screaming phenomenon) when she left him as a child for frequent vacations. He stayed behind with a Scots maid who was a strict disciplinarian, severely obsessional, and upset by the boy's masturbation, continually punishing him for it.

In early childhood he often dressed up in his mother's clothes. He liked dolls and had a family of

Teddy bears he played with to the age of nine. He
always had a marked interest in clothes and could
remember over many years a particular costume that
either his mother or her friends wore. He always felt
that his mother wanted to "keep me at home."

When he was thirteen, his mother "fell in love with
another man." The man's wife would not agree to a
divorce and the patient's mother became "a part time
mistress." At first Campbell was proud of this
relationship and wished his mother would marry her
lover because of his wealth and position. In retrospect
he professed to being "neutral" about the arrangement
but suspects that he had been jealous of her affection
for the man.

In adolescence the patient developed a strong desire
to dye his hair. "I bought a bottle of peroxide and
dumped it on my hair but washed it out immediately."
The following day he cut his hair shorter and shorter in
order to get away from the "exquisite torture" he had
heaped on his head. He began dyeing his hair at
boarding school and continued into graduate school.
He felt that with dyed hair he became much more
attractive, resembling a boy he had met a few years
before entering treatment, a blond, attractive boy he
felt "love" for. With blond hair, he would be "terribly
successful and terribly popular and exercise power."
This was one aspect of the patient's identification with
the mother.

In college he became increasingly unable to adapt
adequately to environmental demands and conditions,
feeling that he was "not enough of a man." Prior to
entering treatment he had failed his last examination
in graduate school and would soon be asked to leave.
Because of his academic failure he faced imminent

military service. Frightened and weakened by these
reality stresses his homosexual urges became more
conscious and terrifying.

He had a profound fear of the female. "I can't even
think of looking at the sexual image of a woman. I'm
scared of kissing, too. Even the thought of the female
form scares me. I look away when I think of it now." He
obviously suffered severe castration anxiety. At school
he never liked "dirty jokes, they disgusted me." As a
child he felt he was treated like a girl. His mother
always took him into women's restrooms and into
ladies' bathhouses when they went swimming. "She
would keep me on the women's side." He recalls seeing
women putting on their girdles. When he later
complained, his mother excused herself by saying that
she had thought of him then as only a baby. "I've
always been so scared of men, too, but if a man wants
me I have a hold on him."

Throughout his life Campbell had been "convinced
by my mother that I have no sexuality at all." He was
terrified of his mother's touch, as it stimulated sexual
feelings. At age fourteen he began telling her not to kiss
him goodnight. When he was fourteen or fifteen, she
invited him to sleep in the same bed with her the night
before his leaving for boarding school. His mother had
always come into the bathroom while he occupied it.
"Mother was always very stupid about that. I was
rather offended that I didn't seem to have any sex at all
to her." It was shortly after he went to boarding school
that his father left home permanently to live a few
blocks away. His recollection from age nine on is that
his father did not sleep in the same room with his
mother.

Since age eighteen Campbell had the "compulsion" to shave the hair off his chest and other parts of his body with the exception of the pubic region. "I realize now that this was a kind of self-destruction, an obliteration of myself. I did not like the hair, did not like having it. It was very dark and ridiculous. I wanted to do it but I did not want anyone to realize it. Both the peroxiding of my hair and shaving the hair off my body were done compulsively. I have to do it. It's such a temptation. It's irresistible." This was a sign of defeat of his masculinity and a protection against the anxiety of not being loved by a man. Only by becoming a woman would he get love from men. He equated the first hair shaving with the first peroxide incident, which occurred after a blond-haired boy rejected him for touching his body, saying to him angrily: "What's the matter with you? Are you a queer?"

"It was my reaction to all this, to the personal cut, a kind of defiance. This would make me considerably more appealing. Peroxiding my hair was certainly a feminine thing, filled me with pleasure and with fright, wondering whether people would notice it. A wet, warm fright, something to do with increasing my physical allure, and that a miracle would occur." These episodes of hair dyeing and hair shaving resulted in a "kind of hysterics" in which Campbell sobbed, cried, felt intensely confused, and occasionally wished for death.

He had numerous childhood fears, for example, that if he left his hands outside the covers when he went to sleep someone would cut them off. Another was that there was someone, especially his father, at the foot of the bed who had come to murder him. Often, upon going to sleep, he would suddenly awaken with a terrifying sensation that his legs were going to drop off. All these fears derived from a fear of castration and a fear of attack by the father. This represented a superimposed negative oedipal conflict on his more basic nuclear preoedipal fears.

He was aware of his "terrible fear" of normal men but felt superior with homosexuals. He felt "terribly vulnerable" with boys who made fun of him for being effeminate, although, in fact, he did not appear feminine. "I can vividly remember every remark about my being effeminate or unmasculine. All the remarks in prep school tortured me terribly and the awful guilty feeling that I might give myself away."

Fears of effeminacy seemed to vanish when he was required to enter the navy after his failure in graduate school. But he had a "year of decline" in the navy, where he worked in a mess kitchen, experiencing homosexual wishes and deeply fearing his effeminacy and homosexuality. He then engaged in a "calculated career" of homosexuality. He was away from home, had lost all his social status, and wanted revenge on the navy. He could now be quite "coldly effective" and "felt unusually happy, although I still had to work in the scullery."

In the evenings he drank a great deal and became "completely animal." He said, however, that homosexuality "saved my sanity. Before, at college, I had reached the end of the world, awful fear. Then I suddenly failed my exams. Then the underlayer of fear, uncertainty, came, that I was going to be at the mercy of people once I got into the service and would have no way to protect myself."

Campbell's adaptive mechanisms were not sufficient to maintain him while in the navy. He regressed and became ill, suffering a severe pneumonia which kept him hospitalized for three months in a critical state. He then had an intense outbreak of homosexual behavior which he no longer fought. In the homosexuality he felt his sanity was preserved. Homosexuality neutralized severe projective anxieties bordering on paranoidal symptomatology, quieted his general distrust, and defended against extreme aggressive outbursts. He had not, on any occasion, become overtly psychotic.

Homosexual Practices

Since becoming actively homosexual, Campbell thought, "If you go home without some sexual escapade you are not wanted." This was a defense against having sexual feelings toward his mother. Even during his earliest homosexual activities the patient was aware of his sadistic ideas. "I had an awful urge to beat these men." Several homosexual partners complained, "Don't bite me," or "Stop pinching me." He engaged in sadomasochistic activities and on two occasions was tied up and beaten. He disliked taking sadistic roles in these situations, and in most instances fled the sadomasochistic scene as soon as it began.

Campbell preferred fellatio or anal intercourse. On rare occasions, when his masochism was intense or when he was intoxicated, he allowed anal penetration. Homosexual encounters frequently occurred when he had been drinking. He often awakened in some strange bed, robbed and amnesic of the preceding events. Most contacts were transient, except in one instance when a relationship lasted approximately a year with "an attractive, intelligent artist" who nevertheless ultimately mistreated him and stole money from him.

During the first year and a half of analysis his homosexual activities mainly took place in a Turkish bath where he engaged in multiple contacts. He was usually reluctant to discuss the details of his homosexual encounters in the analysis, feeling embarrassed and humiliated. These incidents were usually precipitated by his feeling threatened by his mother or weakened by job difficulties involving conflict with authority figures at work. He frequently forced himself to abstain from homosexual contacts for two or three months.

He came to many conclusions concerning his homosexual behavior. He saw it as a way of controlling men so that they would not attack him, especially when he felt vulnerable. The homosexual act sometimes saved him from "some sort of chaotic, mysterious fragmentation. I will fall apart if I don't have it." Almost magically, after homosexual intercourse he felt relieved, whole again, and strong. He often experienced a "split" in himself, as if two selves existed side by side. On the one hand, he believed himself to be benevolent, gentle, kind, attractive, interesting, powerful, and heterosexual. On the other, he was homosexual, defeated, and frightened, and "belonged to Mommie." It was as if he didn't know *who* he was (splitting of the ego). He noticed that homosexual feelings came on whenever he was afraid of his mother "turning around and engulfing me." He felt a weird excitement when his mother approached him if he were half-asleep at home, or if she suddenly sat on the bed or walked into the bathroom when he was there. This "excitement" had, in several instances, proceeded to a conscious awareness of a sexual feeling, of which he was "terribly afraid." Simultaneously, the erotic sensation was mixed with aggression: "I don't know quite what I would do to her." He came to see that his homosexuality related directly to incestuous and aggressive feelings toward his mother. He feared he would either have intercourse with her or perhaps "murder" her. The meaning of the following dream is evident: "In a room looking out there are two seals walking by, a white and a black one. The baby seal is with children. I fear the children will hurt the seals, who are lovable. Then there is a large bed, big enough to hold Mommie. A black man tries to kiss me. I am bent in an arc and his comment is 'I guess you only do this for Mommie.'"

In this dream the patient clearly substitutes himself as the man's object of desire to protect his mother. Simultaneously, he vicariously enjoys the seduction of his mother. In this connection he remembered that at age nine or ten, when his father was violent toward his mother, he got between them, declaring to his mother that he would save her. He recalled that he specifically meant that he would save her from the father's sexual attack, bearing the force of this assault on his own body.

He used to be fascinated by pornographic pictures. He would "look at the woman and go through the woman to the man." He thought that this meant he would perhaps become the woman. This resulted in considerable confusion in his mind. Why should he be more interested in what happened to the woman? He had always been with his mother too much, engulfed by her, and assumed her outlook. There was insufficient self-object differentiation.

Whenever the patient attempted to concentrate on

women and sexual intercourse with them, "the picture of mother would flip into my mind" and his interest abruptly ceased. On several occasions, however, it did not "flip out of my mind and it seems I had an erection at these times." He was unable to have sexual intercourse with men toward whom he felt friendly, as he found that homosexual intercourse was really a "hostile and aggressive act." In these acts he felt superior, and that he had a weapon on his side which enabled him to disarm the partner. He did not like to touch other men's penises and at the beginning of analysis it made him feel uneasy to look at his own. The wish for power over other men derived in part from his desire for power over his father. As a child the only power he had over him was by irritating him. "Father would always resent that I'd read a lot. I'd deliberately curl up with a book in front of him."

He equally feared castration and penetration of his body. Anything coming toward his eyes—a pencil, a gesture, or an article—caused severe fright. "It unnerves me." He had an irrational fear of children being run over. "It almost makes me jump out of my skin." This was a reaction-formation to feelings of murderous rage and was also an expression of his own masochistic desires of being penetrated, castrated, and destroyed.

Both psychic and sexual masochism were strong currents in his homosexual practices and his feminine orientation. Campbell sacrificed himself and became his mother through identification. He did not need her for direct sexual gratification; he had her in himself. Dyeing his hair or shaving it off turned him into an alluring, exotic woman masochistically used and loved by men. He then wanted done to himself what he fantasied any powerful, sadistic man could do to his mother: impale her, cut her up, and subject her to bloody pain and pleasure which he unconsciously imagined to be the fate of women in heterosexual intercourse. In this ultimate self-sacrifice he hoped to make up for the lack of paternal love.

The sexual role of the father and mother were acted out simultaneously on his own body. He enjoyed the violence directed against him vicariously as well as directly. It was an expression of his own sadistic aggression against men. Many times in adolescence he enjoyed fantasies of cutting his wrists and allowing himself to bleed slowly to death in a hot tub of water. In this suffering he experienced a "delicious" form of pleasure. Being in the bathtub symbolized his reunion with the mother; he was in the quiet, comfort, and warmth of her body.

During the sessions Campbell frequently experienced severe shudders and chills and a fear of physical attack. Upon leaving a session he would hurriedly go to the Turkish bath. "I was afraid. I nearly ran to the Turkish bath. I feel better when I'm through. I suddenly have a feeling when I'm here or when I'm with other men or when I feel weak that I'm acting like a girl. I'm feminine and defenseless. I'm like my mother. The anal business is the only thing that satisfies me, anal intercourse. I can have an ejaculation the other way but it doesn't satisfy me. I feel it has something to do with being frightened before I go, relieved that the decision is then made to go. I feel somehow I'm going to be *engulfed* and that I may lose my mind. I'm so mixed up. I've got to go. This reestablishes my sexual identity."

The patient, when weak and defenseless, regressed and feared engulfment and a loss of self in the mother. He reestablished masculine identity by incorporating the penis and body of a more powerful male. In this manner he was able to resist the pull toward his mother.

He often had fantasies of his mother dying or of his somehow murdering his father. These evolved from his negative oedipal orientation. "I think fundamentally I'd like to throw something at him and run. I think I'd scream. I can just see him. I was always afraid of him way back in my mind, afraid—it is crazy—but that he'll find out that I'm a girl, that he suspects it and he will do something awful to me. This occurred to me last night. With men I'm scared that they'll find out I'm a girl. They'll screw me and annihilate me." Consequently in sexual intercourse with men he was raping them instead of being raped by them. During the oedipal period Campbell denied having a penis in order to avoid sexual assault by his father and incestuous feelings for his mother. In adolescence his only aim was to be loved and protected from both fears. Later, when he assumed an active sexual role, he penetrated men anally instead of passively enduring sexual attacks.

In the first two years of analysis the patient was subject to "spells of confusion." These would begin with severe tension headaches in the back of his neck, sometimes extending to the front. Occasionally they were one-sided and migrainous in nature. At these moments he felt he might "crack up," fragment into a "million pieces." He lost a sense of direction and felt disoriented. Lights could appear blindingly bright. The room might shift somewhat and he would become frightened. "I feel terribly sick, as if I'm going to crack up. It's a sort of terrible fright and then a compulsion to homosexual activity. Somehow, it's like I'm going to be destroyed or as if I'm going to be attacked. I'm in terrible danger. Shivers and shudders will shake my body and I'll get into bed, pull the covers over my head and curl up like a fetus. It feels like if I don't then go to a homosexual activity—I do it for my self-preservation. At that point I'm at my breaking point, If I don't I may go insane. It's not an indulgence at all. I have to do it. I might explode or I'll go crazy. It's as if all time and space are mixed up, as if things are shifted and I am in the deepest, direst trouble."

These attacks might occur even when Campbell thought he had mislaid something. He would become increasingly irritated, begin to look everywhere, feel panicky, and then develop his "confusion." His extreme reactions to minor frustrations occurred in the general emotional context of feelings of insecurity and weakness; loss of power; threats of loss of the mother, her anger at or disapproval of him; or threats from the external world. The attacks would miraculously disappear as soon as he made homosexual contact.

Disturbances of Ego Functions

Campbell's description of these episodes revealed severe disturbances in ego functions typical of the Preoedipal Type II homosexual. *Reality testing* was impaired; the boundary between fantasy and reality was indistinct. *Impulse control* was extremely poor; impulses were poorly bound and grossly acted out in instant discharge patterns. These patterns also seemed to be expressed in symbolic psychophysiological reactions. *Thinking* processes showed severe impairment, although of a temporary nature, and predominately of a paranoid type. His *self-concept* was distorted, diffused, and even bizarre. *Ego boundaries* were fleetingly absent, severely impaired, or showed signs of iminent fragmentation. *Affect* and *affect control* showed extreme anxiety, depression, emptiness, and poorly bound aggression. *Object relations* were severely impaired and there were tendencies to externalize parts of the self. There was a preponderance of primitive mental mechanisms such as projection, introjection, and splitting. In periods of psychological decompensation the patient complained: "I feel primarily apprehensive at first for no specific reason. It takes a lot of forms. Then I feel that I'm unwilling to move...I have to move with effort...and it sort of frightens me. My mind suddenly gets fatigued. It's as if I'm in a period of block. The first sign that the block is broken is a rush of thoughts and ideas, like water in a main which can't get through, it goes around the edges." Bodily efforts become uncontrolled. "The idea of something jumping all through my body. It is as if my heart suddenly hits a bit harder. It's as if you're hungry and you suddenly eat food and suddenly you're conscious of blood in your stomach." He felt that he was impelled to act irrationally, "like I might want to kill you and I know you're not going to attack me but I somehow feel this or fear this. I get frightened of myself."

He experienced severe splitting of the ego. "It's like I walk out of the framework of my face, as if there was a space between my face and there's a mask in front of it. I'm in back of what's around me and I wish I could go away. A trememdous lack of interest, sort of a split, a break, a distinct impression of withdrawal within my face. The new face, it is blank and unhappy, it is frightened. The feeling of resignation, a bitter resignation. Sometimes I can rejoin the two faces, the mask and the face, and this can click and they become as if I'm in the face. It doesn't actually happen but it's a terribly strong impression. I lose contact with the other face. I feel the two faces are working autonomously. You can snap me back by a direct question or ask me to reply. The last time it happened was when I was with a girl I knew showed too much interest in me and wanted me. It frightened me. I felt as if I wanted to run away. I suspect I'm really playing the part of a man when I act like a man, but then I have to show my hand and I get frightened and then I want to retreat as if I'm over-extended and then the confusion comes on."

Campbell's inability to deal with a girl's wish to make love or at least to become better acquainted with him initiated this incident. His own desire to do so propelled him into extreme conflict producing autonomic reactions, both visceral and cardiac, splitting of the ego, feelings of generalized collapse, feelings of panic, and severe disturbances in identity, self-concept, and ego boundaries.

He reported a further description of these phenomena following a girl's rejection of him for another man. He had been attached to this girl for a number of years and had felt closer to her than to any other woman. During the analysis he had attempted to draw closer to her and succeeded in overcoming some of his fears. "I had this attack on Saturday. I started writing it down as I felt it. The urge came on at the end of dinner as she gave me the news of her engagement. I had a feeling like a 'get out of here' feeling, a feeling of being trapped.

Simultaneously and strangely I felt an antagonism to my mother, as though she were trapping me. Perhaps it was my mother, then, I was pushed back toward. I felt terribly nervous, and then a desire to sleep and then a fast heartbeat. This went into the feeling that I 'deserve' to go to the Turkish bath. The desire itself does not dissolve the feeling, however. I went to the bathroom four times, each time I had a small bowel movement. Concentration became fitful. This feeling disorganizes every other thought. It leaves the compulsion to homosexuality my only answer and outlet. This feeling reminds me of a mean child that wants its own way.

"It goes all up over my body. It seems to sweep through all my nerve centers. I feel it everywhere. It could be compared to water rushing through the rooms of a house. It activates certain things first, like certain centers, first my stomach, then my head. Within an hour or two my hands are trembling. There's tension in the pit of my stomach, a diarrhea feeling, a terrible feeling at the base of my spine, a pain. And also, strangely enough, a feeling of intense genital excitement. It's as if I've been hit at the base of the spine, too. My headaches then begin and are very intense and I'm almost in a state of hysterics. If I go out and walk around I can suddenly feel very depressed and feel aches and pains. I feel so mad, so disgusted with myself, I'm being so childish. But I can't calm my mind unless I give in to my compulsion. In this state it is as if I am under control in a zombie way. I have absolutely no interest in women whatsoever. The only sensory sensations I have are sexual feelings. Otherwise I am completely dead, I am completely automatic, a robot. My mind is completely blocked. I don't remember a thing that I've thought of."

On this occasion the patient fled to the Turkish bath. "Afterward I felt wonderful, healthy, clear-minded, relaxed, a feeling of security, the way you could imagine a man full of energy would be. I went to the public library later and worked for about an hour. I felt very well, concentrated well, then suddenly my mind started draining away again. I started trembling. I started being automatic again. I felt as if I would fall forward. I felt an involuntary thought that I'll kill myself, then became balanced somehow and pulled myself together by thinking of you." Clearly, in this instance, the patient's disturbance in, and loss of, object relations are regained through the reestablishment of object relations in the transference.

To the patient, this last episode supremely exemplified the power of his homosexual "compulsion." This, together with a severe disturbance in thinking processes, produced the sensation of being "robotized." His homosexuality could no longer be explained through rationalizations or pretense of pleasure-seeking. There clearly was no other way out.

Other attacks came on whenever he felt that he would be demeaned by other men or when he perceived them as more successful than he, as well as whenever he felt castrated or at the mercy of his mother, who could "invade" his privacy. Because of the danger of his regressive attempt to merge with his mother he was forced by his fear to turn to a homosexual outlet.

Regressive States and Regressive Reenactments

After two and a half years in analysis the patient began to experience severe regressive phenomena and was able to understand their meaning and function.

His seeking a closer contact with his mother or attempting to leave her precipitated regressions. He thus had to maintain an optimal distance from and closeness to her in order to ward them off. He had never succeeded in making the separation from his mother. While he wished to return to the earlier closeness to the mother he feared a catastrophic merging with her. The latter evoked a terror of dissolution of self, loss of identity, and complete annihilation.

Insights arrived at in the following session proved decisive for the development of a new psychological equilibrium. He called the analyst on a Saturday for an emergency appointment, sounding nearly incoherent on the telephone. He was seen immediately. When he entered the consultation room he was distraught, nearly foaming at the mouth, face flushed, severely agitated, and complaining of an excruciating headache in the back of his head. He alternated between crying and bitter and childlike half-laughing; tears were streaming down his face. He was unkempt and tended to fall from the couch to the floor.

He had just returned from the country. His mother was exceedingly angry at him for wanting to return to the city, as he would be away on a business trip and would not see her again for a month. "I felt as if Mother were saying that if I left her she'd leave me to Daddy. She compared me to him, saying how thoughtless I was." While in the country the day before, he had a dream that a rabbit, whose rotting teeth had been knocked out, had died. He readily equated this to his feelings in his dreams of his own teeth being knocked out. "Mother was exceedingly angry but I still decided to return. I felt apprehensive on the drive back. She had lost her driver's license and asked me to look for it in her dresser." Upon entering the bedroom he opened the drawers of her bureau only to find the lingerie and underwear mixed up as if they had been thrown in there. He compared it to the garbage can fantasy he used to have as a child. In this fantasy he was immersed in a garbage can, filled with garbage up to his mouth. If he tried to move he would sink deeper and the garbage would go into his mouth. This had always filled him with disgust and extreme fright. "This was the garbage can, the underwear, being inside her. I began breathing very hard, as if I were there, as if I were inside her. I was breathing very hard and fast like I was going to be sick to my stomach and that I would be compressed and choked and die. I think I'm going to faint now, like I'm going under an anesthetic. The garbage can, that's what I see."

He began to scream and cried uncontrollably. "I've got to get back myself, I'm losing myself. And then before that I lay down on the bed, her bed, and I felt I would be engulfed." At this point, hands clenching spasmodically, he moved his head and rocked back and forth. He choked, sputtered, and cried. He said he felt better crying, as if he was restoring himself to himself, and continued sobbing saying he felt terrible and recalled that he had experienced something like this before.

He began to roll on the floor, was finally induced to rise, and then slumped and collapsed on the couch. "I'm a child, I'm a child. Mommie's coming back to the room. She's got to come back, I think I'm yelling. It's that funny yell, like a child's yell, I think it's rage." It was, however, quite easy to bring him back to reality, although the affect continued. "I had a terrible ear abcess and the pain was like this pain. I remember I used to yell. I'm yelling now. A terrible abcess and the pain wouldn't go away. This happened to me when I was about two, I think. You know, it's almost like you've given me some sodium pentathol and I'm under. I'm just as glad you did. This has been in the back of all things, this state, this is what I'm afraid of, that I'll sink into this. It is Mommie. If only she would come back to me." Now the patient's voice is that of a baby. "If she'd only understand me, protect me." At this point he is pleading and whimpering, his face is contorted, and his eyes are staring and wild.

The patient continued: "She must protect me. She said this morning she will leave me to Daddy. Yes, this is what I've been afraid of, that Daddy would kill me and that she would leave me. I kept wanting to turn back to go to her but my mind just became blank. I said I won't. It's such a private thing. I keep on thinking I was drooling like a baby. Was I drooling? I was never allowed to chew the blanket. My mother saying, 'Don't chew the blanket,' something to do with losing my teeth. Last night I felt some of this, some of her disapproval. I must be under an anesthetic, just as if I were under ether. It's all true what I said, it's like losing myself, like I'm all novacainized. The picture I have is a wish to lie in mother's arms and her loving me and her enfolding me but it scares me. The conflict is I want to love her terribly but we can't because of the sex business. It's a childish thing. I want it so desperately that it links through all this to the fright of the sexual thing. Today I was in acute pain. When I went into the bureau drawers, the childish impulse....As I saw the drawers I felt a terrible impulse to get inside her. I think I was *entering her.* I wouldn't ever open her pocketbook or any drawers. I actually was acting out the rejoining of her and I couldn't do it. Before I came here I went out to the store and bought some peroxide and I put the peroxide on my hair. Then another conflict began...that I shouldn't do that any more. Then I felt terribly depressed. I couldn't change my sex [transsexual wishes]. I thought I'd then go back to lie on her bed and I'd die there, die there like in her arms...and I looked at myself in the mirror and I was shaking and I felt, 'Oh, you bitch.'"

During this scene the patient felt that he actually became a baby. The scream was the sound he made when he had had his mastoid infection or when he had felt afraid of his father. In this session he enacted his fear of abandonment, his being allowed to suffer, and his "being given over to Daddy." Out of all this, including his mother's rejection, came an intensification of the wish to be close to her, even to join her, and finally merge with her. This wish gave rise to feelings of massive anxiety as the wish to merge became the fear of merging, the fear of exploding, the fear of dying, and the fear of personal annihilation (threat of self-object dedifferentiation). At other times he developed sensations of being paralyzed.

The patient terminated this regressive episode within a few hours and returned to his former equilibrium with a new sense of relief and well-being. It seemed apparent that this reliving allowed affective discharge and relief of previously isolated, repressed material. The verbalization of these affective phenomena allowed the patient to experience them at the level of conscious thought rather than of preverbal images. This allowed for their assimilation into conscious thought. Verbalization, followed by interpretation and discussion, reinforced his orientation to the present rather than to the past. His relationship to the analyst, who has shared the reliving, allowed him to undergo similar experiences on several occasions with decreasing disruption of reality and easier and safer returns to the present.

The regression tended to reappear the next day, but upon talking briefly with the analyst by telephone the threat of personal dissolution vanished. His pain and fear of abandonment, the fear of being left to the father, led him to the wish to forcefully merge into the mother as the only way to find security. The wish was a terrifying one, as it involved complete loss of self. It was not that he once experienced this merging that kept him ill, but that he continued to experience it not as conscious thought, but only as a repressed affect, as if he were still in danger. His defensive maneuver was the homosexual act, which reassured him against bodily and ego dissolution; was a substitute for reunion with the mother; allowed for the expression, alleviation and discharge of severe aggression aroused by the imperative need to merge; and established temporary object relations. With progressive desensitization the tendency to such regressive reenactments disappeared.

Therapeutic Course

During the first year of analysis a series of dreams on the same night portrayed Campbell's severity of psychopathology as well as his overwhelming distress, fright, and dire predicament. The dreams were captioned. The first caption was "What Have I Done Wrong?" In this dream black and white men engaged in various forms of sexual perversion. Parts of bodies were visible and there were suggestions of sadistic practices taking place. Black and pink "behinds" were aimed in his direction and men approached him sexually with erect penises from which he looked away in fright mixed with anticipation and pleasure.

The second dream was captioned "See Her Finally Deceived and Humiliated." In it, he was being approached by a man with long pants, a man he had met in a Turkish bath, who "desperately wants to make a pass at me." He ejaculates as the man approaches. He felt that the caption connoted his identification with his mother and her humilitation if she were to discover the full extent of his homosexual actitivites. He got a strange pleasure out of her embarrassment and severe disappointment in him, as if he were "taking out some kind of resentment on her."

The third dream was entitled "See the Last Agony of This Man." In this scene a man who apparently is Hitler is being hanged by the neck. "His head is in the noose—broken—he had been hanged. The only reason he is there, it seems to me in the dream, is a device to show some sexual sadism and my anger." The hanging man also signified a limp, hanging penis.

The most terrifying aspect of these dreams to Campbell, however, was not their content but the fact that they were "blurred"; they came in and out of focus and consisted of partial or superimposed images. He saw mutilated parts of bodies and a conglomeration of black and white bodies. These dreams made him despair. He did not see how he possibly could get well or improve, but felt doomed to go deeper and deeper into the quagmire of his homosexual relations "and the underworld of homosexuality." He felt "justifiably depressed" at this point in therapy and could see no hope for the future.

Over succeeding years Campbell became aware of the meaning of his castration anxiety; his fears of merging and the threat this posed to him; and his use of masochism both to punish himself for homosexual wishes and to keep himself the weakened masochistic slave of his mother. He improved in his work and social relationships.

During the third year of analysis he began to enjoy the company of a young woman with whom he had his first heterosexual intercourse. She gently coaxed and playfully enticed him to sexual intimacies. He was potent in the sexual act, even touching and kissing her breasts, a part of the female body which he formerly could not tolerate thinking about. This relationship continued for three or four months. Because of his diminished aggression he was able to accept sexual assertiveness from her without its evoking in him the retaliatory impulses originally aimed at the mother. With decreased fears of merging, he was able to relate sexually to a girl who appeared independent, undemanding, and not possessive.

She eventually became pregnant and expressed her desire to get married. Upon his rejection of her proposal, she obtained an abortion and the relationship was abruptly terminated.

A long period ensued in which he felt "soured and bitter" about this experience. He knew, however, that he could now enjoy sexual relationships with women. He could have intercourse without constantly fantasying the intruding image of his mother and felt that he had conquered his fear of incest. He grew progressively away from his mother in many respects, although he could still be "invaded" by her whenever "down and out." When he felt threatened by her he would stand up for his rights, declare himself a man, demand that she not treat him as a child, and on occasions order her out of his apartment.

He realized that in masochism he passively controlled others: his mother, his analyst, and his friends. Through masochistic passivity he had also managed to avoid being a male. In subsequent sexual encounters with women his fantasy life was preponderantly heterosexual, although homosexual images would sometimes intrude. He no longer experienced fearful periods of "confusion" which originated from the regressive pull to a symbiotic relationship with her.

Campbell was subject to fresh attacks of his infantile anxiety in a number of instances throughout his analysis. Once, when he unfortunately lost a greatly prized job through no fault of his own and was attempting to make renewed heterosexual relationships, he felt considerably weakened and afraid. In this emotional context he was arrested by the police through the process of entrapment and had to appear in court.

In the following session he reexperienced the original infantile trauma but exercised significant objectivity through remembering the previous regressive experiences and their meaning. His verbalizations were not simply a repetition of analytic interpretations but were entirely his own productions. He was able to pull himself out of the affective state by listening to the analyst's comments and could go in and out of the depth of regression and its intense affectivity, emotions, and bodily discharge phenomena.

He had been awakened by his mother, who telephoned and told him to get up and look for a job. She called him a number of times after that but he did not answer the telephone. The calls seemed quite frantic.

The doorbell rang and when he buzzed the latch his mother walked in. Despite his reluctance to see her she immediately put her foot in the door and demanded to be admitted. "She came at me as if she were about to envelop me. I felt I would dissolve. She still came on. I said 'Leave me alone.' She said, 'You lose your wallets to bums. I don't know where you are. You lose your job.' I felt like I was going out the window, as if she had almost caught me with a man. I had to tell her she was not welcome. You know I really want her, I really want to know she is there, but I don't want her *too close* and she knows better than to do what she did and she is so cruel. I think I became stimulated by this fight [the patient shudders]. I think I'm going out of my mind. What does she want? What does she want? She wants me. She was like a mad person. She was hateful. She got on the bed...oh, oh I'm now so frightened, when I leave here I think I'll be so frightened...I'm so vulnerable...I don't have a job." The patient squirmed and moved his head back and forth. He was flushed and crying. He appeared nearly to be drooling.

"It is awful. It's this sexual thing, I think, it's so awful. She just shouldn't have been there, that's all. It was gruesome. I just had a feeling I was going to *swallow my hand* [incorporation anxieties]. I felt like masturbating after she left and I also felt I had to kill her if I ever wanted to get married." The patient cried and sobbed bitterly.

"Or I also thought I might have to kill myself. It's awfully hard to be a man in a situation like that. She was telling me I wasn't a man and also that I was unfaithful, somehow, by her coming over. [Swallowing his hand connoted swallowing the mother, swallowing himself or being swallowed, thereby reestablishing the mother-child unity.]

"She's a cruel, destructive, castrating bitch. As we are fighting...and why, why, why, I said to her, 'Why are you going back to treating me like a four-year-old? Stop it.' And she said, 'I guess I'll just have to kill myself. You're making me so unhappy and maybe the few thousands of dollars you get, maybe that will make you happy, but I know you'll waste it and then you'll kill yourself.' I guess this is the engulfing mother that we've talked about. I truly had the feeling this morning that she was capable of killing me, of being capable of destroying me. I had the choice: if I started crying and I was just like a baby, she would let up. Crying...crying. If I did that she'd rescue me. But I had to be myself, I had to be a man even though she attacked me. I started to get up and I was going to wear father's suit which he had given me. She said, angrily, 'Don't wear that suit. Don't wear his suit.' This is all the same thing that happened to me as a child: 'Don't be anything like father because he is nothing.' Many years of psychoanalysis did pay off this morning. I've been awful to you in many ways and awfully nutty but I'm very grateful. This is what made me crazy and in the mood I'm in now I probably will get married. That is, I'm damn mad and I want to get rid of her. But the spirits that she let loose are more powerful at times. But right now I can cope with this difficulty. When I said today, 'Mother, you're a castrating bitch,' I still loved her but she still was a castrating bitch. But she was so out of control. She doesn't like me. She's so angry. She wanted me all the way back to the tiny tot. She wants to make me a child. She tries to castrate me and when she does all this and when I felt it I got aroused sexually. Why? I'm so all aroused now as I think of it. I'm so jacked up, I tingle. She's coming at me...closer and closer...something awful is going to happen and something delicious. My legs are tingling now. I'm almost convulsed, *like thowing myself over into another body*...fuck me...not in the rear, in the front. This has a terrific discharge in my body, like a convulsion [erotization of anxiety]."

The patient terminated the analysis after nine and a half years of treatment when he procured highly desirable employment in Europe. His overall psychological functioning was vastly improved and he was able to function heterosexually. Several follow-up interviews during the ensuing five years revealed that he maintained the progress achieved, but that under conditions of severe emotional strain he engaged in infrequent and isolated homosexual encounters. All in all, he had profited greatly by increasing his performance and functioning in the major areas of life and he felt increasing confidence and pleasure in living.

Recapitulation

Campbell was unable to pass through the developmental phase in which he could separate his identity from that of his mother. This defect in development led to later difficulties. Out of the inability to separate and the need to identify with her came a threat of identifying and a threat of merging. The preoedipal fear that crystallized was then added to by the later castration fears of the oedipal period.

Campbell entered late childhood with an inhibition of self-assertion and aggression and a pronounced feminine (maternal) identification. He had a strong inhibition of all male sexuality to avoid his fear of merging. He achieved a spurious masculinity, acquiring a penis and affection from men, thereby avoiding the dangers connected with his mother, but he still wished to maintain a close tie to her. In his homosexuality he tried to rid himself of the damaging, destructive urge toward union with her and attempted to ward off his incorporative needs. When the pressures of adaptation and appropriate masculine role functioning became too pressing in adulthood he tended to regress to the less demanding period of maternal closeness. This period, fraught with more primitive unconscious fears, led to homosexual acting out.

Attributing this patient's condition to preoedipal factors does not minimize the importance of the oedipal period and its castration fear. Campbell suffered severe castration anxiety. Upon entering the oedipal period he was assailed by many fears related to his "cruel" father, in part a consequence of allegiance to his mother and murderous wishes and guilt feelings toward his father. Campbell expressed this fear of the father in his negative oedipal attitude, in which he unconsciously offered himself sexually to the father in place of the mother. At the same time he could be more like his mother, exaggerating and emphasizing his feminine identification, with the hope of gaining safety and protection. Unconsciously he was not only castrated by the father but also attained sexual pleasure from him masochistically through substituting male partners. This was in part responsible for his dread of and his desire for anal rape. He successfully fought off conscious awareness of his dread of anal rape by attacking other men anally and by transforming them from threatening figures to "loved" figures.

Chapter 13
THE CASE OF ROGER
(Preoedipal, Type II)

At the age of twenty-five Roger had become moderately successful in his artistic vocation, but was severely anxious and troubled for fear his homosexual behavior would be discovered. Married for three years, he sought treatment because his homosexuality continued despite desperate attempts to terminate it. Most of all he feared discovery by his wife; he felt that this would not only destroy her feelings for him but would also "contaminate" her with the ugliness and misery of his homosexuality. The latter was a thought he could not bear. He became unable to work and concentrate, experiencing periods of depression, violent feelings, irritability, extreme moodiness, and a tendency to tears. He was impressive in appearance, intelligent, witty, charming, at times jovial, and often humorous.

Three years prior to starting analysis he had graduated from a major university and despite his markedly spotty performance in collage there were many who considered him a genius. He loved his talented, creative wife and felt she was the only important person in his life. She introduced him to heterosexuality, was patient upon their first attempting intercourse, and helped him to gradually overcome his fear of and repugnance toward the female genitals. She encouraged and assisted him in achieving erections and adequate functioning.

During the year before entering treatment his heterosexual performance had been unreliable and faltering. Most of the time he had no desire for intercourse unless his wife was fervently passionate and told him that she "needed" his penis and sexual orgasm. Whenever her menstrual period was delayed his potency increased; he felt more masculine because she might "have my baby inside her and that makes me more of a man."

Developmental History

Roger was an only child, conceived during his father's military leave during World War II. Because his father was on combat duty overseas, Roger did not see him during the first two years of life. During that time he lived with his mother, who was employed intermittently in a minor administrative capacity in an industrial plant.

As a young child, according to his mother, he would lie on his stomach, lift his "heavy head" and drop it sharply, striking the bed. This head-bumping, which still occurred occasionally in adulthood, went on for many years. His head would become sore and he would develop headaches. He later was very ashamed of this activity and continued it in secrecy.

In childhood he also developed the habit of rocking. He would sit on his bed with his knees under him and make rhythmic motions of the body backward and forward. Between the ages of six to ten he began bed wetting for several months. "I remember all this kind of activity in terms of violence."

His earliest and most significant memory at age four or five was still an extremely traumatic one. His father, who no longer lived with him and his mother, visited them. "My father came in one day and apparently they had broken up. The scene I remember occurred in the living room. He may have been drunk or out of control. He had come to ask her for money and she wouldn't give it to him. There was a fight, a huge, huge argument, which got absolutely out of control. He jumped on her and started pulling her hair and I can feel the incredible tension. He's really a kind of introvert and they both got hysterically violent. I see a similarity in me. He started pulling her hair merciless-ly and I stood there frozen. It went on and on and I started screaming and I ran out on the porch and shook and shook and I was screaming at the top of my voice. It was full of the most frightening violence. He was pulling her hair and she was whimpering like a dog. I can remember all the details of the room and I can still feel the screams and then there's a complete blackout."

After this incident the parents eventually divorced and the patient saw his father on only two occasions. The first occurred at the age of seven when, with his mother, they encountered his father on the street. "Mother abruptly turned me around and we ran for the subway." At the age of twelve, "Father called her and he told her he wanted to see me and then she tells me, of course, he never really wanted to see me. She always tells me that. He never cared about me. She told me this for as far back as I can remember. My father was an alcoholic, a sick man...I feel so sorry for him. She said she married him out of sympathy. He said that he really wanted to see me and she said she just wanted to protect me and he was a bad influence and he was a drunkard and she got rid of him."

The memory of his parents' fight had an important meaning for Roger. Whenever he saw any violence he would have a resurgence of powerful emotions. "When I see people fighting I feel all the things I did when my father was fighting my mother—a sinking feeling of helplessness—and then I think 'I wish they were hitting me rather than hitting each other.' The feelings are hate, shame, murder and guilt. I guess I needed to be killed by my mother. She's coming by today to see me. I hate myself so much, I called my mother and now I won't be able to do anything all day. I just hate, hate, hate. I don't remember hating my mother for leaving me but I hate my wife for now wanting to leave me. I feel, however, I've got to make some kind of effort in my life. You know what I'd like to do? I'd like to rock and hum or bang my head and by rocking I hold on. It's a way of controlling, by rocking and humming, preventing myself from hurting myself. I've had the most murderous feelings toward myself and others because of this childhood memory. If she wants me to die, okay, show me the coffin. I don't have any feelings. I just want to kill someone. You know what I want to do? I want to scream. I want to destroy something, smash my head against the wall. I'm afraid to let go, I'm afraid it would be awfully ugly."

After the parents' separation Roger was sent to a prekindergarten school for what he termed "other displaced children." He was removed from the school when he developed a mastoid ear infection but the following year his mother sent him to a private school in a distant community. He lived there from age six to ten with his maternal grandmother "to convenience my mother." His grandmother was nearly senile and gave him little attention or affection. He was extremely grateful when his mother would occasionally visit, but she had an active social life and had become involved with a man whom she subsequently married, after her divorce from Roger's father. The mother's suitor hardly ever saw the boy and rarely took him anywhere. Roger felt lonely and isolated. In reaction to feelings of helplessness he had fantasies of being gigantic and huge. In what he called his "Superman Game" he could rip trees out of the ground by their trunks and toss them over buildings. He had many such fantasies of omnipotence, hate, and power (narcissistic grandiosity).

Roger yearned and wept for his absent father. One of his earliest dreams or memories, he could not tell which, was of his father and him together in the bathroom. The father was urinating and the boy was looking at his father's penis. The father had a pleasant smile on his face. This represented the boy's desire to be loved by the father, and to be endowed with masculinity through identification with the father and his penis.

At the age of eleven, Roger returned from private school to live with his mother and stepfather. He never felt close to either of them. His first homosexual experience occurred at this time when another boy lay on top of him. Roger suddenly developed a sexual feeling in the genitals and feelings of "love." He recalled intense feelings of aloneness, a sense of being "terribly self-contained and alone, a sense of needing my father and also being very shy and timid. I was in awe of all the world around me and I had a sense of my own oddity, specialness, a sense of difference in an individual way. I felt very much as if I were in a fantasy world of my own—a world of make-believe."

This continued to the second year of high school; after school he played alone, "like a small child."

Once, after an altercation with his mother, he stayed in his room for an entire month. Neither his mother nor his stepfather attempted to interrupt this self-imposed exile. "I don't feel loved in any way. In my room was myself. I was going to deny them the pleasure of me. I wanted her to love me. I wanted her to be more maternal and she tended to be authoritarian and logical and not terribly affectionate at all. She'd dragged me out of that other environment and given me nothing and now I had nothing here, even in this so-called home."

This period of staying alone in his room followed soon after the second accidental meeting with his father. "My father was carrying a brown package under his arm. I remembered him to be tall and I remembered his face, a very, very shy, gentle, tender face and he impressed me as a very sensitive person with a kind of ashamedness and guilt within him. We shook hands and I was probably frightened. I have since thought I would have liked to have thrown my arms around him."

His mother had engaged in a verbal vendetta against his father ever since he could remember. The father was "no good, he never did anything any good, there was nothing good about him."

Roger was beset and troubled by another recurrent memory. At the age of six, when he was about to be sent away to school, he recalled that he "drowned the book," *The Little Engine That Could.* His mother had given it to him and then she decided to send him away. "I remember I filled the tub and drowned the book. The color came out red. I hurt her by drowning the book. I can remember doing it. I filled the tub. I put water in the tub and I put the book in it. I held it down and I ripped it apart while it was in the water. I can remember the bathroom and the basin being higher than me. I could barely see into it. The water turned red and now I often see red and blood in my dreams."

At sixteen, he was sent to a military academy where he occasionally engaged in homosexual relations. He often was obsessed with an intense feeling of love for a particular type of boy who looked clean-cut, well protected, and well cared for. Upon his return home from the military school on leave, at the age of eighteen, his mother found a letter written by a homosexual friend. She became extremely angry and hysterical. She screamed that he was a homosexual and started to attack him physically. He suddenly became violent. "I threw her down on the floor and I beat her and beat her just like my father did once. I beat her and there was a minute that I could have killed her but then I looked in her eyes and I saw she was frightened. That was just after I felt that the moment of murder might be there, and when I saw her frightened I started to cry hysterically and I was sobbing and I said, 'Forgive me, forgive me. You don't love me. You are my mother. Please be my mother.'" His stepfather called the police and Roger was sent to a hospital in a straitjacket. By then, however, he felt completely calm. He recalled tearfully that he had had many fantasies as a child and even in his teens about how nice it would have been to marry his mother.

He was continually beset by feelings of weakness and inferiority during military school, interspersed with sudden periods in which he felt an intense sense of power and male identity. During these times he was elated. There was a kind of "exultant power" (development of pathological internalized grandiose self). His voice was full, his faculties sharpened; he was fulfilled, happy, and had a sense of dignity and importance. "I felt like a god and the full brilliance of my mind came into play. I would get a lot of love this way because others admired my strength and I felt I made many friends."

During his four years in college he did exceptionally well while euphoric—but not during depressions and when in "need of a man." He twice attempted suicide. Once, when he felt rejected by a schoolmate who did not come to see him when he had promised, Roger became drunk and cut his wrist superficially in order to be discovered bleeding by his neglectful friend. In the other instance, while drinking, he became jealous of a homosexual partner's interest in another boy. "I was jealous. I couldn't stand it any more. I started to leave the room and the other boy wouldn't let me. I ran and threw myself through the second floor window." He broke the glass, cut himself severely, and was rendered unconscious. "I strangely enjoyed the whole experience, jumping through the window." This theme, of jumping through windows or into space, frequently appears in the dreams, fantasies, and acting out of homosexual patients. Behind it lies a rebirth fantasy: in returning to the mother (death), rebirth then becomes possible (Glauber 1956).

Roger was unable to establish any relationship with his stepfather and believed that the new father did not want to have anything to do with him and would like to see him dead.

Roger often consciously wished he were a girl because "boys like girls. I like boys because they are gruff and funny. As a girl I think about being sentimental and how I would be loved. I remember my mother used to put her tongue in my mouth when she kissed me. I feared that. I used to hear my mother and my stepfather having sex and she was crying. She was weak and horrible and I got terribly upset. She sounded like she hated it but she really liked it and I think at times I've been jealous."

Homosexual Practices

In many of Roger's homosexual relations he wished that the man would simply put his arms around him, hold him tight, and make him feel secure. This was in direct contrast to a very aggressive sexual move he would make when angry and "vicious." These abrupt, violent sexual encounters usually occurred when he was "frantic, fragmented, and furious." He felt that he would collapse, disintegrate, or fly apart at these times, that he was only "put together again" when he saw the penis of a homosexual partner (restoration of the self through incorporation of the penis). He alternated between passive enjoyment of his partner's embrace and active, violent grabbing and forcing. In both cases his partner was, in unconscious fantasy, his father, from whom he desired love.

He could not reconcile himself to remaining homosexual but found that despite his inner struggle against it he increasingly frequented public toilets or waited on subway platforms for homosexual contacts. He would wander through subway stations and have two or three contacts a day whenever he felt weak or "unmanned," picking up anyone, deliberately choosing those most unkempt and disheveled. These homosexual excursions took much time from his work and he became depressed, defeated, and angry at himself. In the subways he would often look at the man's penis while he masturbated; otherwise he would feel "too open" to the other man, who might tear off his penis or testicles. On a number of occasions he allowed anal penetration and penetrated others. He had practiced fellatio and mutual masturbation since the onset of adolescence.

During analysis Roger became aware that in his homosexual relations he was angry at his father and yet was trying to find him and love him. His homosexual partner represented a fusion of maternal and paternal images. In sucking a man's penis (father's penis) he was also possessing the good and giving maternal breast through substitution. He relieved aggression by forcibly seizing the penis and became whole again through identification with the male partner.

Roger harbored profound fears of homosexuality represented in dreams as the fear of being bitten by poisonous snakes. At these times he would cry out for his wife and ask her to save him.

He felt most masculine after relations with a man and after he had masturbated. He was then able to have intercourse with his wife with much more ease. However, he continually felt that his wife might at any time be unfaithful to him and frequently dreamt that she was flirting with another man and he would lose her. In these dreams her behavior was wild, giggly, cold at heart, and cruel—completely the opposite of what it was in reality. She showed none of her sensitivity, gentleness, and concern for him. These dreams of jealousy and deception represented his own wishes to vicariously possess the other man. They also served as punishment for his homosexuality. At times his feelings of "love" for a man were more intense than feelings of love for his wife. On these occasions he often felt he was in competition with her for the affection of men. This related to his negative oedipal position. Turning toward the male (father) meant gaining masculinity, women (mother) offering only cruelty, deprivation, and deception.

Regressive Phenomena

Roger, like Campbell (chapter 12), showed severe regressive phenomena due to a preoedipal fixation. In times of exceptional stress, his voice changed and he became angry, bitter, snarling. "As I'm talking I feel my hands getting bigger now. The fingers are clasped like there's a penis in a hole. In my dream I was thinking the man with my wife is faceless, the one who gets her, who goes away with her, there is no detail in his face. It seems to me that he is laughing at me, that he knows something about me, that he has taken my wife away from me and he doesn't have a face or identity and somehow I get pleasure out of her deceiving me. I feel like a little boy...a little boy...I'm sinking, sinking, my whole body's going down, almost as though I'm shriveling up. I feel like I couldn't get up, like I'm embedded in this couch and tons of weight are on me and as I was about to cry a second ago I felt a relief feeling as if by your interrupting me that you are going to say something to make it clear and all this would go away now and I'd come back somehow. And I feel now like I am being rolled on a ship. I have nausea. My hands have gotten very cold. I'm swinging now. I love and hate all men. I like to beat them. I got very upset as I said that. It's as if I'm at the bottom of a hole. The opening is way up and it's very dank and warm and wet and my head is out, however, it seems at times. My penis is covered and I'm lying flat."

Regressive phenomena appeared on numerous occasions: when the patient felt the need to be closer to his mother, when he was overwhelmed by her, or when he felt weak and hopeless. When regression became too intense the analyst asked him to sit up for most of the session. This was a true fixation at the preoedipal period and did not represent a regression from the oedipal conflict. These phenomena reappeared in forms similar to those in other cases cited. The change in bodily size and shape, the loss of sense of identity, the feeling of sinking, the loss of orientation, and the outright fantasy or near hallucination of being inside the mother's womb proved to be unmistakably preoedipal in origin.

Course of Therapy

Continually and pervasively troubled by the traumatic memory of the assault by his father upon his mother in childhood, Roger experienced an insistently recurrent dream: "I was on a plain, a plateau, and it stretches for miles and miles with splotches of cactus and grass. It was a nightmare. This whole dream seems like death. The landscape means death. Lots of sand and I'm standing there on the plain and there is before me a hard prickly nightmare plant, ugly looking. In the middle of this a little sandy area. There is a mother chicken and little chickens and the mother chicken's head is cut off and her feathers plucked out

and she's bleeding blood out of her neck and in spurts."
The spurts reminded him of sperm and the chicken with the head cut off reminded him of the time when he was four or five, watching chickens being beheaded in a butcher shop. "There was blood all over the place and the little chickens running along and the feathers all plucked out. That's the real horrid part, soggy with blood, matted, and it's disgusting. It's all so unhappy and the mother was dying." The plucking of the chicken refers to his father pulling out his mother's hair. The patient wished her dead for many years but he knew he could not bear to lose her.

The injuries to his mother could also be visited upon himself, as in the following dream: "It took place in a subway toilet. Lots of people there. A policeman there, too, and a man is standing in front of a urinal with his penis out and someone had slashed it with a knife or pin and I got frightened but morbidly fascinated. The color, the poetic redness, was very fiery and very beautiful, a sort of vermillion. Yes, I think of the pin being stuck in him or a knife, like blood running out of Christ's hands."

Having recounted this dream he expressed a sudden impulse to show the analyst his penis and then he suddenly felt like crying. He felt childish. He felt angry and aggressive toward homosexual partners' penises and at times angry at his own. He had had fleeting thoughts of cutting his penis, hurting himself, and slashing his wrists. He felt the same angry resentment toward his mother's breasts which he recalled having seen occasionally when he was living at home. They were the penis that was denied him. It was the penis which he was angry about and searched for. The presence of the policeman in his dream was his superego defense against committing these sadistic acts.

In the transference he experienced feelings of warmth and love traceable to his yearning for his father. "I'm also afraid of you and I became nasty to you and violent and extremely critical. I feel I could tear you apart with my tongue because I would love to love you as if you were my father and I would like you to love me back and I'd like to be held like a baby and comforted and I'd like you to take me into the bathroom and give me a bath and hold me and love me and I know you won't and you can't. I'm afraid to give you this love. I'm scared of being rejected by you and ultimately it involves sex and I'm afraid of the rejection. I'm afraid you'll say, 'You're mad. You're a homosexual.' And I want to kiss you and it upsets me."

Alternating with his love feelings the patient had tremendous destructive urges toward men. "I want to kill a man in battle, perhaps, and then to have intercourse with the dead or dying or murdered. I'm helpless and you see I'm crying (he is sobbing hysterically). It would be nice if the man were crying, too, and we'd cry together. I would bite off his penis. I'm just so violent and it's of a sexual nature, too. A lot of love and kisses. His arms, chest, his lips. I'd want him to be helpless and immobile. Why would I want that? I think it's because my father's dead, I think, although I don't know where he is. He's dead for me, in a sense. I would like to be able to act out on him all the things I wanted from my father, that is, the being loved part. He's always away or dead. Also if he were dead or dying or unconscious I could do all these things without his knowing it. Perhaps he then would have no choice but to love me. And it's about the only way I could get a normal man and he couldn't hurt me or laugh at me or hurt me in some way." The lifelong search for his father was filled with a limitless poignancy and despair.

As the analysis progressed the intensity of homosexual impulses decreased: "This morning when I went into the subway nothing happened. I couldn't do it." He cries and whimpers. "It's getting harder and harder to do anything homosexual. I've tried asking myself how I felt and I felt rotten. I think I just want to be held in my father's arms or to hold my father's hand as I walk down the street. Perhaps someone strong next to me. I'm so ashamed. Oh, I don't hate him at all. I hate her but I don't hate him. But they both hate me. One left me and one never paid attention to me." He starts an hysterical, high-pitched laughter. "He should have pulled her hair out and pulled her legs out and shoved them down her throat. He should have killed her and taken me with him. I can see his head balding if I imagine him. I don't like the way he looks. He looks like me and I'd like to look like him. I wonder what his hands look like, what his chest looks like. I wonder what it would be like to put my hands on his chest or to be kissed. I'm getting dizzy now. I feel as if I'm floating away [regressive phenomenon]. He had nice blue eyes. I think she killed him. She made him drink. She cut his penis off the way she has tried to cut mine off. I think the reason he left her was that if he didn't he would have killed her. I'll kill her now." He cries and sobs. "He loved me. I kept thinking I ought to see my mother this week but I guess it's because I'm lonely."

Roger was in analysis for approximately two years.

He showed considerable improvement and a beginning ability to refrain from homosexual relations except when "pressed to the limit" by external circumstances such as visits from his mother, her attacks against him, or feelings that his wife had become unfaithful or was about to be. His wife decided to enter analysis and as a result their financial difficulties increased. It was her money that he had been using for treatment and as she now needed it, he reluctantly terminated therapy. In the last few months of analysis he became increasingly able to detach himself from his mother and her demands. For weeks he had no need to see her and when he did he "stood up to her like a man" and did not "become a child."

Unfortunately Roger could not complete therapy. He returned to the analyst on several occasions for single sessions. His wife divorced him and although he suffered intensely from this loss he remarked that he "felt good about it," saying he "could not offer that lovely, intelligent, attractive, and creative girl any chance for happiness."

He continued to communicate with the analyst for four years after terminating treatment and eventually reported that he was living with a somewhat older woman with whom he regularly had sexual intercourse. He felt fond of her, as she was a rather gentle and maternal person.

His homosexual activities seldom recurred. He had enough insight, he said, to realize that he could not find either his father or his mother "in these deluded acts of self-destruction." Whenever he felt homosexual inclinations he attempted to have heterosexual intercourse, discharging much of the energy of his residual homosexual wishes in this way. At times he missed his former wife intensely but "disciplined" himself not to think about her excessively. He felt content with his circumstances and expressed the hope of eventually marrying the woman with whom he was now living. He had attained increased ego strength. His artistic endeavors continued and he produced several finished works, although he masochistically withheld them from public display.

Chapter 14
THE CASE OF DAVID
(Latent Oedipal)

David's case history is an example of the confusion that can arise around the diagnosis of latent homosexuality.

David adopted early in life a "preacherlike" attitude which led others to admire his "maturity" while still in high school. Although desiring to make a favorable impression on women throughout his teens and into his twenties, he felt himself to be awkward, lacking in experience, and unable to gain acceptance by them. He was not aware of any homosexual conflicts or unconscious fantasies prior to or during adolescence. He was, however, extremely shy and lacked confidence to a severe degree in all relationships with females. He was very fond of his older brother, who was killed in an accident when David was nineteen. He continued through adulthood to mourn this loss and longed for the love and affection of his ego-supporting brother.

While there were no homosexual fantasies regarding his brother, the first twenty years of the patient's life were marked by suppression of all sexual expression.

At the age of twenty-six, he was moved to marry a girlfriend through feelings of guilt and responsibility but never felt comfortable with her sexually or otherwise because of what he felt was her "different sociocultural background" and "limited intellectual status." When she decided to leave him after his career required his moving abroad, he developed an attack of bronchial asthma, a repetition of a childhood condition which had lasted until he was ten. He felt severely depressed over the separation but ultimately was able to accept the divorce. In the course of treatment the depression lifted.

David suffered from severe castration anxiety and had feelings of guilt upon entering sexual relations, ardently wishing for passive satisfaction and wanting a woman to make seductive maneuvers toward him and show him by her interest that he was a "man" in every way. This sexual passivity was in direct contrast to the aggressivity he demonstrated in the vocational area of his life. He feared heterosexual intercourse, experienced dreams of castration, and chronically worried over the size of his penis, its strength and effectiveness.

He feared rebuff and rejection by all women whom he admired. At times he was unable to have an erection and realized that his guilt about heterosexual desires was the cause of his failure to respond. On occasion he would awaken from dreams of being surrounded by Indians or other tribal males about to attack him (unconscious wish and dread for penetration), or dreams of being rejected by women, with pains in his rectum of such intensity that they would produce a near shocklike syndrome (Proctalgia fugax). This condition consisted of a massive spasm of his anal canal or rectum, and perhaps his sigmoid and lower colon. The pain was so severe that it caused faintness, sweating, increased pulse rate, alterations in consciousness, and other signs of a shocklike state. These phenomena represented a defense against anal rape. The syndrome usually occurred during sleep, when he was not in conscious control. This was verified by dream material preceding the spasm and concomitant with it which clearly reflected his dread of and/or wish for anal penetration. This condition was erroneously attributed to an organic ince in the autonomic nervous system involving the lower intestinal tract. Significantly, this author has seen several cases of this disorder occurring in latent homosexuals of the oedipal form. It is a response in passive latent homosexual individuals in the throes of the negative oedipal relationship who have an accompanying intense conflict over assuming the less demanding role of the woman in sexual intercourse. It was quite clear, even to the patient, that at times he feared being assaulted and degraded by more powerful men pushing their penises into his rectum.

On isolated occasions David was able to function heterosexually with complete competence, orgasm, and pleasure, and he had an affective interest in women. It could be demonstrated, however, that there were conscious or unconscious fantasies for persons of the same sex for sexual intercourse. As a result of therapy, he ultimately achieved his best sexual functioning with the diminution of infantile guilt in the alliance with the analyst's more permissive superego and with a resolution of his oedipus complex.

David suffered from homosexuality in its latent form. His defensive structures were basically of the obsessional type, involving strict and severe superego control, an exaggerated capacity for impulse control, and postponement of affect and a split between affect and thought. As a result he was almost always able to repress and/or suppress homosexual desires. As noted above, prior to therapy he was capable of meager heterosexual performance with very little or no pleasure and was plagued by convictions of his own sexual inferiority.

Chapter 15
THE CASE OF CLAUDE
(Oedipal Form)

Claude, a thirty-five-year-old engineer, showed a pronounced identification with his older brother. His history revealed the typical secondary identification with mother and the presence of a weak father. His father suffered severe business reverses at the time the child was born. The mother, who was the matriarch of the family, had helped her own younger siblings to complete college and to launch their careers. She was always domineering in the relationship with her husband. She appeared masculine in many ways and dominated the family. The father assumed a quiet, benevolent, passive role but was extremely attentive to his older son, who became, in time, prominent in athletics of every description and very popular in his home community.

Claude always felt inferior to his brother. On the positive side, he had been able to develop a strong affective life with emotionally rich social relationships, especially with older women, his grandmother, and teachers. The father had unsuccessfully attempted to force him into sports. His brother had also attempted to teach him games, especially those in which he himself excelled. Claude complained that his father had been overly permissive with him in many ways, allowing

him undue "free choice" as to beliefs and range of
interests because "my father was mostly tied up with
my brother."

Beneath his oedipal problem there was no evidence
of any failure in traversing the separation-individuation phase. Female identification with the mother
was due to a flight from oedipal strivings, the lack of a
masculine father with whom to identify, a murderous rivalry with an older successful brother. A male
teacher seduced him at approximately age seven and
he later experienced a number of seductions by older
men at his places of summer employment while still
attending school. He was pleased with the affection
men gave him but would develop severe anxiety on
being fondled, caressed, or otherwise sexually approached.

When he was thirteen, his brother was drafted into
military service. One and a half years later the patient
was severely traumatized when he answered the
telephone call advising him of the brother's death in
action. This tragic event had a strong influence on his
subsequent development; he developed severe anxiety
over the death as well as intense guilt. His guilt was
due to his unconscious ambivalent wish for his
brother's removal as a rival for the affection of the
father. He suffered from an oedipal structural conflict.
Since that time his homosexual activities, except for an
interval of two years in the armed forces when none
took place, were motivated by the unconscious search
for replicas of his brother with whom he could make
reparations in an attempt to alleviate his guilt.
Furthermore, there was a strong identification with
the brother; in his homosexual activities he was
searching for narcissistic self-restoration. Over the

years his physical resemblance to his brother had become striking to those who knew them both.

His anxiety during homosexual relations increased as he reached the end of his twenties, and for several years he found himself wishing to achieve a heterosexual orientation. It was as if he had been doomed to pleasing other men by giving himself sexually to them, doing penance and sacrificing his masculinity because of his guilt over wishing to usurp the older brother's preferred family position. He had been punishing himself for his infantile hostility toward his brother, aggravated by the almost magical fulfillment of these wishes by the brother's death. Expiatory attempts were evident in a series of automobile accidents, some of them nearly fatal, and in subjecting himself to the sadistic practices of a particular homosexual partner with whom he lived for ten years.

One year before entering analysis, Claude unsuccessfully attempted to terminate this masochistic homosexual relationship and leave his sadistic partner. During this temporary separation he met a woman for whom he developed considerable affection and was able to establish a sexual relationship with her. In this instance, and in other intermittent relationships with women, he could become involved only with those of a different race or nationality—women in no way reminiscent of his mother or of other females of his own cultural or familial background. This pattern rendered any lasting or meaningful relationship unlikely.

He always carried out his homosexual acts when partially intoxicated. In his homosexual activities he often sought out heterosexual men, tested them to see if they would have homosexual intercourse with him,

and was relieved if they would not. On numerous
occasions he succeeded in "making heterosexuals
homosexual," but only to subsequently suffer intense
guilt.

Claude was disturbed by the early exciting and
frightening childhood memory of his brother masturbating and by his belief that his brother had wanted to
have homosexual relations with him. During analysis
he discovered that he felt guilty in not having gratified
what he perceived to be his brother's homosexual
wishes for him. There was no direct evidence for this
assumption; later it became clear that this was a
projection on the part of the patient of his own
homosexual desires and a fear of homosexually
seducing his brother. The brother's death actively
relieved his unconsciously anticipated and dreaded
homosexual encounter with the brother upon his
return from the service. The unconscious relief at his
brother's death further augmented his guilt and
produced a need for expiation, a need for punishment, a
need to remain homosexual, and a need to suffer
throughout life.

His unconscious guilt had far-reaching effects.
Claude had been unable to finish important projects
which would have occasioned career advancement and
professional acclaim. He was unable to accept professional offers which would lead to prominence in his
field because, consciously, he feared exposure as a
homosexual; unconsciously, he could not permit
himself the exceptional success for which he was both
endowed and qualified. He wandered for years in a
maze of homosexual dread and desire, guilt and
atonement. At times he initiated experiments with
heterosexuality resulting in some pleasure. But these

attempts were followed quickly by guilt and wishes for self-punishment, as exemplified by his sadomasochistic submission to a homosexual partner who exploited him mercilessly.

Prior to entering treatment Claude had undergone a period of about six months of continual drinking, yearning to break away from the bondage of his homosexual life and to fulfill himself in meaningful relationships with women. In fact his autotherapeutic attempts (through homosexuality) at cure of his deepest conflicts had produced a sense of ego depletion rendering him well motivated for psychoanalytic therapy and treatment of his disorder. Unfortunately, every time he attempted a successful advance into heterosexuality it was accompanied by tragedy. On several occasions dearest friends died just as he was trying to free himself from his deteriorated life situation. His first heterosexual experience in adolescence coincided with the sudden news of his brother's death. His homosexual partner for the past decade had threatened to kill himself were the patient to leave him. He became filled with self-loathing and disgust during homosexual contacts, all of which were preceded by anxiety and accomplished only by the use of alcohol. There were episodes in which he endangered himself with homosexual pickups by inviting police entrapment as well as physical abuse and loss of personal property. He came to realize that homosexuality "is valueless, cheapening, aggressive, asocial, demoralizing, and self-destructive. I have never met one happy homosexual."

During analysis he became aware of his identification with his mother, and his incestuous conflicts which inhibited relations with women; he was able to tolerate the infantile unconscious guilt provoked by both situations. To become heterosexual like his brother, he felt, was tantamount to murdering him. As a result of working through this material in the analysis he no longer felt he must retain the intense identification with his brother (an effort to keep him alive) and began to see himself as a different and independent person who could live a rewarding heterosexual life once freed of guilt and anxiety. He urgently desired both parents to recognize him as a strong and mature man rather than a weakened, depreciated homosexual.

As a result of a five-year analysis, Claude was completely cured of his homosexual impulses and was able to successfully cathect with libido a heterosexual love object. His subsequent marriage to a young women in a related field of work has produced a fully affective and fulfilling life and his success in his professional activities. A five-year follow-up interview revealed that the cure of his condition has been uninterruptedly sustained.

Chapter 16
THE CASE OF SUMNER
(Preoedipal Type II with Severe Narcissistic Character Pathology)

Sumner, a thirty-nine-year-old engineer, was the eldest of three children born into a Catholic, Irish-American immigrant family. A brother was born when he was two and a half, and a sister five years later. His mother, an "emotional woman," was given to angry outbursts, violent temper tantrums, "throwing pots and pans around the house" whenever she felt over-burdened by the demands of her household tasks. She was callous and indifferent to her children for long periods of time, and apparently suffered from some depressive episodes. She had been a professional athlete before her marriage and apparently resented the maternal role. She was subject to the most extreme attacks of rage, in which she would break bottles on the kitchen table when frustrated by the demands of her children. As for the father, he was an aggressive, driving man who was intent upon making his fortune and paid little attention to the children, except during summer holidays and when the boys were old enough to work for him. Sumner felt abandoned and "unloved" after the birth of his brother, clinging even more intensely to his mother and screaming if she ever left his side. Sumner's relationship to both brother and sister was always superficial. The younger brother, apparently heterosexual, has always been detached, aloof, and has attained much less success in a similar profession. The patient feels his brother resents him. The brother's interest has been mainly in sports activities that the patient early in life deplored or felt beneath him. His sister joined a convent at the age of sixteen, only to leave it a few years later, and is now active in the feminist movement.

Sumner's memories of his earliest years are of being misunderstood, misjudged, and disapproved of. He felt "different" from other boys: feminine, awkward, and unathletic. In his early childhood, he recalls surreptitiously dressing up in his mother's clothes with exhilaration. He developed a severe sense of shame and guilt over his "femininity." When criticized he would run away to hiding places in the house—beneath staircases, into secret cubbyholes in the attic—where he could cry, suffer, and nurse grievances. He magically relieved these periods of intense suffering by fastening upon grandiose fantasies of becoming a "beautiful ballerina" and dancing before vast, admiring audiences, the center of all eyes and attention. At the height of suffering, he fantasized the Virgin Mary coming down a staircase from heaven and selecting him to rise with her above the multitudes. At other times, he would relieve suffering by imagining himself as a beautiful young man on an enormous white horse, proud, defiant, and all-powerful. He frequently thought of himself as the martyred St. Sebastian. Grandiose fantasies alternated with fantasies of suicide in which everyone would remember him as filled with purity and innocence and tragically misunderstood. When laughed at and teased by children, he frequently imagined putting his arms around a huge tree, pulling it out of the ground, and smashing his persecutors.

As soon as he entered secondary school, his father required him to take part in the family business, working outdoors at hard labor. Although he resented this enforced activity, he is now proud of his "masculine physique," a product of those earlier years.

An incident in childhood demonstrates his tendency to engage in masochistic injuries whenever frustrated. While washing the floor one day (at age nine), he accidently stepped backwards into a pail. He became so furious at his predicament that instead of trying to extricate his foot from the pail, he angrily thrust his other foot into it, causing him to fall over and severely strike his head.

His first sexual experiences, in which he seduced younger boys, began at prepuberty. Despite strong guilt feelings and expiation through confession, he was unable to stop his imperative need for sexual contact with neighborhood boys.

At age fifteen he entered a Catholic military academy, but was deeply afraid that his classmates would discover his homosexual inclinations. He was surprised and pleased to discover that he was an extremely competent swimmer and achieved prizes and awards in this activity. At eighteen he entered college to become an engineer like his father. After the intense activities of being pledged to a fraternity during the first one or two months of college, he was unable to study. He and his new roommate enjoyed considerable popularity and success; but with the cessation of these glamorous activities the patient became intensely and acutely depressed and sought to intensify his relationship to his roommate through sexual contact. Rejected, he became desperate, ashamed, enraged, inferior, empty, and attempted suicide by ingesting large quantities of aspirin. Forced to interrupt college, he returned home and received psychotherapy of a supportive nature for a year. During this period, his therapist treated his homosexuality as if it were simply a fear of heterosexual relationships which would go away if his self-esteem were elevated. Therapy enabled him to return to college, and he acquired his degree four years later. During this period, he carefully avoided intense involvement with any students, either sexually or socially, and limited his homosexual contacts to vacation periods while away from school. A professor who was especially fond of him depicted him in a cartoon as a complex student with a brilliant mind, filled with ingenious thoughts, plans, and projects, all of which he would be unable to deliver. It was during this period that Sumner became known as a charming connoisseur of art and the classics, a voracious reader, a driver of fast cars, and an arranger of weekend parties. He became a striking figure, enthusiastic, attractive, sophisticated, but, inwardly, never involved with his associates or peers.

When he was twenty his father died of cancer of the intestinal tract. This had a particularly traumatic effect on the patient, as just before his death his father had begged Sumner to take him home and allow him to die "in his own bed." The patient, afraid to challenge his mother's authority, did not grant the father's wish. He later felt he had let his father down, and shortly after his death he launched into intense homosexual activity with constant cruising, engaging in anal intercourse, fellatio, and so on in public bathrooms and whenever and wherever homosexual activity offered itself. His homosexual activities continued essentially unabated from age twenty until entry into analysis.

Graduating from college at the age of twenty-four, he almost immediately married a distant cousin. The patient himself behaved as a "benevolent parent" to his young bride, but occasionally they engaged in sexual relations quite successfully, especially following their marriage. He had told his wife of his homosexual inclinations before the marriage, and she readily accepted his explanation that he had conquered his sexual problem. Heterosexual functioning on his honeymoon, however, had to be buttressed by several homosexual experiences.

Endowed with a natural charm, grace, and verbal ability, Sumner gained employment almost immediately after graduation in a small, prosperous company. It was required, however, that he "deliver" and "produce," and he became anxious and depressed when such performance was demanded of him. He fled this job, but ultimately secured employment in this field with a renowned firm led by a world-famous professional man. Again, his handsome and commanding appearance and air of confidence and superiority enhanced a gradual upward progression; finally he reached the ranks of junior executive. Although outstanding as a planner and organizer, he was unable to follow through and had begun to feel depressed over his failure to reach the heights of which he knew he was capable. By age thirty-three, he had two daughters who he felt were "both brilliant and exciting."

Sumner has always had difficulties in sustaining work for which he bore total responsibility, although

he could delegate responsibility. As he approached
forty he experienced a severe decrease in his self-
esteem and a beginning sense of failure because of his
inability to achieve "great success." His homosexual
life had become increasingly more intense, involving
pickups on the street and cruising in public restau-
rants, theatres, and gay bars. During these episodes he
almost always played the active role, penetrating his
partner anally. When a partner performed fellatio on
him, he experienced both feelings of triumph and the
need to demean his sexual partner. The need for
homosexual experiences was an imperative one,
occurring at almost any time during the day. It was
especially acute when he felt himself slighted, humiliated, or criticized by superiors or even associates.
Following the homosexual act he felt "restored" and
complete, and was able to return to his office and carry
on his duties. However, he became progressively
depleted by the multiple and endless search for
partners in the most "disgusting places." He wondered
whether a "prolonged relationship" with a "good,
suitable partner" might be possible, thus sparing him
the endless and tiring search. A gay counseling service
told him that gay marriages were working out.
Choosing an office colleague, Malcolm, as a possible
permanent homosexual partner, he embarked on a
plan to seduce Malcolm and then enlist his participation in a homosexual-heterosexual partnership with
himself and his wife. Malcolm first accepted but after a
few months rejected Sumner, plunging him into
masochistic despair. Sumner's wife responded with
shock and disbelief.

Course of the Analysis

Sumner entered analysis with severe anxiety, pain, and suffering following this double rejection. Intermittent episodes of failure of erection with his lover compounded his narcissistic humiliation. He engaged in a masochistic orgy of begging and pleading with Malcolm, beseeching him for compassion, admiration, and affection. Episodes of masochism alternated with bouts of intense, overwhelming narcissistic rage in which he felt he could kill his lover, his wife, or himself. Both regressive and masochistic tendencies quickly disappeared with the beginning of the analytic work. Gradually, identification with the analyst and the analytic work promoted self-esteem. Beneath this, however, were grandiose fantasies of achieving a rapid and miraculous cure of his homosexuality and attaining new and even more wonderful powers through the analytic work.

He was an ideal analytic patient in many ways: verbal, articulate, "hard-working," responsive to interpretations, and productive in his dream material and associations. Analysis soon demonstrated that his perverse sexual life was an important source of internal regulation of self-esteem. Through his sexual escapades, he attempted to secure narcissistic balance, overcome an overriding aggression, and handle an instinctual tension which he was beginning to recognize bore little resemblance to that of normal instinctual drives. Of even greater importance, analysis re- the homosexual act to be (as in other homosexual patients with narcissistic character pathology) a substitute for the inner ideal he was searching for, an externalization of his inner need to be powerful. This substitution, however, did not produce an enhancement of self-esteem, despite the hundreds of homosexual contacts he had engaged in over a twenty-year period. In fact, such escapades continued to rob him of his own external ideal, his power and perfection, through its sexualization. As noted above, these temporary feelings of narcissistic balance induced by homosexual performances had already begun to be inadequate to sustain him through the middle phase of his life. Furthermore, they constituted a severe block to successful functioning in work, social relationships, and competition. As a result of the identification (mirroring and transference) with the analyst, a quiescent period in the analysis ensued, and the patient's family life assumed a more normal course and his work effort became somewhat more productive. During this phase he began to understand the meaning of his insistent demands for approval of his values and goals by various father figures, including the analyst. His grandiosity and even arrogance and feelings of superiority, all of which were gracefully disguised by a pleasantness of manner, high intellect, and capacity to express some tender, affectionate emotions, could be understood as a reaction against deep feelings of inferiority, impotence, smallness, and emptiness.

In spite of his intense homosexual life, Sumner had long yearned for an end to his homosexuality. This was in part because of his strong religious feelings from childhood and intense feelings of shame in relation to his father, who had disapproved of his femininity and often teased him about it. Despite this teasing, however, the father never completely abandoned his son or turned away from him, demanding of him the same masculine efforts that he did of his other son. Similarly, he offered rewards for successful achievement in work. The reawakening and strengthening of his desire to get well allowed Sumner to diligently pursue the meaning of his homosexual episodes. He began to perceive them as orgastic experiences whose meaning was to gain strength by draining it from fantasy images of strong, powerful, handsome men. In pursuing them and conquering them, he acquired their penises and felt restored. They were sexualized statements of a deeper psychological defect within himself, and their aim was to shore up a failing self-representation; all of this was an attempt at buttressing threatened self- and object-representations.

By the end of the first year of analysis, Sumner's failure to be magically cured of his homosexual desires resulted in a severe devaluation of the analyst and a more vehement turning toward homosexual activities. In this phase, he experienced the analysis of these homosexual encounters and their infantile components as criticisms and coercive attempts by the analyst to make him cease his homosexual life. They tended to produce severe narcissistic blows and consequent masochistic regressions marked by crying and sobbing, loss of all executive functioning, withdrawal and depression, and agonizing scenes of a helpless little child being beaten, struck, hurt, misunderstood, and abused. These affective experiences relived in the analysis were replicas of earlier childhood experiences when he would run away from home or hide in cubbyholes around the house. Alternating with these affective states he experienced overwhelming rage in which he felt that he would break everything in the room, attack the analyst, his wife, or any person of

authority. On these occasions he would stay away
from work and remain in bed; he was unable to tolerate
the slightest criticism or comment on his behavior by
anyone.

Despite these stormy sessions, a major aim of the
first two and a half years of Sumner's therapy was to
promote empathic responses and shared experiences,
thereby enabling him to reach a stage where his
representational world could be structured in such a
way that structural conflicts belonging to the oedipal
period could be defined and analyzed. It was apparent
that Sumner was unable to find, achieve, and actualize
a real self. When faced with tasks of actual performance such as applying for a new job, writing a new
curriculum vitae toward an application for a special
prize, and so on, he experienced severe anxiety,
inability to function, and feelings of emptiness, panic,
and worthlessness. At such times he noted that he
would disengage himself from the analyst, in a sense
lose his object relationship to him, and would develop
regressive attacks, crying, whimpering, falling to the
floor during the analytic session, rolling himself into a
fetuslike position, crying out like a baby, grunting and
groaning in pain and anguish, and closing his eyes
with his head cocked backward in the position of a
martyred saint on the cross. He also engaged in
convulsive kicking motions of his arms and legs.

"I'm between regressions. Although I feel quiet I feel
depressed and I'm very angry. A little act of will and I
could get out of this maybe. I don't want to sit here and
complain any more. I don't want to feel any childhood
emotions though I don't give a shit. I'm petulant, I
don't give a fuck, hate you all, nobody loves me [the
patient looks around the room slowly, observing its

details]. Bloody, fucking women! I don't care what happens, I'm not going to suffer anymore, to cry or be hurt, all that shit of suffering, suffering, suffering, regression, a waste of time—I'm not going to say anything because I don't want to be hurt again. Ugh, ugh [grunt and scream] Everybody accuses me of everything; I'm the great lover, though. Ha! [jerking body movement, propelling the pelvis somewhat forward]. I won't regress any more and I feel bitter. My marriage is a wreck: she says I'm judgmental, putting down everybody, that's the way I've been behaving. Ugh, ugh [grunt, movement of the feet, kicking upward]. I wish when I wrote those plays during therapy that I'd quit—everything. I've done what I want to, I don't want to feel anything if I don't feel good things! I had a dream the other day that I was on a street in Brooklyn. I was a little kid again, sitting there. Ominous clouds in the sky and it started to rain and pour and I was holding something to my chest. The rain was terrible. All this reminds me of my childhood and how I'd run away and hide and console myself and dream of wonderful things and how I would get back at everyone. Why can't she understand, my wife? I want to be loving and affectionate. I don't believe any of this in a way [he makes a sudden movement of the feet]. I used to run away in the rain.

"I was trying to think of B., my lover. I could make love to him and that would make me feel better. How do I get back to myself? I know this is all child's stuff. I know I can handle everything when I get back to myself. A few days ago I felt so solid, I felt the real self for only a few hours but it was marvelous. I don't know why they all are so mad at me all the time, why they're so nonloving, oh, oh, like my mother. I don't care what happens, I'm just disappointed that I can't have the things that I want when I want them. I never thought I'd let myself get this down, this down, as far as I've gone since I've been here. There is no room, no room, no room! Everything is potentially disastrous, every feeling is like the childhood anger and oh [patient sobs, cries, falls to the floor in agony] I don't want to kill myself, I don't care how many guys I fuck, it's so hard to live all the time on the outside of things! But nothing is so bad. I could turn these things around, but I'm so lost, there's no one. I want to cry out for help but nobody's there to hear. I wish I could just DIE! [The patient yells at the top of his voice. He then growls and says] Maybe I'd kick that woman and give her what she deserves. [Kick what woman?] My mother, my mother."

In the above session the patient demonstrates: (1) his unconscious, ever-present desire to remain a child; (2) his turning to creative activities (writing plays) in part to lessen destructive feelings; (3) his overwhelming fear of responsibility and his hostility toward both his wife and mother; (4) his tendency to regressive episodes as an escape from both homosexuality and responsibilities; (5) his temporary turning away from the analysis and its possibilities for alleviation of his distress by assuming a narcissistic grandiose stance; and (6) his proneness to severe bouts of masochism and narcissistic rage.

In the following session, Sumner reveals the centrally important lack of empathic responsiveness from his mother during his early childhood. As a consequence, he failed to separate from her and desired to merge with her in order to achieve a lasting fusion and attenuation of his overwhelming oral cravings for love. Simultaneously, he presents two unintegrated representations of the self: an older, callous, silent, angry, powerful, threatening, and cruel man, and a helpless, crying infant. We see these two selves in the following dream: "An old farmhouse. There's this guy, standing outside, imperious, near a fireplace, totally withdrawn, throwing things in the fireplace. There is a woman there who is silent, filled with silent anger. This guy is desperate, however, and begins to appear as if he's at the end of his rope. In other words, he changes. Then he is suddenly on the ground, becoming a baby, trying to paddle away somehow. The woman says, in a sarcastic tone, 'There he goes again!' The action then turns to inside the house. Someone is putting firewood into the fire and the child or baby is thrown into it and he shrinks to just a few inches. This fellow in the fire who is now a baby starts to sing, howling in the night, 'Love me, Momma, love your little baby!' But two people who come in just sit there and as I look at the scene I'm horror-struck: they are just sitting there, it's too late. Meanwhile the woman simply goes upstairs (as my mother used to do whenever she was upset or wanted to get away from us). She's adamant, refusing to respond, and self-content."

The patient's associations were that the man was obviously himself and the woman was a combination of his wife and his mother. He expressed the desperateness, the sense of isolation in his being thrown into the fireplace, or somehow climbing into it, being consumed by need, desire, and destructiveness. No one cares.

"Sexually, what you get out of a guy is like being in the fire. It's a kind of burning. The two people in the room are perhaps you and me, younger and older, or perhaps two aspects of myself. After this dream I went to the beach and I wanted to cruise; also I had the

fantasy of being a ballerina* dancing to music as I
used to when I was a child. But then I somehow got out
of it. I decided I didn't want the homosexual thing. I
then somehow, *magically* almost, started to feel
myself, pride and pleasure in this, about my children,
my fatherhood, and I had a feeling I'd make it, no
doubt about it. When I'm feeling gay I think I'm feeling
this small and then I suddenly try to become bigger by
actually having a homosexual relationship. But that
way I don't sustain my real self very long, like these
few minutes, moments we've been talking, I feel very
good, I really have my self. These feelings about being
a little baby, love me Mommy, even about my mother's
estate: if things do not go just right for me I'm
intolerant; if things are not perfect I become frustrated,
disappointed, and afraid."

Summer was filled with unintegrated self-
representations, consequences of defensive splitting
for the purpose of warding off severe ambivalence
conflicts (structural conflict). At other times these
partial self-representations constituted early prestages of splitting (Stolorow and Lachmann 1978)
characterized by an inability to integrate contrasting
images of the self. Similar considerations applied to
unintegrated object-representations. Both these forms
of psychopathology are evident in this verbatim
material from a single session midway in the analysis:

"The first scene of my dream is quite clearly the front
of my own house in Queens. My wife looks marvelous.
She is smiling and busy, that is to say she is very much
herself as I like to think of her. She is perhaps saying

* A close examination of this fantasy revealed it to be a "self-doll ballerina"
fantasy, first utilized in early childhood as a compensatory device preliminary to
the development of a full-stage narcissistic grandiose object relationship—the doll
being used as a transitional object similar to cases described by Natterson (1976)
and Volkan (1973).

goodbye to me and I to her but in the manner of a typical day as I leave for work. All this somehow has the tone and quality and warmth of what I think of as normal before the Malcolm incident. The whole scene is observed somewhat at a distance and it takes on for me a kind of idyllic tone.

"The next scene, I'm walking down, I'm beginning to walk down the street on my way to an appointment with you. As I begin to walk down the street I observe over the fence and in the front garden a cupboard, or what we used to call breakfront, a large storage unit. As I continue down the street my eye is caught by a bowl, a rather large bowl of tulips sitting atop another piece of furniture, rather like a dining room sideboard or buffet which stands in the sidewalk, its back to the street so that anyone moving along the sidewalk would pass between it and the front garden of my house. The bowl of tulips is seen in close-up, as it were; that is to say that while I observe all the other things I focus on this. A fellow walking up the street, that is to say coming towards me, sees my interest in the bowl of tulips, smiles a very friendly but very knowing smile and says, 'I know where you can get some of those.' I look away without responding, somewhat embarrassed at his having observed my interest or fascination [ambivalence conflict].

"I can think of two possibilities, or should I say three for whom this fellow resembles. He has rather short-cut blond hair and facially in some way reminds me of Malcolm's roommate. In another way, he suggests this fellow in my neighborhood with whom I have been making it recently. He is, by the way, a florist.

"Of course, he is really 'another aspect of myself' or my wishful self, who has all the time in the world to wander about, making knowing and friendly glances at other fellows' flowers, i.e., cruising, and I don't have to rush off to an appointment with you. I would contrast, however, his easy, relaxed attitude with my embarrassment at his having observed my glance.

"Then I seem to have taken the subway and inadvertently gotten off too early, for I am downtown at the office and I am late for an appointment (severe ambivalence). I am rather frantically searching for a cab and it is then that I come upon this truck driven by this girl. I ask her rather nicely if she'd mind, as I'm terribly late for an appointment, at your office, to give me a lift uptown. She says, 'Sure, get in,' and as I do I notice that there are some other fellows in the back, among whom may be my brother. The girl driving the truck has cutoff bluejean bermuda shorts and a tee shirt or sweatshirt. She has dark hair and glasses and now I know who she resembles exactly: she is the perfect image of my brother's wife's younger sister who is a real tomboy and who is well on her way to becoming a dyke. As we begin to drive toward your office suddenly we are driving through suburban housing and then up and up into remote hills. I express my concern about the lack of similarity to Madison Avenue but she assures me that it is just a shortcut. I accept without protest this assertion. As we drive higher and higher on what appears to be less and less a road we are on rolling hills, somewhat desertlike, no real trees or wood. At this point I have severe anxiety and lack of full attention to what is happening. I remember the truck is without doors and as we veer from the perilous crest of the hills from one side to another I can see down into the valleys between the hills [fears of engulfment, ego dissolution, and loss of ego boundaries]. Some vague suggestion of lights and a city or town below. These mountains or hills continue above and below; it is as though we and the truck were a tiny cork in an ocean of massive waves, and we are in a sense simply riding them [fear of merging and ego dissolution]. Next thing we are out of the truck and she is going down on me [attempt to restore the self-representation]. I feel quite adolescent now as this rather butch girl 'does me.' I see she is still dressed in her jeans and shirt and she is saying 'Wow, what a cock!' I can't understand this since to me it is hardly even hard and I find it false admiration, not pleasing but offensive [injured narcissism].

"The next scene is the scene with you. The room resembles to a great extent the dining room of my house. I am lying in a sort of chaise lounge, my back to one wall and my head resting on an arm, and I'm telling you the above dream. You are sitting right next to me, your profile facing me, your head bent forward listening, engrossed, thoughtful. And I am feeling intimacy, warmth, engagement but also the sense, somewhat, of a confessional atmosphere. At my head is the door by which one enters the room. On the same wall is another—'opening?' But it is there that I see your face full front [split object-representation]. You are peering at me. Smiling, I think, out of a mirror or an open door. This mirror or room is filled with sunlight and as I think of it, it is the only real source of light in the room, or at least the brightest spot.

"As we continue our intimate discourse, he enters the room, as I said: he is tall, a man about my age, but has a mustache. He moves across the room behind you, oblivious of our presence, and walks to a chest of drawers at the wall opposite my feet, or at my feet as it were. He takes a cigar out of the drawer, lights it up and takes a self-satisfied puff. You have been taking notice of his presence with some annoyance and you finally say to him, with annoyance but not anger, 'Do you mind?'

"He is rather piqued, and responds, 'Oh, was I interrupting? I'm sorry, don't mind me,' or something to that effect. In addition to all those associations which I made before having to do with *The Secret Sharer*, Conrad's *Secret Sharer*, these additional things come to mind: your face seen in full, you have a sort of curly red hair and blue eyes which remind me of my father's friend who treated me more like a man than my father did. You look like the father of the girl whom I've just told you about. She was a tomboy and a kid I grew up with and with whom I had a very real sexual attraction in my teens, surprisingly enough. As you recall, I know who that other man is: he is the narcissist in me. He's a split-off me [split self-representation]. I realize now what has been confusing me over this period: the guy with a cigar is a guy my age, the narcissistic person. I identified the grown-up part of me with the narcissistic self and the other self is the adolescent self. You were like a priest—confession, guilt, like my real self is the narcissism, though, the homosexual. This is where I've been making a tremendous mistake: the real self should not be the narcissist. In the normal relationship the narcissistic self does the functioning, e.g., I have a bad reputation of breaking up conversations when I feel like it, interrupting other people, and a just total disregard for others—haughty and imperious. And then I begin to examine all these things, that they interfere with my friendships, as we have done here, with my relationships with people. However I continue to relate to you as a little boy, castrated, and you are the father. But in putting myself in this position I cannot relate to you as a whole man [unintegrated self-representation]. Then I come back at other times as a narcissistic self, like I'll tell you how to write your books, how to expand your theories, etc. At other times when I confide painful parts to you it's simply I'm a good little child to relieve the pain. Also I do the same thing to others: I can be extremely submissive and frightened of anybody, even if he is not clearly an authority figure, when I feel this way. Not only when in pain—when I'm facing important questions in my life. I act like a son to a father, not like equals with another man which is what it should be. Furthermore, the narcissism protects me against feeling masochistic, like the time it forced me to take the pills and the Malcolm episode, when I became masochistic to him and wanted to kill myself and leave my wife if she wouldn't stay married in that homo-hetero relationship. What comes to me very strongly is this: when I relinquish my narcissism I feel a threat, I feel I have to deny the strong aspects of myself and that's my confusion, that my narcissism is equated with my real strength which it really isn't [inability to integrate contrasting self-images]."

It is important to note that although contradictory images of the patient and an ambivalence toward the analyst were present, they were not as severe and rapidly alternating as in earlier sessions. The patient felt he had gained new insights and had made progress after the session. He had been feeling better all day, not verging on regression; he felt very much restored to rational, "analytic thinking," as he put it. Perhaps, however, he might feel "even better" if he were to go out and get a fix, a homosexual encounter, perhaps at a "tearoom or bathroom somewhere" in order to firm up his sense of self and the good feelings he was already experiencing.

"I'm still afraid I might possibly set up a regression if I don't. But I feel I don't belong in a gay bar. You know, to be really successful in homosexuality you have to give up your real self. I did go to a porno movie, though, and ultimately, I went to the bathroom there. It didn't work. I wasn't interested. I went to another place and I couldn't get an erection. I was totally out of the proper emotional state of mind to function homosexually. I began to feel that homosexuality wasn't doing anything for me. But then I began to feel somewhat paranoid, suspicious, distrustful, and uncertain. 'Jesus! Now you have lost your passionate self. You are tamed, weakened, and enfeebled all because of the analysis—and because of you. Also I began to feel tired and weary because I was going home to my wife and potential sex with her and I'm not up to it.'"

The positive transference and the working alliance had produced progressive improvement in this patient. He underwent experiences which he legitimately needed but missed because of his ego developmental arrest, experiences related to self-object differentiation, and his need for grandiose objects to restore an omnipotent self. The positive object-representation with the analyst had to be repeatedly reinforced. For example, he felt the analyst would abandon him as he believed he was by his real father. The following dream reflects his difficulty in maintaining a positive transference and his turning to archaic mechanisms in order to incorporate the analyst's penis, which he then responds to in an ambivalent way with revulsion and the need to vomit in order to expel the incorporated image of the analyst:

"I'm in a room with you, sitting. You are sitting with your back to me. It is like a cocktail party; or at any

event, there are a number of other men whom I take for
your students there. They are all talking in animated
tones. There are two in particular, one on either side of
you, both talking and laughing with you. One puts his
arm around your shoulders to emphasize a point,
smiling and laughing and talking. He glances back at
me with a smile. It is as though he lets me know that he
is where I'd like to be. Suddenly they have all left or are
leaving and I am alone. As the last one leaves he looks
at me and says, 'My God, your analysis is amazing," or
something to that effect (need for narcissistic reinforcement). There is some sense that the conversation
that has been going on has been about your work in
general, but that in some way it has been about me in
particular. Next I am physically ill, crawling across
the room to a bathroom in the corner (infantilization)
feeling like I am going to vomit. I am desperately
wondering where you are, thinking to myself, 'Can't he
see that I am sick!' You are in a bathroom next to the
one I am moving towards, taking a leak, and I want to
shout out to you to come and help me."

This dream reminded Sumner of a recent dream he
had had only a week before: "I go down a corridor and
turn left. Another corridor leads to a room in which my
father is lying on a sofa. I'm astounded to see him, and
angry because I had given him up for lost. I berate him,
'Where the hell have you been? Why did you go away
without saying a word?' He does not respond with any
kind of vigor or defense. He seems not to care at all.
This dream recalled reminds me of earlier dreams,
perhaps in the last couple of years, repeated more than
once, in which I discover that my father is still alive
somewhere when I have given him up for dead. That he
just took off one day, abandoning us, and I had learned

to live with the fact only to discover that he was there somewhere all the time now *but I didn't care.*"

The second dream was accompanied with a strong affective discharge: tears, anger, and bitterness at his father for not rescuing him from the fearsome women in his household, his mother and sister. The dreams represented an attack against the analyst, a fear of being let down by him, and a wish to sadistically destroy him as a significant figure to identify with and believe in. Such an identification could lead to the formation of a satisfactory internalized ego and superego. Associating further to this material, he remarked that his father was the first man he knew who was not cowed by the puritanical sexual ethics of the Catholic church. However, he could not recall either his father or his uncles ever making an aggressive or sexual remark with respect to women. It was as if women were all put on pedestals. "If my father revolted against his childhood, it never fully went beyond the sexual puritanical values I associate with him. I associate you with my other values, and that's what I need."

After approximately one and a half years of analysis, the patient was becoming increasingly cognizant of additional unconscious meanings of his homosexuality: to find the perfect narcissistic and grandiose self-representation in the partner; to relieve depression, feelings or emptiness, and isolation; to ventilate aggression; to merge with an idealized self, thereby protecting himself from the wish to merge with the mother; to alleviate masochistic tension; to reduce a rising narcissistic tension through a "perfect experience"; and to acquire a full, powerful sense of masculinity, enhancing the grandiose aspects of the self.

He felt that narcissism was his main problem—
homosexuality was simply one way of expressing it.
He had to eradicate homosexuality as a necessary step
toward the solution to finding his true self. Attempts to
cease homosexual activities, however, were fraught
with danger. Preceding the following dream he
engaged in an orgy-a-trois with a neighborhood
homosexual and a pickup, only to feel humiliated,
inept, and dirty after the act. The experience completely lacked the grandiose superpleasure he had achieved
on so many other occasions. The sexual acts were
performed peremptorily, without much passion, and he
felt considerably demeaned. He dreamt: "I've entered a
bathroom where there are young boys. They ask me to
open a package and it is difficult to do so. There is
something like a sausage in it and somehow it has to be
cut and a lubricant will come out. Then the kids run out
and one looks around at me and I become very upset. It
looks like one of the children I once exhibited myself to
when I was eleven or thirteen years of age, and he just
ran away. In the dream, they run out and they cry out,
'Rape, rape!' But I haven't done anything. I am being
unjustly accused. They are furious at me (projected
harsh superego). Then I am outside and there is a glass
partition that I am standing in front of, almost right up
to it, and a gush of sperm comes out of my erection and
splatters all over the glass. Then on the other side of
the glass wall there are two other men doing the same
thing (his homosexual partners a few hours before).
They are a little bit further back; I'm up next to it. There
are people spurting sperm and they kind of look like
penises, their entire bodies, yes, that's what they
looked like (body equals penis equation). I suddenly am
standing up there, however, without my clothes on and

there are raw vegetables cut up into pieces, including meat pieces, on my body. They form a tight compact, like a bathing suit, and then they gradually turn into coals and they light up and they flare up. I have a lot of coals all over my body, with a pattern like a bathing suit. I am being tortured but in a sense I don't show it. I am powerful and defiant; in fact, I take a couple of sausages and put them right in the flame coming from my body. I am hurt and angry and suffering. Inside me real suffering begins now, yes, maybe like St. Sebastian but I won't show it, I won't give them that satisfaction. But I'm like trapped. Then I become more frightened. I won't let them see at this point that they have succeeded in torturing me. It's almost like a Hindu attempting to walk through coals but I can't do it. It seems like a defiance, my defiance, a defiance which doesn't work. However, I think, 'I won't give you the satisfaction of knowing how much you're hurting me—torturing and paining me, all these people watching and smiling and grinning and mocking me.'

"Suddenly at that point I come on as an observer from the side. There is a woman there, too, like my mother. She is doing the same thing, grinning with the audience like the others, and the whole thing now loses all proportion and becomes a horror (the patient begins sobbing, screaming, and crying during the recitation of his dream). Suddenly this person to the side, I guess me, I guess, this split-off part of me, grabs a branch or a twig and shouts, 'Stop it!' They all stop grinning and stop and look. They suddenly realize they are torturing a human being. I am legitimately angry but now the guy is not defiant and the whole thing is over and everybody has come to their senses."

Sumner resorted through regression to the exhibitionism of his childhood, in which he had attempted to shore up his failing self-representation by exhibiting his penis to other youths. This was later transformed into a homosexual symptom. He projected his own harsh superego onto those he would exploit sexually and had them persecute him, denounce him, and threaten to destroy him. He had the choice of masochistic suffering or grandiosity and at first chose the latter. He quickly saw that the man with the girdle of coals was really Jesus Christ in a crucifixion position with garments would around his pelvis. He himself was the crucified Jesus Christ. He recalled that from ages four to eight he had fantasies of being rescued by the Virgin Mary, becoming a saint, being elevated to heaven, and having everyone feel sorry for him. It is apparent that he projected his harsh, sadistic superego and ego ideal onto the onlookers, including his mother. He failed to see the unreality of the expectations of his own ego ideal and sensed severe humiliation and self-deprecation because he is unable to endure the tortures which he had made for himself. In a sense, he had been unable to integrate ego ideal with superego and felt mocked, shamed, and humiliated. Ultimately, intense masochism appeared, to become nearly paranoidal suffering. The patient saw that in his homosexuality, when it was functioning "properly," there was a "place" for the depression and the rage which consumed him, and that he acted out upon his partner both powerful emotions. The failure of his previous night's sexual encounter exposed his underlying conflicts and needs and their attempted resolution through homosexuality.

At approximately the three-year mark in analysis Sumner became increasingly able to face the knowledge that his narcissistic rage was of such a destruc-

tive quality that it threatened both object and self.
When acknowledged and understood in terms of his
early childhood feelings of vulnerability, he could
begin to control it.

"For the first time I feel I have a complete model of
what I'm going through. It gives me confidence, but it
is not the cure. I am now testing and 'becoming,'
hopefully; but I now have some confidence in what I
consider narcissistic and what is not narcissistic, what
is my true self and what is my grandiose self which
makes me very vulnerable to feelings of inferiority and
failure in everything I do....The other morning I woke
up and thought of the problems at work, you, my boss,
my wife, and a paranoia came on. Everything loomed
impossibly large. I then had an image that I was in my
dining room, my wife and my mother are there and are
chatting. I pick up a candlestick and I express my rage.
I smash all the windows in the house and I start
beating my mother in a violent rage and then I turn to
my wife and she says, 'Wait a minute.' But I'm going to
attack her, slaughter her and even slaughter my
children. And then I have some convulsive-type
movements like the kind I have here. I'm still lying in
bed, however, I'm only thinking this, and I start
groaning and I feel panic and terror and that the edge
of the abyss is there. I start drifting off and sort of lose
connection with everybody. No images or verbalizations or thoughts. However, this time I begin to make
out the verbal connections and can almost begin to
stop them. I realize that if I really say what I think,
what's on my mind, that it would be destructive of all
those relationships. As a matter of fact, I act them out
but do not say them, in my homosexuality, in my
regressions and in other things. Then I started to jump

out of bed and my wife tries to restrain me. I'm still very angry. But I realize I've been here before, I've done it before. I'm shaking. The image of the slaughter is there, the narcissistic rage. I walk downstairs, I'm frightened by it, but I'm already starting to analyze it. I begin to get hold of myself. Slowly I begin to have a sense of relief. I begin walking around downstairs. I start thinking I don't really...these images of my mother—are all archaic. They don't apply to my wife, to you, or even to a real situation but to an infantile situation. At other times I felt these emotions were much more powerful than me. Also I felt the fact that I'm homosexual justifies my rage at everyone. My wife comes downstairs and comes over to show me compassion. She's terrified, however; it's like I'm Dr. Jekyll and Mr. Hyde. I begin to gain control of myself and develop a patience. I begin to feel clarity and a sense of connection and somehow that the relationship with reality is better than what I'm feeling. I feel there is a point at which the relationship with reality is something to be wished for and to be controlled. My problem seems to be to detach from myself all the great power demands I make on myself of every sort."

Beneath the patient's narcissism was a hungry infant at the mercy of insatiable cravings for the mother, for union with her, and fear and distrust of her. His grandiosity protected him against these infantile demands. His homosexual encounters largely expressed in a condensation the multiple facets which lie within the infantile personality and the grandiose personality.

Sumner was able to form a transference relationship to the analyst proceeding through the narcissistic transference phase. His narcissistic attack on the object, however, led to fear of retaliation and a fear of guilt reactions. Most of all, he dreaded a sense of loneliness and abandonment derived from his frightening relationship with his sadistically perceived mother image and the absence of a caring father. It was some time before he was able to tolerate his own feelings of hatred toward everyone, as he felt his feelings might destroy the analyst and destroy his own capacity for caring. On the surface the latter was developed to a high degree, although it lacked depth and commitment to anyone prior to analysis. After the more superficial aspects of the narcissistic transference to objects were analyzed, a period of analysis of the transference neurosis and the oedipus complex occurred. He began to see himself as an independent object but one who had made himself vulnerable through the adoption of a narcissistic, grandiose object relationship. He perceived the unreality of the expectations of both ego ideal and superego and attempted to make a more legitimate goal for himself. Beneath his idealization of the analyst Sumner needed to externalize pathological grandiosity onto the analyst. His failures led to attacks of oral rage while success of this pathological projected self led to feelings of envy, both of which had to undergo subsequent transformation in the transference neurosis. The narcissistic transference tended to return repeatedly until it was fully worked through at later stages of the analysis.

During a period of relative well-being, Sumner arranged for the entire family, including mother, sister, brother, and in-laws to rent a home for the summer. During this vacation both mother and sister "took command," attempting to run the home and telling the children what chores to do, how to make the beds, and so on. Sumner revolted angrily and openly challenged them. While holding his own for several weeks, the intensity of their verbal denunciations of him as a "chauvinist" and "dictator" finally had its effect, and he was reduced to periods of crying, and feelings of smallness and emptiness, alternating with severe episodes of rage in which he fantasized punching, kicking, and even killing his mother and sister. These attacks of rage were short-lived and he would again become a "little boy," pathetic, defeated, mocked, humiliated, empty, and afraid. After weeks of such confrontations he felt so weakened that he wished to beg their forgiveness and acted like a "good little boy." He was successfully dissuaded in therapy from playing the penitent, masochistic, helpless child in relation to his mother, sister, and brother when the analyst pointed out to him that his narcissistic omnipotence had failed in producing a perfect situation in which he was to be triumphant over the others and others would only obey his orders and demands completely. It proved of great value to Sumner to ascertain that in his rage he felt he would destroy both external objects and the self. In his destructiveness he was continually placing impossible demands upon himself by insisting that external objects respond perfectly to his omnipotent demands. If they did not, he attributed the failure to their malevolence and destructiveness (a projection of his own narcissistic rage) or to the meanness, smallness, and inferiority of the self. Thus he was placing a tremendous and impossible demand upon himself, making him unnecessarily vulnerable to disappointment. This considerably relieved his tendency to treat with hate and fear all external objects who did not agree with his wishes and omnipotent demands. The interpretation was made in this manner, for to stress the overwhelming quality of his rage would often lead to feelings of shame, guilt, and an increase in his homosexuality.

As the analysis progressed, he began to tolerate "being stood up" by men because of strength gained through identification with the analyst. This identification allowed him to endure refraining from his homosexual encounters for long periods of time.

It was not necessary during regressive periods to offer physical contact with the patient. Instead, a warm, empathic, understanding, caring, and soothing attitude sufficed to return him to a higher level of ego integration. Simultaneously, the analyst provided a running commentary on the meaning of his motions, actions, and verbalizations. It was obvious that such regressive episodes also constituted a form of resistance to the forward movement of the analysis and to the ultimate relinquishing of both the narcissistic character disorder and the homosexuality. Regression in the service of resistance could only be interpreted later, at approximately the two-thirds mark during the course of analysis.

Sumner's narcissistic personality disorder revolved around his failure to integrate the ego ideal and superego. Whenever he attempted to make a statement about his real worth, cruel and harsh internalized figures assailed him, making him feel small, inferior, and frightened. He engaged in primitive splitting of all-good and all-bad self-images and object-images. He appeared to be superficially protected by his inflated self-concept, but it was soon discovered that, similar to other narcissists, there was within him a deeper level, a "deprived, hungry infant at the mercy of tension that stems from oral-aggressive conflicts" (Volkan 1976, p. 239). (He dreams of himself as a howling baby: "Love me, Momma, love your little baby.") This inner need, tension, and hunger led him on a continual search for narcissistic supplies which he was then unable to use for fear of self-depletion. Beneath his air of superiority he feared people and was unable to get close to them; he dreaded that others, especially women, might smother him. Simultaneously he craved love and admiration from both men and women. When frustrated by external objects, he would feel assailed by their badness, hatefulness, and evil. His narcissistic defense mechanisms were projective identificaion, omnipotent thought, splitting, control of external objects by devaluation or idealization, and denial.

He suffered from archaic, severely regressed, primitive, punitive superego forerunners which he attempted to exclude from consciousness through externalization. When he attempted important tasks, when Sumner in a sense was asked to "deliver," he felt berated, attacked by these archaic superego forerunners who castigated, demeaned, and diminished him. This produced an incapacity to act. During these emotional crises Sumner felt paralyzed and overwhelmed by contradictory affective states. When he identified with the external primitive superego parts, he was certain that an attack from the external world was imminent, or that he would be unable to meet external challenges and would be destroyed if he tried. This led to apathy, withdrawal and regression.

As noted by Volkan (1976), the difference between the defense mechanisms of the narcissist and the borderline, both of whom may suffer from an inability or failure to integrate ego ideal with superego, is that

the narcissistic patient is able to both "see and feel the
unreality of his expectations of his ego ideal."

Sumner's primitive splitting made it difficult, if not
impossible, to integrate elements of superego with the
elements of the ego ideal. This integration proved to be
an important therapeutic task throughout the analysis. It could be achieved only through reliving these
experiences in the transference in the later phases of
the analysis. The analysis revealed the inflated self-
concept to be a way of protecting himself from harmful
tensions going back to early childhood in which he saw
the world through fearful eyes, a world populated by
evil, large women, ferocious animals preying upon him
and threatening to devour him. This failure to
integrate all-bad and all-good units and his externalization of these all-bad units onto the outside world
created a terrifying external world of his own making.
The need to cope with such a world awakened in his
hungry self an impotent rage reflected in his dreams
and in his everyday behavior. Analysis gradually
revealed the inflated narcissistic self-concept to be a
pathological formation to defend against severe
aggression. What ultimately had to be achieved was a
surrender of his narcissistic defense for reality—a
reality which would provide him real achievement and
normal self-esteem.

Specific transference problems arose throughout
Sumner's analysis. While he idealized the analyst he
also externalized the pathological grandiose self,
including the pathological grandiose "bad" self, onto
the analyst and therefore loved, feared, blamed, and
hated him. The full-blown narcissistic transference
was allowed to develop for a time and was ultimately

replaced by a transference neurosis. Sumner was dominated in his self-esteem regulation by the aim of attaining a *perfect* self image, a perfect experience, both in his narcissistic behavior and especially in his homosexual behavior. This can be likened to a state of being in which the nursing infant only sees the perfect image of the mother's breast in his mouth (de Saussure 1971).

The homosexual encounter itself was intimately related to the pathological narcissism. It represented a search for the narcissistic self-representation and for the grandiose self-representation. In uniting with another man, there was a fusion of the self with various images of both mother and father without facing the imminent danger of loss of self at the hands of the mother. Suffering from a severe loss of normal narcissistic self-esteem, and filled with pathologically disturbed relations to internalized objects, Sumner remedied his sense of emptiness and inertia by giving pleasure to an external object and the self simultaneously. In the homosexual act, he induced dependence in his partner and compelled an external object into instinctual surrender. This augmented his sense of power, reduced his sense of isolation, and captured a pseudoempathy for the external world through a "primitive mode of communication" (Khan 1965). What was lacking, however, as in all homosexual encounters, were the abilities to trust and to surrender himself to emotional experiences. Thus the encounter, while averting an intrapsychic trauma and constructing a pseudo–object relationship, always failed in achieving true gratification and true object relations, except in the most transitory fashion.

For a further discussion of the therapeutic problems posed by severe narcissistic character pathology, the reader is referred to chapter 22, "The Selection of Patients and Problems at the Outset," and chapter 23, "Modification of Technique."

Chapter 17
THE CASE OF HARRY
(Schizo-Homosexuality)

Schizo-homosexuals are those homosexuals whose fixation point is in the symbiotic phase. Accordingly, their symptom is part and parcel of a psychotic condition. They are often seen in the psychoanalyst's office for an evaluation of the part played by the homosexuality in the causation of their psychosis. Of overriding importance is the treatment of their schizophrenic decompensation with its associated delusions, hallucinations, ideas of reference, and other secondary symptoms of schizophrenia. With the return to a compensated state of schizophrenic adaptation, their homosexual symptoms may remain unaltered alongside the primary symptoms of schizophrenia. Paranoia and paranoid symptomatology are striking features in such cases.

Harry was a thirty-five-year-old white male of Mediterranean extraction who was admitted to the hospital in an acutely psychotic, delirious state, following an overdose of hypnotic medication the previous evening. He was detoxified within twelve hours. This suicidal gesture was the product of his rage

I am indebted to Arnold Merriam, M.D. and Denise Phillips, M.S.W., of the Jacobi Hospital, Albert Einstein College of Medicine, Department of Psychiatry, for the use of this clinical material.

at his parents for attempting to restrain a rigid, obsessional, compulsive housecleaning ritual. Although his obsessive cleanliness dated back to early childhood and his parents had disapproved of his cleaning habits, they had never attempted to restrain him in this manner. Four years previous to hospitalization he had moved back into his parent's home. The continuous intrusion of his cleaning and sweeping prompted his parents to "put a stop" to his compulsive rituals; this prompted Harry, in a fit of rage, to "teach his mother" a lesson by attempting suicide. He had experienced increasing psychological pressure, having developed both hepatitis and syphilis during the previous year. Both diseases had apparently been contracted during homosexual relations with anonymous men. The forced cessation of his obsessional rituals produced an exacerbation in hallucinatory material, present for years, and resulted in flagrant bizarre behavior of a psychotic nature. Harry aimed at "drowning out" the voices in his head by his suicide attempt. He reported that these chronic auditory hallucinations of grandiose and derogatory content had become more intense and unsettling. The kitchen stove told him "You win" and a picture of Jesus and the Last Supper said "Up—you're a Saint!" For months before hospitalization he heard both male and female voices telling him to "take abuse" or "take shit" and interpreted these as the trials he had to pass to earn status. He felt that since the world was already destroyed, everyone he saw was dead and his parents were "impostors."

A close perusal of Harry's history revealed that since the age of thirty he had suffered from a complicated delusional system. This first began as referential ideas which led to feelings of persecution and then to world destruction fantasies. At this point he had delusions of grandeur in the setting of new world reconstruction fantasies. The latter state constituted a quieting delusion of grandeur. In his new "kingdom" all wishes would be instantly fulfilled and all disease and unhappiness nonexistent. He populated the world with people "all pink, without sexual organs." The men would be dressed in long robes, like popes, and the women in flowing gowns. He would go to church, lie down on the altar, and "give everything to everybody." It appeared this delusion relieved him of deep shame and guilt for wishing to be a woman and for his homosexuality.

The developmental history revealed that he was considered "strange" from early childhood, had never had a close male friend, and had always liked to be with women. As far back as he could remember he was ashamed of his body and did not feel it would be accepted by his peers. He was overly attached to his mother and at four years of age his mother, anxious over the size of his penis, took him to a doctor for an examination. His academic performance was poor and spotty and by the eighth grade a priest told him that he was probably a homosexual. His father, a weak, distant, and cold man, was in the Army and absent from the home when the patient was two until he was four and a half. Upon the father's return the patient was so frightened of him that he dared not look him in the eyes. By four and a half there was a strong female identification and extreme closeness with his mother. By five he liked to stay at home and help his mother in the tasks around the house. Also at five another male child was born, with whom he never got along.

It appeared that his mother was well aware of her son's tendency to effeminancy and homosexuality from his early years but seems to have fostered rather than discouraged it.

At the age of eleven, while still prepubertal, he willingly performed fellatio "on older men in the bushes" and was "amazed" at the size of the men's organs. A year later he engaged in anal intercourse as the passive partner. By age twelve he masturbated, always with fantasies of naked men. Throughout his teenage years he had frequent homosexual contacts. He asserted: "I like doing what makes *him* happy—I just want him to accept me and my body." His favorite fantasy was that of a big strong man with construction boots. He felt alienated from overtly feminine homosexual men and said, "there's a mix-up in their genes. They hate their mothers and I *love* my mother—as a mother only."

Harry was overconcerned with his body and with maintaining a slim figure in order to be attractive to other men at the sauna clubs he frequented. In his adult life he had three sexual contacts with women and two of the three were with prostitutes. The third involved anal intercourse without vaginal penetration. He regarded women as dirty and sexually unattractive. His longest sexual relationship was with one man for six months on an intermittent basis. He frequently cruised and had relations with up to three strangers in one evening.

During his six-week hospitalization Harry gradually lost his delusional system. He still maintained, however, that there are "bubbles" in the sky which he could not get rid of. He stated that neither his homosexuality nor his obsessive cleanliness was a problem for him. Auditory and almost all visual hallucinations vanished during the period of hospitalization. No attempt was made to alter his homosexuality during hospitalization and he was discharged as recovered from the more intense and florid aspects of his psychosis.

Harry's symptomatology directly relates to his lifelong symbiotic attachment to his mother. His primary feminine identification with her, as well as a wish and/or dread of merging with her with a threat of loss of self, persists. His greatest security is in emulating the mother. In his feminine identification he attempts to form relationships with external objects through homosexuality, incorporating the body and masculinity of a man, thereby defending himself against disruptive incorporation by the mother. In his homosexuality he is attempting to stabilize a fragile and chaotic ego structure and to create object relationships which are essentially fusions, as they have been destroyed by the schizophrenic process. (See chapter 26 for a complete discussion of the schizo-homosexual's severe ego deficits and incapacity to establish object relations.)

This patient presented paranoid symptoms coexisting with homosexuality. A study of his delusional system in comparison to Freud's (1911) study of Schreber's delusional system reveals a striking similarity in that both individuals harbor unconscious and later conscious wishes to be women. The function of their quieting delusion of grandeur was to decrease the pressure and conflict over homosexual urges. It is now well known that paranoia may be a defense against passive homosexuality, may coexist with homosexuality, and in certain instances may be present without homosexuality.

As early as 1895 Freud suggested that paranoia is a neurosis of *defense*; its chief mechanism is projection. On November 21, 1906 (Freud 1911, editor's note), he presented a case of female paranoia before the Vienna Psychoanalytic Society in which he made a connection between paranoid and repressed passive homosexuality. In Freud's account of the Schreber case the idea of being transformed into a woman was the salient feature and the earliest germ of his delusional system.

Harry's object relations were alternately bizarre, absent, and distorted. His homosexual contacts attempted to create an object relation by finding a narcissistic representation of himself. Object relations conflicts dominated his life, and anxiety and guilt were associated with the failure of development in the phase of self-object differentiation. There was a gross impairment of thinking with hallucinations and delusions. Thinking was predominately of the paranoid type with bizarre ideation; his self-concept was lacking and ego boundaries were severely impaired.

Finally it should be noted that in some individuals of inherited schizophrenic disposition the sexual organization remains at a rudimentary level because at least two of its essential constituents, pleasure and love, are innately defective (Rado 1956). Therefore, sexual activity is blurred or floundering and a chaotic sexual organization is present. Schizophrenics try to make human contact and will try many forms of perversion but with very little or no affect and with little empathy for their partners.

Bleuler (1911) was the first to note that "perversions, alongside the manifestations of normal drives, are much more pronounced in schizophrenics than in neurotics. The homosexual components, especially, play an unexpected large role" (pp. 410-411).

Discussion

Aside from the importance of the case of Harry as an example of schizo-homosexuality, its particular value lies in the observation that the history of his homosexuality, its emergence, and its enactment bear striking similarities to the homosexual activity of preoedipal homosexuals, Type II, at least on superficial examination. For example, Harry, like preoedipal Type II homosexuals, had an early, intense fixation to his mother; severe separation anxiety; early pronounced feminine identification; severe difficulties in relating to the opposite sex from his earliest years; homosexual interests beginning in childhood; and essentially exclusive homosexual relations through life. Such surface manifestations should, however, be viewed against the backdrop of the degree of ego-pathology present; this is strikingly dissimilar from that found in the preoedipal Type II homosexual and should not be confused with it. In this instance, the presence of overt psychotic processes obviously militates against any significant similarities.

A chart comparing schizo-homosexuality and preoedipal homosexuality is supplied in chapter 26. It is useful at this point to summarize these differences, which were brilliantly defined by Bak (1971) in his important paper, "Object Relationships in Schizophrenia and Perversion." There he noted the following qualities in homosexuality in the schizophrenic in comparison to nonpsychotic homosexuality: (1) Homosexual impulses as well as other sexual impulses are a frantic attempt to maintain object relations. (2) Homosexual impulses so often seen in paranoid schizophrenia are not "etiological" but these conflicts and their delusional elaboration are "consequences of the schizophrenic process rather than causative of it." (3) Perverse actions in schizophrenics with self-object dedifferentiation show significant differences from the well-organized perversion in people who have better object relations and considerable ego functions. (4) There is a basic qualitative difference between the schizophrenic process, the perversions and the neuroses, and the incidental psychoses. In the incidental psychosis there is a temporary abandonment of object-representation. (5) In true perversions object relations are maintained despite a fused body image and confusion in genital representation in contrast to perverse activities in the schizophrenic, where object relations are not maintained . (6) Paranoid delusions with homosexual content do occur in schizophrenics. In those instances, however, an object relationship may be highly pathological and yet nevertheless be preserved. The delusions are an attempt to maintain object relations in the face of (a) severe regression, (b) attempted destruction of object relations, (c) the presence of a primary defect or deficiency in the autonomous functions of the ego, and (d) the inability to maintain a protective stimulus barrier. If the regression is severe, the delusional content contains a less experiential basis and a well-structured delusion cannot be formed or maintained.

Chapter 18
THE CASE OF ANNA
(Preoedipal, Type I)

Anna entered psychoanalytic therapy at the age of twenty-four with complaints of moderate depression and feelings of self-depreciation. She was an attractive young woman with a figure of average proportions and a bright, winning personality. For the past six months she had begun to feel intensely drawn toward a girl and "wanted a caressing thing with her."

The patient had not worked for several months and felt "lost, unable to function and with no direction. I want to love somebody and I want them to love me. No one will love me because I'm nothing." She was attracted to women but at the same time felt that she liked men. She was not "a part of this world, not coping and achieving like others," and she urgently desired success. A few days before deciding to start treatment she had felt "terribly affectionate" toward a girl who hugged her. On occasion, when her anxiety became intense, she felt she was in a state of "no relatedness, dizziness, and something like 'unreality.'"

She had become increasingly concerned over the number of affairs she had had with men during the past three or four years.

Immediately preceding entry into analysis she had

the feeling that she was "walking as if in a dream, everything seemed so strange" (feelings of depersonalization). She was dizzy and felt very depressed. "I just couldn't relate to anyone and I hadn't talked to anybody for weeks." In actuality, she was overwhelmed by her wishes for homosexual relations and concerned about the direction her life was taking. "The day before I came to you I wasn't noticing a thing. I was completely removed from everything. I had terrible guilt feelings about my family, about my mother. I met a girl to whom I had declared my undying love last winter and she had said to me, 'You're a phony' because I wouldn't go through with it."

Developmental History

When Anna was born her father had so wanted a boy that he had chosen a name only for a son. Her mother was planning to separate from her father but her pregnancy intervened. The mother "wore the pants in the family" and was, in fact, the matriarch dominating the home. Anna had two sisters, one four years older and one six years younger. She pictured her parents as a martyred mother and a rejecting father. One of her earliest memories was of crying over her lost galoshes and nobody wanting to help her.

At around age two and a half she recalled watching her father urinate and she would hold his penis while he was doing so up until the age of four. At this time she experienced a severe trauma. The father suddenly turned upon her when she attempted this act, shouting, "Leave me alone, you slob." She was dimly aware that this persistent memory had somehow influenced the course of her entire life. She was extremely hurt, crestfallen, and guilty over having done something "dirty."

After this incident she gave up trying to hug and kiss her father or get close to her mother, experiencing a keen sense of loneliness and deprivation. She developed nightmares of falling from high places and obsessional and compulsive acts such as having to count all the tiles in the bathroom. At five she was a problem eater and would occasionally vomit upon being forced to eat. She recalled her mother continually saying, "You'll be sorry when I'm gone." At about the same time she developed crushes on girls and a horror of insects.

She remembered being thrilled when a girl of eighteen approached her lovingly. "She was just lovely. I really felt like a boy and that she wanted me as a boy." She also recalled being kissed by a girl of ten and feeling immensely pleased. At the age of eight or nine she had crushes on boys in her class and would "beam" when an older boy paid attention to her.

At the age of six an especially significant incident occurred. Her older sister nearly drowned while Anna helplessly watched her sink into the water. "I saw her going down and just stood there." She felt guilty for doing nothing and for watching her sister thrashing about in the water. Also at this age her younger sister was born. The father again showed great disappointment that he still did not have a boy. Anna complained bitterly that the father "paid very little attention to us." Shortly after the birth of the sister the mother left the home temporarily. The patient felt abandoned, rejected, and "terror-struck. She really did leave us."

At seven she recalled how ugly she felt. "I had buck teeth, a very long neck, dental braces. I felt unwanted and unlovable." She remembered an incident in which her father, angry that she had not moved from the living room floor where she was lying, suddenly kicked her in the head. She had harbored a profound resentment toward him for this over the years. At age eight she struck her sister full force with a baseball bat and the sister was ill for a number of days. The patient became extremely remorseful. In the same year her father developed a "semi-nervous breakdown." She remembered his crying, head between his hands, and moving agitatedly around the room. He was prone to depressions and would constantly complain "there is nothing to live for." This produced severe feelings of anxiety and helplessness in Anna. Negativism permeated her life; she repeatedly commented to the analyst that "no good will come from other people or from the world and no happiness can ever come from men."

At the age of nine she was subjected to two traumatic events. Her appendix ruptured and she required extended hospitalization. She then suffered a fractured skull when she fell off a bicycle. At the age of ten, in the fourth grade, the class was divided and she was separated from her favorite teacher (the good mother); she developed severe anorexia and lost twenty pounds. In the fifth grade she was very unhappy. "I had a miserable teacher, very unloving. She would yell all the time at the students and had a very bad temper." Anna did not want to go to school and would complain of stomach cramps and headaches, and would cry and vomit. Until this change in teachers she had been the teacher's pet.

Her father tended to treat her more like a boy than a girl, occasionally taking her to ballgames. "I was a good baseball player and even boxed with boys." At the age of twelve, at the time of puberty, she stopped playing with boys and spent a great deal of time alone. She began to develop headaches due to what she now perceived as anger. She became depressed whenever she observed someone whom she thought was "great," a female movie star or an attractive, confident-looking woman on the street. She knew she could never meet them.

By thirteen, when she had developed a feminine figure, she was unable to take her clothes off in front of her sisters and would undress only in private, believing herself to be gawky and unattractive. She loved to be with older people. Upon entering high school she felt severe inhibitions in getting up in front of others. She had nightmares about her teeth being crooked and ugly and about having a long nose and a long, skinny neck. Up until the age of sixteen, she recalled, she "would have given anything to be a boy" and it was an amazing revelation at this time "that I was becoming attractive." She had to accept the fact that she "was becoming physically attractive. I don't think I wanted to be a boy any more."

She felt she could not wear sweaters or any clothing which hugged her body closely and required loose-fitting garments to conceal her attractive figure. Since age eighteen she had not known how to deal with her increasingly attractive appearance. She was pleased, but at the same time upset, with the full development of her breasts. She tended to be critical of them, resenting them because of her male identification. The presence of breasts would make it more difficult to acquire the feminine love she so urgently desired; masculine love could only be disappointing and depressing. Also at eighteen her older sister attempted suicide and was hospitalized.

When she first had intercourse at twenty-one she felt it was "great." But within a week she developed strange stomach pains and fears of having a cancer of the genital system. Both reactions disappeared within a short time. Following this first relationship she had intercourse with a number of men, which exacerbated her guilt. Although the attention given her by men was stimulating and exciting, it confused her because she felt she was interested in becoming a man herself. Simultaneously she had an intense preoccupation with being loved and accepted by prominent women of the stage or screen and she vowed that she would somehow go into the theater or movies. She undertook the relentless pursuit of contacts with well-known women in the theatrical world, which led indirectly to homosexual involvement with one of them a year and a half after beginning therapy.

During the course of analysis Anna became prominent in her professional field with proportionately high financial rewards. Even this, however, was not sufficient gratification to quiet her anxiety and feelings of deprivation.

A year prior to starting analysis she met a "lesbian with whom I had a big physical thing. It made me furious and excited, too. I usually fantasied kissing the breasts of this girl but at the same time she would be me" (identification with the female partner). "If I wasn't with men I usually would think about women and their breasts and sucking them. If I have an attraction to a man I cannot eat if I've seen him only a few times and have no security with him." The problem of eating was intimately connected with her feelings of gratification and worth. Whenever deprived, food was bad and made her nauseous, just as love from women was bad and love from men was not possible.

She bitterly complained that she could not show affection but that she desired to do so. "My father was not a demonstrative person and he stopped us from being demonstrative and mother had nothing to offer at all. Why can't I show affection? I get terribly affectionate when I'm out, especially with a girl. I feel uncomfortable even with a man. I'm so conscious of it, I'm conscious that I'm doing something that it was taboo to do, feel these things for girls."

Major Psychodynamic Factors

The nucleus of Anna's fears was the repressed emotions centered around her oral deprivation, and her severe aggression and anxiety over the wish to merge with the bad mother. She feared abandonment by the mother, which she consciously experienced as a fear of starvation and a lack of protection. As a child she constantly imagined that her mother would leave her; this reinforced the wish to merge with her. It also frightened her, as it would mean her own destruction, loss of ego, and subjection to being "nothing" but a piece of excrement. There was no support to be expected from the father, no help, no reassurance, no protection, no feeding, and certainly no love.

During the oedipal period she was subject to severe rejection, shame, and guilt over her sexual curiosity and feelings toward her father which he himself had provoked. She could find salvation in becoming a boy.

Until puberty she played baseball and went to ballgames with her father, but nevertheless felt that he basically disliked her because she was a girl. Since she could not attain his love even though she tried to please him by acting like a boy, she instead began to seek love from other girls. In this way she gained the identity of the beloved woman and was orally gratified. It was the reemergence of these tendencies during her late teens and early adulthood and the conflicts and symptoms which they produced which led her to seek psychoanalytic treatment. Whenever she tried to feel like and be a woman she developed anxiety and fears that she would only be abandoned and hurt.

In the male position she unconsciously endowed herself with a penis and tried to find protection, love, and pride in herself. Her wish to be a boy and have security had survival value; in the feminine role she could anticipate only rejection and loss. To be a female meant subjection to intense anxiety expressed in dreams as castration, attacks by women, fears of death, and becoming feces. It was a sign of unworthiness, unlovability, and vulnerability. To be a girl also exposed her to tremendous aggression toward her mother. She often commented that "I am afraid to let out the hate toward my mother's ineptitude, self-concern, and lack of love for her children."

Anna attempted in childhod to become feminine but this was too dangerous; she feared her mother would attack her, and she would retaliate with murderous impulses. During her active homosexual episodes she would allow herself "to be walked all over in order to get love," to diminish her rage and guilt, and to rid herself of abandonment anxiety. To her it was the choice of the lesser evil. The homosexuality revolved around two factors: fear of merging with a depriving, destructive, and abandoning mother and the murderous hatred behind it; and disappointment at the hands of the father.

She was compelled to deny her sexual identity and even at an early age had displaced the penis to the breast and imagined she possessed a penis. Her aim was to forcibly extract from women their femininity, love, affection, and narcissistic and oral supplies. She had an unconscious rage at men; because her father originally rejected her, she felt she would always be rejected by men. Her preferred sexual activity with men was fellatio, except when the man proved "much more powerful" than she. Then she could have vaginal intercourse with orgasm on occasion, as a more powerful man neutralized her own sadistic impulses. By sucking the penis (breast) she was incorporating it and being "filled up."

Anna vacillated between severe self-depreciation and a narcissistic overvaluation of the self. "One of the things I fear about myself is that there is nothing I cannot do if I want to but I have severe inhibitions. That's the way I feel about my work. If I get down to the point of doing it I will be great. I want to express myself."

Anna's aim in life was to prove that men would only disappoint her, degrade her, and make it impossible for her to find happiness as a woman. She could achieve satisfaction, support, and gratification of dependency needs only through women. From women she wanted food, love, milk, and breasts, but in her dreams women often turned into frightening animals that would attack her. If, in a dream, she felt loved by women she would soon find herself "being attacked by them, by a cat, angry and mad, tearing me apart." In her dreams of men she wished to attack the penis; at first she wished to play with it, but then to strike at it or to appropriate it for herself. She dreamt of castration and death at the hands of her mother if she dared to become a woman. When deprived by both male and female lovers, she dreamt of loss of food, starvation, and emptiness. She vacillated between, on the one hand, intense feelings of love for women and a wish to be close to their breasts, and, on the the other, equally intense feelings for men who would satisfy and protect her.

The following dream typifies her strong penis envy: "I was washing a little boy, about two or three. I was giving him a bath. He was fighting. I think he had a grown-up face. I was scrubbing his back very hard. He was relaxed. I massaged his back and shoulders. There was a sexual connection. I shouldn't be doing this. I also thought I wanted to wash his penis but I didn't dare. I was very curious to see if he had an erection. I looked down. There was a penis there and it was not attached. I thought 'Now they're going to know what I've done.' Then it didn't look like a penis, it was something else."

Whenever she felt she had no one, neither man nor woman, she had unconscious fears of "being attacked by a woman and being eaten by her, becoming feces and being abused." Futhermore, she dreamed of swirling into a large whirlpool-like abyss which would engulf her. This was quieting, dependent, and loving, but at the same time most frightening. She felt that it represented a fear of merging with her mother, of becoming one with her, but this meant becoming dissolved, impotent, unable to function, incompetent and a "nothing" (regression to the amorphous undifferentiated phase).

Her dreams indicated a strong wish to possess a penis. "I had strange warts on my stomach and they began to grow like on a stem. I was upset when I saw them and my father said, 'Why don't you cut the stems?' I said, 'No, it would hurt.' To cut off the stem it would hurt me." Anna easily deciphered the meaning of this dream. She would not give up her masculinity because she could not trust men and would only suffer at their hands were she to become feminine.

Another dream referred to her oral needs and the deprivation which provoked them: "A little girl is going down on me. I don't know who—it was either my niece or a little girl in a show I had seen. We had been joking with each other in real life. I was being pursued by this child. I knew that's what she wanted to do to me and I didn't want her to. I didn't want her to suck me but I seemed to remember someone encouraging me to do it. Finally I let her and I became very excited by it. I tried to get away and she kept pursuing me. I used to find that very, very exciting with men—finally it was so exciting I'd have to have intercourse right away." It seemed to her that the penis must be a breast. She tried to take femininity from women in sucking their breasts. "I thought maybe this kid tried to take my femininity. I seemed to be the woman and this little girl last night, when I looked very feminine and I got a lot of admiring looks at the theater, was also then interested in me because I was good, attractive, charming, and lovely. In the dream there was a lot of fluid coming out from me, like it was milk, and the little

girl was sucking it. Perhaps I was the little girl." Her
homosexual oral incorporative wishes were desires to
suck and be filled up by the maternal milk displaced
from her mother onto a little child.

A typical dream follows: "Ladies with blond mus-
taches, homosexuals hugging and kissing each other
on the train, and I'm hugging and kissing my younger
sister and Mother is nodding approval. I'm thinking 'I
haven't done this in years' but I feel very funny. I am
then eating fruit salad sensuously and sitting down
with two Puerto Ricans who own the place and who I
had assumed were poor slobs. They wanted to put the
bill on the house after friendly conversation. I was
buttering up to a girl, not making it too well. I was
insincere. A stiff piece of fruit is in my mouth and I am
mortified." She demonstrated here her oral needs and
her feelings that her mother would approve of her
becoming obedient, but demonstrated at the same time
her inability to accept the role of making love to a
woman. She wanted to stop but could not. Men, on the
other hand, were simply foreigners, lowly in caste, who
really wanted things "on the house" and who did not
want to give to women.

She urgently desired in most of her dreams to become
female but could not produce proof that she was
desirable as a woman. She expressed this in the
following dream: "The proof to my mother that I was a
female was to show them that I had my diploma. It's in
a tan leather cover with another document. My mother
tells me to find it. I begin searching the house and
they're nudging me and I can't find anything.
Suddenly I remember I took it to my apartment where
it belongs. The other document is a birth certificate.
They're mine and I want them with me. Daddy is mad

at me. I go home to find it but I cannot." The dream and the associations made evident that the deprivations in the dream were a form of retaliation and vengeance against the father. She hurt herself in order to hurt him and thereby showed him what he had done to her by not accepting her as a girl.

Course of Therapy

In the transference Anna resented the analyst's not becoming the good mother and father to her by supplying all the needed satisfactions and gratifications for which she yearned. These needs, met by her homosexual partner, had the impossible price of a sexual transformation which she was unable to make, feeling repelled by playing an anatomical role contrary to reality. During the course of therapy she renewed her determination to find a male who could offer enough protection, strength, and love for her to marry. She has learned at first hand that "homosexuality was futile."

At the beginning of treatment Anna's resistance consisted of feeling wronged, of blaming the analyst, and of suffering at his hands. She wanted to evade all psychodynamic material which she found disturbing and whenever pressed to reveal her feelings, she stated she "felt nothing." She repeatedly asserted that the analyst wanted to "put things in my mind." She taunted him by saying, "I know what you want me to say but I just won't give it to you."She felt no one had ever really cared about her, and the analyst certainly would not, so why should she expose her intimate thoughts and feelings? She likened him to her father, who wanted to seduce her into holding his penis but who would, in the end, reject and debase her, and make her feel ashamed. Beneath these feelings was a strong affection and transference love. On occasion she imagined that the analyst was taking advantage by making fun of her or even masturbating behind her back. Furthermore, he was rejecting her by not enjoying her sexually or by not allowing her to enjoy him.

She had immense oral cravings for love and feared expressing this imperative need. Unconsciously she imagined herself as a very aggressive, unattractive, destructive, and "smelly" object. She "gave off smells" and was filled with bad things. "If I show my evilness everyone will abandon me." Simultaneously she angrily insisted that everyone give her love and take care of her. She wanted to yell and scream her hatred of her mother. Most of all she feared that there would be "no response" from either parent were she to show her affection and love. She projected this fear onto all important figures in her life. She felt that in her anger "I will lose my mind and explode" and that certainly as a result she would not be accepted by anyone.

Anna continually chose men whom she knew were afraid of women and who were no threat to her. During the early phases of therapy, whenever a relationship with a man grew emotionally intimate, she would destroy it with the rationalization that, "He will see my dullness." When attracted to a man she usually felt elated, but it never lasted. Despite her self-accusation of dullness she had always somehow felt creative even while feeling she wasn't. "Other people have a base from which they operate—a big thing which they have—but I don't have anything that I really love to do and I have no one to say to me, 'Boy, you're good.'"

Whenever feminine wishes were stimulated during the course of analysis she attempted to deny her warm and heterosexual feelings and would be upset by them. She tried to deny her positive feelings for the analyst by imagined abuse and she accused the analyst of bad treatment. For long periods of time she blamed the analysis for her frustration and continually expressed a chronic pessimism as to its outcome.

Anna's relationship to men began to improve markedly midway in the analysis. In the setting of a pronounced feeling of rejection by a man she hoped to marry, she became involved in a homosexual relationship with a somewhat older and "glamorous" woman. This was the patient's only sustained homosexual relationship. It lasted for a year and a half and it both "terrified and gratified" her. The rejection by her male lover led to a regressed and renewed search for good maternal love which required extensive psychoanalytic work to overcome. The female partner was wealthy, popular, and insistent. She represented a grandiose and narcissistic object choice. Despite the patient's later protestations that she be allowed to continue her heterosexual life concurrently, the partner managed to isolate her from contacts with men. During this homosexual relationship she interrupted the analysis for months at a time, traveling with her lover to distant cities and returning to therapy only intermittently.

Most of all Anna enjoyed the feeling of being held like a child, sucking her partner's breasts, and being gently soothed. Introduction of the partner's finger into the vagina with orgasm and mutual cunnilingus left her somewhat depressed and repelled. The lover's intense jealousy and inability to tolerate any contact with men on Anna's part forced a separation and ultimate break. The patient suffered feelings of loneliness and despair. She renewed her anger toward men. While she condemned them as "immature and weak, unable to offer fulfillment," she still raged at their lack of interest in marrying her. She consistently chose men who were unsuitable or unavailable for marriage. For example, prior to this homosexual affair she had lived with a married man, the father of three children, for over two years.

From her female lover she received much help in her work and became quite successful both professionally and financially. It seemed that only through women could she be gratified, taken care of, protected, and loved. Her partner continually reassured her of her deep concern for her and her wish that she be happy. Here was "a dream come true," but with the important feature that it was provided by a female, a fact she found impossible to completely accept. She both enjoyed and abhorred vaginal penetration by the finger or tongue of her partner. Upon awakening in the morning and finding herself entwined with the body of a female she felt anxious and depressed, but welcomed the protection, solace, and concern as well as the orgasm.

Following one brief separation from her partner Anna reentered therapy, complaining of severe weight loss, intense stomach cramps, excruciating headaches, and anxiety. The only relief from her anxiety was the analytic sessions and her work.

During breaks from her partner she began to regularly have successful orgastic experiences with men but continued to choose men who were unsuitable. She complained that there were no desirable men around to marry and that she had no interest in marrying in any case, as a man would only treat her like her father had. She did not trust men and their promises. She wished she could somehow enjoy a friendly maternal protective relationship with a female without the sexual component.

In the later phases of the analysis she recalled with great affective release that she used to watch her father urinate. "I used to ask to hold his penis and he let me. This must have gone on for about a year and then suddenly I asked if I could and started to and he said, 'Oh, leave me alone, you slob.'" She was "extremely hurt and insulted" and her "face felt very warm.... You know my father was really a very modest man." After that there was "the no kissing thing" with her father. She felt "like a slob. I felt like I wanted to do something dirty and I wanted to be a boy definitely. I would go out and sell papers and things like that." She connected this incident to her inability to give to anyone since that time. She was stingy about food and money. She did not feed herself and was "a skinny maverick. I'm always so conscious of what it's costing me and I'm always getting by on the bare minimum in life."

She then dreamed: "My older sister is eating next to my father. I am across from them. Her food drips on his leg. He is very annoyed and states, 'Why are you such a slob?' and he wipes food off his knee very thoroughly. I feel for her as her eyes fill up with tears. She cries and tells him off, 'What's so important about your lousy clothes? Is it so important that you should hurt my feelings?' I'm with her as she keeps on and I look at Daddy who feels very bad and then I'm with him." Obviously she projected onto her sister this very incident. The timeless indestructibility of the unconscious became manifest: the dream revealed to her that her father actually experienced an ejaculation (the spilled food) when she had handled his penis. His guilt had led him to blame her for his sexual excitement. By calling her a slob," he had attempted to deny his ejaculation and had projected his guilt onto her. She now understood the traumatic incident correctly and realized it was he who was the "slob." The source of her deep and abiding bitterness against him and other men was this unfair and hypocritical condemnation.

Anna realized that she could be protected from her homosexual drive by the love of a strong man, as the following dream revealed: "I was grown up. I was with a man, an elderly man but not my father, maybe a boyfriend. I was looking for a place to spend a vacation. I said 'Why not the place I used to go when I was a child?' I wanted to go back [the patient cries and sobs]. Back where we used to go when my father would come up during the summer for two weeks, a big, round-front car, swimming. I don't know what set me off. I am very happy. It reminds me of all the wonderful things he could have given me, if he only could have loved me. I just wanted him, to throw myself at him, and he would grab and hug and kiss me. It's the first time I've thought of that in years. I'm so happy to be back there. I'm just dying to go back there sometime and see it again.

"I'm crawling in the dream. I'm just like a little child. I'm crawling toward my father. Isn't it funny I can't walk on the ground, just on a sort of plank. Then a terrible fright. Mother and a man in an adjoining room. I thought Mother might walk in when I'm hugging my father and ask 'What is this all about?' [oedipal conflict]. Oh, fuck her. I want father to explain to mother that I wasn't doing anything. In the dream I was dying to get back to the place where my father hugged me nice and firm. I think the man was you, the man with gray hair, helping me across. I guess helping me to heterosexuality. He was telling me to stand up and walk across and I wasn't afraid of falling off but I just wanted to stay on the plank that I was on. A round lawn and a hole in it. It's all like a vagina. Somehow it had something to do with the boy-girl thing. This is not intellectual. I think perhaps it's rebirth, coming out of a vagina, and you're finally joined with a man. I must have been very happy there when I was a child."

After four and a half years of psychoanalytic treatment Anna terminated therapy because her employment required her to move to a distant city. The initial symptoms with which she entered therapy, such as anxiety, depression, feelings of worthlessness, attacks of depersonalization, distortions in body image, and feelings of emptiness, had all disappeared. Only minor fluctuations in feelings of self-worth were evident; narcissistic grandiosity as well as profound feelings of inferiority had profoundly diminished. Object relations, impulse control, ego boundaries, reality testing, and capacity to sustain affectionate contacts with both men and women were markedly improved. Successful performance and financial and professional reward reinforced her self-concept. She had developed the capacity to love a man and hopefully looked forward to marriage.

Recapitulation

Anna had been unable to successfully traverse the separation-individuation phase of development. In addition, she utterly lacked the support, reassurance, protection, and strength of her father. Her mother, upon whom she depended for oral gratification, denied and deprived her. This intensified her oral cravings and her desire to be close and never separated from her mother. Anna experienced any attempt to move away from the dependency toward her mother as grave anxiety from both the fear of retaliation and the fear of her own aggression toward her mother. She had to substitute teachers, older girlfriends, and other females for love and affection. Her father reacted to her with severe aggression, kicking her in the head, deploring her femininity, openly wishing for a boy. becoming depressed and severely rejecting, and shaming her for her sexual interest in him during the early oedipal phase. She could only regress to the previous fixation to her mother, but her image of her mother was filled with malevolence, inadequacy, and martyrdom. As a result she searched for other women (good mothers). She greeted all signs of femininity, including the wearing of feminine clothing, development of her breasts, and menstruation, with antagonism. She felt these could lead to further devaluation and demeanment. While unconsciously desiring femininity, she equated femininity with extreme worthlessness.

Anna represents those patients who suffer from the form of homosexuality designated in my classification as Preoedipal Form, Type I. Her deep unconscious tie with a malevolent mother represents a fixation with a concomitant nuclear wish for and dread of merging with her. She expressed this as a fear of loss of self, being swallowed, becoming a fecal mass and so on. Her salvation lay in finding the good mother in the form of a loving and caring female in homosexual relations.

Superimposed on her preoedipal conflict was an oedipal conflict of severe proportions which could be discerned only during the course of analytic therapy. Her denial of tender, affectionate, and loving feelings for men arose from traumatic incidents suffered at the hands of a rejecting father whose love she urgently desired, attempted to acquire, and finally surrendered in despair. The successful working through of the oedipal material was of paramount importance to the ultimate solution of her problems.

Chapter 19
THE CASE OF SARAH
(Preoedipal, Type II)

Sarah was in her mid-thirties when she first entered analysis. She complained of anxiety, fears of losing her girlfriend, migraine headaches, depression, and phobias concerning food contamination. Though her symptomatology appeared very severe, she performed, throughout her analysis, in a demanding position in the field of economic research.

Sarah might well be placed in the group of homosexual women who identify themselves with the female love object, not with the male. The external object relationship to women is very imperfect, merely representing her own femininity through identification. This particular group has little or no interest in men and their libido centers exclusively on women, employing other women to exhibit their femininity. One notes here the correspondence to the male homosexual who identifies himself with the maleness of his partner.

The patient had been overtly homosexual since the age of nineteen, and had lived with approximately seven partners, her relationships ranging from one to two years except for her present relationship, which had lasted a decade. She experienced little sexual contact or enjoyment except during the first years of this relationship, the union being essentially that of a companionate pair. The companionship, however, was riddled with strife and intermittent episodes of envy, hostility, and jealousy.

Developmental History

Early in life Sarah was told that her mother's milk had disagreed with her and that she had frequently vomited in infancy. Although breast-fed, she did "not get much milk" and lost weight, "screaming all the time." At the age of one year she overturned a teakettle and severely burned most of the skin on her hands. This injury required prolonged and painful treatment and mechanical restraint, which undoubtedly increased her sense of deprivation. From birth to two years of age she suffered from an eczema over the entire surface of her body. At approximately twelve months she had worms, for which she was given antihelminthic medication which produced considerable chronic abdominal pain. She sucked her thumb up to the age of six and was cured only after her mother put "bitter medicine" on her thumb. She still remembers this as having caused "a queer feeling in my head."

She reported a screen memory, between the ages of two and three, of a violent flood which she thought was her actual first memory. Her father was knocked down, the house inundated, and she recalled clouds "dipping down" and her cowering in the attic. Around the age of three she felt very close to her father and believed that her mother was "jealous." Sarah's father was a rather unhappy, withdrawn person who, apart from one reversal during his daughter's adolescence, had been a successful businessman. He was very fond of the patient but as a child she rejected him because of unconscious guilt. This was due to her fear of retaliation from her mother, whom she saw as a cold, unsympathetic woman, subject to episodes of acute depression.

Between the ages of two and three she developed a fear of feathers. Her mother, in order to prevent her from venturing from the top floor to the lower floor of the home, piled feathers at the head of the stairs; this would terrify the child. At the age of five a brother was born toward whom she developed considerable hostility. Between four and five she remembered that she was frequently constipated and forced to drink castor oil. She then developed obsessional thoughts concerning the death of her mother. These continued up to the age of eleven: "If I step on a crack I'll break my mother's back."

Between ages four and five she still felt very close to her father and considered her mother "a terrible creature." For example, "Mother would pour boiling hot water on a spider when she saw one on the porch." At age six the patient recalled actually hating her mother and wanting to kill her. She had fantasies of putting glass in her mother's orange juice in the morning so she would die.

At age five a severe tomboy, she often had fantasies that she was not really a member of her family but belonged to some other family. She hated her little brother, as her mother always seemed to take his part. "I felt I could actually kill him." At seven, another brother was born, whom she liked and dominated. At the age of nine she was aware that she was extremely attracted to a girl of approximately the same age and, in an episode of teasing, took a piece of chocolate away from her, ran away, and ate it. She suddenly felt severe guilt and could not stand to be seen.

From ages eight to twelve, there was a reversal of an
overt fear that she might kill her mother; she began,
instead, to dread that her mother would kill her. On one
occasion at about this time she fell off the roof of the
garage, was knocked unconscious, and suffered
several broken bones. This was in expiation for her
chronic aggressive fantasies toward her mother.

At age nine she had a tonsillectomy and she was sure
she would not survive the surgery. Around that time
she had recurrent dreams of a bear chasing her. She
now felt that this bear was her mother, who hated her
and wanted to murder her. Another recurrent dream
was of standing on the tips of her toes and being
"swished down a long passageway like a penis."

Between ages eleven and twelve she was repelled by
her mother's body and could not stand the sight of it.
She had a very vague recollection of swallowing iodine
at about age fourteen, feeling "terrible and angry at my
mother." At age thirteen, upon first menstruating, she
developed a horror and fear of death and consciously
wished to be a boy. During high school she was a good
student but felt "awkward and different." She became
very interested in religion. Another girl, two years
older than she, told her she was a homosexual and she
felt very relieved and close to this girl.

In early adolescence she had "a vague thought of a
knife and wanting to kill my mother." Also, lying in
bed, she thought, "I will be killed. Up to the time I was
thirteen, whenever my mother would punish me I often
thought she intended to kill me. I sort of had a feeling
that the sausage patties in the pantry—I thought of
them as being poisoned. I've always felt that my
mother didn't love me and she really wanted to kill me.
The only person who was really nice to me was my

grandmother, my father's mother. When my first brother was born I loathed him. He was awfully mean. I think I actually could have killed him if I could have found a way. He was always the baby and I was always left out."

When she was sixteen her father, who had suffered a business reversal, was drinking excessively and there was frequent parental discord. At age eighteen, she entered college and for the first time felt a degree of pleasure and security within herself. She had no crush on anyone during her first year away from home. It was at nineteen that she had her first homosexual contact. She felt terror that she would be "engulfed by the passion" of her homosexual partner during love-making.

A series of affairs with other girls followed this contact. She left college just before she would have received her degree. At the time, she claimed to have lost interest in completing her courses, but came to recognize in treatment that this self-defeating act was due to guilt for the unconscious murderous hatred of her mother and siblings. After leaving college she met the woman with whom she continued to live until entering analysis.

During the father's military service in World War II, when Sarah was in her mid-twenties, they corresponded frequently. She was startled, overwhelmed, and guilty by the evidence of loving feelings in her father's letters. She also felt unaccountably "frightened" by these tender and affectionate messages.

By age twenty-seven, completely immersed in her homosexual way of life, she was often frightened by the possibility that previous homosexual partners might seek retaliation for her having rejected them. A

year later she began to have difficulty with her present
partner, fearing that the woman would leave her,
making her "terribly upset." This was a reflection of
her own ambivalence in the relationship.

Whenever another girl kissed her passionately the
patient would have sudden feelings of panic, terror,
and guilt. This reaction was due to her unconscious
fear of the oral destructiveness of both the other girl
and herself.

In her late twenties she felt threatened by the
developing political factionalism in her place of
employment and her being singled out by the owners
as a troublemaker. She developed feelings of bodily
weakness, a severe degress of apprehension, and a
rash which erupted over her entire body; she was
hospitalized with a diagnosis of erythema-multiforma,
an illness with a potentially fatal outcome. When all
somatic therapies failed she was seen by the attending
psychiatrist at the hospital and with daily psychotherapy she recovered in four weeks.

Sarah had always been jealous of her partner, except
in the very early years of their relationship. Signs of
love and tenderness would temporarily quiet her
jealous fears. Her partner had said that if the patient
were ever unfaithful to her she would "somehow get
even." At age thirty-four, for the first time in her adult
life, she had a conscious fear of being poisoned. This
had been a preoccupation during childhood. Now she
thought her partner would poison her. At this point she
entered psychoanalysis.

Major Psychodynamic Factors

It was evident that Sarah's deepest conflicts consisted of oral incorporation fears of the poisonous bad

maternal object. She feared both incorporating the mother and being incorporated by her (merging with her).

The fear of incorporation is well illustrated in a late childhood experience. "This girl...I felt attracted to her. I felt I loved her very madly. I asked her one day to take my lunch to school. I was teasing her. The girl had little squares of chocolate. I grabbed one and ran and she couldn't really catch me. When she came close to me I popped the chocolate into my mouth. I felt guilty. I felt like a thief. I couldn't stand to be around her after that."

As a consequence of the patient's oral destructive urges she developed a profound sense of guilt. This was in direct correspondence to the degree of her oral sadism. From hating and wishing to destroy the mother (homosexual partner) she instead wished to be desired and loved by her as a reaction-formation.

The childhood event described above represented this patient's inhibitions against taking enjoyment for herself, including sexual or other pleasures in life. "The chocolate...how horrible I felt...absolutely obsessed with guilt. I had taken the chocolate to tease her. Ever since then I've been allergic to it." She had also, until late in the analysis, been afraid ever since of taking oral medication under any circumstances.

The mechanism of homosexuality did not afford the patient more than a marginal degree of comfort and gratification because of the strength of the oral sadism inherent in it, and the fear of the incorporated object (the mother) and its destructive effect upon her. Very often she projected her fear and developed expectations of her partner's retaliation and aggression (paranoid mechanism). While severely inhibited and

constrained sexually, the patient felt extreme rage
when she was not satisfied sexually on those infrequent occasions when she desired sexual relations and
attempted to initiate them. "My feelings of love are so
strong, at these times, more than they should be, so
intense, I feel that I may be raping the girl. I feel that if
I moved toward her and she said no, I think I'd have to
stop and think what to do. I think I might frighten her.
I have a feeling I would rip her vagina with a knife or
kill her or beat her up."

Sarah suffered from the most intense feelings of
inferiority. "A feeling that I'm no damn good and that I
never was, that people have laughed at me all my life
and they know I'm homosexual and they never have
accepted me. I'm afraid of kissing any of these girls.
When I start to kiss them I'm terrified and when I kiss
them I sometimes suddenly grow cold. I guess I'm
afraid of feeling too much, a feeling of great fright. It's
not a fear of being rejected; it's a wave of vulnerability.
I'm afraid of the woman, I guess, and isn't that strange
that I should be since I'm homosexual."

These feelings revealed that the patient was afraid of
her own oral aggressive desires toward the mother
which, carried too far because of her oral sadism,
involved the destruction of the mother, fusion or
merging with her, and loss of identity. Because of her
inhibitions, all sexual partners moved away from her
as the relationship continued. Her jealousy and
aggression then increased and she would get migraine
headaches. They would come on especially when she
was jealous, frightened, feared the loss of her partner,
wished to attack and destroy, or had to suppress her
rage responses. Any attempts to become sexually
intimate with other women terrifed her. "I'm afraid of

my own feelings, I guess. I'm afraid they may not like me and then what couldn't I do?"

Sarah's dreams revealed many of the essential features which regularly appear in female homosexuality. In one dream she is trying to have intercourse with a girl who was not her longtime partner. As she put her hand on the girl's vagina her father walked by. "I woke up with a great desire for this sexual affair but I am terribly frightened at what I have done to my father." The *desire for revenge* against the father's "not loving enough" was a central feature in Freud's study of a homosexual girl (1920b).

Another dream revealed her identification with the partner, *fear of orgasm, intense jealousy,* and recurrent anxiety of impending breakup with her partner and resulting murderous rage: "It's a summer resort, I was looking for my girlfriend. No one would say where she was. She heard I was looking for her. She was having an affair with somebody else. Would I sign a paper and release her for this? I said I would but first I wanted to talk to her. After all, we'd been together for many years. I had almost decided then that she must come back to me and then I woke up."

There was a second part to this dream: "I felt very excited when I got her in bed with me. Then all of a sudden I didn't feel anything any more. I had difficulty in reaching an orgasm." The third part followed: "She and I were going to a movie and walking around to find a seat. It was very precarious, as we were in the balcony. She slid down, it seems, five or six stories. As she slid down there was a loud crash. I went down there and I found her dead. The sound as she hit was like a terrible crash. It reminded me of falling off the garage, which I did as a child...the horrible feeling as she fell away...nothing now to do. She would fall in the street and be killed. I couldn't reach her. I couldn't grab her. She was gone. It was death. I couldn't see her body as she fell between a couple of cars. I wonder if that's why I can't do anything...if I'm so afraid that I'll bring about this terrible punishment to her."

Sarah's ambivalence about experiencing any satisfaction with her partner—her wishes to give her up and at the same time keep her—led to her feeling that if the partner (mother) desires to love and satisfy someone else the punishment is death.

On occasion the patient desired women other than her partner. "I feel terribly in love with H. It was almost as if I didn't have any control. I felt perfectly horrible about feeling this way for someone, almost physically sick, kind of like she was cold, however, and I had to make her warm. If she's cold I can't stand it. I must make her warm. These people ought to be warm, as though they feel something, like it's their duty (an obvious reference to her mother's coldness and a projection of her own coldness). Also you could make them feel more than anybody else could. However, when this happens and they don't get warm I get scared. Somehow, I feel that if they don't get warm I might hurt them."

Another dream revealed her *fear of poisonous substances* which will attack and destroy her as she incorporated or is incorporated in the body of the mother (fear of fusion). "There was a bath in the kitchen and water running into it. It was very dark brown water. I was waiting for it to clear up, then I turned it off. The water had seeped out of the tub and come out of the bottom and had come out of the two drains instead of one and there was something about a roast that my girlfriend was cooking, a roast that was supposed to be sliced by me, and I realized that it was very hot and that it shouldn't be sliced the way I was slicing it, and then I wondered whether she had cooked it in this terrible water." The patient's associations concerned the water of a cistern in a town in which she had lived as a child. It also reminded her of the color of her grandmother's face when she was dead. Someone had lifted her up to see it as a child and she had been horrified by the terrible color.

Other dreams reflected her *guilt over her homosexual relations* with her partner. "The dream occurred after some sort of sexual relationship yesterday when I felt so bad. However, after it was over I wanted to call home....my girlfriend and I on an elevated thing, a car, I think, going downhill. Then we stopped in a washroom. She washed her hands. All of a sudden a reddish mold growing all over my hands. I started ripping it off. It was feathery-like. It's all right if I can rip it all off. A big thick layer and she had it on, too. I ripped it off the hands. Something about fire and something burning underneath."

The female homosexual must love the attacking, hostile mother but fears the poisonous substances that will come from the mother's body. Therefore, she faces an extremely dangerous love object, in part a product of her own destructive aggression. "I was in a rather civilized place. There were parks and trees. I went into this bathroom which was long and narrow and was washing something in the sink. I put on some rubber gloves, skin-colored, so that my hands wouldn't become contaminated or get wet. I realized they were my mother's rubber gloves and that I didn't know what they had been used for. She might have used them for something poisonous and I would get it on me. The water was running over in the sink and people outside heard it and opened the door to see who was in there. I hid in the corner so they couldn't see me. This happened twice. Finally I found the stopper and pulled it out so the water could run out. I pulled off the gloves, held them up, and was appalled at having used them."

Because of the danger of aphanisis (total extinction of the self) upon loss of the love object, homosexual women show tremendous *destructive aggression toward the partner*. This aggression arises from the preoedipal period and is heightened by the oedipal conflict.

She dreamt this after suspecting her partner of an infidelity. "I was living with my girlfriend in a large house with other people. I came home from work one evening and noticed that she and M. had been throwing each other fond glances. M. asked if we were going to have a salad and I said that I didn't think it would be necessary because we had plenty of other vegetables. I noticed that there was cellophane curled up in the dishes of food and had been cooked with them. I asked who has done that and my girlfriend laughed and said she guessed either she or M.

"This made me angry since they were so unconcerned. I took my girlfriend into another room and pulled down the blinds. Then she said that I shouldn't treat M. that way, the way I did. I realized that she loved M. I got so violently angry that I started fighting her. Then I threw her out of the room and pulled M. in and started fighting her. I hit her and was crying and acting like an insane person yet I couldn't help myself. I kept realizing the way I was acting could only drive someone away from me, yet I couldn't stop. I threw her around the room and the next minute I would act more rational and try to reason with her.

"I realized I was just bringing all this out in the open instead of keeping it under cover and trying to make my girlfriend love and respect me. I finally asked her what she intended to do and she just smiled at me and said 'Have a place of my own by next summer.' She was exuberant and I was a miserable wreck. I told her that I had spent so much money in analysis in order for us to have a better life. She said 'You can't have a life on only foundations of an old life,' and I said you had to tear everything down to the bare foundations in order to build a new life, that I loved her and that I wanted to build a new life with her. I knew she still intended to leave me for M."

Other dreams frequently referred to certain themes: castration; penis envy; the acquiring of a fictive penis; poisoning; becoming insane, losing control, and destroying the mother; and penis identification.

Course of Therapy

Sarah underwent psychoanalytic treatment for four years and has returned for periodic visits for over a decade. From the very beginning she expressed an interest in securing help only for the relief of her associated symptoms; she did not wish to attempt a reversal of her homosexual condition. She readily perceived that she was in a state of decompensation in terms of her psychological functioning, and that she felt miserable and extremely paranoid. In accordance with this request the analyst made no attempt to directly alter her sexual orientation.

During the course of treatment, however, heterosexual interest had been observed and at one point—approximately the third year of treatment—she felt strong affectionate interest in a male college associate with whom she had a social acquaintance. This affection was not reciprocated and, feeling rejected, she continued her former relationship with her female partner. She also expressed heterosexual desire toward the analyst, which caused her to become embarrassed and to have guilty fears toward her partner. Typically, she had guilty dreams of an oedipal nature about her father.

During her fourth year of analysis her father became seriously ill and she experienced intense feelings of love and sorrow for him. These were the first genuine positive feelings she could remember ever having had for him which were completely acceptable to her. She had never permitted any appropriate physical closeness between her father and herself but realized now how much she wished she had had such contacts. She felt that she deeply loved her father but had completely repressed it. Subsequently her dreams consisted of yearnings for love from men but she felt "it was probably too late to find a suitable man." She derived very little pleasure from her homosexual partnership but still occasionally felt a "female love" for a new woman. She could imagine meeting a man who might be quite suitable for her, a consideration that would formerly have been terrifying and entirely disagreeable.

It is important to note that although psychoanalysis did not fully open the pathway to heterosexuality, it was instrumental in both the alleviation and removal of paranoidal and phobic anxieties in this patient.

Recapitulation

Similar to male homosexuals, female homosexuals have nuclear conflicts belonging to the earliest period of life which force them into choosing partners of the same sex for ego survival. The female homosexual, unable to pass successfully through the separation-individuation phase of early childhood, has suffered maturational (psychological) failures and thereby incurred severe damage to her ego functions.

Sarah represents those cases of female homosexuality in which the basic disorder and fixation occurs in the earliest period of infancy. Compared to milder preoedipal forms of homosexuality, in which the fixation is likely to have occurred in the rapprochement phase (just prior to the formation of object constancy), the fixation in this instance may have occurred in a period closer to the symbiotic phase. Such fixation indicates a greater tendency to psychosis. Sarah's conflicts revolve around the most primitive aggressive, destructive, and incorporative urges of the infant toward the mother and the resultant defenses against them.

The anxieties associated with these patients resemble those seen in borderline cases. This type of homosexuality is frequently seen in patients entering therapy for concomitant symptomatology rather than because of a desire for heterosexuality. Attempts to change or challenge their homosexual state should proceed with great caution as there is marked possibility of severe decompensation and an efflorescence of paranoid and phobic symptomatology bordering on the psychotic.

Sarah's fear of destruction by the female is clearly a fear of poisoning and incorporation. The fear of merging is represented as fear of contamination and death at the hands of the woman. Because of her fear of her projected sadism there is a compensatory death wish for the destruction of the homosexual love object.

Sarah's homosexuality would be classified as Preoedipal Form, Type II. It carried with it a guarded prognosis as to therapeutic reversal, as there was a severe degree of pathology of internalized object relations and object relations were severely impaired and sometimes bizarre and distorted. The Preoedipal Type II homosexual loves the partner in order to achieve narcissistic restoration. There is a failure in the development of sufficient self-object differentiation and when regressive states appear they may completely disrupt the analytic relationship. Projection, introjection, and splitting are common defense mechanisms, and impulses and aggression are poorly bound in this type.

Chapter 20
THE CASE OF JOANNA
(Oedipal Type)

Joanna was a nineteen-year-old college student when she entered psychoanalytic treatment following a period of hospitalization after attempting suicide by slashing her wrists. This was a second attempt after release from a sanitarium. There she had received electroshock treatment following a prior suicide attempt using tranquilizers and aspirin. After the first attempt she had received psychotherapy but her condition remained unaltered. During psychotherapy she had been silent and uncommunicative, hostile and scornful of any efforts to help her.

The patient, an attractive, cultured, intelligent girl, was condescending in manner toward everyone, including the analyst. Her father was extremely wealthy, as were other family members, a factor which she subtly referred to in most of her therapeutic sessions. From this wealth she derived the power and strength to do "whatever I please," especially in her sexual life. She furthermore felt herself quite special by virtue of her intellectual cultivation and artistic temperament.

Joanna's intellectual ability was indeed appreciable, but her achievements were at this point nonexistent.

Much to her annoyance and disappointment she had to attend a college she regarded as beneath her. She was particularly unhappy about this, as a slightly older cousin, with whom she compared herself, enjoyed an enviable academic success at a more renowned school, as well as great social success with an elite group of men and women. The patient suffered from intense shyness in relation to men and developed acute anxiety upon entering a room where there were new men to meet.

Two and a half years before her first suicide attempt she had traveled abroad with her uncle and her cousin, whom she envied and resented. Throughout the three-month tour, when they were guests of prominent residents of the foreign countries they visited, she felt lacking in poise and grace compared to her cousin. She complained that she felt humiliated and demeaned.

Joanna had a sister, four years younger than she, whom she ignored or treated as if she were a small child. There was, however, an intense rivalry with this younger sibling who received a greater share of the limited affections of a rather cold and passive father. The mother, from all accounts, appeared to be a psychotic or prepsychotic individual who, during the patient's childhood, would often threaten her daughters with knives. The patient felt her mother was "inferior" and had little affection for her. When not afraid of her, Joanna had actively taunted, teased, and been hostile to her for many years. Her father she described as calm and reserved, displaying little emotion; she gave a perfect picture of the cautious, prominent, but passive patrician of their rural upper class community.

The patient first announced her difficulties at school by informing her parents on the telephone that she was "a homosexual" and was going to live her life any way she pleased. She found this harder to accomplish than she had originally anticipated. She became the "dupe" of numerous homosexual girls on the campus, discovering "I was unable to dominate or control them in any way." She suffered from feelings of being "left out" if a girl made love to her and then rejected her. After being scornfully abandoned by one of her "conquests" she experienced mounting anger for six months prior to her first suicide attempt. She then suffered a severe depression with impulses to cut her wrists or to take sleeping pills. She felt no desire to do anything, "to make anything of myself." She wanted women "not because I like them but so I would have them and have them care for me. I don't really care about them anyway, nor do I care for Mother. I like women more than men, mostly because I'm not afraid of women." This statement was made during a rare moment of candor, as Joanna was intent, throughout the early phases of treatment, on "demasculinizing" the analyst, on showing him he had no strength in the situation and could "not possibly make me into a heterosexual."

Course of Therapy

Shortly after starting analysis Joanna defiantly began a homosexual relationship with a woman ten or fifteen years older than herself, a friend of the family, who was known by the patient to be a homosexual. The patient preferred to be the active one in the relationship, making her partner achieve orgasm through her caresses and through her manual manipulation of the partner's vagina. In this strong masculine role she felt she possessed a penis, which pleased her. On occasion she submitted and played the passive role but this was not nearly as gratifying.

She felt intense dislike for men, cursed them for having a penis, and similarly derided the analyst. Her major ambition in life was to show that all men were weak and ineffectual, like her father who had not protected her from her cruel and sadistic mother. In essence she was asserting that she was a man and therefore did not need a man.

On several occasions she attempted heterosexual intercourse expressly to show the analyst that she was not impressed by it and did not feel much for the man or for the situation. She would passively submit to heterosexual intercourse and then laugh about it to the analyst, insisting that there was nothing to being heterosexual; she insisted that she could be either homosexual or heterosexual. To Joanna it was simply a matter of "preferring" the love of her women partners where she would be the man. She came to sessions dressed as a man, minimizing any semblance of her true attractiveness and obvious femininity.

Her suicidal feelings substantially disappeared within the first four months of treatment. Despite a homosexual relationship with the family friend and her insistence that she was interested only in women, she simultaneously harbored unexpressed heterosexual wishes. There were transference feelings of an intensely erotic nature toward the analyst, whom she wished to make into the perfect heterosexual partner, that is, the loving, caring father.

After a year and a half of treatment she abruptly withdrew from the analysis only to return two years later to continue her therapy for a period of eight months. During this period of interruption she returned to see the analyst at six-month intervals to discuss current external life problems. She was leading an active homosexual life with her partner and had not resumed college. She no longer suffered from depression, although at times she felt considerable anxiety as she could not entirely accept her homosexual role, especially when her partner took over the active masculine role and asked her to remain passive.

Joanna obviously has a need to thwart her progress; she interrupted her treatment before she could realize her potential for heterosexual adaptation. However, her suicidal acting out had apparently been eliminated, as had the deep depression which had precipitated it. Her defensive self-aggrandizement would not permit her to face the infantile incestuous longings (structural conflict) for her father, and she desired to show the analyst (father) that she had no further need of him. She said she felt well and happy and would be able to manage her life herself.

Joanna returned to analysis for the second phase of treatment following her "successful escape," as she termed it, from her homosexual lover, who had become progressively jealous, increasingly paranoid, and even assaultive to her. During this interim period sexual activity between them was infrequent and without interest for her. She had not only engaged in heterosexual activity with pleasure but had begun to "fall in love" with a man with whom she was considering marriage. The subsequent months of therapy were concerned with the establishment of a stable heterosexual orientation and the working through of her oedipal conflicts both in the external world and in the analytic relationship. Most striking were her personality changes. She became a vivacious, outgoing young woman of considerable wit, charm, poise, and intellectual ability. Hostility toward men had completely vanished and she was capable of warmth, affection, and a cathexis of her love object.

Psychodynamic Factors

Beneath Joanna's facade of imperious masculinity she suffered from intense feelings of inferiority as a female. Being a woman meant to her an active identification with the psychotic or prepsychotic hateful mother. She harbored both loving and angry, resentful feelings toward the father for not having loved her enough as a child and for not protecting her from the depredations of her mother.

The immediate precipitating cause of her homosexual behavior was her intense feelings of envy and rivalry toward a more successful, attractive, and powerful female cousin. This resulted in a loss of self esteem and a deep sense of worthlessness. Underlying these symptoms were lifelong wishes to excel over everyone, possess a penis, and not be subjected to what she imagined would only be humiliation and lack of love at the hands of men. By controlling women she no longer needed men; she could acquire all the love she wanted and obtain relief from her severe aggression toward her mother. Her homosexuality was the choice of the lesser evil (despite conscious protestations of being happy in this role), preferable to facing her deep conviction that she would fail in the heterosexual world. Her underlying sense of inferiority and her frustration in trying to gain and hold the love of women during college, together with her unconscious conflict over being homosexual, produced an agitated depression which culminated in attempted suicide.

Careful examination of this case revealed that Joanna suffered from a structural conflict. It arose from oedipal period disturbance, and whatever preoedipal symptoms she experienced were due to regression. Such regression brought her closer to her mother and consequently she experienced feelings of doom. The acquisition of a good maternal substitute in her female partner was "reassuring" and comforting. "Doom" feelings were signaled by tremendous "voidlike" emotional states in which she felt she would be engulfed in a whirlpool of disgust and destruction by getting so close to her mother. She feared her mother's presence and especially her breasts, finding them "strangely malevolent" in every way. She had experienced these sensations as far back as she could remember.

The following dream reflected her heterosexual yearnings and the conflicts they engendered. "A father was having intercourse with a daughter. It was more or less forced on her but not in the sense of rape. She put up with it and tried to forget it and she couldn't do anything about it." Her associations were that when the father or any man came close to her she sometimes wished she could cut off his penis, not in actuality but certainly in fantasy. The sex act in her dream was performed "in the usual way, once or twice," and then "the man asked if he could just hold his penis there for a while and I could do nothing about it. I was on my stomach, like a child, it seemed."

"I recall one time when my mother was away, around the time I was ill. I was fairly young and I was a little bit shorter than Father since I have always been quite tall and I was a little jealous of my sister when I grew up. We used to take showers with Daddy and around age eleven I said, 'Okay, I'll take a shower with them.' Then I suddenly remembered and I realized I was too old for that. I try to pretend that Father doesn't have a penis and I don't like the idea of his having one because that makes him like the other older men and there's the possibility that I might think of it and be disgusted [reaction-formation].

"The one-time college friend of my father would come to see me and I had a crush on him at about eleven. He used to carry me on his shoulders and I remember thinking that I had to hold myself away from his neck because I couldn't stand the idea of someone touching me there. He used to hug me very tightly, almost as tight as he could, and I used to get a sexual thrill out of that. I've made myself try to forget all these kinds of things. I remember thinking that when they were in bed together, Mother and Father, that there was something between his legs and I could feel it there between mine. I was afraid of the possibility that it might bother me and I tried to put it out of my mind. When I was in college the first year there was a persistent desire to have a penis inside me. I didn't want to give myself up to a man, however, at the same time."

This dream illuminated the oedipal conflict: her fear of her father's penis and her wishes to have intercourse with him. She was jealous of the favored place of her younger sister, who had not yet reached puberty and could still enjoy intimacies with the father that she was now denied. Growing up meant getting rid of any fantasies which concerned her father and other men. It

became quite clear that she then developed a severe
envy and hostility toward the penis which would
threaten her. She wished for love but could not have it.
Her oedipal rivalry with the mother and fear of her
retaliation further augmented the patient's incestuous
fears.

The crisis provoked by her severe rivalry with her
cousin reactivated the previous conflict with the sister
for paternal affection. She turned to homosexuality in
college so that she would not worry about the
possibility of being tied up with any man (father). "I
wouldn't have to worry about the time when he would
no longer be able to love me." She was unable to
transfer her feelings from her father to other men and
as a result turned to homosexuality as a partial
solution and relief. This was also, in part, revenge
against the father who was unable to give her a strong
feeling and acceptance of femininity.

Joanna was a severely repressed individual whose
sexuality had sought expression but for unconscious
reasons had been unable to find a suitable object. Her
incestuous wishes toward the father produced more
conflict, and she regressed to a mother-child relationship with women. In her homosexual activities she
wished to be the man, the proud possessor of a penis,
and thereby avoid union with the mother and an
unconscious identification with her. She detested and
despised the mother and expressed murderous feelings
toward her which she knew, of course, she would not
act upon in reality. Her depression was a mixture of
intense rage and loss. She directed this rage toward her
mother, toward her disastrous and damaging upbringing in early youth, and toward her lack of any
personality traits with which she could buttress her

femininity. She hated her father for his coldness, indifference, and lack of appreciation of her sexuality and attractiveness.

Summary

Joanna's homosexuality would be classified as an oedipal form of homosexuality. Genital oedipal conflicts dominate the clinical picture, in which there is a renunciation of her oedipal love for her father. She experiences a structural conflict between aggressive and libidinal wishes on the one hand, and her own inner prohibitions on the other. There is no fixation at a preoedipal level but there is, at times, a partial regression to that earlier period. Her homosexuality represents a failure to resolve the oedipus complex and castration fears leading to a negative oedipal position. This involves a sexual submission to a parent of the same sex. (This form of homosexuality is the only type in which it can be accurately stated that the flight from the opposite sex partner is a major etiological factor.)

The tendency to severely regress is mild, although there is some regression, as in neurotics.

In these cases, although the homosexual symptom appears to be ego-syntonic, it is, upon careful analysis, revealed to be ego-alien, that is, consciously quite unacceptable.

Since the self is bound and cohesive and there is no impairment of ego boundaries, the orgasm does not fulfill the unconscious purpose of buttressing a failing self-representation, as in preoedipal homosexuals, and the patient can much more easily terminate homosexual activity when the underlying neurotic symptomatology is analyzed.

Joanna, like other oedipal homosexuals, developed potentially analyzable transferences which were ultimately dealt with effectively. The reactivation and reenactment in the transference of oedipal wishes led to their resolution. Her object relations, as well as other ego functions, were unimpaired.

Part III
PSYCHOANALYTIC THERAPY

Chapter 21
GENERAL PROBLEMS

In 1955 Gillespie, at the International Psychoanalytic Congress in Geneva, remarked that the subject of perversion and homosexuality, although not neglected by psychoanalysts, had received surprisingly little attention, especially since it occupied a place of central importance in Freud's theories, both of sexuality and neurosis. The explanation was simple; Freud had written a masterpiece on this subject during the pioneer years of psychoanalysis, the "Three Essays on the Theory of Sexuality" (1905a), an outstanding example of his genius, in which he clearly perceived "the intimate connections between the manifestations of earliest sexuality, of adult sexual perversions, and of neurosis and psychosis" (Gillespie 1956a).

For many years the lack of a systematic study of ego psychology and the absence of a concept of ego development comparable to the phases of libidinal development presented difficulties in the application of structural concepts to homosexuality and to the other sexual perversions.

Since the founding of the American Psychoanalytic Association in 1911, only four panels of our Association have been devoted to either the clinical, theoretical, or therapeutic aspects of perversion or homosexuality. These occurred in 1952 (Arlow 1952), 1958 (Socarides 1958), 1960 (Socarides 1960b), and in 1976 (Payne 1977). Fortunately there have appeared in the psychoanalytic literature brilliant theoretical and clinical essays which illuminate one or more facets of this multidimensional disorder. Indeed the state of our current knowledge of the therapy of these ineluctable conditions would not have been possible without these theoretical, clinical, and therapeutic observations. Until the present time, however, there has been no psychoanalytic text devoted entirely to the treatment of homosexuality as exists for the treatment of transference neuroses, psychoses, borderline conditions, and narcissistic personality disorders. The answer to the relative scientific neglect of this subject may lie in the following observations: (1) Psychoanalysts found that patients who experienced pain and suffering from their condition are motivated to change; others very often are not. (2) The homosexual symptom itself is ego-syntonic in well-structured cases. (3) These patients are intolerant of experiencing anxiety; the relief from anxiety when acting out is engaged in has previously led to therapeutic nihilism and countertransference reactions. (4) The neutralization of conflict allows for the growth of certain ego-adaptive elements of the personality, so that some homosexuals may appear on the surface not ill at all except for a severe deficiency in sexual functioning. (5) Of all the symptoms of emotional origin which serve simultaneously as defenses, homosexuality, like other perversions, is successful for limited intervals in providing a neutralization of profound psychic conflicts and struggles for the purpose of attaining a pseudoadequate equilibrium; it also produces a high pleasure reward (orgasm).

The major reason for the scientific neglect of the homosexual seems to revolve around the questions of the therapeutic effectiveness and the therapeutic techniques to be employed in the psychoanalysis of this disorder.

In 1905, Freud (1905a) wrote that the only possibility of helping homosexual patients was by commanding a suppression of their symptoms through hypnotic suggestion. By 1910, he believed that psychoanalysis itself was applicable to the treatment of perversions, including homosexuality (Freud 1910), but later expressed caution about the possibility of complete cure (Freud 1920a). His criterion of cure was not only a detachment of the cathexis from the homosexual object but the ability to cathect the opposite sex. Freud recognized that it was especially difficult to analyze an individual while he is at "peace" with his perversion; a combination of neurosis and perversion, according to him, presented a more hopeful therapeutic possibility.

An early analyst and author, Boehm (1926), concluded that homosexuals leave treatment at the time heterosexual tendencies begin to emerge along with hatred and castrating wishes directed against the analyst-father. In 1950 Anna Freud (1951) lectured in New York on the recent advances in treatment of homosexuals, stating that many of her patients lost their inversion as a result of analysis. This occurred even in those who proclaimed their wish to remain homosexual upon entering treatment, having come only to obtain relief of their neurotic symptoms.

A consensus emerged over the years that homosexuals could be treated most like phobics. However, this

presented considerable difficulty, including the proba-
bility of premature termination of treatment and the
production of excessive anxiety. A major difficulty in
treating homosexuality has been the misconception
that this disorder was of hereditary origin, the patient
commonly believing that he "was born that way."

It is widely agreed that to achieve therapeutic
success it is necessary to interpret to the patient his
fear of castration; his fear of oral dependence; his
disgust with the opposite sex; and his fear of his own
destructiveness and sadism. But the interpretation
that best achieves a relaxation of his resistance is that
he (the male homosexual) is attempting to acquire
masculinity through identification with the partner
and the partner's penis in the homosexual act. A
similar mechanism is present in the female. After this
interpretation is worked through the patient may be
able to function heterosexually, going through a
strong narcissistic-phallic phase in which women
serve the "grandeur" of his penis. The unconscious,
fearful fantasy of homosexuals that they would
dissolve into a woman at the height of the sexual act is
another crucial interpretation in all treatment of male
homosexuality.

Numerous authors have reported a significant
proportion of successful results in the psychoanalytic
treatment of homosexual patients (Bacon 1956,
Bergler 1956, Bieber 1967, Bieber et al. 1962, Bychowski 1956b, Deutsch 1944, Freud 1933, Lorand 1956,
Nacht, Diatkine, and Faureu 1956, Socarides 1969). An
unpublished and informal report in 1956 of the Central
Fact Gathering Committee of the American Psychoanalytic Association was one of the first surveys to
compile results of treatment. It showed that out of fifty-

six cases of homosexuality undergoing psychoanalytic therapy by members of the Association they described eight in the completed group (which totaled thirty-two) as cured; thirteen as improved; and one as unimproved. This constituted one-third of all cases reported. Of the group which did not complete treatment (a total of thirty-four), they described sixteen as improved; ten as unimproved; three as untreatable; and five as transferred. In all reported cures, follow-up communications indicated assumption of full heterosexual role and functioning.

In 1962, Bieber and his co-workers presented a systematic study of 106 male homosexuals. Their results do much to clarify the progress in therapeutic knowledge and effectiveness. Out of the 106 homosexuals who undertook psychoanalysis, twenty-nine (27 percent) became exclusively heterosexual.

My own clinical experience with homosexual patients in private practice may well be (with the exception of Bergler) one of the most extensive. During a ten-year period, from 1967 to 1977, I have treated psychoanalytically fifty-five overt homosexuals. Thirty-four of these patients were in long-term psychoanalytic therapy of over a year's duration (average 3.5 years). The number of sessions ranged from three to five per week. In this group there were only three females.

The remainder (eleven) were in short-term analytic therapy (average 6–7 months) at two to three sessions per week. Three were female.

In addition, full-scale analysis was performed on eighteen latent homosexuals, in which the symptoms never became overt, except in the most transitory form. Thus the total number treated in long-term analysis, whether overt or latent, was sixty-three.

In addition, over 350 overt homosexuals were seen in consultation (averaging one to three sessions) during this ten-year period.

A definitive breakdown and analysis of the therapeutic results in these various groups is currently being written. One can report, however, that the forty-four overt homosexuals who have undergone psychoanalytic therapy, twenty patients, nearly 50 percent, developed full heterosexual functioning and were able to develop love feelings for their heterosexual partners. This includes one female patient. These patients, of whom two thirds were of the preoedipal type and one third of the oedipal type, were all strongly motivated for therapy.

The structure of homosexuality consists of neurotic conflicts involving both anal and genital stages of sexual development and the oedipal phase (structural class of conflict). These are superimposed on the preoedipal nuclear conflict (object relations class of conflict). The remnants of the preoedipal conflict pass through the later developmental periods and complicate, add to, and give a particular configuration to the later conflict. All oedipal conflict contains the preoedipal danger. Therefore psychoanalysis is the treatment of choice for this disorder. Both preoedipal and oedipal anxieties can be relieved through the revival of infantile memories and traumatic states and developmental arrests; and the reintegration and growth of the individual can be achieved. Treatment of preoedipal damage requires, in addition to the uncovering techniques of psychoanalysis, educational and retraining measures, more intensive supportive interventions, and modifications in the handling of transference, resistance, and regression.

In 1945 Fenichel (1945) summarized the central issues in the psychoanalytic treatment of homosexuality as follows:

1. The treatment of perversions is complicated by one factor not present in the neurosis, namely, the very symptom itself brings pleasure in perversions and treatment not only threatens to remove it but to rekindle the very conflicts the patient had evaded by means of his illness. Treatment also threatens to destroy the only sexual pleasure the patient knows. The possibility of normal sexual pleasure may seem most remote to him.

2. The prognosis depends upon the patient's determination to change or to what extent this determination can be awakened. A trial analysis will have as its main tasks the evaluation of the will to recover.

3. Some patients ask that psychoanalysis rid them of their neurosis but wish to preserve their perversion. The very nature of analysis makes this impossible.

4. The analysis of perversions is, on the whole, no more difficult than that of "pregenitally determined neuroses."

5. The prognosis for psychoanalytic treatment of homosexuals is better than generally assumed. Certain modifications in technique become necessary, analogous to those suggested by Freud (1919a) for hysteria; the analyst may suggest at a certain point in treatment that the patient seek the normal sexual situation representing the phobically avoided situation.

6. The need for reassurance expressed in perversions is frequently due to an intensified narcissistic need (related to self-representation) and a weakness of reality testing. In consequence, there are many

patients who show in their transference a character
disorder or a borderline picture. In such cases psychoanalytic treatment meets the same difficulties as it does
in the borderline conditions or psychoses.

Edward Glover, in his book, *The Roots of Crime*
(1960), devotes considerable attention to the problem of
therapy of male homosexuality. The Portman Clinic
Survey in England reached the following conclusion:
"Psychotherapy appears to be unsuccessful in only a
small number of patients of any age in whom a long
habit is combined with psychopathic traits, heavy
drinking, or lack of desire to change."

Glover divided the degrees of improvement into three
categories: (1) cure, that is, abolition of conscious
homosexual impulse and development of full extension
of heterosexual impulse; (2) much improved, that is, the
abolition of conscious homosexual impulse without
development of full extension of heterosexual impulse;
and (3) improved, that is, increased ego integration
and capacity to control the homosexual impulse.

In conducting focal treatment (brief therapy aimed
at the relief of the homosexual symptom), Glover
commented on the significance of social anxiety
present in these patients. This social anxiety, despite
its apparently rational justification, however, is based
largely on a projected form of unconscious guilt. The
unfortunate punitive attitude of society enables the
patient to project concealed superego conflicts onto
society and the law.

Glover felt that almost from the outset the therapist
must decide whether to conduct the treatment through
the regular and prolonged course of analysis or
through focal therapy of the symptom. In following the
latter course, he would soon find that having uncov-

ered some of the guilt, he would then strike against a core of sexual anxiety, and, in particular, the multifarious manifestations of the castration complex. At this point the history of the individual familial relations, traumas, frustrations, disappointments, jealousies, and so on, would come to the surface or should be brought to the surface.

It is necessary to demonstrate the defensive aspects of the homosexual situation, for only by uncovering the positive aspects of his original relation to women (mother, sister) and by demonstrating the anxieties or guilts (real or fantasied) associated with the hostile aspects of these early relations can a path be cleared for the return of heterosexual libido.

Regarding psychoanalytic treatment proper, Glover drew the following conclusions, which because of their unique contribution to therapy will be reported in considerable detail.

1. Given appropriate selection of cases, the ultimate success (or failure) of the psychoanalysis of male homosexuality lies in how thoroughly or inadequately the analyst explores the unconscious libidinal phases of the negative oedipus complex and the reactive aggression associated with them. The effect on ego and superego structure of identifications and introjections that are laid down during both positive and negative phases of the oedipus complex must also be fully analyzed (Glover 1960).

2. The technique of psychoanalysis proper precludes a focal attack on the symptom itself. It is not possible to direct analytic attention to any one phase of mental development to the exclusion or neglect of other material. This can be attempted only in the cases of

short focal treatment. In any case, the requirements of psychoanalysis cannot be satisfied by libido analysis only, or for that matter by the analysis of the unconscious hostility and aggression that run in series with libidinal development. Glover remarked that if the course of psychoanalysis can be said to be directed at all, it is directed by the vicissitudes of anxiety and guilt and by the defense maneuvers (resistances) which these affects engender. Effective interpretation of resistances may, in this sense, be said to guide the analysis, but effective interpretation is regulated at all times by ad hoc considerations, not by preconceptions of the symptom picture (Glover 1960).

3. Despite the priority of homosexual object choice, homosexual psychic organizations comprise a wide range of component impulse. There is consequently a wide scope for regression to various contributing fixation points. It follows that there can be no standard course in the progress of analyses of homosexual cases considered as a group. In this respect the analysis of homosexuals differs from the analysis of most transference neuroses, where fixation points are more clearly localized at definite ego levels. Concentration at the genital level of the homosexual patient's development cannot succeed until the pregenital regressions are fully ventilated. One can obtain some hint of the pregenital regressions from study of fantasy systems and actual sexual practices. Behind these conscious fantasy systems and manifest practices, however, lie more primitive unconscious systems, the analysis of which is essential to the loosening of defensive regression. It is at this point that the analyst finds some of the most intractable resistances, since these early unconscious sexual fantasies, if sufficient-

ly charged, can disturb the patient's reality sense, giving rise to prepsychotic reactions (Glover 1960).

4. The factor which tides the patient over such crises is the degree of transference rapport. As fixation points in homosexuality vary, so do the transference manifestations. Reactions corresponding to hysterical, obsessional, depressive, and paranoidal transferences can be observed in different types. On the whole, the obsessional type of transference seems to be the most commonly encountered in Glover's view. There are some transitional forms in which obsessional reactions and perverse sexuality seem to overlap, for example, the patient converts his associations into a running obsessional commentary on his manifest homosexual reactions and on his generalized hostility toward women. By so doing he blocks the approach to his underlying hostility to men and attraction to women (Glover 1960).

Transference reactions of the obsessional type very rarely reach the intensity observed in the hysteric or in the fulminating crises of the prepsychotic type. Manifest erotic transferences between a male homosexual and a male analyst are seldom observed and rarely exceed the compulsive expression of fantasy or, at the most, a transient episode of pseudoexhibitionism.

We are confronted at the outset with apparently formidable difficulties in the psychoanalysis of all those with well-structured sexual perversions. For example, the homosexual bears characteristics that are present in most individuals who suffer from impulse neuroses, addiction, delinquency, and narcissistic personality disorders, as well as in some borderline cases. Because of their narcissism they seem to be unable to maintain a continuous analyzable transference relationship. Their relationship to the therapist, therefore, often abounds with fusion of self- and object-images, primitive forerunners of identification. They often suffer from poor object relation or lack of object constancy. The symptom is ego-syntonic and there is a great deal of acting out. Furthermore, they appear at times intolerant of postponement of impulses. From clinical experience I believe these formidable issues can be met and solved, as they have in many instances of borderline conditions and impulse neuroses.

For example, the need for homosexual activity is often of extreme intensity and is often carried out in states of utmost necessity. This requires modifications of technique which depend upon the individual underlying structure and meaning of the homosexual act (A. Freud 1954). In most homosexuals it is wise to neither encourage nor prohibit homosexual activity. The patient, through the analysis of the unconscious motivation and fantasy leading to the homosexual act, at a suitable point in therapy, will be able to decide on a course of action. Also, the patient must not engage in what may be experienced as a self-castration through self-prohibition of homosexual acts until this facet of the unconscious problem has been understood and thoroughly analyzed. Our aim is that the patient not flee therapy as a result of unwise prohibitions against homosexual activity.

One of our basic concerns is that the resisting forces which may be necessary for maintaining ego boundaries are not suddenly overwhelmed. We do not intend a sudden, unopposed breakthrough of id derivatives (as seen in prepsychotic cases). We need variations of technique, therefore, when manifestations of transference or resistance exceed in force or malignancy the amounts with which the patient is able to cope. In order to more adequately control transference and resistance there may be an increase or diminution of sessions, and the patient may occasionally be engaged in face-to-face therapy, for shorter or longer periods of time, instead of lying on the analytic couch. In this manner anxiety can be lessened; distortions and appearance of negative transference can be kept at a manageable intensity; regressive episodes can be more easily managed; and face-to-face discussions may dissipate distrust and lessen the severity of projective anxieties. Using these modifications, the analysis of dreams, fantasies, transference, and resistance proceed as in any other psychoanalytic therapy.

One of the major resistances continues to be the patient's misconception that his disorder may mysteriously be one of hereditary or biological origin or, in modern parlance, a matter of sexual preference or "orientation" that is a normal form of sexuality. The analyst must deal with these views almost from the very beginning. They often stem from the fear that destruction of homosexual pleasure will leave the individual with no pleasure at all.

During the course of therapy of the well-structured homosexual perversion (preoedipal form) there is a revival and working through of the following psychodynamic issues:

1. Persistent stimulation of the child's aggression by the mother throughout early and late childhood, resulting in an unalleviated guilt binding the child to her; any attempt at separation induces severe anxiety.

2. The substitution of the male partner for the

mother as a love object to avoid both oedipal (incest) and preoedipal conflicts.

3. The conditions under which the imperative need for homosexual relief occurs.

4. The destructive aggression inherent in all "love" relationships between homosexuals.

5. The ubiquitious presence of the distorted body ego.

6. The homosexual's often quite open demeaning and degrading of the father. He identifies with the aggressor (mother). This, however, produces guilt, which is an impediment to his feeling entitled to be a man.

7. The identification with his partner in the sexual act. Homosexual contact promotes a transient, pseudostrengthening of his own masculinity and identity which must constantly be repeated lest a psychic decompensation occur. The male homosexual seeks masculinity, not femininity and knowledge of this unconscious motivation becomes a potent source of strength, reassurance, and determination for change in the direction of heterosexual functioning. (Anna Freud (1949) made the important discovery that the interpretation that most achieves relaxation of resistance is that the homosexual attempts to acquire masculinity through identification with the partner and his penis in the homosexual act.

8. The primitive fears of incorporation, threatened loss of personal identity, engulfment by the mother, and personal dissolution which accompany any attempt to separate from the mother. While the analysis of oedipal fears of incest and aggression is of paramount importance in the analytic work, it is vital to the understanding and termination of homosexuality that the above nuclear preoedipal anxieties be revealed.

9. The substitution of the penis of the partner for the feeding breast of the sought-after good mother (breast-penis equation). The homosexual thereby escapes the frustrating cruel mother and makes up for the oral deprivation suffered at her hands.

10. An intense yearning for the father's love and protection at unconscious levels as a further frustration of the need for masculine identification. The homosexual act, as a consequence, dramatizes the aggression and yearning toward all men.

Given the appropriate selection of cases, the ultimate success or failure of psychoanalysis of homosexuality lies in the thoroughness with which the analyst explores not only the unconscious libidinal phases of the negative oedipal complex and the reactive aggression with which these are associated, but also the effect on ego and superego structure of those identifications and introjections that are laid down during the preoedipal phase of development. One can obtain the meaning of the preoedipal factors from a study of the conscious and unconscious fantasy systems.

Of paramount importance is the degree of transference rapport which can be established. Ideally, an active analytic rapport will take place in the form of father transference in which the positive element predominates. It is essential to uncover the negative elements of the father transference so that the patient may delve into the deeper mother transference and preoedipal material.

A process of sexual reeducation may be necessary at certain points in the analysis. This may consist of a systematic sexual instruction since the unconscious fantasies of homosexuals tend to promote a number of conscious myths of a phobic nature which inhibit any attempt to put heterosexual impulses into action. The best means of accelerating the education or reeducation of homosexuals, however, is to uncover and decrease inhibiting anxieties and where possible, uncover the sources of infantile guilt.

Ferenczi (1914) was the first to correctly emphasize that "homosexuality gains its significance from the content of the unconscious fantasy which is realized in the perversion." This fantasy must be analyzed in great detail. A minute examination of the practice and its fantasy proves to be an acting out of drives, infantile and polymorphously perverse in character; concomitant anxieties; and guilt feelings. Anna Freud (1949) suggested that, "The basis for classification of homosexuality should not be the overt practice carried out with a partner but the fantasy which accompanied the act...."

Our aim is to mobilize the patient's feelings and fantasies which accompany his sexual contacts and masturbation. We direct the patient's interest to a minute investigation of his aims in his perversion and in his acting out. We will find that many of his fantasies originate around incorporating or being incorporated and around an intense interest in the breasts of the mother. In the male homosexual, therefore, we will see that there was once a very strong attachment to the first hererosexual object, the mother. He must reexperience and understand the early frustrations, intimidations, and fixations; give up his attachment to his mother; and transfer his libidinal interest to other women. Before this aim can be achieved all developmental phases have to be investigated, including his identification with the father (analyst) in the transference. Analysis of the homosexual patient requires a total analysis of the personality at all stages.

Chapter 22
THE SELECTION OF PATIENTS
AND PROBLEMS AT THE
OUTSET

It must be remembered that the treatment of any perversion threatens to rekindle the very conflicts from which the patient has fled by means of his perversion and to destroy "the only sexual pleasure the patient knows" (Fenichel 1945). However, even such individuals "at peace" with their perversion may have a determination to get well. Central to the issue of prognosis and selection of cases is to what extent this determination can be awakened. The determination itself may have multiple motivations and in every case a trial analysis will have, as one of its aims, the evaluation of the will to recover.

Even if the patient is influenced by others to seek help, a number of rationalizations and a maze of defensive attitudes are invariably found beneath the presence of a desire to alleviate his suffering.

The most promising cases are those in which it seems that the patient feels "worse" not only from the point of view that his perversion may be accompanied by neurotic symptoms but that he can no longer tolerate his homosexual adaptation. Such a patient seeks analysis because he is unable to achieve any form of true ego satisfaction in his perversion. The instinctual discharge via homosexuality has led to a sense of depletion, exhaustion, and a wish to turn away from the homosexual object. This reduces his satisfaction and his expectations in life and leads ultimately to despair and a need to undergo treatment.

Even the most serious cases of homosexuality will yield to therapy if the patient seeks therapy when he feels severely distressed about being homosexual, not only because of guilt or shame but because he finds his homosexual life meaningless and alien to the biological realities of life around him. Hopefully, he may have more than a vague awareness that he is the victim of internal psychic disturbances which have left him no choice but to engage in homosexual activities.

An important criterion is that the patient experiences inner feelings of guilt available for analytical use. This strong inner feeling of guilt derives from unconscious wishes of an aggressive and libidinal nature experienced under the guise of homosexuality. The absence of conscious guilt usually does not mean that the patient does not suffer from guilt, but instead that it is experienced by him as a need for punishment. Once the patient sees that his guilt arises from internal conflict and not simply from the mores of a condemning society, he is on a path toward at least the beginning of resolving his homosexuality.

Ideally, homosexual patients should voluntarily seek therapy and not be coming under duress from parents or other authority figures, for these patients are beset by savage unconscious drives against their parents, a hatred that is in direct proportion to the self-damaging tendencies their aggressive homosexuality camouflages.

Beneath an apparent willingness to get well, the real intent of some patients may be to prove that homosexuality is as rational as heterosexuality. It is obvious that as long as the patient remains committed to the idea that his interest in same sex partners represents the expression of an inherent biological choice, the benefits of therapeutic help are limited. It must be made clear to the patient that neither homosexuality nor heterosexuality is innate; rather, both are learned behavior.

Another criterion is the degree of self-damaging tendencies in the patient. Hopefully, if the patient views this damage socially, personally, and in the work area as arising from his homosexuality, there may be strong motivation toward change.

Another criterion relates to the strong preference for homosexual reality rather than homosexual fantasy. With therapy the patient ultimately moves in the opposite direction; first he prefers homosexual fantasy instead of acting out the irresistible impulse, next he attempts heterosexual fantasy, and ultimately he achieves heterosexual reality. Despite a decrease in societal condemnation, most homosexuals suffer from a sense of inferiority and guilt over their disability due to their infantile fears which have isolated them from the social-sexual relationship of the majority. This remains a constant and deep-rooted source of shame, humiliation, inferiority, and discontent. He strives for semiautomatic and conscious repair of this damage to self-esteem. As a consequence of these maneuvers the patient may present a facade of pseudoconfidence and self-aggrandizement. He may do everything in his power to convince himself and the therapist of the validity of his face-saving rationalizations.

The analyst should make an early interpretation that the patient's lack of sexual interest in women is not due to the absence of heterosexual desires but to his fear of women, which militates against desire. Often the patient may then begin to reappraise his "commitment to homosexuality" and begin to make the acquaintance of women beyond the narrow and preconceived fashion which has so far characterized any contact with them. This redirects his anxiety from his fears associated with being homosexual to his fears of the female and reopens a long avoided avenue fraught with anachronistic dangers related to the preoedipal and oedipal mother.

The analyst must not permit the patient to use his self-deceptive rationalizations as a threat to terminate treatment. Nor can the patient be permitted to belabor arguments that the analyst is biased against homosexuality and is interested only in its eradication. The homosexual's confrontation of the analyst with arguments that certain famous men were or are homosexuals can be disposed of by pointing out that such achievement did not ensue because of their homosexuality but because of their abilities.

From the outset the patient tries to rely on infantile omnipotence to save him from an assortment of humiliations and fears. Not only does he attempt to feel superior; he tries also to appear all-powerful. He casts himself in the role of being super-attractive and irresistible to others. Underneath this bravado he fears external punishment. At a deeper level he fears internal punishment, as the homosexuality itself is a product of conflict; an unconscious part of his superego may continue to object to the basically aggressive meaning of the homosexual act. Beneath the patient's often voiced declaration of approval of his homosexual acts lies a deeper fear of being unable to change; if he admitted disapproval he would experience shame, frustration, and despair.

The Problem of Narcissism

In preoedipal homosexuals there is a weak ego structure based on narcissistic and prenarcissistic dispositions. The archaic narcissistic ego structure makes the ego vulnerable to the impact of libidinal stimulation, and renunciation of primitive gratification becomes difficult if not impossible. In his repetition compulsion the homosexual dramatizes a repeatedly unsuccessful attempt by the ego to master libidinal and aggressive impulses and the originally archaically cathected objects. In place of object cathexis the ego seeks gratification in a short circuit between the self and pseudo-objects—for example, between various substitutes for the ego and for parental images (Bychowski 1954). The ego, when faced with the task of object cathexis, experiences a threat of further impoverishment. Concomitantly we find a lack of neutralized energy indispensible for control, postponement, and anticipation of gratification.

The homosexual, alongside those with narcissistic personality disorders, has specific assets which differentiate him from the psychotic or borderline individual. Unlike the latter, homosexuals have "in essence attained a cohesive self and have constructed cohesive idealized archaic objects"; they are not seriously threatened by the possibility of an "irreversible disintegration of the archaic self or of the narcissistically cathected archaic objects" (Kohut 1974). Furthermore, they are able to establish specific, stable narcissistic transferences, which allow the therapeutic reactivation of the archaic structures without the danger of their fragmentation despite regressive episodes. In two earlier papers, "A Provisional Theory of Etiology in Male Homosexuality" (1968) and "Sexual Perversion and the Fear of Engulfment" (1973), I described, using clinical examples, the homosexual's tendency to severe regressive episodes during therapy; the episodes proved not only reversible but of extreme therapeutic value. This also jibes with Kohut's observation (1974) that "the analyst is particularly effective...if he is capable of broadly reconstructing archaic ego states...." Thus, like patients with narcissistic personality disorders, homosexuals are analyzable. Agreeing with Kohut's conclusions that narcissistic disorders are analyzable, I maintain that in the treatment of homosexuality there is also a spontaneous establishment of a stable narcissistic transference. This is one of the most reliable signs which differentiate these patients from psychotic or borderline cases on the one hand, and from ordinary transference neuroses on the other. Therefore, a trial analysis is of greater diagnostic and prognostic value than overt behavior.

The homosexual, like those with purely narcissistic personality disorders, suffers from "specific disturbances, in the realm of the self and of those archaic objects cathected with narcissistic libido (self objects) which are still in intimate connection with the archaic self objects which are not experienced as separate and independent from the self)" (Kohut 1974). Archaic overestimated configurations have not become integrated with the rest of the personality and result in an impoverished adult personality. Consequently this hampers realistic adult activities by the "breakthrough and intrusion of the archaic structures and of their archaic claims."

The two major pitfalls in the analysis of narcissistic personalities are similarly of paramount importance in the analysis of homosexuals. The first concerns the analyst's readiness to take on an ethical or ethically tinged realistic stance toward the patient's narcissism; the second concern his tendency toward abstractness of the relevant interpretations of the material provided him. Kohut warns against the triad of value judgment, reality ethics, and therapeutic activism such as educational measures and exhortation in which the analyst feels he must step beyond the basic interpreting attitude and become the patient's "leader, teacher and guide." He makes the proviso, however, that in areas where metapsychological understanding is not lacking altogether but is merely incomplete, the analyst may supplement his interpretations and reconstructions with suggestive pressure and the weight of his personality.

In some patients the sexualization of pathological narcissism through homosexuality may appear to be the central clinical problem. Careful scrutiny will reveal whether we are dealing with an erotized statement of what is basically a narcissistic personality disorder (many narcissists may fleetingly engage in homosexual activities without suffering from the true pervesion), or whether the pathological narcissism is a major aspect of the homosexuality, lending a particular stamp and configuration to the clinical picture. In such instances one is confronted with important theoretical and therapeutic difficulties requiring special handling. (See chapter 16, The Case of Sumner, and chapter 25, Modifications of Technique.)

Kohut warns that it is unwise to confront the undisguised narcissistic manifestations of the split-off sector "with reality in the form of educational persuasion, admonition and the like..." (Kohut 1974). The exception is when a "chronic defensive grandiosity" has secondarily become surrounded by a system of rationalizations analogous to the disguise in a phobia.

The analyst's interpretations regarding the narcissistic transference should not become too abstract. This requires an acceptance with equanimity of what appears to be repeated acting out and to understand and respond to it as an archaic means of communication. To summarize Kohut's valuable suggestions (1974), interpretation should (1) clarify to the patient in concrete terms the significance and meaning of his acting out messages; (2) demonstrate the back-and-forth flow of the cathexis of the narcissistic positions; and (3) demonstrate to the observing ego that these archaic attitudes consisting of grandiosity and overestimated narcissistically experienced objects are comprehensible, adaptive, and valuable within the total context of personality development.

Chapter 23
MODIFICATIONS
OF TECHNIQUE

Ideally, in psychoanalysis theoretical advances should be closely followed by advances in technique; conversely, every technical rule should be considered valid only when solidly founded on a specific piece of analytic theory. Deviations from classical technique become necessary to meet variations in a patient's ego structure. Technical experimentation may lead to new insight into the abnormality of structure. However, modifications of technique should be firmly based on the structure of the particular condition and firmly rooted in the theory of the disorder (A. Freud 1954).

The position of the analyst with regard to modifying the traditional psychoanalytic stance must be examined from the sides of ego and id variations (resistance and transference, respectively). This has been done with schizophrenia, where patients' narcissistic withdrawal makes them nearly inaccessible; with paranoid patients, where the transference may not remain within controllable limits; and with delinquents, where the destructive quality of id urges poses serious problems. Variations in technique become necessary whenever the aspects of a case lead us to expect manifestations of transference or resistance which exceed in force or malignancy the extent with which we are able to cope effectively. At the beginning of analysis, before we have insight into the structure of the condition, it is impossible to predict how the patient will respond. There is no guarantee that two homosexual patients or any two individuals with the same symptomatology will react similarly to the same technical procedure.

Let us take, for example, the traditional rule of asking a patient to desist from any activity in which he derives pleasure but which is also self-damaging. We base such a prohibition on the belief that there is little chance of successfully treating any disorder in which we allow the gratifying aspects of it full scope. For many years psychoanalysts believed that homosexuals should be treated for the most part like phobics, the feared activity, heterosexual intercourse, being faced and undertaken, and activities involving phobic avoidance, homosexual intercourse, being interdicted. This approach, while of considerable value in the treatment of phobics, can have disastrous consequences in the course of therapy for the homosexual. Applying the rule of prohibition to two hypothetical homosexual patients illustrates this point and provides a basis for comparison. In one patient, an attempt to prohibit his homosexual activity will move him to outbreaks of hostility and anxiety which threaten the continuation or the effectiveness of the analysis. To insist upon it would be a grave technical error. In the other, although he experiences intense anxiety, such prohibition results in decreased frequency and duration of homosexual episodes, the analysis penetrates deeper, and heterosexuality may more readily be achieved. In the latter case, cutting down on homosexual practices will play a beneficial part. It seems here that identical symptomatology is based on somewhat different psychopathology and it is the latter, not the former, which decides how a case should be dealt with technically. In the first patient the outburst of homosexual practices serves to reduce the anxiety aroused by active, aggressive masculine urges. Passive advances to male partners served as reassurance in lessening anxiety.

It will be possible for the patient who wishes to be constrained and protected during treatment to reduce homosexual practices because of the transference; a new attachment, that to the analyst, has taken place. The analyst would then be in the role of protecting him against dangerous destructive impulses. When the analyst fills this role in the patient's imagination the patient does without the male partner. This implies that the analyst be available to the patient at all times and that the patient cannot tolerate interruption of the analysis for long periods.

In the other patient the perverse activity may serve a completely different purpose. He may fall into that group of men whose homosexuality represents the investing of other men with the attributes of their own phallic masculinity. They cannot bear to be without these ideal male figures and pursue them unremittingly. By urging a patient of this type to restrict his homosexual practices, one urges him to self-castration. What then ensues is an immense resistance and hostility to the analyst if he insists on imposing the restrictive edict. Interpretation of the origins of the patient's projection of masculinity has to come first and will enable him to assume his own phallic properties; thus, he is no longer dependent for his masculine identity on the homosexual partner. Male partners will begin to lose their importance and the patient will be better able to do without them.

To summarize this issue: the question of prohibiting homosexual activity should be decided on the basis of its unconscious meaning to the patient. Outbursts of hostility and anxiety may threaten continuance of therapy if the therapist prohibits activities the patient considers necessary for psychological survival. Prohibition, if it induces or connotes an active self-castration, is not recommended. Ideally, prohibition should be first suggested by the patient; analyzed fully before it is attempted; and undertaken only when a full knowledge of the underlying structure of the symptom is known and understood by both patient and analyst.

This modification in technique has been commented on by several authors, including Lorand (1956), Clyne, (Socarides 1960b), Socarides (1960b), and Anna Freud (1949, 1954).

Controlling the depth of regression in order to offset its utilization as resistance in the transference relationship is another modification. The depth of regression will reveal important psychodynamic material, but the patient's degree of anxiety must be manageable. His tendency to regression to the earliest paranoid anxieties must constantly be watched and dealt with. Regressive episodes are often related to severe dependency wishes, as these patients have intense oral conflicts. As long as their orality is fulfilled they do not rise to a higher level of integration. Dependency strivings should be adequately controlled inasmuch as our goal is to achieve a higher level of integration. Prolonged oral regression is not advisable.

An additional modification is the use of extraanalytic transferences. Bacon (1956, Socarides 1960b) has observed that the homosexual must be induced to set up a "triangular relationship once again," for he "can never love a person of one sex and simultaneously a person of the other sex." He must always be "taking sides." If he feels love for his mother, he cannot love his analyst (father) or feel any warmth toward him. If he feels close to the analyst he will have nothing to do with his mother or any other female, and will despise and hate her.

The analyst must stress to the patient that the resolution of his problems will ultimately have to take place outside the analyst's office. At the same time the analyst must reduce the depth and intensity of the patient's regression in the transference in order to enable him to carry out this very interaction. To accomplish this, the sessions may be intermittent or decreased in frequency in order to diminish regression and dependency and to direct the patient's attention toward the external world, especially when there is not excessive castration anxiety present or exceedingly intense aggressive feelings.

Modification by decreasing sessions and by suggesting interruptions in therapy depends upon the current motivational state of the patient. During intervals of severe aggression the analyst should increase sessions so that the patient can ventilate aggressive discharges with their concomitant psychic material rather than suppress or act them out. Behind this aggression is a deep need for love which the analyst neither condemns nor criticizes. Running away from extraanalytic problems by regression to an identification with the good mother and becoming an infant must be constantly interpreted. The continuing identification with the analyst increases the patient's strength and he finds that his aggression does not kill the analyst (father); nor does it destroy the mother or himself.

The female homosexual, even more than the male, suffers from intense feelings of inferiority and self-depreciation, which may be completely unconscious and result in a proportionately intense reaction-formation of superiority and grandiosity. She suffers, therefore, with an initial hostility toward the therapist which may be quite powerful. The analyst must be prepared for this from the start, not allowing it to impair or disrupt the beginning therapeutic alliance.

This hostility has another source: the feelings of rejection and depreciation by the father. Much of the transference revolves around this basic fear, resentment, and vengeful attitude arising from the experience of having been forsaken by the father. In these cases the father could not allow his daughter to exhibit her feminine wishes in the oedipal situation with his tolerance, acceptance, and love.

The female homosexual will ultimately enact in the erotic transference her relationship to the father much more vividly than the male homosexual will. Fearing rejection, she will test the analyst by attempting in some instances to act out directly with him her reawakened oedipal wishes. The analyst must interpret the meaning of her erotic and dependency demands before they have attained an overwhelming peak of intensity, as they are mixed with the most bitter and savage retaliatory affect aimed at the father. If not interpreted early enough the patient can then claim a new humiliation at the hands of the analyst (father) when these demands are not met. The male homosexual patient very seldom makes such importunate demands for direct libidinal gratification by the analyst. Sustained, insistent demands for sexual gratification by a male homosexual patient directed toward the male analyst usually connote a conscious wish to destroy the therapeutic alliance and flee the therapy. On the other hand, an erotic transference between a male patient and female therapist may represent a reawakening of oedipal wishes.

The female's primary identification with the mother does not necessarily change her basic anatomic identification and capacity for heterosexual functioning. Therefore, oedipal material should be analyzed immediately and frequently. With the resolution of her aggressive and incestuous feelings toward the father, heterosexual relations may be brought about sooner than can be anticipated in the male homosexual patient whose primary identification with the mother has inevitably impaired such activity.

The female homosexual does not have to undergo a change in gender identification, as does the male. Of course, her primary identification with a hateful sadistic mother and her fears of being incorporated by and merging with the mother must be analyzed in order to bring lasting improvement or cure.

It should be noted that many homosexual women with a marginal heterosexual adjustment and functioning suddenly become overtly homosexual as a result of their disappointment in traversing crucial phases of life—menstruation, first intercourse, marriage, and motherhood—situations in which they may once again experience a feeling of rejection and abandonment by the male (father). The overtly homosexual woman may be restored to heterosexual functioning by the direct analysis of these precipitating events.

It is erroneous to assume that homosexual women do not experience the intense anxiety of their male counterparts. It is precisely the female who, upon losing her female partner, experiences anxiety of total extinction—aphanisis. This condition, because of its implications for suicide, is usually the reason for entering analysis. Aphanisis can also occur if there is a premature attempt on the part of the patient during therapy to separate from her partner. Thus prohibitions as to continued homosexual behavior must take into account both the same principles as prescribed for the male (depending upon the individual dynamics) and the danger of massive anxiety leading to panic and suicide. As this danger is very great, the anxiety must be worked through as thoroughly as possible whenever separation is contemplated.

Modifications in Homosexuals with Narcissistic Character Disorders and Concomitant Preoedipal Developmental Arrest

Narcissistic preoedipal homosexuals (Type II) present more complex and serious therapeutic problems (dependent on the degree of such narcissistic investment) insofar as they include various types of character pathology in addition to object relations pathology.

The most severe type of homosexual pathology, except for that in the schizo-homosexual, is the preoedipal homosexual with a narcissistic personality structure. While patients with narcissistic personality structure and pathological grandiose self often present a better surface appearance, seemingly functioning at a higher level than other homosexuals with less pathological internalized object relations, their prognosis may be worse.

Sumner (chapter 16) typified this group of homosexuals, who are often considered quite resistant to therapy. The intrapsychic conflicts common to other preoedipal homosexual patients were compounded in Summer's case by a severe ego developmental arrest (preoedipal fixation) and by problems peculiar to patients with a severe narcissistic character disorder.

It is important to treat the preoedipal developmental arrest with supportive measures until the patient can begin full psychoanalysis (Kolansky and Eisner 1974, Eissler 1953, Kohut 1971, Dorpat 1974, Atkin 1975, Stolorow and Lachmann 1978). In some instances the signs of preoedipal developmental arrest may not be apparent at the start of the analysis. In general, these patients make excessive demands of the analysis and the analyst. The analyst encounters severe countertransference problems in dealing with the transference. The analyst is put under great stress by being devalued, and his interpretations are often treated as meaningless or responded to with contempt. He may be provoked into excessive concern and intervention in response to a patient's provocative and perhaps even dangerous behavior. In such instances, a longer psychoanalytic treatment may be necessary in order to first break through the developmental arrest and the pathological character structure activated in the transference (Kernberg 1970).

All such patients suffer deficiencies in ego functions. Among the most prominent of these is the patient's intolerance of anxiety. While this may have neurotic determinants it is largely a consequence of a more profound damage to the personality—an inability to delay immediate responses because of severe early ego damage. The deficiency in self-concept and in body-ego boundaries require interpretations of a supportive and empathic nature in accordance with the patient's feelings and imperative needs. Kolansky and Eisner (1974) have noted that it is "useful to educate" the patient with preoedipal developmental arrest to the nature of his specific vulnerabilities in order to minimize his "asocial and self-destructive tendencies." Ego-syntonic areas of immaturity, when probed, produce severe anxiety and only later structural conflicts become manifest—when the conditions have been converted into a neurosis. These patients often express rage directly in response to a slight frustration. Such severe bouts of rage threaten to destroy both the object and the self; a common defense against them is masochism and regression.

As Stolorow and Lachmann (1978) noted, defenses in these patients may be immature—in a prestage of development, a prestage of defense. Consequently, ego and superego functions are unable to participate in the production of intrapsychic conflict because of previous unsuccessful self-object differentiation and integration. Appropriate self-object differentiation and integration have been interfered with because these patients did not receive particular empathic responses from the environment in childhood (see chapter 16). "Developmental *prestages* of projection and incorporation as defense mechanisms can be found in the normal symbiotic ego states of early infancy, in which self- and object-representations are merged, and in the somewhat later infantile states of partial self-object differentiation and partial self-object boundary confusion" (Stolorow and Lachmann 1978, p. 74).

For example, Sumner (chapter 16) often used projection, incorporation, and splitting, not in the sense of true defenses but in the sense in which self- and object-representations were merged so that he could not tell the source of his feelings. On several occasions he accused the analyst of "not believing" him whenever he made a serious or incisive comment, or felt the analyst might laugh at him behind his back as he left the consultation room.

He was unable to integrate contrasting images and thoughts, attributing them alternately to himself and to others. He frequently projected a split-off harsh superego onto others whenever he attempted to make a positive statement affirming strength and normal self-esteem ("They are laughing at me" or "They hate me"). He located his ambivalence in an internalized bad self personified by an inner image of an arrogant man taking satisfaction in all of Sumner's failures.

He viewed the analyst as fluctuating between being all-good and all-bad. This type of splitting of the same external object is due to a developmental deficiency in self-object boundary maintenance, with a confusion between self and object, ego ideal and superego. It would be erroneous to interpret the patient's splitting as due to a defense against instinctual structural conflict.

In dealing with structural conflicts, our aim is to reactivate infantile experiences which have been repressed and defended against, and to analyze them in the transference relationship. However, in instances of ego developmental arrest, "experiences that the patient legitimately *needed but missed* or prematurely lost are understood within the transference in order to assist the patient's ego in its belated development."

This exposes certain configurations so that they can ultimately be modified into mature forms of self-esteem regulation. It is necessary to deal first with what the arrested ego needs to achieve and to interpret only later what the defending ego needs to ward off (Stolorow and Lachmann 1978).

In these cases the need to engage in homosexual activity and narcissistic grandiose behavior should be treated as a manifestation of an arrested developmental phase, in a sense as a developmental necessity, at least for the time being, and not as a resistance. This basic principle is a major consideration in the treatment of all preoedipal homosexual patients, but Sumner's sensitivity to even the slightest comment on his encounters made entry into these discussions extremely hazardous, as he regarded them as narcissistic injuries.

Special techniques are necessary to promote the growth and maturation of such arrested ego functions. The aim of these techniques is to promote structuralization of ego functions sufficient for a later exploration of the defensive aspects of the patient's psychopathology in terms of the instinctual conflicts it serves to ward off (Stolorow and Lachmann 1978). Sumner had to discover the developmental stages he had failed to successfully traverse before he could deal with his pathological defenses. Developmental imbalances could be reconstructed from memories, dreams, and the transference, and could then be placed correctly in the specific developmental stages to which they belonged. For example, self- and object-representations were vulnerable to regressions in which he yearned for self-object dissolution and a mystical oneness and reunion with the saints (Jesus, St. Sebastian, Hindu mystics, and so on). Vulnerability to such regressions vitiated or blocked his progress. He neded archaic self-objects for self-esteem regulation and as a result a long period of symbiotic-like idealizing transference had to be promoted. This helped him gain the feeling of an individual idealized self (a real self) first based on identification with the analyst.

The transference situation provides opportunity for new paths of growth, for it "insures a process of developmental unfolding, free from the anxieties, perils, threats of the original situation..." and "the anaclitic factors operating in the transference relation enable the patient to reestablish his object relations also at that level at which his development was deficient" (Spitz 1959, pp. 100–101).

In view of the lack of structuralization of the psychic apparatus in these cases, the analyst must "facilitate the structuralization of their representational worlds by promoting the gradual differentiation and integration of self and object representations within the therapeutic relationship" (Stolorow and Lachmann 1979). In order to do this, "the patient must be permitted to revive in relation to the analyst those archaic phases at which his representational development has been arrested." This revitalizes development that has been aborted. During this period it is necessary that the analyst restrict his interpretations to an empathic understanding of the patient's "primitive, arrested representational configuration," which the patient attempts to restore.

Furthermore, he should acknowledge to the patient successfully reached developmental milestones—for example, the patient's acknowledgment of his *own* penis. "Neutrality" and "consistent understanding" of archaic states contribute to the formation of the patient's representational world. "The therapeutic action of this environment is to provide a facilitating medium reinstating the developmental processes of representational differentiations and integrations that had been traumatically aborted and arrested during the patient's formative years" (Stolorow and Lachmann, 1979). The aim is to foster the gradual internalization of a differentiated image of the analyst as an understanding presence and, eventually, the development of an autonomous capacity for empathic self-observation, a crucial milestone which makes possible the patient's entrance into a therapeutic alliance" (Stolorow and Lachmann 1979). At this point, since sufficient structuralization has taken place, one can proceed with the analysis of transference manifestations and of libidinal and aggressive conflicts.

Chapter 24
TRANSFERENCE
CONSIDERATIONS

In his 1962 "Survey of Psychoanalytic Literature on Overt Male Homosexuality" Wiedeman noted:

There are not too many reports on transference, course in therapy, and treatment results from homosexual patients. . . .It seems that further study of homosexuality from the point of view of structural theory, the consideration of early phases of libidinal and ego development, and examination of transference problems will bring further progress in our understanding of homosexuality.

Wiedeman cites four papers dealing with transference: Anna Freud (1949, 1951) has provided examples of several overt homosexuals in therapy in which certain essential transference interpretations were necessary to effect a change from homosexuality to heterosexuality. Boehm (1926) observed that some homosexual patients break off treatment just when their heterosexual tendencies begin to emerge. This is often due to an increase in the hatred and castrating wishes directed

Paper presented as part of the panel entitled Psychoanalytic Treatment of Male Homosexuality, American Psychoanalytic Association meeting, May 7, 1976, Baltimore.

against the analyst-father. Lagache (1950) described a
similar transference development in which the patient,
during his efforts toward heterosexuality, developed a
brief but violent jealousy ("a defense against a passive
homosexual fixation on the father") directed against
his "rival," the analyst.

It has become clear over years of clinical investigation of homosexual patients that no matter the form of
homosexuality, it is the *degree of preoedipal fixation*
(Socarides 1960a, b, 1969) that plays an important part
in the clinical picture, affecting transference manifestations and resistance.

The Nature of the Transference

Crucial to the analyzability of homosexual patients
is neither the presenting symptomatology (even
apparent extreme femininity), nor the life history of
the homosexual, but the nature of the spontaneously
developing transference. Do transferences develop in
the psychoanalytic treatment of homosexuals and, if
so, what is the particular nature of these transferences?

The preoedipal homosexual has a capacity to
differentiate between self and object world and has the
ability to displace reactions from a past object-
representation to an object in the present. He has,
therefore, an organized, differentiated self, an entity
separate and distinct from his environment, with the
capacity to remain the same in the midst of change.
This is a hallmark of his capacity to form a transference neurosis, in contrast to psychotics who have lost
their internal object-representations and strive to fill
up the feeling of a terrible void by creating new objects

(Kernberg 1975). The homosexual object stands for the self; it is narcissistic but still an object relation—that between mother and child. (This is a more serious disturbance in object relations than is found in oedipal homosexuals whose object relation is between the infantile submissive self and a domineering prohibiting father—self to object.) Thus the object relationship is between object and self or, in the severest forms of homosexuality, those marked by a great deal of narcissism, between a "pathological grandiose self to self" (Kernberg 1975).

When he misunderstands the present in terms of the past this misunderstanding is only partial and temporary. When he suffers regressions in ego functions they are circumscribed and largely limited to certain aspects of his relationship to the transference figure. He may allow himself to regress in his object relations and ego functions and may renounce certain of his reality testing functions partially and temporarily; he is, however, able to work with and understand these reactions with his observing ego (Greenson 1967).

One can observe in his transference behavior and fantasies early forms of ego, id, and superego functioning. Temporary regressions as well as progressions are usually circumscribed, and he may rebound from them or simply express them during analytic sessions. Such primitive mental mechanisms as projection, introjection, splitting, and denial are commonly encountered in moderate and severe cases.

The tendency to act out the transference reactions indicates a loss of impulse control. The tendency to somatize as a transference manifestation is also a regression in ego functions. The externalization of parts of the self—id, ego, and superego—may be another sign of this regression. The more regressed the transference becomes, the greater the preponderance of hostile, aggressive strivings in the homosexual. The regressive features of the transference provoke superego reactions of shame and feelings of being contemptible.

Of great importance in working with homosexuals is the maintenance of the working alliance (Greenson 1967, Dickes 1975, Socarides 1975). The patient forms this relatively nonneurotic rational rapport with the analyst through a motivation to overcome his homosexuality, a sense of helplessness, a conscious and rational willingness to cooperate, and an ability to follow the instructions and insights of the analyst. The medium which makes this possible is the patient's partial identification with the analyst's analytic approach as he attempts to understand the patient's homosexual behavior. The maintenance of the working alliance is of special importance in the analysis of homosexual patients since his presenting symptom is ego-syntonic, affords orgastic release, and creates a temporary equilibrium within the warring intrapsychic parts of his personality. Thus, the patient may on many occasions react negatively to his therapist, who may be viewed as a threat to the only sexual pleasure the patient knows.

Shifting Transference Manifestations

In the early stages of analysis there are many indications of spontaneous transference, some of which can be recognized as essentially maternal in origin (Glover 1960). However, the more common type of transference manifestation is a positive paternal transference to a male therapist (Socarides 1968). At the beginning, in the latter instance, there may be a passive receptive attitude toward interpretation which alternates with disappointment when this is not forthcoming. The most active analytic rapport takes the form of father transferences in which the positive element strongly predominates. It is essential, however, to uncover the negative elements of the father transference, as only when these have been fully ventilated is it possible for the deeper mother transferences, both positive and negative to appear (Glover 1960). It seems quite clear that most analytic failures, in the sense that the patient retains his homosexual symptom even if in a less marked form, are due to the failure to uncover and analyze these potential mother transferences, which at first are almost exclusively saturated with pregenital sadistic fantasies. With the successful overcoming of these deeper regressive phases the prospects for successful outcome are greatly improved.

While the patient's productions are likely to be limited during the early stages of therapy to material centering around oedipal conflicts, both positive and negative, it is most important to bear in mind that they represent accretions to the difficulties originating in the preoedipal phase. They therefore reflect aspects of the unresolved primitive excessive anxieties and aggressions so prominently a part of his earliest psychic functioning. For example, a homosexual's (oedipal) love for his mother is fused with the most disturbing aggressive, incorporative affect. The analysis of phallic and anal material is necessary but only supplementary to the analysis of oral fantasies, which in many instances derive from phallic stage fantasies. For example, I agree with Arlow (1963), that it is important to realize that in many instances we are dealing not with an actual regression to an oral fantasy which originated during the oral phase, but with one which originated during the phallic oedipal period derived from the preoedipal phase difficulties.

As a rule, the first sign of a fundamental improvement is the appearance of anxieties which would ordinarily set up neurotic defenses. These differ from the earlier manifestations of social anxiety encountered at the beginning of the analysis of most homosexuals. These deeper anxieties gradually give way to guilt reactions and it is at this point that superego analysis can be most effective. This calls for persistent ventilation of the projection system by means of which the patient covers his guilt. During this period the patient may manifest a number of transitory symptom formations of the conversion type and his inhibitions in work and social contacts may be exacerbated. Once these have been worked through the way is open to analyze the genital kernel of his oedipus complex, which the homosexual has used every unconscious mechanism to conceal.

As Glover (1960) has noted, success in treatment depends upon (1) the effectiveness with which the purely psychological disposition to homosexual object choice can be uncovered; (2) the degree to which current ego difficulties and frustrations can be offset; and (3) the degree of transference rapport which can be established and analyzed.

What is essential is that the degree of potential accessibility in each case be maximized. The analyst must provide the homosexual patient the opportunity to admit to the transference figure the extent of his desolation. A somewhat lengthy interval will be required before the patient's unconscious material reveals aspects of himself which he abhors and wishes to change. The patient should begin to suspect that he is suffering from irresistible impulses in which the striving for security and the striving for instinctual gratifications are intimately commingled. He begins to perceive that this tension is like a dangerous trauma intruding into every aspect of his conscious life and producing in him an overriding aim to rid himself of tension and to achieve sexual gratification. Gradually he becomes aware that he does not experience these drives in the way he experiences his other, normal instinctual drives, and he wishes to change them. When these conditions are met he will become even more curious about the unconscious factors responsible for his homosexuality.

Homosexuality requires full-scale, thoroughgoing analysis of all phases of development. This does not mean that symptomatic improvement may not be achieved early in therapy. Symptomatic cures, usually transient in nature, in which a patient who previously engaged exclusively in homosexual acts is able to participate in heterosexual intercourse, may be due to his overcoming phobic avoidance of the female genitals because of reduction of incestuous (oedipal) fear of his mother. The working alliance and positive transference relationship may facilitate the patient's feeling of strength and ability to face these oedipal dangers. However, the patient may still remain homosexually motivated; it is misleading to regard this change as anything more than partial and probably temporary.

Transference and Acting Out of Impulses

It may be possible for the patient who wishes to be constrained and protected during treatment to reduce homosexual practices because of the transference; a new attachment—to the analyst—has taken place. The analyst will then be in the role of protecting him against the dangerous destructive impulses. When the analyst fills this role in the patient's imagination the patient does without his male partner.

In other instances men have invested other men with the attributes of their own phallic masculinity. They cannot bear to be without these other male figures either bodily or mentally and they pursue them unremittingly (A. Freud 1968). If the analyst urges a homosexual patient of this type to restrict his homosexual practices, or if the patient attempts to do so on his own as a result of the working alliance and the positive transference, the patient is either being urged or is urging himself to commit self-castration. An immense resistance and hostility to the analyst ensues. Interpretation of the origin of the patient's projection of masculinity has to come first, thus enabling him to assume his own phallic properties. Therefore he is no longer dependent on the homosexual partner for his masculine identity. Abstaining from homosexual activities should be decided on the basis of its unconscious meaning to the patient and must not be attempted prematurely.

In a 1954 paper, "Problems of Technique in Adult Analysis," Anna Freud described the cessation in an alcoholic patient of passive homosexual practices. His outbursts of alcoholism served to reduce the anxiety aroused by his active, aggressive masculine urges which he regarded as destructive to the female partner as well as to himself (heterosexual behavior had already begun):

Drink as well as passive advances to male partners served as reassurance and lowered his anxiety....During the treatment it became possible for him to reduce the addiction to alcohol because in the transference a new addiction, that to the analyst, took its place. He gave me the role of protecting him against his dangerous masculine destructive impulses, in short, of holding him down. While I filled this role in his imagination, he could do without alcohol or male partners. This implied, of course, that I had to be at his disposal without fail, and that interruption of the analysis could not be tolerated. He would find me at the other end of the telephone even in the middle of the night which was of course the usual striking deviation from the orthodox technique, whenever it is applied to an addition. Where the relationship to the analyst takes the place of the satisfaction or reassurance gained from the system, the analysis turns into a battle between the two addictions, the addiction to the analyst holding the fort temporarily until the unconscious material appears and is analyzed. [pp. 389–390]

It is useful to educate the patient with preoedipal developmental fixation to the nature of his specific vulnerabilities in order to minimize his asocial and destructive tendencies, such as his frequent acting out under dangerous and masochistic situations. Psychoanalysis is most useful as a technique when there is sufficient neurotic conflict stimulated to be analyzed (Ostow 1974). Therefore the concept connoted by the phrase "spoiling the gratification of the preoedipal developmental arrest followed by analysis" (Eisner and Kolansky 1974) has special importance in the therapy of homosexuality. Such therapeutic activity may lead to discomfort and anxiety in relation to previously ego-syntonic areas of immaturity. Its purpose is to convert the entire entity into neurosis.

The basis in part for the homosexual's masochistic self-defeat is his wish for immediate gratification, his easily wounded pride (high degree of narcissism), and his intolerance of frustration and anxieties. This interpretation has to be given with tact, without further injury to his pride. Kohut (1974) advocates giving interpretations to those with narcissistic disturbances "with correct empathy for the analysand's feelings," a useful technique in uncomplicated neuroses but imperative in cases in which there is a combination of neurotic manifestations and ego disturbances characteristic of "ego developmental arrest." Such a task is difficult, as the relationship of easily wounded pride to the way of compensating for it by feelings of omnipotence make the patient further vulnerable to wounds inflicted by its interpretation. These patients live in a vicious cycle which must be interrupted if this phase of treatment is to be successful.

My own approach is to not interfere with the narcissistic transference at a very early stage, proceeding along the following lines. The narcissism of homosexual patients can be attacked as a resistance only after the working alliance is strengthened and maintained. There must be (1) a systematic interpretation of the defensive functions of the grandiose self; and (2) an investigation of the devaluation of parental images and real parent figures both as they occurred in real life and in the transference. These patients, similar to the narcissistic personality disorders, "reveal dramatically the total devaluation of the transference object for the slightest reason and, thus, the intense, overwhelming nature of the aggression against the object" (Kernberg 1970). It is then possible for the patient to express direct rage and the need for omnipotent control of the object which reflects defenses against his aggression. In Kohut's opinion (1974), "The narcissistic transference, in other words, first activates past defenses against deeper relationships with the parents, and only then the real past relationship with them" (p.263).

In agreement with Kernberg (1975) the optimal technique for the narcissistic resistance seems to be the systematic interpretation of both the positive and negative transference aspect, rather than focusing exclusively on libidinal elements.

Transference Manifestations During Regressive Episodes

During periods of severe regression, the analyst increases sessions so that aggressive discharges and their concomitant psychic material can be ventilated rather than suppressed or acted out. Behind this aggression is a deep need for love which the analyst neither condemns nor criticizes. The analyst must constantly interpret the patient's running away from extraanalytic problems through regressing to an identification with the good mother and becoming an infant. The continuing identification with the analyst increases the patient's strength, and he finds that his aggression neither kills the analyst (father) nor destroys the mother or himself.

A short clinical vignette of a twenty-five-year-old
homosexual professional man (whose case history is
reported in detail in chapter 13) illustrates a variety of
transference reactions containing painful and frightening libidinal and aggressive impulses. Roger experienced feelings of warmth and love for the therapist
traceable to a search for his father, who was forced
from the home by a domineering and phallic mother
when the patient was only two; the patient was allowed
to see him for brief intervals on only two occasions at
ages ten and twelve.

I am afraid of you and I've become nasty to you at the same time I
love you. And I become violent and extremely critical. I feel I could
tear you apart with my tongue because I would love to love you as
if you were my father. And I would like you to love me back. And I
would like to be held like a baby and comforted. And I would like
you to take me into the bathroom and give me a bath and hold me
and love me. And I know you won't and you can't. I'm afraid to
give you all this love. I'm scared of being rejected by you and
ultimately it involves sex and I'm afraid of the rejection. I'm
afraid you will say "You're mad. You're a homosexual!" And I
want to kiss you and it upsets me.

Alternating with his libidinal feelings the patient
had tremendous destructive urges in the transference,
not only toward the analyst but toward other men.

I want to kill a man in battle perhaps and then have intercourse
with the dead or dying or murdered. I am helpless and you see I am
crying. [He is sobbing hysterically.] It would be nice if the men
were crying too and we'd cry together. I would bit off their penis. I
am just so violent and it's all of a sexual nature too. A lot of love
and kisses, his arms, his chest, his lips. I would like to be able to
act out on him all the things I wanted from my father, that is, the
being loved part. He has always been away or dead. Also if he

were dead or dying or unconscious I could do all these things without his knowing it. Perhaps he then would have no choice but to love me. It's about the only way I could get a normal man and he wouldn't laugh at me or hurt me in some way.

The lifelong search for his father was filled with poignancy and despair. In another session, midway in the analysis he dreamed:

It took place in a subway toilet. Lots of people there. The police were there too and a man is standing in front of the urinal with his penis out and someone has slashed it with a knife or pen. And I got frightened but morbidly fascinated. The color, the poetic redness, was very fiery and very beautiful, a sort of vermillion. Yes, I think of the pen being stuck in him, or a knife, like blood running out of Christ's hand.

Having recounted this dream he expressed a sudden impulse to show the analyst his penis; then he suddenly felt like crying. He felt childish. He felt angry and aggressive toward homosexual partners' penises and at the same time angry at his own. He had fleeting thoughts of cutting his penis, hurting himself, slashing his wrists. He felt the same angry resentment toward his mother's breasts which he recalled seeing occasionally when he was living at home (breast-penis equation). They were the penis which was denied him. It was the penis that he was angry about and searched for. The presence of the policeman in his dream represented a superego defense against committing these destructive acts. The dream elements also represented a castration fear and a masochistic submission in a grandiose narcissistic fashion. The exhibitionism was an attempt to ward off castration

anxiety and also at deeper levels it was a defense
against his primary feminine identification with his
mother and his oral need for the breast (penis).

Both positive and negative feelings toward the
analyst emerge during regressive episodes. The
positive feelings are prerequisites for the maintenance
of the therapeutic alliance; the emergence of strong
negative feelings necessitates prompt measures to
reestablish the positive transference relationship. The
attitude of the patient toward his regression—whether
he passively accepts it or struggles against such a
passive acceptance—is important.

Although regression may at times take on the
appearance of resistance and may actually prove to be
such, these episodes most often enrich the transference. During severe regressive states childhood events
may be relived in the transference with dramatic
impact and vividness and with profound meaning for
the patient, not only permitting a degree of abreaction
but also furthering understanding. A basic trust is
often implicit in the patient's regressive episode and
this, of necessity, includes transference elements. On
other occasions distrust may appear and regressive
states may represent resistances.

Reactivation of infantile material and modes of
functioning may become so archaic that the guardian
function fails and a brief psychotic-like episode may
appear in the most severe types of preoedipal homosexuality. Persistent psychotic episodes, however, have
not occurred in the homosexual patients (nonschizo-
phrenic) that I have analyzed, even during the most
intense regressive episodes—although severe ego
disturbances, merging and fusion phenomena, and
splitting mechanisms are common. One of the great

values in the reconstruction of these phenomena is to demonstrate to the patient how he has coped with the difficult situation in the past. In many instances homosexual patients experience regressive states with great anguish and often in horrifying detail. In the patient's restitution, as in the handling of regressive states during psychoanalysis of other conditions, "we hopefully plan not simply to seal over but to reverse and undo the damages inflicted in the compulsive reenactment of earlier traumatic situations" (Weinshel 1966).

Chapter 25

THE ANALYSIS OF
REGRESSIVE PHENOMENA

As noted in chapter 24, on transference, the severity of preoedipal developmental fixation with its associated ego disturbances may be crucial to the outcome and forward movement of the therapy as regards the formation of a working alliance (Dickes 1975, Greenson 1967), transference, resistance, analyzability, and the capacity to undergo analysis without succumbing to overwhelming severe regressive episodes which border on psychotic manifestations. Most obligatory homosexuals show some signs of preoedipal developmental fixation together with neurotic symptomatology. In the milder forms, the presence of ego disturbances and regressive episodes may be fleeting or intermittent. The majority of cases seem to lie in the group which might be termed *transference neuroses* marked by libidinal fixations with an underlying, more limited fixation in ego structure. As a result, the overall personality differentiation has not been halted. Those with a minimum degree of preoedipal develop-

This chapter was first presented as a paper before the American Psychoanalytic Association, December 1976, entitled "Considerations on the Psychoanalytic Treatment of Overt Male Homosexuality. Part III: The Analysis of Regressive Phenomena." It is for the most part restricted to an examination of regressive phenomena in homosexual patients of the preoedipal form, Type II.

mental fixation seem to have the best prognosis, as a transference neurosis can be easily maintained and worked with in psychoanalytic therapy; the worst cases, which require our special concern, appear to be those in which there are frequent regressions or manifestations of ego disturbances which lend a definite borderline coloration to the clinical picture together with the appearance, on occasion, of clinical features similar to transference psychoses.

In comparison to the psychotic, the preoedipal homosexual's regression in ego functions is circumscribed and limited largely to certain aspects of his relationship to the transference figure. (These observations pertain also to his transference.) He may allow himself to regress in terms of his object relations and ego functions and he renounces certain of his reality testing functions partially and temporarily, but he is able to work with these reactions and to understand them with his observing ego. Temporary regressions as well as progressions are usually circumscribed, not generalized, and he may rebound from them or simply express them during analytic sessions. Primitive mental mechanisms like projection, introjection, splitting, and denial are commonly encountered in the more severe cases.

Developmental failures leave the patient subject to two consequences: (1) the development of perverse practices and/or fantasies, and (2) regressive episodes experienced as engulfment, merging with the mother in the earlier phases of child development, and self-object dissolution. In patients who are unable to form stabilizing, well-constructed perversions (Socarides 1973) or in those where the perversion no longer serves as a successful repressive device (Sachs 1923) against

deeper anxieties, there appears an increasing vulnerability to regressive episodes in which engulfment
phenomena, loss of ego boundaries, the tendency to
loss of self, body disintegration anxieties, splitting of
the ego, and diffusion between sexual and aggressive
drives occur. Thus it is of the utmost importance to
fully comprehend the meaning and function of these
phenomena as their successful handling is vital to the
resolution of the homosexual's difficulties.

In a previous paper (Socarides 1975) I suggested that
the manifest perverse behavior in homosexuality has a
specific relationship to its unconscious hidden meaning which can only be likened to the relationship which
exists between manifest content of a dream and latent
dream thoughts (Joseph 1965). Joseph (1965), in a Kris
Study Group Monograph report, is of the same opinion
regarding beating perversions. The "latent dream
thoughts" of the perversion are compellingly revealed
during the regressive phases; their meaning can then
be fully revealed to the patient.

Concentration at the genital level of the patient's
development cannot be successful until the preoedipal
regressions to which these patients are subject are
fully ventilated. Some hint as to the meaning of the
preoedipal regressions can be obtained from the study
of the fantasy systems and actual sexual practices.
Behind these conscious fantasy systems and manifest
practices lie the more primitive unconscious systems,
the analysis of which is essential to the loosening of
defensive regression. It is at this point, however, that
one finds the most intractable resistances, more
particularly since these early unconscious sexual
fantasies, if powerfully charged, are capable of
disturbing the patient's reality sense to such a degree

that, if persistent, would give rise to psychotic-like reactions.

Some homosexuals may not readily portray the merging phenomenon in its most dramatic form. However, fears of engulfment and merging are seen in their derivative forms—for example, dreams and fantasies of being surrounded by snakes, of being sucked into whirlpools, of being enclosed in caves, of traveling at express speed in elevators whose sides are collapsing, and so on. Other patients may never approach these experiences if they do not seriously attempt to interrupt their perversion. Others greatly fear facing this overwhelming anxiety and will prematurely terminate psychoanalytic therapy in a period of resistance, with many rationalizations for the interruption. Some of the latter will return to therapy for shorter or longer periods of time to relieve their suffering, only again to escape from facing their deepest conflicts. The failure to successfully resolve these may be largely responsible for the inevitable later continuance of the perverse practice. On the other hand, once this material has been worked through, the way is open to analyze the genital kernel of the oedipus complex, which the homosexual has used every unconscious mechanism to conceal.

Clinical Examples of Regressions

Roger (see chapter 13) used the couch during most of his sessions, although at times of severe regression he would spontaneously sit up for short periods of time, unable to tolerate disturbances in body ego and spatial relationships. On most occasions he felt relieved through the affective discharge of memories and would spontaneously allow himself to drift off into reveries, fantasies, and affective experiences. With the progressive elucidation and understanding of the unconscious meaning of his homosexual act, its substitutions, its displacements, its function as a repressive device, its attempt to create an equilibrium for both his libidinal and aggressive drives, and its aim of incorporating both maternal and paternal images in one act, he began to lose the intensity of his homosexual urges.

This morning when I went to the subway nothing happened. I couldn't do it. [He cries and whimpers.] It's getting harder and harder to do anything homosexual. I've tried asking myself how I felt and I felt rotten. I think I just want to be held in my father's arms and to hold my father's hand and to walk down the street, perhaps someone strong next to me. I am so ashamed. Oh, I don't hate him at all. I hate her but I don't hate him. But they both hate me. One left me and one never paid attention to me.[He starts an hysterical, high-pitched laugh.] He should have pulled her hair out and pulled her legs out and shoved them down her throat. He should have killed her and taken me with him

It became clear to Roger that he was attempting in his homosexual object choice—in the most distorted way—to find the primary reality of his narcissistic relationship with different images of his mother (and later of his father). He saw that he desperately needed and sought a contact whenever he felt weakened, frightened, depleted, guilty, ashamed, or in any way helpless or powerless. During the course of psychoanalytic therapy the homosexual symptom had become progressively less ego-syntonic, its magical and narcissistic triumphal powers had begun to diminish, and his increasing reluctance to utilize the perversion left him susceptible to a great danger, namely, a regressive pull to the preoedipal fixation point where there was a desire for and dread of merging with his mother.

On most occasions these regressive phenomena did not alarm the patient; he wished to investigate them and actively cooperated in their analysis. He felt profoundly relieved by the elucidation of their meaning and by the knowledge that he was overcoming previous profoundly disturbing fixating emotions of his childhood.

On several occasions his voice suddenly changed pitch. He became angry, bitter, snarling:

As I am talking I feel my hands getting bigger now. The fingers are clasped like there is a penis in this hole. I feel like a little boy now, a little boy and I'm sinking, sinking. My whole body is going down, down, almost as though I am shriveling up. I feel like I couldn't get up, like I'm embedded in this couch and tons of weight are on me and I was about to cry a second ago and I felt a relief feeling as if by your interrupting me that you're going to say something to make it clear, that I will come back and all this will go away, and I will come back somehow. And I feel now like I'm being rolled in a ship; I have nausea. My hands have gotten very cold. I am swinging now. I love and hate all men. I'd like to beat them. I got very upset as I said that. It's as if I'm at the bottom of a hole. The opening is way up and it's very dank and warm and wet. And my head is up. However it seems at times my penis is covered and I'm lying flat.

On other occasions he experienced changes in bodily size and shape, a loss of sense of identity, feelings of sinking, loss of orientation, and an intense fantasy bordering on hallucination of being inside the mother's womb. These were accompanied by terror, sobbing, crying, and severe anxiety.

In the case of Campbell (see chapter 12), regressive states were especially prevalent during the first two years of analysis and gradually reduced in both intensity and duration. They often began with severe tension headaches, usually one-sided and migrainous in nature. At these times he felt he would crack up or fragment into a million pieces. He felt a loss of direction or orientation. Lights became exceedingly bright. The room sometimes appeared to shift and he became frightened (spatial orientation disturbances). At these times, "I feel terribly sick, sort of terrible fright and then a compulsion for homosexual activities. Somehow it's like I'm going to be destroyed, I'm going to be attacked and I'm in terrible danger. It feels like if I don't preserve myself, if I don't have a homosexual relationship, I may go insane. It's not an indulgence at all that I do this but I have to do it or I might explode or go crazy." In regressive periods he developed strange feelings that he would swallow parts of his body such as his hand or his foot (incorporation anxieties and body schema disturbances), and that he could lose part of his face or be separated from his face, or that in separating from his face, another face would be found to exist beneath it (ego splitting).

On one occasion after an emergency telephone call, the patient arrived at my office nearly screaming, alternating between crying and bitter childlike half-laughter. Tears streamed down his face. He was unkempt and tended to fall from the couch to the floor, unable to walk. He could not take a step without complaining that he felt paralyzed. His mother had been extremely angry at him for wanting to return to the city and not accompanying her to a cocktail party.

In this session he relived previous fantasies or actual experiences. He choked, stuttered, cried, and felt terrible. He was unable to get up from the couch, began to roll on the floor, finally was helped to rise, but soon collapsed. "I am a child. I am a child. Mommy is coming back to the room." He was easily brought back to reality by a comment from the analyst, although he easily slipped back into this affective state. He suddenly cried out in pain, grasping his head, as he reexperienced a long-forgotten memory of a mastoid infection while around the age of two and a half. He felt he was under sodium pentathol and that the analyst had anesthetized him.

This is what I'm afraid of—that I'll sink into this, that I'll sink into Mommy. I keep thinking that I'm drooling like a baby. I must be under an anesthetic. It's as if I were under ether. It's like I'm losing myself. I got increasingly anxious after I left her. She asked me to find her driver's license and when I looked into Mommy's bureau I saw her underwear and I felt a terrible inpulse to get inside her. Not intercourse like but of totally entering her. I remember I would never open her pocketbook or her drawers as a child. It was like I was rejoining her but I douldn't do it. I remember a terrible garbage fantasy as a child—being immersed in it up to my mouth and could not move or else I would be swallowed up by garbage. Before I called you I tried to stop these feelings by putting peroxide on my hair, wanted to shave my hair off my body and going out and having a man. But I realized I shouldn't do this any more and I washed it out. I also felt she is closing in on me, will not love me anymore if I try to leave her. I felt terribly depressed and I can't change my sex. But then I go back to lie in her bed and I lie there, like in her arms, and I look at myself in the mirror and I am shaking.

This regression gradually ceased over a two-hour period. It tended to reappear the following day, but upon telephoning the analyst the threat of personal dissolution vanished. In this and in similar regressions Campbell became completely aware of his fear of abandonment by the mother, and at the same time, of a wish to merge forcibly into her. The only way to escape and achieve security was through the homosexual symptom. The regressive material appeared when the patient, aided by the positive transference, attempted a premature separation from his mother, openly defying her.

Conclusions

In the psychoanalytic treatment of these patients it is important to assess the degree to which these regressive episodes are primarily defensive reactions in the face of danger, consequences of severe ego deficits, or a combination of the two. If the ego deficiency is severe it may be necessary to temporarily support the patient in his desperate struggle to maintain contact with reality and to preserve the object, that is, the self. Thus, the analyst may answer questions more readily, support reality contact by utilizing the sitting-up position, combat fears of separation and object loss, and allow contact with the analyst by phone. Under these special circumstances it may be vital that the analyst be continually available to the patient. Later on, one may return to the traditional and basic psychoanalytic techniques. This is in agreement with the views expressed in several panels devoted to the comprehension and management of all severe regressive states during analysis

(Weinshel 1966, Calder 1958, Atkins 1967, Dickes 1967, Frosch 1967, Peto 1967, Wallerstein 1967).

At the outset it is important to realize, as noted in chapter 24, that these regressions do not necessarily connote regression to the earliest period of life, that is, to oral fantasies which originated during the oral phase. They may have originated during the phallic oedipal period and may consist of "regressions to an oral fantasy which originated however during the phallic-oedipal phase" (Arlow 1963). Thus they do not necessarily mean a reliving of conflicts or events of the oral period itself. It is important to trace back the fantasy of the neurotic symptom to the time of its origin in the history of the patient, placing it within the framework of the immature ego organization which existed at that time. These regressions are reactivations of earlier childhood regressive experiences which, because of the loss of maturational gains and secondary autonomy, represent a return to the helplessness and dependency of infancy. Although they may be termed *regressive reenactments* these regressions are characterized in the Weinshel Panel Report (1966) as follows: (1) There is a pointed intactness in the ego's relations with reality, but reality testing is consciously and/or unconsciously temporarily ignored (to save the pleasure principle); (2) "Object relations are impaired to the point of dedifferentiation and disruption in the boundaries of the various psychic structures"; (3) "More archaic ego states, functions and defense mechanisms" make their appearance; (4) "The nature of the anxiety seems related to problems of preservation of self and identity rather than oedipal conflict not unlike that seen in psychotic states" (Weinshel 1966, p. 538).

In general, patients who can handle these experiences successfully demonstrate: (1) "a capacity for self-observation"; (2) "the ability to verbalize" that which they have experienced; (3) "a high intelligence, synthetic and sublimatory capacities"; (4) "a capacity for thought symbolization"; and (5) an ability "to keep hallucinations distinct from fantasy and fantasy from reality" (Weinshel 1966, p. 544). The absence of enduring psychotic episodes in my patients who have experienced similar regressive states in the course of psychoanalysis of their homosexuality tends to support Arlow's viewpoint.

The revival and affective discharge of such primitive emotions leads to a gradual diminishing of their force, especially if combined with a new understanding of chronically persisting and highly disturbing childhood memories and fantasies. The patients reintegrate to the extent of living an organized life, often being able to marry, having sex with women, and ridding themselves of their perversion and symptomatology.

What is vitally important is that these severe regressive states should not lead the analyst to give into the "temptation either to abandon the analysis or to modify the basic analytic approach" (Weinshel 1966, p. 555), although some supportive measures may be given. The eventual acquisition of the capacity for object relationships is reflected in the therapeutic alliance. It must be seen that this is the patient's way of reliving in his analysis his infantile disturbances and his early relationship with his mother and father, discovering his infantile self-image, and his primitive identifications. In the patient's restitution we do not simply seal over but reverse and undo the damage "inflicted in the compulsive reenactment of earlier traumatic situations" (Weinshel 1966). The various ramifications of the early damaging fantasies become a crucial part of the reconstituted efforts.

As with other patients with severe regressions, the analysis of homosexual patients "focuses on the regaining of relinquished capacities and aspects of the self, rather than being a reeducation or a filling in of ego defects" (Weinshel 1966). Such a focus involves a bringing together and acceptance by the self of repressed, denied, and projected parts of the personality. If the regressive transference revival of the traumatic infantile disturbances remains unanalyzed, analysts may "in a sense be guilty of abandoning the helpless patient to himself, leaving him vulnerable to possible enduring fixations."

The ultimate value of these regressive phenomena lies not only in the removal of symptoms but in their function as a vehicle for furthering psychoanalytic knowledge of the perversions. As correctly noted by the Weinshel (1966) panel:

The specific protective set-up of the analytic situation offers the patient's ego an opportunity to face the previously repressed material in a more constructive manner than at the time of the original fixation. Thus a patient proves to himself that his ego is stronger and more adaptive than he considers it to be. This in turn permits some reintegration of previously split-off representations and the abandonment of somatic symbolizations in favor of higher forms of feeling and more mature affect mobilization and control....The flow and continued emergence of regressive material may be controlled by a balance between content and resistance interpretation as a means of discouraging such material. The analyst's accepting attitude and resilient empathy encourage the continuation of the regressive process, and while there may be certain misunderstandings which temporarily disrupt the analytic relationship, they can be readily balanced by the analyst's genuine efforts to follow and comprehend the various archaic details. [p. 545]

Regressive episodes have a beneficial effect on the development of transference in the course of analysis. New material is elicited; the repetitive aspects of the regression increase the opportunity for the controlled working through of material and its more propitious integration. In many cases the regression constitutes the vehicle for the channeling of hitherto repressed forms of object relations and drive gratifications. This regressive dedifferentiation is a necessary preliminary to the introduction of "better neutralized structures into the ego and into the drive organization" (Peto 1967). Furthermore, with many homosexual patients an integrated, consistent and meaningful self-image will emerge only after this phase has been traversed. Thus, with the gradual passing of these stormy periods what begins to make its appearance is the relative peacefulness of emerging adaptive reintegration.

Chapter 26
DIFFERENTIATING CRITERIA OF THE HOMOSEXUALITIES AND THEIR IMPLICATIONS FOR PSYCHOANALYTIC THERAPY

In this final chapter I shall limit myself to ten differentiating categories which separate, contrast, and clarify the three major forms of clinical homosexuality. This grouping in an integrated fashion reveals, I hope, what can be expected in a well-conducted psychoanalysis of these patients; provides information as to the ultimate outcome regarding the removal of homosexual impulse, the establishment of heterosexual functioning, and the capacity of the individual to cathect a heterosexual love object; notes types of resistances; describes transference manifestations; notes the depth and frequency of regressive experiences and the capacity of the individual patients to use them therapeutically and recover from them; informs us as to the basic nuclear conflict that will be

The material was first presented before the American Psychoanalytic Association, December 1977 in a paper entitled "Considerations of the Psychoanalytic Treatment of Overt Homosexuality: Part IV: A Provisional Classification and Differentiating Criteria of the Homosexualities."

affectively revived during therapy and the capacity of
the individual ego to deal with it; specifies the class of
conflict to be met with (structural vs. object relations);
and indirectly provides information as to the presence
of areas of healthy object relatedness which will serve
as our therapeutic allies during the course of psycho-
analysis. Ongoing clinical observations and data
collecting will undoubtedly lead to further clarification
and refinement of the distinctly different homosexualities and thereby increase the efficacy of psychoanalytic treatment.

The essential ingredient of homosexuality is the
unconscious and imperative need to pursue and
experience sexual pleasure and orgastic release with
individuals of the same sex. This act expresses, in a
distorted way, repressed forbidden impulses and most
often brings temporary relief, either partial or complete, from warring intrapsychic forces. The homosexual mechanism for the relief of unconscious conflict
exists at any level of libidinal fixations and ego
development, from the most primitive to the more
highly developed levels of organization. The underlying unconscious motivational drives are distinctly
different depending upon the level from which they
arise. Oedipal homosexuality arises from the phallic
organization of development and must be differentiated from preoedipal homosexuality which arises from
preoedipal levels of development. We associate narcissistic neuroses and impulse disorders with the latter.
The homosexual symptom can operate at an anal level,
especially when it represents a regression from genital
oedipal phase conflict. In the schizophrenic the
symptom may represent an archaic and primitive level
of functioning, a frantic and chaotic attempt to
construct object relationships.

Thus, there is a wide range of clinical forms of homosexuality, from those which derive from very archaic, primitive levels to those which are a product of more highly differentiated ones. Each individual case is hierarchically layered with dynamic mechanisms stemming from multiple points of fixation and regression. We can conclude that the clinical picture of the homosexuality itself does not necessarily correctly describe the origin of the particular mechanism responsible for it. This requires a study of the developmental stages through which the individual has passed, the level of fixation, the state of his object relations, and the status of his ego functions.

The challenge which confronts us is to understand the various clinical pictures of homosexuality from the mildest to the well-structured perversion to that occurring in an individual with a florid psychosis. Greenacre (1968) succinctly stated the difficulties facing any investigator in the course of describing general genetic and dynamic aspects of perversions. She noted that (1) the multiplicity of forms and varying intensities of the perversion, from the slightly deviant to the extreme or even bizarre, confuse us in understanding its essential character; (2) the analyst usually treats the the relatively pronounced cases in which "perverse development is clear and definite" (p. 47); and (3) while careful psychoanalytic investigation of a small number of well-structured cases is very important, "it is nonetheless difficult to accumulate sufficient experience on which to base broader generalizations" (pp. 47-48).

Three contributions have set the stage for attempting a psychoanalytic classification of homosexuality. The first, by Gillespie (1965a), was entitled "The General Theory of Sexual Perversion." As I have previously noted (Socarides 1968), Gillespie's theory was remarkably comprehensive, taking into account infantile sexuality and affirming that the problem of perversion lies in the defense against oedipal difficulties. It underscored the concept that in perversion there is a regression of libido and aggression to preoedipal levels rather than a primary fixation at those levels. He provided all-important insights into ego defenses, the Sachs mechanism, the role of the superego in perversion formation, splitting processes, and the relationship of perversion to psychosis.

In a summing up of her extensive clinical research in 1968, Greenacre concluded that "our more recent studies of early ego development would indicate that the fundamental disturbance is in this [sexual development] area and that the defectively developed ego uses the pressure of the maturing libidinal phases for its own purposes in characteristic ways because of the extreme and persistent narcissistic needs.... Probably in most perversions, there is a prolongation of the introjective-projective stage in which there is an incomplete separation of the 'I' from the 'Other' and an oscillation between the two. This is associated with a more than usually strong capacity for primary identification" (Greenacre 1968, pp. 48-49).

In a 1967 paper presented before the American Psychoanalytic Association, entitled "A Unitary Theory of Sexual Perversion" (Socarides 1978), I proposed that the genesis of well-structured perversions including homosexuality may well be the result of disturbances which occur earlier than had been generally assumed, namely, in the preoedipal phase. This unitary theory grew out of my intensive work with homosexual patients and others with perversions in which the preoedipal nuclear conflict emerged dramatically and repetitively in individuals showing no evidence of psychosis. The pillars of the preoedipal theory described in 1968 are as follows: (1) Nuclear conflicts of all those with sexual perversions derive from the earliest period of life, before the age of three, forcing these individuals into later sexual behavior which not only affords orgastic release but also ensures ego survival. (2) The primary fixation occurs in this period; a regression may occur to this early period under conditions of stress. (3) The sexual pervert has been unable to pass successfully through the separation-individuation phase (Mahler 1967) or early childhood. (The level of fixation may vary according to the type of perversion and this fixation creates the original anxiety from which the sexual perversion arises.) (4) The source of the pervert's original anxiety emanates from the preoedipal period. As a result of this maturational (psychological) developmental failure there are mederate to severe impairments in ego functions and the presence of a faulty or distorted sexual identity. (5) Sexual perversion including homosexuality serves the repression of a pivotal nuclear conflict, the urge to regress to a preoedipal fixation in which there is a desire for and dread of merging with the mother in order to reinstate the primitive mother-child unity. The phenomena I observed in homosexuals and other perverts in their acts, dreams, fantasies, and other symptoms did not appear to be due to a regression from a previous, more mature phase of development. On the contrary, it impressed me that the primary preoedipal fixation dominated the life of the individual in his search for identity. It was my impression that a disturbed preoedipal phase in these individuals contributed to producing a disturbance in sexual identity, a matter central to the homosexual's difficulties. Subsequent clinical observation of an increasingly large number of homosexual patients during a ten-year period (1967 to 1977) has led me to conclude that this hypothesis, although correct, was too narrow. The preoedipal theory casts light on the content and meaning of well-structured and pronounced cases. The heuristic value of applying this formulation both in clinical practice and in teaching was that it led irresistibly to the search for explanations for other forms of homosexuality which did not fulfill the characteristics and criteria of the preoedipal form. In a 1974 article I divided the homosexualities into oedipal and preoedipal forms and described the characteristics of each (Socarides 1974).

Specific forms of homosexuality must be seen in relation to other forms. A comprehensive classification system must correlate, integrate, and group many factors in a logical fashion. Such a system must explain homosexuality which arises from oedipal sources, preoedipal fixations, or schizophrenic processes. It appears likely that a similar system will help explain the various forms of other perversions; for example, pedophilia may be classified as oedipal pedophilia, preoedipal pedophilia, and schizopedophilia. Above all, it should answer the question as to whether the same phenomenology has different structures in different individuals with the same perversion.

A psychoanalytic classification of any disorder cannot derive from a single frame of reference, such as the symptom alone—whether it be a phobia, a conversion reaction, or a perversion. Neither can we fully comprehend the condition by a knowledge of the processes of symptom formation, for example, defenses. Rather, as outlined by a 1960 panel on nosology (Ross 1960), we must adhere to a multidimensional approach. This should include data derived from a number of sources including: (1) the level of libidinal fixation or regression (instinctual framework); (2) the stage of maturation, fixation, or regression of the ego (developmental framework); (3) the symptom itself as an "end product"; (4) the processes of symptom formation; and (5) an inventory of ego functions.

The homosexualities may be listed as follows: (1) preoedipal form Type I and Type II; (2) oedipal form; (3) schizo-homosexual form; (4) latent form; (5) variational form; and (6) situational form. The general criteria for each form have been previously described (with the exception of schizo-homosexuality) in chapter 5.

Briefly, both situational and variational forms are nonobligatory in nature and do not represent a true sexual perversion in the clinical sense. Both have strong determinants in conscious motivations and heterosexual functioning is possible and preferred. Latent homosexuality, properly defined, has the underlying psychic structure of either the preoedipal or oedipal form but without overt homosexual practices.

Schizo-homosexuality, the coexistence of homosexuality and schizophrenia, is a term coined by the author. The major contribution in this area has been provided by Bak (1971). He noted that (1) homosexual conflicts and their delusional elaborations are "consequences of a [schizophrenic] process rather than its cause" (p. 239); (2) perverse actions in schizophrenics with self-object dedifferentiation show significant difference from those in people who have better object relations and ego functions; and (3) in true perversions object relations are maintained despite a "fused body image or fused genital representations" in contrast to perverse activities in a schizophrenic where they are not maintained (p. 242).

It seems evident that schizo-homosexuality may be explained by its relationship to autistic and symbiotic modes of adaptation. This may connote a fixation at the autistic and/or symbiotic phase in order to ward off the fear of dissolution of the self-representation. This is in striking contrast to the fixation in the preoedipal form of homosexuality which appears to have taken place during the later phases of the separation-individuation process.

In contrast to my 1974 classification (Socarides 1974), the preoedipal form here is divided into Types I and II. In the milder preoedipal form, Type I, while the preoedipal fixation is etiological, the clinical picture is largely one of oedipal phase conflict, and regression does not involve severe impairment in object relations or other ego functions. In the more severe preoedipal form, Type II, preoedipal fixation is of prime importance both etiologically and clinically, constantly dominating the psychic life of the individual in his search for identity and a cohesive self. Oedipal conflict and castration fears may defend against deeper fears, and preoedipal fantasies may defend against the emergence of oedipal material (Hoffer 1954).

Oedipal homosexuality is a different form of homosexuality and may be approached therapeutically as one would the neuroses. It occurs secondary to the temporary regression and does not represent a developmental failure due to a primary fixation. Although the repressive compromise (Sachs mechanism) is operative, it does not defend against primitive archaic anxieties and self-object differentiation conflicts.

A detailed examination follows of the differentiating characteristics of the preoedipal Types I and II and the oedipal type with the aim of further demonstrating and clarifying both their similarities and their differences. Some comments will be made on schizo-homosexuality for the purpose of clearly separating it from preoedipal homosexuality, Type II.

Status of Object Relations

In oedipal homosexuality object relations are unimpaired and consist of a relation of self to object, more precisely, from the "infantile submissive oedipal self" to the "domineering prohibiting oedipal father" (Kernberg 1975). In preoedipal form, Type I, object relations are mildly impaired and consist of an object relation which fits the formula of object to self. In preoedipal form, Type II, object relations are moderately to severely impaired and consist of a relation of object to self. In both preoedipal Types I and II the homosexual object stands for the self; it is a narcissistic one but "still an object relation, i.e. that between mother and child" (Kernberg 1975). In schizo-homosexuality the psychotic has lost his internal object-representations and strives to fill up the feeling of a terrible void by creating new objects (Kernberg 1975). There is a lack of adequate separation of self and object. The author acknowledges here the valuable contributions in the area of internalized object relations and narcissictic personality disorder made by Kernberg (1975), Kohut (1974), and Volkan (1976) among others. Kernberg suggested in 1975 that male homosexuality may be classified along a continuum that differentiates the degrees of severity of pathology of internalized object relations.

Prognosis for Recovery

In the oedipal form the prognosis for the removal of the homosexual symptom and the attainment of objec t love is often excellent. In the preoedipal form the prognosis varies from good to more reserved. Similar to the oedipal form, the preoedipal form, Type I patients usually do not require specific modifications in psychoanalytic technique. In the more severe cases (preoedipal, Type II) the analyst may use modified techniques on occasion, as with the borderline conditions. Those with a "severe narcissistic personality structure proper" (Kernberg 1975) may pose special problems in that the attempted removal of the narcissistic character neurosis produces severe depressive attacks, feelings of emptiness and worthlessness, and attacks of narcissistic rage.

In the schizo-homosexual the prognosis is poor since there is a qualitative difference in the homosexual symptom in these individuals. One should keep in mind that homosexual symptoms are consequences of a psychotic process and not causes of it (Bak 1971). The schizophrenic process itself has undone repression, destroyed object relations, and laid bare both the pregenital phase and primitive ego states. Even with the disappearance of the secondary symptoms of schizophrenia it is not unusual for the homosexual symptom to remain during compensated phases of the psychosis (see chapter 17). The advisability of attempting to remove homosexual symptoms during compensated phases of schizophrenia must be carefully weighed against the possibility of exacerbating the psychosis. One takes exception to this observation in those who experience "incidental psychoses"

(Bak 1971) as they have retained their capacity to restore object relations.

Meaning of the Homosexual Act

In the oedipal form the homosexual symptom is due to the failure to resolve the oedipus complex and to castration fears which lead to a negative oedipal position. There is a sexual submission to the parent of the same sex. Genital oedipal conflicts predominate.

In the preoedipal form, Type I, oedipal conflicts are prominent and superimposed on more basic preoedipal anxiety. In Type II, preoedipal conflicts predominate over genital ones. The pursued partners in both types of the preoedipal form represent the patient's own self (narcissistic) in relation to an active, phallic mother. Identification with and incorporation of the partner's masculinity in the sexual act is essential to both Types I and II. Anna Freud (1954) first introduced this major mechanism of preoedipal homosexuality. In addition, preoedipal homosexuals unconsciously enact the mother-child role (breast-penis equation). The Type II homosexual loves the homosexual partner as an extension of his own "pathological grandiose self" (Kernberg 1975). Splitting processes of the ego, object, and superego are especially prominent.

In schizo-homosexuality the patient attempts to make relationships to external objects through homosexuality, defending himself against imminent disruptive incorporation by the mother.

Degree and Level of Fixation

In the oedipal form there is no fixation at preoedipal

levels but often a partial regression to the preoedipal phase. In the preoedipal form, Type I, a fixation may be mild to moderate and is probably located in the later phases of the separation-individuation process in the rapprochement subphase. In the preoedipal form, Type II, the severity of fixation is considerably more intense and damaging in its effect. In schizo-homosexuality the fixation may, in all likelihood, be in earlier phases of the separation-individuation process, possibly the symbiotic phase. There are severe to moderate ego disturbances, and symbiotic relation-ships are based on the degree of fusion.

The basic nuclear conflict that is effectively revived during therapy in the preoedipal Type II homosexual does not represent an actual return to the undifferen-tiated phase, despite the appearance of symptoms of fe fears of merging with the mother, threatened loss of ego boundaries, feelings of fragmentation, and fears of annihilation. As Arlow (1963) notes, such primitive and regressive experiences and fantasies apparently derive from phallic or late prephallic phase fantasies and do not originate in the oral phase. My own clinical experience supports this view: preoedipal Type II patients do not become psychotic despite these frightening experiences.

Class of Conflict

It has become increasingly apparent that there has been "no satisfactory set of concepts...proposed for the study of the psyche before its differentiation into id-ego-superego" (Gedo and Goldberg 1973). In his clear exposition of this problem, Dorpat (1976) notes that Modell (1968), Jacobson (1964), Fairbairn (1954), and

Gedo and Goldberg (1973), among others, have already laid the foundation for a systematic theory of such early conflicts. Dorpat notes: "At a higher developmental level, the hierarchical model includes the tripartite model, and at a lower level it includes an object-relations model.... The object-relations class of psychic conflict covers the phase of psychic development prior to id-ego-superego differentiation" (p. 837).

In the oedipal homosexual a structural conflict exists which involves the major psychic structures of ego, id, and superego. The conflict is between the subject's aggressive, sexual, and other wishes and his own prohibitions and ideals. The nuclear conflict may consist of the renunciation of oedipal love for the mother in the male and a corresponding conflict in the female.

In both types of the preoedipal form an object relations conflict predominates. This consists of anxiety and guilt "associated with the failure of development in the phase of self-object differentiation" (Modell 1968, p. 328). As a consequence, the nuclear conflict in this form is a preoedipal fixation in which there is a desire for and dread of merging with the mother in order to reinstate the primitive mother-child unity (Socarides 1967, 1968). (It is of interest to note that, as in this instance, conclusions arrived at by clinical research methods can precede their theoretical explanation.)

The Sachs Mechanism and Ego-Syntonicity

In preoedipal homosexuality the intense attachment, fear, and guilt in the boy's relationship with his mother bring about certain major psychic transformations which are effected through the mechanism of the repressive compromise. It is a solution by division whereby one piece of infantile sexuality enters the service of repression, that is, it helps to promote repression through displacement, substitution, and other defense mechanisms. Pregenital pleasure is thereby carried over into the ego while the rest is repressed. Sachs first described this major mechanism in the development of homosexuality in 1923. It is the basic mechanism in producing preoedipal homosexuality of both types in both males and females (Socarides 1967) and in promoting ego-syntonicity.

Clinical observations reveal that the Sachs mechanism may play a minor role in oedipal forms in which regression takes place and that it is partially effective in schizo-homosexuality. It is infrequently utilized successfully in the oedipal form and the homosexual symptom remains ego-alien. Although unconsciously determined in oedipal forms, the anxieties which are held in repression through the Sachs mechanism are not those concerned with primitive archaic conflicts and fixations. The symptom may remain at the level of unconscious thoughts, dreams, and fantasies and is not a disguised, acceptable representation of a deeper conflict. When the symptom threatens to break into awareness, anxiety develops. Under certain conditions of stress and feelings of helplessness, homosexual acts may take place. Such acts, however, do not achieve the magic symbolic restitution of the preoedipal types. They may, in fact, exacerbate the situation through loss of pride and self-esteem.

The less successfully functioning Sachs mechanism in the oedipal form makes the task of removing the homosexual symptom a much easier one, once the unconscious motivations for the homosexual desire are analyzed, since the magical restorative and equilibrium producing functions of this mechanism are less effective.

Otto Sperling (1956) described a special form of homosexuality which he termed *induced perversion.* Here there is a splitting of the superego in which a leader in group perverse activities replaces the patient's superego. This reactivates a split in childhood which had remained latent. "Induced" homosexuality can be either oedipal or preoedipal.

Tendency to Severe Regressive States

In the oedipal form the tendency to severe regressive states is mild, and when it occurs it is similar to regression in neurotics. The threats of the oedipal period have disrupted the already formed identity; a regression to an earlier period occurs as an escape from the dangers of the oedipal period. This is a partial, preoedipal regression to anal and even oral conflicts.

In the milder preoedipal form the tendency to regression is moderate and temporary while in Type II it is moderate to severe although the patient has an adequate capacity, in most instances, to circumscribe these regressions. In the more severe cases these regressions are often chronic and not easily removed. They may temporarily disrupt the analytic relationship and reintegration may be difficult (Weinshel 1966).

The severity of the preoedipal developmental fixation may be crucial to the outcome and to the forward movement of the therapy as regards the formation of a working alliance, the transference, resistance, analyzability, and the capacity to undergo analysis without succumbing to severe regressive episodes which border on near-psychotic manifestations. In most instances these episodes may be fleeting or intermittent. One can find detailed study of regressive phenomena with clinical examples in chapter 25.

In schizo-homosexuality deficiencies of the ego in forming, maintaining, and investing object-representations has led to a "paucity of object-representations" and a "predominance of fused self-object-representations" (Bak 1971, p. 241). This "defective capacity" is later experienced "as a danger to the self" and there are frequent "regressive adaptations with a further destruction of object representations" (p. 241). Thus, the tendency to to severe regressive states in schizo-homosexuality is extreme and occurs concomitantly with manifest secondary symptoms of schizophrenia.

Degree of Potential Analyzable Transferences

In chapter 24 I noted that crucial to the analyzability of homosexual patients is not the presenting symptomatology (even apparent extreme femininity), nor even the life history of the homosexual, but the nature of the spontaneously developing transference.

In the oedipal form transference manifestations are similar to those in the transference neuroses and therefore the degree of potentially analyzable transference is ideal. In preoedipal Type I there is also an analyzable transference because of sufficient self-object differentiation and internalization of object-representations. In the preoedipal form, Type II, analyzable transferences are present to a fair degree but the outcome depends on the tendency to externalize parts of the self and on the presence of severely regressive episodes.

Fortunately, however, we have sufficient clinical experience to conclude that the preoedipal homosexual has the capacity to form neurotic transferences. The relationships that exist between transference, object relations, and ego functions so well described by Greenson (1967) regarding neurotics apply as well to preoedipal homosexuality. For example, the homosexual differentiates between the self and the object "and has the ability to displace reactions from a past object representation to an object in the present" (p. 173). Therefore, he has, for the most part, "an organizing differentiated self, an entity separate and distinct from his environment, which has a capacity to remain the same in the midst of change" (p. 173). In contrast to psychotics "who have lost their internal object representation" (p. 173), he has the capacity to form a transference neurosis.

Therefore, if the preoedipal homosexual "misunderstands the present in terms of the past this misunderstanding is only partial and temporary" (p. 174). When he "suffers regressions in ego functions" they are "circumscribed" and largely "limited to certain aspects of his relationship to the transference figure" (p. 174). He may allow himself to "regress in terms of his object relations and ego functions" and he "renounces certain of his reality testing functions partially and temporarily," but he is able to work with these reactions and to understand them with his "observing ego" (pp. 173-175).

Capacity of the Orgasm to Restore
the Sense of Having a Bounded
and Cohesive Self

In the oedipal form the sense of self and ego boundaries are essentially unimpaired and therefore the orgasm does not function as it does in the preoedipal form. In preoedipal Types I and II there is a strong capacity for the restoration of self but in the severer form, Type II, the effect may be transitory, leading to an insistent and imperative need for multiple and frequent sexual contacts. In the latter instances boundaries between self-object–representations may be very fragile.

The greater the capacity of the orgasm to restore a sense of a bounded and cohesive self (Stolorow 1975, Eissler 1958), the more difficult it becomes to remove the homosexual symptom. Conversely, the less the orgasm functions in this manner (in those with a better structured ego), the greater will be the success in early removal of homosexual symptoms. The analyst must consider this factor in any attempted cessation of homosexual activity during therapy, as the patient (especially preoedipal Type II) may suffer greatly or withdraw from treatment due to the eruption of intolerable anxiety.

Status of Ego Functions
Other Than Object Relations

In the oedipal form of homosexuality reality testing and impulse control are intact.* *Thinking* is unimpaired and is dominated by the reality principle. Self-concept and ego boundaries are essentially unim-

paired and conflict is internalized. Affect is appropriate and responses of anxiety and depression are
frequently encountered. Aggression is essentially well
defended against. These findings are similar to those
in the transference neurosis.

In the preoedipal form, Type I, reality testing is often
intact but "consciously or unconsciously ignored to
serve the pleasure principle" (Kolansky and Eisner
1974). In Type II the boundary between fantasy and
reality can be indistinct; severe anxiety results in a
flight from reality in these instances.

Impulse control may be incomplete or partial,
leading to "acting out of impulses and pursuit of
instantaneous gratifications" (Kolansky and Eisner
1974) in preoedipal Type I. In the more severe type,
impulses are grossly acted out in an instantaneous
manner suggesting the complete loss of ego and
superego controls.

In the milder preoedipal Type I thinking may be
"clear but dominated by the pleasure principle"
(Kolansky and Eisner 1974). Such thinking combined
with poor impulse control leads to actions which
involve a denial of reality. In less severe cases thinking
may reflect the patient's own projective anxieties. In
the more severe cases greater impairment of thinking
may occur with occasional and fleeting semidelusional
convictions.

In preoedipal Type I patients, self-concept frequently
fluctuates between an elevated sense of self-esteem

---

*The author acknowledges his indebtedness to Kolansky and Eisner (1974) for the
use of their chart and listing of categories of "changes in ego functions" in their
paper, "The Psychoanalytic Concept of Preoedipal Developmental Arrest."
Although their paper deals with the differences in ego functions which exist
between "preoedipal developmental arrest" and "ego disturbances" I have found
their differentiations of great value when applied to homosexuality.

bordering on omnipotence and feelings of extreme self-depreciation. Ego boundaries are mainly intact and there is a strong need for narcissistic supplies. Occasional feelings of grandiosity may appear. In preoedipal Type II patients, there may be an unconscious and severe sense of worthlessness and emptiness with an extreme disturbance in self-concept. Under stress, ego boundaries may show severe impairment with the removal of the narcissistic facade.

In affect and affect control in both types of preoedipal homosexuality there is an inability to bear "external frustration" (Kolansky and Eisner 1974). In Type I, patients respond to anxiety and depression with aggressive action. In Type II patients, bursts of rage are frequent, as they have lost the capacity to neutralize aggression.

A schematic representation of the material cited above follows in a form which clearly distinguishes the homosexualities according to the criteria listed above.

CLASSIFICATION OF CLINICAL
FORMS OF HOMOSEXUALITY

CLASSIFICATION OF CLINICAL FORMS OF HOMOSEXUALITY

A Schematic Representation With Differentiating Criteria and Therapeutic Implications

	Oedipal Form	Preoedipal Form: Type I	Preoedipal Form: Type II	Schizo-Homosexuality (coexistence of homosexuality and schizophrenia)
Status of Object Relations	(1) Unimpaired (2) Self to object (from infantile submissive oedipal self to domineering prohibiting oedipal father)	(1) Mildly impaired (2) Object to self (homosexual object stands for the self) (3) A narcissistic one, but still an object relation, i.e., between mother and child	(1) Moderate to severe impairment (2)–(3) Same as Preoedipal I (4) Complicated often by severe degree of narcissism in which object relation is from pathological grandiose self to self	(1) Severely damaged, impaired or absent (2) Lack of adequate separation of self and object (3) "Regression of object relations" (Bak) (4) Psychotic has lost his internal object-representations and strives to fill up the feeling of a terrible void by creating new objects (Kernberg)
Genital Oedipal Conflicts	Dominate clinical picture	Oedipal conflict present with underlying preoedipal anxieties strongly evident	Preoedipal conflicts predominate over genital ones	Oedipal and preoedipal conflicts subject to severe distortion by psychotic process
Prognosis for Recovery	Excellent	Good to excellent. Patients usually do not require specific modifications in psychoanalytic technique	Not unfavorable, but more reserved than Type I. Can be treated successfully using modifications of technique as with borderline conditions. Most severe type, most commonly found in association with severe narcissistic personality structure proper	Poor. Homosexual symptoms are consequences of a psychotic process and may remain, appear, and disappear dependent on the psychotic process. Exception: incidental psychoses found in association with retained capacity to restore object relations

Meaning of the Homosexual Symptom	(1) Failure of resolution of oedipus complex and castration fear leads to negative oedipal position (2) Sexual submission to parent of same sex	(1) Pursued partners are representative of patient's own self (narcissistic) in relation to an active phallic mother (2) Identification with and incorporation of partner's masculinity in the sexual act (3) Unconscious enactment of mother-child role (breast-penis equation) (4) Splitting processes of ego, superego, and object prominent	(1)–(4) Same as in preoedipal Type I (5) The homosexual partner is loved as an extension of the patient's own "pathological grandiose self" (Kernberg)	(1) The patient attempts to make relationships to external objects through homosexuality, defending himself against imminent disruptive incorporation by the mother (2) Regression of self-nonself leads to adaptive reintegration attempt through perverse fantasy or action
Degree and Level of Fixation	No fixation at preoedipal levels but often a partial regression to preoedipal phase	Mild to moderate fixation, probably in later phases of separation-individuation process (rapprochement sub-phase)	More severe fixation which is more damaging in its effect. Rapprochement subphase	Fixation to earliest phases of separation-individuation with tendency to regress to symbiotic phase whose "essential feature... is hallucinatory or delusional somatopsychic omnipotent fusion with the representation of the mother and in particular, the delusion of a (cont.)

	Oedipal Form	Preoedipal Form: Type I	Preoedipal Form: Type II	Schizo-Homosexuality (coexistence of homosexuality and schizophrenia)
Degree and Level of Fixation (cont.)				common boundary between two physically separated individuals" (Mahler 1975, p. 45)
Class of Conflict	(1) *Structural conflict:* between major structures of ego, id, and superego. i.e., between subject's aggressive, sexual and other wishes and his own prohibitions and ideals (2) Nuclear conflict consists of renunciation of oedipal love for mother and corresponding conflict in the female	(1) *Object relations conflict:* anxiety and guilt associated with the failure of development in the phase of self-object differentiation (2) Nuclear conflict consists of a desire for and dread of merging with the mother in order to reinstate the primitive mother-child unity (separation anxiety)	(1) *Object relations conflict:* same as in Preoedipal Type I	(1) Primary deficiency in the autonomous ego, especially in the ego's capacity to form and maintain adequate object-representations (Bak) (2) Various anomalies of the ego produce impairment of (a) stimulus barrier (b) defensive functions (c) formation of psychic structure which leads to a defective capacity to deal with both the internal and the external world. This is experienced as a danger to the self, and regressive adaptation results with "further destruction of object representations" (Bak)

| The Sachs Mechanism and Ego-Syntonicity | (1) Although unconsciously determined, the anxieties which are held in repression through the Sachs mechanism are not those concerned with primitive archaic conflicts and fixations. (2) Ego-alien symptom (3) Symptom unacceptable to superego. No splitting of the superego | (1) Utilized successfully. It is a mechanism of repressive compromise—a solution by division whereby one piece of infantile sexuality is enacted and in so doing is helpful in promoting repression of a deeper, more dangerous conflict through displacement, substitution, and other defense mechanisms (2) Ego-syntonic (3) Symptom acceptable to superego due to splitting of the superego. An unconscious part of the superego stemming from the parents is demanding the perversion. Therefore, treatment task is to establish a conscious split in superego and analyze the part of the superego that supports the perversion and strengthen the ego against its commands | Same as in Preoedipal Type I | Only partially utilized and effective due to schizophrenic defects |

	Oedipal Form:	Preoedipal Form: Type I	Preoedipal Form: Type II	Schizo-homosexuality (coexistence of homosexuality and schizophrenia)
Tendency to Severe Regressive States	Mild. Some regression as in neurotics to anal and oral conflicts	Moderate and temporary. Adequate capacity to circumscribe these regressions and recover from them	More severe regressive episodes. More chronic and/or intermittent and more difficult to recover from quickly. Intensity borders on psychotic-like manifestations with full affective experiences of earliest fears and aggressions. Contact with analyst maintained but regressions threaten to temporarily disrupt the analytic relationship	Frequent regressive adaptations with tendency to further destruction of object-representation. Secondary symptoms of schizophrenia may appear
Degree of Potentially Analyzable Transferences	Ideal. Similar to neurotics	Good. Sufficient self-object differentiation and internalization of object-representations.	Fair. Has for the most part an organizing, differentiating self and has not lost completely internal object-representations	Poor. Lack of adequate separation of self and object
Capacity of the Orgasm to Restore the Sense of Having a Bounded and Cohesive Self	Sense of self and ego boundaries is essentially unimpaired. Orgasm does not function in this capacity	Strong capacity of the orgasm to restore sense of bounded and cohesive self	Same as in Preoedipal Type I. The effect, however, may be more transitory, requiring frequent repetition due to the imperative need for restoration of self-representation	Partially effective, if at all

Status of Ego Functions Other Than Object Relations (after Kolansky and Eisner 1974)				
A. Reality Testing	Intact	Often intact, but consciously and/or unconsciously ignored to serve pleasure principle	Less intact than Type I; boundary between fantasy and reality can be indistinct with some misperception of reality (high degree of anxiety leads to withdrawal from reality)	Severely impaired as a result of the schizophrenic process
B. Thinking	Unimpaired, dominated by reality principle	Clear, but dominated by pleasure principle. Such thinking combined with poor impulse control leads to actions which seemingly deny reality. Thinking reflects patient's projective anxieties	More severe than Preoedipal Type I	Gross impairment with occasional delusions, hallucinations (temporary and/or fleeting). Paranoid thinking may predominate
C. Impulse Control	Essentially well controlled. Capacity to delay gratification	Incomplete or partial control leading to acting out of impulses and pursuit of instantaneous gratification	Impulses grossly acted out in an instantaneous manner suggesting complete loss of ego and superego controls	Controls minimal or absent. Distortions of control mechanism seen
D. Self-Concept	Essentially unimpaired	Elevated sense of self-esteem bordering on omnipotence alternating with feelings of self-depreciation. Need for narcissistic supplies and narcissistic restoration	More severe than Preoedipal Type I	Extreme lack of self-worth; distorted, bizarre, or diffuse

STATUS OF EGO FUNCTIONS (cont.)	Oedipal Form:	Preoedipal Form: Type I	Preoedipal Form: Type II	Schizo-Homosexuality (co-existence of homosexuality and schizophrenia)
E. Ego Boundaries	Essentially unimpaired	Somewhat impaired but remain intact	Under stress boundaries may show severe impairment especially with removal of compensatory pathological grandiosity	Absent or severely impaired
F. Degree of Internalization or Externalization of Conflict	Internalized conflict	Relative freedom from internal conflict. Reactions and thoughts lead to conflict as a result of external frustration at which point internal conflict occurs (externalized conflict—Kolansky and Eisner)	More severe than Preoedipal Type I	Often extremes of conflict regarding concepts of self, ego boundaries, incorporated images
G. Affect and Affect Control	Appropriate; responses of anxiety and depression frequently encountered	Intolerance of external frustration may arouse anxiety. Action is substituted for normal anxiety or depression	Extreme anxiety, depression with feelings of loss of self, emptiness, remorse, guilt. Sublimation generally absent	Often inappropriate. Chronic symptoms of anxiety, depression, guilt, pananxiety, panneurosis
H. Aggression	Emotionally well defended against	Tendency to respond to anxiety and depression with object-directed or self-directed aggression (sadism and masochism)	Poorly bound. Bursts of rage frequent as capacity to neutralize aggression has been largely lost. Violent acts may appear	Severe impairment in control of aggression

References:

Bak, R. (1971). Object-relationships in schizophrenia and perversion. *International Journal of Psychoanalysis* 52:235–242.

Kernberg, O. (1975). *Borderline Conditions and Pathological Narcissism*. New York: Jason Aronson.

Kolansky, H., and Eisner, H. (1974). The Psychoanalytic Concept of the Preoedipal Developmental Arrest. Unpublished.

Mahler, M.S. (1967). On human symbiosis and the vicissitudes of individuation. *Journal of the American*

Appendix A
A TEN-YEAR FOLLOW-UP INTERVIEW WITH A SUCCESSFULLY TREATED PATIENT

Paul, now aged forty-three (see chapter 11), was seen seven years after the successful completion of his psychoanalysis in two follow-up interviews one week apart. What follows is an excerpted verbatim account of those two sessions. He supplies a moving description of his former homosexuality, his psychoanalysis, and his present rich and gratifying heterosexual life. In a lively exchange with his former analyst he supplies a valuable source of information on (1) the fate of the homosexual impulse; (2) the turning points in therapy; (3) the significance of the transference relationship; (4) the homosexual's ability to achieve normal object relationships; (5) the neutralization of aggression as a result of therapy; and (6) the capacity to cathect with libido an opposite sex partner.

Paul: I had a very unpleasant night. It was really strange. I'm not sure if it was connected with my coming here this morning. Like this morning raising up the past. Do you have the tape on now? (CWS answers.) I got those pains in my chest and I don't remember the last time that I have had them. I can't remember the last time. It must be years. Last night was the worst time I ever remember.

Socarides: Was it the idea about coming and discussing the past?

Paul: I was feeling a lack of affection from my wife and we had a little bit of a problem along those lines, giving each other affection and showing affection more. There was really no good reason for it though.

Socarides: You mean about coming here?

Paul: This morning it rang a bell. Maybe it was because I was coming here and we were going to discuss the past and—all I could think about was the terrible parts of it that we would discuss. And it was painful obviously and it produced pain in me, physical pain. It was so painful. I guess what I was thinking about was the compulsiveness of it. (Chest pains were a frequent somatic expression of conflict during an early period of Paul's analysis.)

Socarides: During treatment you ask if you would be free forever from the homosexual symptom and I said that you would not have any imperative need to express it nor any real desire to do so. For example, a person who has a street phobia and gets rid of the street phobia then under severe stress later on in life can then have a temporary tendency to return to something that functioned as a solution before. And the phobic avoidance is one type of solution. And certainly an idea or a fleeting homosexual thought could return under severe stress but one's life can, in my opinion, be tremendously changed, the whole of one's life.

Paul: Well, what happens when I get those occasional thoughts, which I almost never do, is that I think of the pleasurable aspects of my life now. I don't think about the bad parts of my so-called previous life. The pleasurable parts of what I have now, that I don't want to lose, get rid of it so quickly that it's unbelievable. It's just gone. I just don't want it. I just don't want it anymore. I sometimes get upset if I get the thought but I really—it goes away very easily. It's not a torture or anything. It's a pleasurable thing for it to go.

Socarides: Let's go back. When exactly were you in treatment?

Paul: We started in 1966 and ended in 1971. It was about three years of four times a week and then maybe a year or two of three times a week.

Socarides: One of your concerns was the return of the homosexuality. Would you say on the whole that it has returned at all in the sense of the way you had it?

Paul: Oh, it's another world.

Socarides: Could you tell me about it?

Paul: Well, to do that I'd have to tell you what it was like. What I remember about it was the compulsiveness. I wasn't married at the time and I was living by myself and I was very successful in my work life. Well, in terms of what it was like, it could never be the same. The compulsiveness of it. I keep using that word but that's what it was. It was coming home at night and suddenly getting this unbelievable urge to go out and find a homosexual partner and walking the streets like a nut. It was like there was almost a viciousness about it. Maybe not showing it on the outside, actually covering it up on the outside. That's an important point because I think that most homosexuals do that. They try to be very cool and sophisticated. They come on very cool and pleasant and unassuming and uninterested and underneath there's this burning urge—if they have seen somebody that they really want to go to bed with. That's what I had and I know a lot of people who had the same experience. Underneath it this burning urge and the need. If I met somebody I was interested in I'd try not to show it, try to be very cool and calm about it because I was always afraid it would turn the person off. And then finally some nights not finding anybody and going home and masturbating half a dozen times during the course of a few hours.

Socarides: With the image of a man in your mind?

Paul: With a homosexual image. Or then finding somebody and having a relationship with him and then after he's gone even possibly going out and looking again. This could go on into the early morning hours. I could be out on the street at two or three in the morning, looking.

Socarides: Did you feel driven?

Paul: Yes.

Socarides: Were you driven at times or was it just a pleasurable need?

Paul: No. I was definitely aware of being driven and I would have a strong urge not to be driven. It would drive me crazy a little bit. It was tremendously upsetting. Not just a little bit. It was tremendously upsetting to feel these urges. And that's why again I always use the word *compulsion.*

Socarides: There was a time though I suppose at the beginning that once you got into it you really enjoyed it. Was it a kind of power play or what?

Paul: Yes.

Socarides: How long were you homosexual before you came into therapy? You thought you were from about seven or eight but I mean practicing. When did you really "come out" and decide that was what you were going to do?

Paul: I was about twenty-three. I had various homosexual contacts before that but nothing so heavy.

I think that I finally realized, I guess because I was finally on my own, that was one factor. And then I realized the availability. I didn't know anything about the homosexual world when I was younger. I led a very sheltered middle-class life. I was brought up in a neighborhood where there was no exterior sign of it. Coming into Manhattan was an occasional thing and homosexuality was not pointed out to me nor was it seen when I went into Manhattan so that my occasional contacts were because of a specific availability prior to the age of about twenty-three, a specific availability of a person and it just happened. It wasn't a matter of looking.

Socarides: It just fell into your lap so to speak at twenty-three. Then at twenty-three you became overtly homosexual?

Paul: At twenty-three I began to—I don't know how I found out but I did find out about gay bars and I started to have friends who also had similar leanings and we started doing some things together. It started to snowball.

Socarides: What age did you come into analysis?

Paul: Twenty-six

Socarides: So from twenty-three to twenty-six was a wide-open homosexual life?

Paul: Yes.

Socarides: You'd look for it. You'd get it. You felt driven to it and all that. And that's when you came to analysis.

Paul: Right.

Socarides: Compare that behavior to your behavior now as regards the sexual impulse. That was one of the things you worried about—that treatment could never get rid of it.

Paul: Right. It's unbelievable that I can think about it intellectually because it's past history and there is nothing in my present that vaguely resembles that past history. I sometimes think about it in terms of heterosexual existence and I sometimes see guys for example who must go to bed with other women that they see. And they can't have a relationship with one woman. The only comparison I can make in my present way of life is—it's funny that I'm talking about it this way because I never really thought about it as one way of life compared to another. It was just an evolution as far as I was concerned.

Socarides: What I mean is do you feel that kind of homosexual impulse at all?

Paul: No. I have never felt it over the last—well, since well before we stopped therapy. No, I don't feel it at all now. I never feel it now.

Socarides: You know it is said about so-called cured homosexuals that what they really have done is just suppressed their homosexuality and they really would be homosexual but have just learned a way of suppressing it. Do you feel you have suppressed it?

Paul: No. I don't at all feel that I've suppressed it. In fact, my thoughts and feelings come out very easily.

Socarides: About everything?

Paul: Yes, about everything. I feel very free, which of course I attribute to my analysis—the whole feeling of freedom. And if those feelings of homosexuality were there at all, as they were, I'm sure they would really surface. Other things surface with me—concerning my relationships with everybody that I know, concerning my work, concerning everything about me, my family, everything comes out of my head. I don't always say it to everybody. Since I'm not seeing you anymore there is nobody that I would say everything to but I know what has surfaced.

Socarides: Do you ever get an occasional thought of wanting to carry out a homosexual act?

Paul: No. I've had a few fleeting thoughts over the years but all that suddenly goes quickly through my mind and the thought just goes. And also I get a feeling of some sort of inner strength that I have learned to cope with it. And I guess that is the most important thing—the feeling of security that I suddenly get—a feeling of self-security and that usually stops it. In fact it helps me to get over whatever problem I have in my mind too—that feeling of self, regardless of whether it's something regarding my wife or something about my work that has come up to act as a slight upset. Generally my work feelings are not that upsetting. I do very well and I'm very successful. Although once in a while there is an insecure feeling and then a secure feeling will come so that really makes me feel so good. It's a great feeling.

Socarides: What about the other areas of your life? What's happened there?

Paul: Well, I started talking about my work. I'm aggressive about my work but not in the same way that I used to be. I'm not a killer—which is how I used to think of myself. And I see a lot of my friends who do the same work that I do who have this overly aggressive drive. And I now look at them—I'm talking about people at my level who have achieved a comfortable status in their profession who are doing well—and they still have these tremendous aggressive drives and want to become the president of this professional organization and they want to control various phases of the profession and they have these huge urges to do so. All of their professional lives revolve around these activities. And that used to be my way and now I want to have my own personal life and enjoy my wife and children. I want to enjoy my profession but I have a lot of parts of my life that I want to enjoy and I don't want one to interfere with the other or dominate the other. So that's a tremendous change in me. That is a very, very big change because I was totally the opposite. And a lot of people who knew me before still think of me that way. I have to tell them that I'm not that way.

Socarides: You had a wild aggression which you would also feel sexually.

Paul: And the satisfaction out of getting somebody which I used to have. I find that I don't have that kind of satisfaction at this point. I just do what I think is right for the people that I work with, myself, my family, but not with the idea of deriving satisfaction from getting somebody. And I see a lot of that around me. And I look at it and understand more about it. Right now we're having a problem with my in-laws and I see it with them. They can't relax and enjoy us and their grandchildren. They're missing out on so much in life.

Socarides: In the sexual thing of course you were getting somebody too, although you didn't realize it.

Paul: Well, I realized it as we went on in my analysis.

Socarides: What's your relationship with your wife like?

Paul: First of all, when we make love we do really well. That's important to me because until I was well into the four times a week analysis I really had never made love or had any sexual contact really with a woman.

Socarides: Was it after about a year that you were able to function?

Paul: Some place within the first year or two.

Socarides: Just to function sexually with a woman, but you were not able to love a woman yet?

Paul: But for me it was such an unbelievable accomplishment that I actually—I never really thought that I was going to be able to have any sexual relationship with a woman. I guess that was one of the things that made me start analysis. I know I had a tremendous fear of that kind of contact with a woman, an actual fear of the sexual contact. As I said, I did have that feeling that I would not be successful. I think that's probably true. A great number of homosexuals of course claim that they have had sex with a woman— I'm not always sure they're telling the truth when they say that. I met men who would come on that way or who if there were women around would really make up to them, would fool around with them. That happened a large number of times.

Socarides: Let's get back again to your sexual life with your wife. You say it's really great.

Paul: Yes. We really do very, very well sexually. We do a variety of sexual acts with no holds barred and a relaxed feeling on both of our parts.

Socarides: Would you say that the sexual experience with your wife is better than any you had with men?

Paul: It's completely different.

Socarides: How is it different?

Paul: I'm trying to think of what it was like with men. It's funny. I think that in a way my homosexual experience had helped me in my technique, as you once suggested it would.

Socarides: I told you that you would be a very good heterosexual lover.

Paul: Yes, I remember, and it's true. I think that oral sex for example was very easy for me to do with a

woman because of my oral sexual things with men. It
wasn't a prohibitive kind of a thing. I often walk
around thinking that I do better sexually with my wife
than a lot of other men do who have always been
heterosexual.

Socarides: You prefer genital penetration?

Paul: Well, that's where it's all at. That's the end
result and I feel unsatisfied unless we do have
penetration. Occasionally I guess I get so aroused that
other things are in the feeling but that's occasional.
For the most part, the most satisfying thing is
penetration, holding my wife very closely—that is the
way I enjoy it most, that is the best. Strong feelings of
love and expressing it.

Socarides: What about your kids? What about your
relations with your kids? You have three children,
don't you?

Paul: Three. I have one six, one four, and one one.

Socarides: Would you talk about that a bit?

Paul: I don't really know how to start talking about
it.

Socarides: About your having them and so forth.

Paul: It's just that for me having three kids is so
wonderful, I don't even know how to say how
wonderful it is. It's so hard to say. I can't describe how
feelings of love, tremendous love, protectiveness,
wanting to teach, most of all, wanting to show them
love, and wanting them to be happy and wanting them
to feel secure. Wanting them to be successful in life, in
all the various phases of life. And watching my oldest
who is sick now as I said, watching him develop along
those lines, watching his tremendous freedom of
expression, his liveliness, thriving on it myself.

Socarides: Would you compare the way you're

bringing up your kids with the way your mother and father brought you up? You must have a very personal idea of what makes a homosexual child.

Paul: I guess all the things I just said I never really felt from my parents.

Socarides: What were the specific factors, would you say, that your mother and father did that you and your wife are not doing? What was done to you, in other words?

Paul: Just a feeling of security and self is one big, big factor, just feeling that I can make it in this world without having my mother around.

Socarides: What did she do to make you feel that you couldn't make it in this world without having your mother around? What happened? I know this may bring up a lot of memories for you, but could you just comment a few minutes on that? Your family setting now is so different from that which you had to endure.

Paul: And it was an endurance, you used the right word. The funniest thing is that you don't realize it's an endurance until you're able to separate yourself somewhat from it. And at the time I was going through it, as an example, when I got a little bit older and I should have been doing things with my friends and being off by myself, I would always be doing things with my mother. And to me that was what you were supposed to do. If you have a Sunday, and you're in college already, and you have a Sunday off and you might do something with your friends, with a girl, whoever, a contemporary, to me it was very natural to go visit the relatives with my parents, with my mother's relatives specifically.

Socarides: You were not independent from your family.

Paul: A total dependence, totally tied to my family, doing everything with my family, with only occasional—almost as if I were on a leash, and occasionally the leash being let out for me to do something. Almost with a feeling, as I look back on it, that I had to be given an occasional satisfaction of freedom or else I'd go crazy or something. I don't know, maybe that was the thought. But I was given an occasional freedom to do something without my family but not too often. I was afraid to, also.

Socarides: You were afraid?

Paul: I think it was both.

Socarides: Wasn't it your mother that was the leash you were held by?

Paul: It was definitely my mother. My father very early in the game, I don't even remember when he gave up, but he just stopped.

Socarides: You were the pawn. Your brother in a sense was given to your father, but your mother took you.

Paul: Right.

Socarides: The younger boy, right?

Paul: The interesting thing is that my brother resents it to some degree because he feels that he never got my mother's love. I told him that any time he wants to have it, he can have it. (Laugh.) The problem is he couldn't get it, and you know, to this day he still can't get it. It's really weird, to this day he cannot be satisfied along those lines because my mother has never given up and will never give up with me.

Socarides: How do you handle your mother, would you say, as an outcome of the analysis, and what insights did it require to do that?

Paul: It required an understanding of what we were

just talking about. First, being able to separate myself. The funny thing was that until I underwent my analysis, even though I moved out of my family—well, maybe I did see subconsciously that there were certain problems, which I never really thought about before. Even though I did very well in school I was not aware of the problems that I had at all. I began after a while to look down on my father as a result of my mother's attitude toward him, and as a result of the way he acted toward her. And my children, I think, obviously love me, and I would never want them to feel that I was inferior, you know. I know too that there are certain problems that are my own, but basically that I love them and basically that they can come to me, they can talk to me. I never had that feeling about my father until about three years before he died.

Socarides: He died about the sixth year I knew you?

Paul: That's interesting, because about three years into my analysis I was able to start having what I considered a wonderful relationship with my father. It was the best I could have at the time but it really gave me tremendous satisfaction that I could love him. I was able to see his good qualities, which I was avoiding to a great degree. More and more the bad qualities had been affecting me. His weaknesses had been affecting me and dominating my thinking. And as I proceeded in my analysis, I began to see his good qualities and enjoy them and love them. And I realized the important parts they played in my life, even though I was denying them. In other words, I denied the qualities, but he obviously had some influence earlier in my life which I never thought about once I had become a homosexual. I just really put him down and put him away. I really didn't think I could get anything from my father. I felt that I really couldn't get any support from him, I guess, against my mother. I really didn't think he had a lot to offer in certain respects, and my mother put those ideas in my head. You know that he had very little to offer, that he was weak. Well, she's stopped now. I think what I've basically done is to realistically talk about my father to other people, to myself, to my mother. She has pretty much come to realize over a period of time that she cannot put my father down to me. She will try, she doesn't stop trying, but as soon as she brings it up, I tell her that she's wrong. There is no question that he had his weaknesses, but he was a really fine person in many respects, and he had a lot of wonderful interests, and my mother can't take that away from me, no matter how hard she tries at this point. She had taken it away from me before.

Socarides: Why was she trying to do that?

Paul: I think she has her own problems, which is kind of naive. She was very basically insecure herself, she was very alone, she—I could tell you a lot of her history again but basically I think she needed me, she wanted me. I don't think she was able to relate to men very well. I don't think she can relate to men very well now. It was easier with a little child whom she molded from the time he was born. She got along with me better than with anybody else. It's not that she was so strong. I used to think of her as being so strong. I think she had certain strengths and she has done certain positive things for me. But I've always said if I had to choose one parent who would still be alive, and this may sound cruel, I'd rather it were my father than my mother, because he really knew how to enjoy a lot of things. She knocked a lot of it out of him. He loved music and art, he loved going to a park and watching people play ball. She didn't like any of those things.

Socarides: She lived her life through you in a way.

Paul: I guess that's true. It's funny now to hear her say some nice things about my father. She never said anthing nice about him. That's really the strange part of it. If I start saying something she'll start saying, "Well, you know, he did take you to concerts and the museums." She always criticized him for taking me to free things, things that didn't cost money. But they didn't have money. So he tried to get me to things that he thought I would enjoy and that would help me to develop, even though he couldn't afford to take me to the paying things. He took me to concerts that didn't cost money or to museums where it didn't cost money.

Socarides: You have a great feeling for life, don't you? You have a wide range of interests.

Paul: I do, yes. I love to experience everything around me.

Socarides: Could you have these feelings if you still remained a homosexual, do you think?

Paul: Well, the homosexual reality took so much of my time, so actually everything else, even if I had had the interests, the dominance of the homosexual feeling and the urges to have homosexual contacts took so much time. As I said, I could be up to two or three in the morning; that couldn't leave me too much time for anything else or the energy for other things I enjoy. Like when we finish up this morning, I'm going home and I'm going to take our oldest son to a special thing at the museum. And if I were a homosexual, I'd be going home and I might go out looking for a homosexual partner even in the middle of the day if I had some free time rather than doing something.

Socarides: Do you remember how some of those

homosexual contacts were very masochistic at times
and degrading and self-demeaning? Remember the
times you'd go to the tearooms and all that stuff, and
also you'd endanger yourself. You'd go with guys, one
guy hit you that tim while the other guy was watching.
You were yourself engaging in contacts which were
dangerous and degrading.

Paul: I'd pick up people who I was basically afraid of,
you know. I'd be afraid that they might do something
to me.

Socarides: Still you'd go.

Paul: I know. I'd still pick them up. At one point I
thought one guy was going to kill me. The one that you
mentioned where one guy was watching and the other
guy—I'm sure that they had that as a possible thought,
that if they killed me they'd just leave. It was in my
own apartment. They would just leave and no one
would be the wiser.

Socarides: You were having sex with one guy and the
other guy suddenly hit you on the head?

Paul: No, it was the guy I was having sex with,
because he was closest.

Socarides: And the other guy was watching.

Paul: I felt the other guy was his teacher almost, as
though one had taught the other one. One was older,
the one I was having sex with was younger, the other
was older. The interesting thing was that the younger
one left first, then the other one started—even after
what had happened I proceeded to have a sexual
contact with the older guy.

Socarides: Even after you had been struck?

Paul: Even after, yes. I guess it didn't matter at that
point, it was as though...

Socarides: What were you looking for in the men you picked up?

Paul: Absorbing their strength. It never works. When it was all through I felt—I didn't feel good. After my contact or the person was gone or I was gone, whichever, I never really had that good feeling. So I guess that was another reason why I kept looking for more and more and more. In one night I could look for it many times over because I was never truly satisfied. And I think that's a big factor, actually the whole of it. They talk about these guys who are married to each other but they never really are satisfied. And I knew married homosexuals, quote, unquote, and I thought they were basically lying to themselves. Of course, someone could say there are heterosexuals who go out looking for other women, too. But I think both are forms of problems. They are doing it because they have problems and they have to try to satisfy them. But this business about being married homosexually, I think it's almost a sort of game. It's like playing house. The ones I knew, and these are pretty sophisticated ones because I'm in a profession and I made contacts with other people in professions, various professions, businesses that were not just running a local retail store or something, but successful people. And they were almost playing at being married. They were trying to relate somehow to a heterosexual existence, I think.

Socarides: They were trying to make a heterosexual existence out of a homosexual existence?

Paul: An imitation of it, I think, because they were unable to satisfy the heterosexual, which they really wanted. I personally never met a homosexual who

wouldn't rather have been heterosexual. But you have
to know them very well in order to have a basic
discussion and that's what would come out. There
wasn't one who was happy being homosexual. They'd
much rather have been heterosexual. They really felt
hopeless.

Socarides: Then the word *gay* is really a reaction-
formation against what—sad or unhappy?

Paul: That's an interesting thought. Yeah, I guess so.
I never really thought about it before. I wonder if that's
true. I wonder where the word *gay* came from, because
it is certainly the opposite. And unfortunately it's not
true. They're not carefree and they're not gay. They
have too many facades. And it's not just that it's an
occasional facade which everybody has whether
you're homosexual or heterosexual. It's much more of a
constant facade when they're out with each other and
when they're in front of other people. And they always
talk about how they can't be themselves. Even when
they're with other homosexuals they're putting on a
facade in order to attract somebody because they're
basically insecure.

Socarides: Let's go back to when you first thought of
entering therapy. What was your motivation?

Paul: I didn't really see myself being happy as a
homosexual. I guess that was part of it.

Socarides: Why not?

Paul: Because I felt there was something missing in
me that—and I think all homosexuals feel that. You
feel that a woman is made one way and a man is made
another way, and it seems just the way that things
should be. That a man and a woman should be able to
get together. And for me not to be able to think about
that or to think of it and be frightened of it...

Socarides: So all female contacts were extraterritorial, as if you were banned from them because of being homosexual.

Paul: Right.

Socarides: You knew there could be no relationship really.

Paul: Yes, but it didn't bother me because I had my mother and my life revolved around my family so much. But then I moved out of my family's home around the age of twenty-six. I finished my professional training and started to earn some money and I suddenly realized that I'm separated from my family to some degree. Now what do I do? Do I continue with this homosexual existence which to me seems not what I wanted out of life basically? But I can't become heterosexual. I can't have sex with women.

Socarides: Any relationship with women.

Paul: I can't have relationships with women. Well, I could talk with them. I didn't have any big problem talking with them but it was very superficial. So that I realized what was happening and I suddenly became frightened that I was going to be basically all alone. And that is what I think every homosexual is, basically all alone, no matter whether they have other homosexual friends or they have heterosexual friends. Whatever they've got, they have a tremendous feeling of being alone.

Socarides: Well, some people say you could make a homosexual marriage or find somebody...

Paul: Well, I had some relationships with men along those lines. I hadn't formed a marriage of any kind but I've had prolonged relationships but they weren't really truly satisfying because you're always looking for something else that's not there. You know basically

that the guy facing you is a homosexual, that he
doesn't satisfy, truly satisfy your needs. And I think
that's true of every homosexual. Also I was upset about
the time I was spending doing it, involved in homosexuality, the telephone calls to other homosexuals,
planning visits to gay bars. We got in the habit of going
once a week. And all these plans during the week,
who's going to go, who's taking the car. We got all
involved in these plans that were...

Socarides: Well, why would you have to do all that?

Paul: Well, what was the big deal it was going to
culminate in? It was going to culminate in possibly the
hope that you were going to meet a guy who you were
going to have sex with. And you know it's going to be
short-lived or it's going to be longer or shorter,
whatever it is, but it's not truly satisfying.

Socarides: And it didn't really involve a relationship,
did it?

Paul: It's a one-sided deal for each person. You're
involved with yourself and satisfying your own needs
basically.

Socarides: And those had to do with a solution of
your own internal problems.

Paul: It's ludicrous to talk about love. It's not love.
It's very selfish with homosexuals. Each guy is out for
what he wants to try to satisfy. It has nothing
whatever to do with the other person at all. But it's a
compulsive kind of thing. It's not a warm feeling. It's
not a relaxed feeling. You don't look at the other person
with loving thoughts.

Socarides: People said you'd never get out of it. Are
you out of it?

Paul: I think people who say that are afraid or
insecure or—I think they've got their own problems.

Socarides: There are people who say that once a homosexual, always a homosexual, and if you dare to get out of it, either you're going to go crazy or you're just kidding yourself or you're neurotic if you want to get out, or you'll wreck your life.

Paul: Well, the people I knew, when they heard—my closest homosexual friends—when they heard that I had decided to go to therapy to get out of it, I had various responses. One of my friends, my closest friends, decided to go to therapy at the same time. Shortly after I started, he started. Unfortunately, I don't think he's been too successful at it. Other friends thought I would never be able to do it, that they'd see me cruising, and they said it nastily. And that helped me because they were nasty about it. Why do they have to be bitchy about it? It came as such a shock to these people that here I was so involved in homosexual life and going with them, and now all of a sudden saying bye-bye.

Socarides: You threatened to invalidate some of their rationalizations.

Paul: Well, as a matter of fact, that came out from a number of them. It frightened them to see that someone was really trying to get out of it. One of the guys that I knew, after I was in therapy, realized the possibility of my getting out of homosexuality. I started to really feel it, that I could get out of it.

Socarides: At what point in therapy did you feel that?

Paul: It was, I guess, shortly after I'd had my first sexual contact with a woman that confirmed it for me, that the possibility was there without any question. That was the most confirming thing to me.

Socarides: But also that you enjoyed it. You've

enjoyed sex with women although the true enjoyment
didn't happen until after you'd done it a few times.

Paul: Well, I was shocked that I did enjoy it even the
first time.

Socarides: Yes?

Paul: Yes. I think that was a shock to me, that I did
enjoy it. I guess I did enjoy it because I never thought I
would be able to have sex with a woman. I thought I'd
never be able to have an erection with a woman. I never
would look at a woman. I guess part of it was that I can
remember just looking at men and getting an erection,
just looking. Again, I think it was because of the
homosexual compulsion end of it. Just looking at
someone I was interested in, I would get an erection
and I could look at women from now to doomsday and
not get an erection, not think about it or think about
why I wasn't getting it.

Socarides: The male-female relationships are a
different sort, aren't they, a different ball game?

Paul: It's a very different thing, and I think that's
part of the problem with homosexuals. It's such an
instant sex thing and it involves inner feelings that
have nothing to do with sex at all.

Socarides: The homosexual object is a sudden
neurotic solution to all your inner problems.

Paul: It's an instant kind of thing which is unreal,
because I think that although you can become aroused
instantaneously looking at a woman, it's not in the
same way. It's a different kind of arousal. It's not
getting an erection—it's also not getting "serious."
Homosexuals get very "serious" and heavy and the
look does not become one of pleasure. It becomes a
really hard look, a grabby kind of look.

Socarides: There's a burst of aggression in the

homosexual desire, an inner need for discharge of primitive tensions and anxieties that have been sexualized.

Paul: Yes, a tremendous burst of aggression.

Socarides: Your mother didn't want you to come to psychoanalysis.

Paul: That's right. She didn't want me—well, she had no choice at that point. But as we went on she never really wanted me to do anything about myself because she saw that it was affecting her relationship with me. My mother is coming in from Arizona. We haven't seen her since last August. She always wants us to come and visit her. She's been there about two and a half years now, and I occasionally get a desire to go and visit with her but nothing burning, no urgent desire to see her. We talk on the phone and we talk very nicely and I have really come to understand—it's a very good feeling for me. Funny how I think about her now. I never thought it was being insecure before because before, as we discussed it, she was really in my head such a dominant person, such a big, overwhelming person. And she's very small physically, about five feet. She looks like a Sherman tank. But her insecurity and the way it comes across in the way she approaches everything in her life—I can talk to her on almost a child-like basis, as though she's a child.

Socarides: One of the questions in therapy was what would happen to your relationship with your mother and whether you should break with her completely. What do you think of our decision?

Paul: I think the solution was the best I could have possibly achieved. It was really the only solution.

Socarides: You wondered whether to get rid of her, never speak to her, never see her...

Paul: Never speak to her, never see her, just completely eliminate her from my life. But it would take years and years of therapy. And you know about that time I had seen that Eugene O'Neill play, I forget the name of it. I remember seeing it; the guy walked around with the black armband for the rest of his life and he really had this attachment to his mother even after she was dead.

Socarides: Was it *Long Day's Journey Into Night?*

Paul: Yes, I think that was it. And he, even though his mother was dead, he still felt firmly attached for all of his life. And it affected his relationship with women. It affected his whole life. And that was not for me. I was just not going to have any of that. So the alternatives were that I completely get rid of her, or, as you suggested, be able to on a very limited basis have contact with her and control the situation, control the amount of contact, control the way the contacts took place, when they took place, how they took place, have the feeling of being in control of the situation. And it worked out very well that way, even when she was living in New York. And my wife will admit that, that it wasn't just that she moved that helped me to control it, but even while she was living in New York when I had completed my therapy, I was able to do the same thing. It was just that contacts would be more frequent here; there would be more telephone calls, but the face-to-face contacts were cut down tremendously on one excuse or another because I really didn't want to spend that much time with her.

Socarides: You still have strong feelings for her.

Paul: I do. I think I even got to warm feelings for her sometimes. Those were the times that I would have to be most careful because as soon as she feels that my guard was let down or that I'm not thinking, just letting my emotional part be there and nothing else, she clamps down. All of a sudden I feel her creeping over me like she's, uh...

Socarides: Like she wants to take you over again? Take control of you...

Paul: She wants a whole bunch of things. She wants me to be her confidant, her tool to manipulate other people, her...her...

Sucarides: Her penis.

Paul: Yes, I guess that's another way of saying her tool. Yes.

Socarides: Her power. Her penis?

Paul: Her everything, yes.

Socarides: Remember the first time you tried to leave home and you walked away one day? It was early in therapy. You had a tremendous anxiety attack and almost...

Paul: Yes, I remember that. It happened in the street and we had a big argument and I was trying to leave and I had a tremendous anxiety feeling. Now that you mention it, I even remember the feeling. It was very frightening; my heart was going a mile a minute.

Socarides: Yes. As if you wouldn't exist separating yourself from her.

Paul: Well, now when she comes for a visit what I do is I psyche my wife up for the whole thing. I explain that my mother is coming in for a few days to stay with us but she is insecure. She's got her own hang-ups. She may say things but saying things doesn't matter, really. She doesn't control us. She can say a lot of things. She can think whatever she wants but it won't really affect us or our children. It's a short-term visit.

Socarides: Do you remember when you told her that

your wife was pregnant and you were going to have a
child, or maybe it was that you'd had the child, and she
said something like, "No son of mine has had a child.
You are no son of mine." It was a very cutting remark.

Paul: I remember something along that line, now
that you mention it. I don't remember it exactly. She
was tremendously upset over the possibility of my
having sexual relations with a woman and that goes
back long before we had a child. That goes back to
calling me at two o'clock in the morning at my bachelor
apartment and trying to find out who the woman is.
She never liked my having intercourse with a woman. I
mean that was just out of the question. It was
obviously hard for her to accept that. She hated it. It
wasn't just a matter of her accepting it.

Socarides: Do you feel that you've been successful in
analysis?

Paul: Do I feel that I've been successful? That's
putting it mildly! It has—I tell people, when I feel that I
can talk to them about it, that it has been the most
important thing that I've done with my whole life.

Socarides: Do you ever feel that you could possibly
return to homosexuality again?

Paul: No. I don't think so, I know so. There's no way
that I could ever return to homosexuality. Even in my
deepest despair or my wildest fantasies I could never
return to homosexuality. It became a matter of facing
reality and because of this confrontation about the
reality of life I'm liking the reality of life, enjoying the
reality of life. I could never return to homosexuality.
There would be no way that I could actually go and
commit a homosexual act.

Socarides: Not because you so greatly fear it...

Paul: Well, I could say that I fear it and not greatly

fear it, but I certainly would fear returning to an existence which I basically hated, and I would think that a significant thing in looking back on it is that all homosexuals that I knew basically hate being homosexual. And I think that's important and I think that is what is not being recognized. And that is what certain homosexuals are trying to cover up. But if you ever get into a deep, friendly conversation with homosexuals—it's one thing for them to say publicly that they're normal, they're fine, they're functioning and all that, but it's another thing to become personally involved with one, to know them, to talk with them, and I think that people do not know that. I felt nervous in the first session because I knew it was being taped, for some reason. Well, not for some reason. The reason was that I feel so strongly about your work. I'm sure there are other people who do work similar to yours, but I only know you in that respect. I feel so strongly about what has happened to me and because of it I really wanted to impress in that tape, impress my feelings and make sure that I'm saying important things, the right things in our discussion about it and for that reason it became very forced. I feel badly about it.

Socarides: Did you feel that the tape might endanger you somehow?

Paul: Maybe. Maybe that was a little of it, too. I certainly wanted to protect what I had achieved and protect my family and me. And I felt badly about that, too, that I have this feeling of protection. In some way I feel badly about it because there are homosexuals, even homosexuals who are in professions such as I'm in, who come out publicly and therefore the image which is being created for the public is being distorted because they're not hearing from people such as myself. In fact, at one point I was so angry about it I called up one of them, the famous Dr. X. I called him. And he spoke with me. I told him that I thought that he was hurting a lot of homosexuals. I was wondering what would have happened to me if homosexuality was thought of as being normal, and I saw it in the newspapers and—I don't know. Of course I had a lot of homosexual friends at that time and was deeply involved in a homosexual life and I was wondering what effect it would have had on me at that time if these things had taken place then, whether I would have said just the hell with it, I'm going to stay with homosexuality. And I resented that a lot.

Socarides: What was it you told him?

Paul: That's what I told him, just what I told you—that I felt he was doing a disservice to the public, to the people, to society by what he's doing. I told him that I was a successfully treated homosexual.

Socarides: What did he say to that?

Paul: He said there is no such thing.

Socarides: He said that to you right on the telephone?

Paul: Yes. He said there is no such thing. He didn't talk—he got very upset talking to me. He was extremely upset and I wasn't. I was very calm. The difference was so obvious between us. As we talked more and more he was getting more and more upset and the more he got upset the calmer I was. I called up with a lot of anger and I realized then that I was talking to somebody that was sick. As he got more upset I realized that he was losing his control, and then he finally hung up on me.

Socarides: Do you think he's probably influenced a lot of homosexuals not to get help?

Paul: Yes, I do think that's one of the problems. And I

said I'm not sure what would have happened to me if I were around when he made his statements. Here was a responsible physician who had a good position with a university medical school making these statements and if I read them, and if some of my other homosexual friends had read them and we discussed them, who knows what I would have done? I might never have sought help. In fact, thinking about it, there's a good possibility that I wouldn't have because one of the motivating factors for me was the idea that I did think that I was ill. I realized it started working on me. After I moved out of my family's home I said now what is the rest of my life going to be like and what am I involved with? Is it really an illness? And am I going to be happy with it? I mean going from one gay bar to the other, meeting people on the street, even if I had a relationship with somebody and I had various short-term, semipermanent relationships with other homosexuals, I would still, if this person wasn't available, I would look for somebody else if I needed it at the time. So that has been my experience with homosexuals in general, even when they have so-called permanent relationships. If that person is not available the problem is that they need whatever you want to call it, a shot or whatever, and they go to look for somebody else to have a sexual relationship with if that person is not available at the time. So it's an abnormal need that comes up because of what's happening in their lives and they're incapable of coping with it in any other way.

Socarides: Did the doctor bother to ask you anything about your therapy?

Paul: He didn't ask me anything.

Socarides: He didn't want to know about it.

Paul: No. He was just interested in defending his position. And he was really totally upset. I felt sorry for him in some way but at the same time I felt that there was no reason for me to feel sorry for him. I felt that he had done a terrible thing.

Socarides: Not that he'd "come out," but that he'd said it was all perfectly normal and that nobody could help.

Paul: Right.

Socarides: Why do you think you got well?

Paul: I think I got well because I related very strongly to you, because I had a tremendous need to get well, and I had to trust somebody and you were the only person I could trust. There was nobody else in my life that I really could trust, nobody that I could really talk to and nobody that I could really feel secure with. So I just decided that I had to do it with you and I decided that if I'm going to accomplish my purpose I'd better just let it all out and not have any holds barred and be extremely open and extremely honest and really let myself go. I think there was something else that you had said that was important—that I really listened to—and that was that as long as I'm accomplishing something I should keep coming. And I did feel that sense of accomplishment throughout my therapy.

Socarides: You're referring now to the last half of therapy?

Paul: Even at the beginning. Even at the beginning there was a sense of accomplishment. Just being able to stop and think about myself from the beginning almost in a much more realistic way. Sometimes I was very proud of the fact that—not from the beginning though—as I went on I realized that not everybody lies down on a couch or is able to. I didn't know that because we had discussed my not reading the literature and I had very little, almost no psychological background even though I went to college. I was proud of the fact that I was able to lie down on the couch early in the game because what I realized later on is that many people are not able to do that or are not ready for that or whatever. So a big part of my therapy was the tremendous encouragement that I got from you in various ways without saying it directly, "You're doing well." It was just constant feelings. And I was confident that you were on my side completely. That was important. That no matter what happened you were always on my side. That was very important to me. That was the funny thing that that was very important to me because I think I sure felt good about it, that this thing was important to me and that was enough. That was the big thing. I really needed somebody to be on my side against my mother! I didn't realize how much I needed somebody for that purpose. Interesting, though, that I related to my own father so much better after a while. For the last three years of his life he and I were real buddies and we could never be that before. And he got tremendous satisfaction out of that, which I enjoy now. Because he didn't get much satisfaction out of many other things in life because my mother cut him off from everything. She cut him off from his own family, his brothers and his sisters and his children, and she really made mincemeat out of him. What I do feel, and I guess partly because of my feelings about you—I guess it's all intertwined—is that he was happy that I did undergo therapy. He realized the importance of it. I don't think he realized it at first. He wasn't very educated and he was not psychologically educated. It was interesting that my mother always said that my father resented it because he never once said it to me. And not only that but my parents helped me financially to pay for my analysis until he died. When my father died my mother stopped, and it wasn't that she couldn't afford to help me. She started telling me that it should only have taken six months. She said it to me several times, that it should only have taken six months, and why am I still going? And I would always say to her, "Because I'm getting better." And I realized that my getting better and my saying that upset her so much. I remember getting a charge out of hearing her response. It would infuriate her that I felt that I was getting better. And I was. I constantly had that feeling of getting better. You once said that the way to prevent neurosis is to keep open the lines of communication between parent and child; that everything is capable of being talked about. When I talk to my oldest son and discuss things with him a sense of relaxation comes over him. He senses a relief as though I've said the right thing and have really relieved him. And he looks for it. He looks for the right thing to be said and he's tuned in to doing that, which is very nice for him and for me and for my wife. She does the same thing with him. We really try hard. It's fun. For me it is a lot of fun. For my wife it's not as much fun. For her it's more of a torture to work with him and to try to help him grow up well. She tries very hard not to let him see the torture. I'm sure—for me it's fun to help him solve things as he goes along, to help him change and develop and meet problems and challenges. And I always try to tell him that, that it's part of the fun of raising children. She recently has been much better. I used to think that if she felt some symptom or some problem then that's it, we've done it. He's ruined now for the rest of his life type of feeling. And it was weird for me that she could think that way. I mean, here is a child that is growing and changing and we're working with him. So if he has a problem, just deal with it, understand it, find out what the problem is and all its ramifications and help him with it. I don't mean go after him and pounce on him and try to solve all of his problems with one fell swoop, but just as different things come up, gradually help him to work out what is on his mind. As a result he's doing very well at school. He is so well-liked by the kids, by the teachers. Here's a free soul, free and easy soul, and he's nice. You know he has a huge desire to learn everything, not just schoolwork, but he just wants to learn, period. He enjoys it. He thrives on it. It's obvious that he really thrives on it, wants to gobble everything up. As much of everything that is going on around him as possible.

Socarides: Is there anything else you want to talk about?

Paul: No. As a matter of fact his grandparents are coming to pick him up in fifteen minutes and I told him I'd be there to say goodbye. Goodbye, Doctor. Have a nice weekend.

Appendix B
ON THE GENESIS
OF PERVERSIONS

by Dr. Hanns Sachs

We are indebted to Freud's "Three Essays on the Theory of Sexuality" for our knowledge that a perversion represents the breakthrough of a too strongly developed portion of an instinctual drive which, instead of being satisfied with forepleasure, has displaced the primacy of the genitals, established in normal development, onto a different erogenous zone, that is, onto a sensual goal that is incompatible with the drive. The accuracy of these findings has been confirmed by all our later experience and has not been limited or changed in any way. Rather, it would appear as though, through the continuing preoccupation of psychoanalysis with perversions, new problems have been added which make certain expansions necessary.

The most important of these problems is that of the relation of the perversion to the oedipus complex, as well as the relation to the unconscious and to repression. Actually, we are confronted by a single problem which can be dealt with differently according to whether we regard it from the material or from the

From *Internationale Zeitschrift fur Psychoanalyse* 19 (1923):172–182. Translated into English by Hella Freud Bernays, 1966, as arranged for by C.W. Socarides, M.D.

psychic point of view. Here, too, Freud has shown us
the way, in "A Child Is Being Beaten"[1]; there he made
it clear that our understanding of the perversions will
remain incomplete so long as this basic complex is not
sufficiently considered, and is not regarded as being
subject to law. In a specific case, he actually demonstrated that we are dealing with an overthrow of the
oedipus complex; that the overstrong partial drive
would not continue in a straight line into the perversion, but that it would, like a ray of light passing
through a lens, have to pass through the oedipus
complex. It would be incumbent on us to determine the
angle of refraction and to draw our conclusions from it.
This corresponds to the fact that the gratification
obtained by the perversion is usually associated with
quite definite, often very strange and narrowly limited
conditions, which in their peculiarity go far beyond the
demands of a partial instinctual drive and cannot be
fully explained by its successful breakthrough. We
must add that partial drives, insofar as they belong to
a very early stage of sexual development—for example,
to the oral, anal-sadistic, or narcissistic stages—break
through to become perversions only in exceptional
cases in the primitive, nonobjective form (autoerotic or
primary narcissistic). For the most part, after a
working over which has raised them to a higher level,
they are capable of the normal libidinization of an
object; indeed, in certain instances, they are capable of
the finest psychic emanations of such a libidinization.
The conception that neurosis is the negative of
perversion, that is, that in the neurotic the same
fantasies which provide the pervert his conscious
pleasure goal are repressed and pathogenic (in other
words, that they are the determinants of symptom
formation), does not answer the question of what the

relation of the perversion is to the unconscious. It is immediately clear that the perversion, although it is capable of becoming conscious, only represents, as does an island in the ocean, the tip of a mountain mass that extends below the surface of the water. The pervert is no exception to infantile amnesia, which we consider a sort of scar of the important process of repression directed against infantile sexuality. The analysis of a perversion leads us, therefore, to unconscious psychic material as does the analysis of a material as does the analysis of a neurosis. Here, too, Freud's remark remains valid; we must only add the realization that it does not fully exhaust the subject.

We can find no better point of departure than to call attention to the antithesis that the fantasy, held fast in the repression, succeeds in breaking through at the expense of the repression, but only as a neurotic symptom that is ego-alien and ego-hostile; and that the fantasy remains capable of entering the conscious, becoming, in the broadest sense, ego-syntonic and gratifying.[2] This becomes even clearer when we go from the perversion—which is only a theoretical construct of uncertain composition—back to the material itself, as we can do by direct observation. We are then contrasting the perverted gratification— regardless of whether it springs from activity or from fantasy—with the neurotic symptom. If we do not consider forepleasure indication, both of them have much in common: they are both offshoots of infantile sexuality which has been completely overcome and repressed; they are both relatively unimportant evidences that remain, from an important developmental process, as representatives belonging to the conscious, of unconscious drives and fates that rest on drives. Both the neurotic symptom and the perversion are only enlargements and strengthenings of processes which occur in every normal psyche. We know that the neurotic symptom has to be endured in the conscious because it represents the possibility of a dynamic adjustment when there is a discrepancy between the ego and the repressed material. Is it possible that the circumstances are similar in the perversion?

First we want to see whether a real and observable similarity corresponds to the evident structural similarity. This most likely appears to be the case in those instances of perverted gratification which are admitted only unwillingly by the individual in question, in a continuing conflict against moral, religious, or esthetic considerations. Even this kind of gratification, reached by way of conflict, is pleasurable, although the pleasure is circumscribed in advance by disturbing defensive conflicts, and afterwards by remorse, shame, and self-condemnation. We get even closer to the neurotic symptom in those instances where certain conditions are overstepped, for example, when the gratification occurs in actuality instead of in fantasy, or when the victim of a sadistic act feels physical pain while the pleasure is tied to the presupposition that he will be spared this. There then appears not indifference, as might be expected, but a defense which clearly bears the earmarks of anxiety, thus putting it very close to the neurotic mechanism.[3] In a case susceptible to psychoanalytic understanding, I was able to observe accurately the transition from neurotic phobia to perverted gratification. A severely neurotic woman suffered from the memory that as a young girl she had beaten a child and had gotten sadistic enjoyment from it; it was, however, done in the course of play and in a

completely harmless manner. She recalled that a little
later, shortly after puberty, she had sometimes beaten
herself on the buttocks at night in bed and had thereby
experienced pleasurable sensations. This patient
was scarcely able to utter the word beating and
particularly the childish expressions that stand for it.
At any sound reminiscent of a beating—for example,
that of a carpet being beaten—in defense and out of
aversion she became inordinately excited. After a
particularly arduous analytic session, her masturbation, which up to that point had been completely
repressed, broke through. The masturbation that the
patient engaged in from then on could be considered a
perverted gratification, for it occurred only when
accompanied by the fantasy that she was being
beaten. From that time on, all the patient's sensitivity
to words and sounds that had any relation to beating
stopped completely; they were treated like any ordinary words or sounds. The phobia had again been
replaced by the perversion, arising from the previous
repression. During the repression process which had
begun only after puberty and which lasted for a long
time, as well as during this particular part of the
analytical work where the repression had again been
stopped, there were intermediate stages where it was
unclear whether one was confronted with a form of
perverted gratification or with a neurotic symptom.
Such a mixture does not appear to be very unusual;
thus, a masochistic patient who, moreover, was not
satisfied with fantasies but went on to realistic
arrangements, was unable to speak, without a vigor-
ous shudder, a dialect word or a childish word that
referred to his favorite instrument of torture.
  In another instance, a patient reported that on his

way home from his first coitus, which had been
completely satisfying, he had been seized with an
irresistible urge to masturbate openly on the street
with his penis exposed. He found the way out of his
predicament once it had grown dark. He stood at a
railroad crossing and masturbated in full view of a
passing train, that is, in front of a number of spectators
and yet, perhaps, unseen by anyone and certainly not
recognized by anyone. In his whole life, there had been
no other breakthrough of these exhibitionist tendencies. He came to me for treatment of psychic impotence
and for a second, rather unimportant symptom,
namely his inability to urinate in the presence of
others, as for example in a public toilet. The perverse
gratification had thus become transformed into a
neurotic prohibition. In the analysis he then dreamed
repeatedly that he—a schoolteacher—was exhibiting
himself in front of his pupils.

I believe that I have come upon a connecting link,
important both in theory and in practice, among so-
called addicts—alcoholics, drug addicts, morphine and
cocaine users, and those with a dependency on
smoking and chewing. In these cases the compulsive
aspect, the overwhelming of the individual by libidinal
forces that have split off from the ego, is so clear that
they have often been counted as compulsion neurotics.
With addicts as with the perversions, however, we are
not dealing, as in the compulsion neurosis symptom
with   a ceremonial toward which the individual is
consciously indifferent—or even, which is more often
the case, with a symptom that is unpleasant, meaningless, and time–consuming. Rather, we are dealing with
an activity that is indisputably gratifying. That this
gratification has been displaced from the real, origi-

nally sexual object onto something harmless, that is, onto something that does not belong to infantile sexuality, and which thus has the character of a substitute gratification instead of a displaced sexual pleasure that has become inaccessible, brings it closer again to the neurotic symptom.

A patient who had taken opiates other than morphine for a long time, and who had always taken them by mouth, reported that he once broke this habit. He began taking morphine and once took it by injection, after a sexual affair that he had had with the wife of a colleague had ended. He was aware, so he informed me, that the woman's husband was a morphine addict who took the drug by injection. I explained to him that, apparently with the intention of punishing himself, he was identifying with "the injured third [party]." He thereupon remembered another episode in his life in which he had suffered temporarily from a syphilis phobia following the breakup of a sexual affair with the wife of someone who was paralyzed by the disease. The relation to "the injured third" is obvious here, too. In a repeated situation he had, in accordance with the material at his disposal, reacted at one time with a so-called addiction which was actually a characteristic change in an already existing addiction, and the next time with a neurotic symptom, namely a phobia. This fact seems to me adequate proof of the similarity of the psychic bases of the two phenomena.

With the help of inserting addicts as a connecting link, we can set up a spectrum, at one end of which there is a perverted gratification, and at the other, a neurotic symptom.

Still another informative element appears from the

clarification of a form of perverted gratification, the most thorough up to that time, Freud's analysis of the fantasy, "A Child Is Being Beaten." We see that in the three stages of this fantasy—(1); the father is beating the child that I hate; (2) the father is beating me; (3) a child is being beaten—pretty much everything changes: the person who does the beating and the one who is being beaten, as well as the motivation, which at first is provided by jealous hatred of the rival, then by the sense of guilt because of the incest wish, and finally by the regressive substitute for the guilt by the act of being beaten. But one element is constant; it already appears in the first phase, passes over into the second, and remains intact in the third, capable of entering consciousness despite its otherwise pale and indistinct outlines. This element is the fantasy of being beaten, and it is precisely to this that the perverted pleasure is attached, almost compulsively leading to masturbation.[4] According to my experience, this pattern repeats in other forms of perversions; their development up to puberty and even beyond may vary, and the setting and characters of the fantasies may change—but a certain element or small group of elements outlasts the changes, and then appears as the vehicle of pleasure. The other components, which are later rejected and which in the further course of development are completely repressed, give off their whole pleasure content to this remnant which remains, standing for them in the conscious—just the way the neurotic symptom stands for the unconscious fantasies. This state of affairs is particularly clear in fetishism where, from a repressed complex, a portion remains intact in the conscious, quite the way a harmless screen memory (*Deckerinnerung*) is faithfully preserved, behind which the essential portion of the repressed infantile sexuality hides. The difference is that in fetishism, a wide displacement of affect attaches to this one portion the whole pleasure that has been preserved from childhood. Thus Freud, years ago, in the Wiener Psychoanalytischen Vereinigung, reported on a case where a man remained fetishistically fixated on the thin and ugly ankles and calves of women's legs. This fixation went back to a scene where he was sitting having a lesson from his English governess who, because of some trouble with her foot, had propped her leg up on a chair (incidentally, the leg was not in any way exposed). The sexual curiosity which made it possible for the boy to travel up to the genitals, and the repressed memory of a similar, earlier experience with his sister, where this wish had perhaps found fulfillment, had completely disappeared for him. In its place remained a harmless picture memory, but one that was closely connected with what had been repressed, as a fetishistic goal that was desired.

We can explain the strange and often grotesque character of some perversions by the fact that we are dealing with a single fragment of infantile experiences and fantasies which, in this one piece, celebrate their resurrection. The single fragment is torn out of context so that it is equally incomprehensible to the one who experiences the perversion and to others. Thus, in an analysis, I learned from a well-educated man that his only sexual gratification occurred when he heard the sound of a woman urinating. The identity of this woman did not concern him; furthermore, he did not have any desire at all to watch her, since the sound itself was pleasure-arousing. When he wanted to satisfy himself sexually, he used to go to a certain public toilet where it was possible to hear sounds through the partitions. After sufficiently exciting himself by listening, he would masturbate in his own stall. This particular analysis had to broken off for external reasons, yet the material that had come to light made it possible to assume with almost complete certainty that we were dealing with a remnant of infantile sexual curiosity directed at the female genital.

Thus, the genesis of the perversion is that a particularly suitable portion of infantile experience or fantasy is preserved through all the storms and stresses of development, especially those of puberty, and remains conscious. The pleasurable sensations that belong to infantile sexuality are displaced onto this piece after the rest of the representatives of the instinctive drives have succumbed to repression, undoubtedly under the leadership of those partial drives which, either because of constitutional makeup or as a result of too strong gratification, have proved stronger than those that prevailed in childhood development. Supported in this way and endowed with a high pleasure reward, this portion of infantile sexuality proves sufficiently strong to compete successfully with the primacy of the genitals. The question remains, of what does the "particular suitability" of this fragment consist, accounting for its success? A part of the answer has already been given: the pregenital stage of development on which the individual is particularly strongly fixated must be embodied in it, and the extremely powerful partial drive must find its particular form of gratification in it. We may state further that some special relation to the ego must have made it possible for this particular fragment to escape repression. In the screen memory, it is the fragment's apparent harmlessness, its indifference, which sets it beyond persecution. The experiences on which the compulsion neurosis is built up are likewise allowed to belong to the conscious. They owe this to the general isolation of affect from the contents of the fantasy, that is, to a mechanism that is characteristic of the compulsion neurosis.[5]

The perverted gratification, however, does not by any means appear to the conscious as harmless and indifferent. Also, its affect content has not in any way been withdrawn, as is proved by its high pleasure reward. We must here be dealing with something else, something special, to which the phenomenon of the perversion is specifically related.

To reach an understanding of what the circumstances are, we must bear in mind the fact emphasized by Freud in his lecture presented before the Seventh International Psychoanalytic Congress, that not only the repressed instinctual strivings have become unconscious, as a result of their being cast out, but also that in the ego itself unconscious elements are present. The two most conspicuous phenomena of this type, resistance and guilt, can be explained by the fact that the factors related to repression come into such intimate contact with their opposites that they, for their part, are no longer able to enter consciousness—as in former times, bailiffs and those who caught thieves were cast out from decent society because of their occupation. This experience indicates that behind the expression *ego-syntonic* can be hidden very different forms and motives of adjustment. We must never lose sight of the fact that repression is a dynamic process, in which it is not the arguments that win, but in which a stronger instinct organization represses a weaker one, only later, at a new stage of development, perhaps to be repressed itself. In such a conflict of instinctual drives, the one wins which imparts the higher pleasure reward. Accordingly, a particularly strongly developed partial drive must also be especially hard to put down; in fact, a complete subjugation of such a source of pleasure is perhaps not possible. If in such an instance repression should be in some way successful, it must resign itself to a compromise; it must allow the pleasure to remain in a partial complex, and allow it to be taken up into the ego, one might almost say, allow it to be sanctioned. The remaining components that have been detached from it permit themselves to be repressed more easily and they remain repressed; they have been weakened by a change-of-party, as it were, of a former ally. This knowledge of the split, in which one piece enters into the service of repression and thus carries over into the ego the pleasure of a pregenital stage of development, while the rest falls victim to repression, appears to be the mechanism of perversions.

The principal and most difficult work of repression is nearly always the detachment of drives from the infantile object choice: the oedipus complex, and, somewhat below that, the castration complex, which have of late been increasingly attracting the attention of analysts.[6] One can expect that a mechanism such as the one described above will play a considerable role in these important repression accomplishments. Precisely where the love fixation and, as a result, the conflict about repression are particularly strong, the fixation of the libido at, or its regressive taking over by, a group of fantasies that lie outside the circle of the later genital gratification will present itself as a way out. Thus the partial drive does not continue directly into the perversion; first it passes through the oedipal conflict and, through the help of repression, reaches definite relationships with the oedipus complex.

This mechanism becomes very clear in the fantasy "a child is being beaten." In its most primitive form it is merely an emanation of the oedipus complex with special emphasis on the hostile sadistic attitude toward the rival. It would probably, like many similar fantasy formations, be subject to repression, but it possesses the characteristic, after only a little alteration, of becoming a means of substituting for the proscribed genital oedipal wish a wish that corresponds to the leading anal-sadistic partial drive. A new working over wipes out the last traits reminiscent of the oedipus complex, in that it eliminates the person of the father and that of the self. The product is now a perverted fantasy that is capable of entering consciousness and that is pleasure yielding. Our attempt at an explanation fits the average case of male homosexuality equally well: the fixation on the mother is too strong to permit the normal process of getting rid of it. For it to succeed at all, the fixation on one's own sex—a product of narcissism and the retreat from castration anxiety—must be sanctioned and incorporated in the ego. In the case of exhibitionism mentioned above, it would appear that the freeing from the mother and the sexual relations with another woman, by the man who was later destined to become impotent, were, one might say, connected with the inner proviso of a one-time breakthrough of the exhibitionistic tendencies. It is quite appropriate that he should have had his first experience of impotence some years later with the same girl, at a time when they went brook-bathing together naked.

The mechanism described above makes it possible for us to understand the transition from perversion to neurosis if we bear in mind that repression, corresponding to the developmental course of the libido, is a step-by-step process. It can then easily happen that the complex that brings about the work of repression, in the course of its further development, can in its turn fall prey to repression. It can also happen, however, that the complex will again be called forth because it is favored by external circumstances. As a result of the failure, as we frequently have occasion to observe, not a neurosis but a perversion ensues. This, however, is only apparently a new construct; at the time of the oedipal confict, its right to exist had already been granted. Later, in quieter times, this privilege was lost and it is now renewed like a patent of nobility of some family that was formerly worthy, but later fell into disfavor.

We are now able to answer the question: why are there more neurotics among perverts than among normal persons? The juxtaposition of the positive and the negative comes about in this way: although in the conflict over repression, the splitting off of a portion that is incorporated in the ego and that is raised to the goal of perverted gratification proves to be necessary and is successfully carried out, the repressed portions nonetheless remain strong enough, or become so in the course of development, to enforce as a compromise their breakthrough as a neurosis. We need not go into the simpler case, where we are dealing with various levels of fixation that are taken care of in various ways, at this point.

The lessening of censorship in dreams represents an

expansion of ego boundaries in the direction of the repressed. Accordingly, it becomes easy for the dream work, in individual cases, to perform something similar to what we have just become acquainted with as a mechanism for solving the repression conflict in general, that is, to take over into the ego (that is, into the manifest dream content) a portion of what would otherwise be repressed. The case reported by Rank[7] as well as the exhibitionist dreams of the teacher mentioned above, are good examples of dream and neurosis confronting each other, as perversion and neurosis do in other cases. In the anxiety dream, the success is again canceled out as a result of a last reinforcement of repression through the change in affect, yet the break-through to the ego remains in the greater ease of seeing through just such anxiety dreams.

Thus a partial drive becomes a perversion through the exceptional position accorded to a portion of the fantasies which are taken up by the ego as a wish- and pleasure-goal, in order to obtain the partial drive's alliance in the repression conflict, especially against the oedipus complex. We must, however, emphasize that this is only the mechanism of, not the motive for, its breakthrough. The perversion does not grow strong only by means of this alliance; on the contrary, its elective choice rests—whether it be through hereditary constitution or through particular experiences of gratification—on the fact that it has been developed beyond the normal degree.

Notes

1. S. Freud (1919): *Sammlung kleiner Shriften zur Neurosenlehre* (The Theory of the Neurosis), 5th series,

pp. 195-228. English translation: 'A child is being beaten': a contribution to the study of the origin of sexual perversions. *Standard Edition* 17:179-204.

2. According to a remark of Freud's, gratification (*Lust*) can only be conscious. There is no such thing as repressed gratification as such; the process of repression changes gratification (*Lust*) into discomfort (*Unlust*).

3. "The witnessing of actual scenes of beatings in school called forth in the child that was watching, a strangely excited, probably mixed feeling, in which rejection played a large part. In several cases, the actual witnessing of beatings was found to be unbearable" (Freud 1919, p. 197).

4. Freud 1919, p. 195.

5. S. Freud: *Sammlung kleiner Schriften zur Neurosenlehre* 3rd series, pp. 156-157.

6. See the works of Staercke, Abraham, Alexander, and others in this journal (In*ternationale Zeitschrift fur Psychoanalyse*).

7. O. Rank: Perversion and Neurosis, *Internationale Zeitschrift fur Psychoanalyse* 8:403-404.

Appendix C
HOMOSEXUAL FIXATIONS
IN NEUROTIC WOMEN
Dr. Raymond de Saussure

Fifty years have passed since the publication of de Saussure's monograph on female homosexuality. It has been an invaluable source of information for French analysts and is presented here in English for the first time. Although written before the development of ego psychology, object relations theory, and current concepts of narcissism, it presents a masterful knowledge of female psychology, and provides important clinical and theoretical material on the relatively neglected subject of female homosexuality.

Ladies and Gentlemen:

I should like to express my appreciation of the honor you have shown me in calling upon me to present a paper to the Congress of French Language Psychoanalysts this year. In working with this question of homosexual fixations among neurotic women, I am well aware of the difficulties not only because it touches upon a number of delicate questions of feminine psychology, but more especially because to date it has been only lightly touched upon by psychoanalysts.

Presented at the Fourth Congress of French Language Psychoanalysts, Paris, 1929. Translated into English by Hella Freud Bernays, 1966, as arranged for by C.W. Socarides, M.D.

To give you an idea of the extent of the neglect of this problem, let me say that Rickman's *Index Psychanalyticus,*[1] which contains 4,700 entries, has only a dozen references on the subject of female homosexuality. I am well aware that the subject of this report does not include everything pertaining to the problem of homosexuality; it is limited to those fixations, temporary or permanent, that we find among so many neurotic women, and that are not accompanied by lesbian practices. However, in that field, too, it is not of much use to go over previous contributions, for the titles of the articles do not indicate whether they are concerned with the same fixations, and to ferret them out, we would have to reread all the cases on neurotic women that have been published in the psychoanalytic literature, a considerable task which, for lack of time, we do not expect to undertake. Accordingly, I offer my apologies for bringing you a piece of work which does not have the richness nor the amplitude that I would have liked.

I. Limiting the Subject

The history of the study of homosexuality has various phases. Up until the time of the celebrated work of Westphal[2] most scientists held to a moralistic viewpoint, and considered sexual inversion to be an acquired defect. Westphal showed that the homosexual individual was not responsible for his so-called vice, but he connected all cases of inversion with a special type of constitution. From then on, we find this thesis upheld by a number of authors.[3] Certain authors, however, seem to consider that this phenomenon in women might be secondary to a phobia.[4] Chevallier[5] also refers to a pederasty of necessity in alluding to the homosexuals of certain periods, notably Greece in Plato's time. Moll,[6] in his significant monograph, has described cases where the homosexuality has been purely physical, comparable to erotomania, but where carnal desire has completely disappeared or at least remained unconscious. Moll considers these types as constitutional degenerates. This idea found so much favor that numerous observations have been published in which the inversion is accompanied by phobias, doubts, scruples, and so on.[7]

Krafft-Ebing distinguishes various forms of congenital sexual inversion:[8]

1. *Psychosexual hermaphroditism* in which one still finds traces of heterosexuality
2. *Homosexuality, properly called,* characterized by an exculsive inclination for persons of the same sex
3. *Effeminacy and virginity,* sexual inversions accompanied by a correlative inversion in the psychic sphere
4. *Androgyny and gynandry,* characterized by the coinciding of sexual inversion with important anomalies of the sexual character and in particular of secondary characteristics

The constitutional theory held sway until Freud and his pupils[9] brought forward a psychogenetic theory for certain cases of inversion. Their idea was not to deny completely this constitutional factor (everyone knows the importance that Freud attaches to the constitutional bisexuality of our personality), nor to apply their views to every case of homosexuality, but only to show that among many subjects, this inversion could be treated by psychoanalysis. In 1920, Freud[10] returned to this question, pointing out the complexity of the homosexual problem which, according to him, has three different aspects: (1) study of the somatic characteristics of the genital organs (disturbed physical hermaphroditism); (2) study of the psychic sexual characteristics (masculine or feminine tendencies); and (3) choice of the sexual object.

Here is Freud's conclusion (p. 23): "Psychoanalysis is not called upon to resolve the problem of homosexuality. It should be satisfied to discover the psychic mechanisms which have led to the choice of object."

In countering the psychoanalytic school which was trying to explore the psychic processes of homosexuality, Hirschfeld[11] sought to find the biological and constitutional processes of the inversion. This difference in point of view has generated polemical writings[12] which we do not have time to take up here.

With regard to the subject that we intend to treat, we can abstract our particular problem, since we are considering only the psychic homosexual fixations.

This question insofar as it concerns men has been better studied than insofar as it concerns women. Nevertheless, it would be useful to begin with masculine inversion from the psychoanalytic point of view. In general, we recognize three mechanisms which precede this psychic inversion: first, the boy does not succeed in resolving the oedipus complex, he remains attached to his mother but he cannot possess her in reality, he identifies himself with her, and, as a result, he plays a feminine role vis-à-vis other men; second, for one reason or another, the fixation of the boy on his mother has not been able to occur, and the fixation on the father persists; third, the fear of castration is so strong that, to avoid this punishment, the boy reverses the oedipus complex and passively submits himself to the father or to father substitutes. These three types explain in particular the mechanisms of a passive homosexuality, but one finds other forms of the inversion where the male role remains active; that is what occurs among boys who feel cheated by the woman's castration, or among men of the powerful-weak type described last year by Laforgue.[13] For the rest, it often happens that the same man alternately acts out the active role or the passive one. There is the case, for example, of Sadger's[14] patient who kept looking for older men toward whom he behaved passively (as he did toward the father), men of his own age, who represented substitutes for his mother, and young people with whom he identified and whom he would woo as he would have loved to woo his mother.

There are other psychogenetic points of view that should be brought out, such as that of Senf.[15] He thinks that all perversion comes from one of the elements of the sexual which has particularly appealed to the imagination of the patient and which has been isolated to become the method of enjoyment for the individual. For a masculine homosexual, it might be the erection which would play the principal role. Sadger[16] has propounded a similar idea that the homosexual overevaluates the penis and has a sense of being deceived at not being able to find it in the other sex.

We do not wish to proceed further with this psychology of male homosexuality which, I hope, will be the subject of one of our future reports to the Congress; we would only like to insist on the fact that in the study of inversion two quite distinct problems are presented to us: on the one hand, the revolt against one's own sex, and on the other, the fixation on the other sex. We shall return to these two problems in the study of female homosexuality, and they will form the two principal sections of our report.

II. The Revolt Against Femininity and the Castration Complex

In his psychiatric or psychoanalytic practice, each of us has come upon women who are in revolt against femininity. You still recall Allendy's case.[17] He says, "Mme. C. recalls having wished to be a man so that she might avoid her feminine role. She would have wanted to be a man of the sea guiding his ship over the ocean. She remembers particularly, when she was a little girl, having wished for a penis and of having amused herself with imagining one, by rolling up her shirt into a point." I might also remind you of the very typical observation of Ferenczi[18]: "This patient often dreamed of little malicious black men and, in one of her fantasies, she experienced the desire to eat them all up. At this thought she associated spontaneously with the idea of eating black stool, then the idea of biting off and of cutting into little pieces the male organ. By this incorporation (of the male organ) she felt, to a certain degree, her own body being transformed into a male penis. In this way she could, in her unconscious fantasies, perform the sexual act with other women."

We could cite still further observations, but we prefer to enter at once into the heart of our subject.

Before 1920, several authors spoke of the feeling of inferiority which femininity produces in certain women. It is to Abraham that we owe the first study summarizing this point of view,[19] which we will present in brief.

We find, among many neurotic women, the conscious or unconscious desire to be a man. The reasons that the women put forward to legitimize this desire are the greater liberty of action and the greater sexual freedom that men enjoy. These are rationalizations. Analysis teaches us, that, in general, the shock of seeing the masculine organ occurs at a very narcissistic phase in which the little girl says to herself, "I must at some time or other have had a member like a boy, but it has been taken from me." As a result, the little girl considers her own sex organs to be like an injury. During the anal phase the girl, through being jealous of the boy, develops an aggressiveness against all men. In her unconscious, she tries to substitute fecal matter for the penis (see Ferenczi's observation, quoted above). Despite that, the girl always keeps hoping that she will grow this member, or that her father will give her one. In proportion to how much she sees herself compelled to renounce these hopes, she becomes more and more aggressive against men.

It is at this moment, by identification with the mother, that the young girl reaches the point of wanting a child with the father, as a substitute for the penis. Sublimation of this process can lead to a normal sexual life, but it very often becomes frustrated.

The idea of an injury or a wound (the vulva) is reinforced by the appearance of menstruation, and later by defloration and lying-in. Not accepting the reality of the anatomical difference, the woman often reactivates her bisexuality and becomes homosexual.

The homosexuality can remain repressed and manifest itself consciously only in a sublimated way (masculine tastes).

The reactions can come to light in two different ways: (1) desire for a penis, with various fantasies for realizing this wish; or (2) vengeance against the male sex. After having manifested itself in various symbolic forms, the desire for a penis is most often externalized (the piercing eye, the nose, the appendages, the legs, the breast and so on).[20]

Abraham then continues on to the study of the sadistic tendencies against the male. He shows that in vaginismus there is not only the idea of repulsing the male organ, but also, when there has been penetration, the idea of punishing the male and depriving him of his organ. One also sees women falling in love with men who have been deprived of an arm or a leg. This amputation, symbolic of castration, permits them to lessen their unconscious aggression.

Many of these patients do not get married because they have the idea that if they had a husband they would be obsessed by the need to do him harm. Aggression sometimes takes mild forms. Frigidity, for example, is a defense on the part of the woman which tends to make the man impotent.

Many of these patients do attract men and when they have conquered them, they drop them in order to have the sadistic pleasure of foiling them. Others, in order to lessen the difference between the sexes, choose husbands who have strongly feminine traits.

These patients, by virtue of believing that they have been castrated, have a great fear of being brought to bed, of being operated on and even of being deflowered. Freud[21] has analyzed this last fear. He has shown that, for the unconscious, the defloration was the analogy to the sexual act committed with the father. That is why the affects which are appropriate to it are renewed in the act of defloration, the anxiety about which has had, for a long time, to be left to a substitute father (the right of the seigneur). These conflicting affects are the deep attachment to the father, the fear of incest, and the need for revenge for a love that has been spurned and for the feeling of castration. Equating the genital organ with an injury also explains certain functional (nervous) amenorrheas.[22]

In a great many women one finds a very pronounced narcissism, the significance of which becomes clear in this remark of one of Abraham's patients, "I should like to be the most beautiful woman in the world so that all men would woo me, and then I would give them all a swift kick."

Certain of these patients displace the erogenous zone and, while they remain frigid, they show themselves as loving orally, making the tongue play the active role of the penis. Here it is appropriate to refer to Sach's observations.[23]

A young girl who suffered from an intense castration complex had an early memory of having bitten an old man on the ear. In the analysis, she recalled that as a child she had believed that one would pull out the penis in cutting it off. One finds this idea in the rites of many primitive people.[24]

Abraham's article exerted considerable influence. Karen Horney (of Berlin) published two articles[25] which partly confirmed Abraham's views and partly shut the door on them.

Horney asks if it is biologically permissible to think that half of humanity suffers by reason of its sex and if penis envy could not be explained in some other way than by the desire to be a male, especially as one also meets this desire among some women who seem, in their childhood, to have completely escaped traumatization.

The boy, every time he urinates, can satisfy his narcissistic exhibitionistic tendency by looking at his sex organ. The girl does not have this satisfaction, which is why she carries back her narcissism to her whole body, but also envies the boy for having this privilege. Another aspect of this jealousy lies in the fact that urinary eroticism brings more satisfaction to the boy than it does to the girl. A woman's décolletage is probably a compensation for the exhibitionism of the man in the act of urinating (see my earlier reference to the breast as compensating for the penis). Also, the wish for the penis is increased by a repressed desire to masturbate; the boy is permitted to touch his organ to urinate, while the same gesture is forbidden to the girl.

Horney thinks that the desire of the girl in the pregenital phase is revived by the later desire for a child which would be given to her by the father. The disappointment at not receiving this child causes the girl to regress to the pregenital desire for a penis. In this connection we believe it would be useful to reproduce the observation that Horney takes up in her work.[26]

This connection appeared to me to be particularly clear in the case of Z in whom, after the disappearance of certain obsessional symptoms, there persisted a tenacious fear of pregnancy as a final symptom. The memory which, in addition to having observed her parents' coitus up to an advanced age, she felt to have been the most important, was the pregnancy of her mother and the birth of a brother when the patient was two years old. For a long time the desire for a penis seemed to be the crucial point of the analysis. The desire for a penis which she attached to the father and the hate against the brother who had dethroned her from her position as the only child, when they were discovered, were discussed with a great deal of emotion, in her consciousness. With this desire, there surged up all the complexes that we are accustomed to come upon in circumstances like these, notably the desire for revenge, the fantasy of castrating the man, the refusal to do the work and perform the function of a woman, the refusal, strongly emphasized, to be pregnant, and finally, unconscious homosexuality. It was not until the analysis, with the strongest resistance, arrived at the deepest layers, that it became clear that the envy for a penis really hid an envy of the father. This last desire had been displaced on to the penis. The hatred against the brother turned into a hatred for the father because she felt herself to have been spurned by him. The hatred is also let out against the mother because she has had the child. It is only the release at the point of this displacement which resolves the penis envy and the masculine complexes, and which, furthermore, gives her the possibility of becoming wholly a woman. What had taken place? To resume our schematic treatment, we can say: first, that the childish envy had been displaced on to the brother, then on to the father's organ; and second, that the mechanism described by Freud had come to pass, namely to know that in renouncing her love object, the patient, through regression, becomes identified with the object.

Horney thinks that if these women do not reach the point of manifest homosexuality, it is because they do not so much want to be a woman as they want to be the father—so much the father, that the fixation on an object becomes more difficult and turns into a regression toward an autoerotic course.

The identification with the father as well as the refusal of femininity cannot immediately put itself at the disposal of the pregenital desire for a penis. The envy of the male organ only facilitates this identification. It must insist on the fact that up to the moment of the wish for a child from the father, the girl takes, with respect to the latter, a feminine attitude. It is not until after the rejection as to the child that has not been granted her, that the narcissistic regression appears, the refusal of femininity, the identification with the father, and the reactivation of the penis envy.

In her second article, basing herself on a work of Simmel,[27] Horney thinks that the psychoanalysis of women has been considered too much from the masculine point of view, resulting in poor treatment of women. To bolster this thesis, she holds that the psychosexual development of the young girl, as it is described in psychoanalytic literature, corresponds to the idea that a boy has of her in the course of his own development. Here is a schematic representation of this idea:

Boy's Thinking	*Girl's Development*
Thinks that woman also has a penis.	For the two sexes, the masculine organ alone plays a role.[28]
Observes the absence of the penis in woman.	Sad recognition of the absence of a penis.
Thinks woman is a man who has been castrated.	Believes that she once had a penis but that she has been deprived of it.
Believes that woman has been punished and that he is threatened with the same treatment.	Castration considered as a punishment.

Holds the woman to be inferior.	Feels herself to be inferior (penis envy).
Cannot think how the woman can escape this situation.	Cannot arrive at surmounting feelings of castration and of inferiority. Always wants to conquer anew her desires for masculinity.
Fears the woman's envy of him.	Would like to get revenge in some permanent way on man because of his power.

Horney then seeks to show that just as the woman has penis envy, the man envies maternity; but it is easier for the man to sublimate this tendency intellectually by supporting his family, than it is for the woman to sublimate her envy of the penis. On the other hand, we must not forget that the man has a much stronger tendency to despise women than is the case the other way around; this could be the result of the man's unconscious tendencies.

Horney insists further on the necessary difference between the pregenital envy of the penis and the desires for masculinity. We know the latter from the analyses of adults. They are a secondary picture which incorporates all that has been frustrated in the development of femininity. It is the desires for masculinity, then, that, by a regression, reawaken as the envy for the penis.

In this problem it is also important that we pay attention to the differences in the oedipus complex in the two sexes.

With the boy, due to his fear of castration, the renunciation is carried only to the object of sexuality, that is, to the mother, and the masculinity continues to be affirmed; it is even overvalued by the reaction to the fear of castration. We can find it in the boy in the latency period, in the prepubic period, but even more in adult years.[29]

In the girl, on the contrary, the renunciation of the father is accompanied by a movement away from the feminine role. The fear of sexual intercourse has often been interpreted, among patients, as a fear of castration, but Horney thinks that what we have here is a simple fear of a too large penis and the memory of incestuous desire which invest the vaginal zone with an affect of fear and of defense, accompanied, as in the case of men, by a sense of guilt.

Penis envy should not be considered solely from the point of view of rejection. It represents, as Abraham has shown,[30] a partial love, a stage of love for an object. If it remains significant in the adult, it is because penis envy often conceals a defense against not satisfying once again incestuous desires for the father.

There are a number of assertions in this second article that one might take up further, but I do not wish to spend too much time on this. We will content ourselves with exploring the ideas of Helene Deutsch, which provide an excellent corrective to those of Horney. First, however, we would like to present the ideas of Bousfield which tie in more directly with Abraham's article.[31] Bousfield remarks that with women suffering from a castration complex, one finds: (1) a conflict between narcissism and the fear of castration; and (2) a conflict between exhibitionism and the castration.

An exaggerated exhibitionism can be a sign of compensation for a feeling of castration. One also comes upon a certain tendency to repress all phallic ideas to avoid revealing the wound to one's narcissism. In this case prudery is exaggerated as a defense, and appears as a movement in opposition to exhibitionism which serves as a compensation. In this connection, Bousfield reports the history of one of his very prudish woman patients, suffering from a very strong castration complex which made her retain her urine in order to have the pleasure of urinating by way of a catheter which, in her fantasy, served as a penis. This person at age seven had seen a naked man bathing in the ocean. She has asked if her father was built like that, and remembered that when she had been very ill at age two she had thought it was because they had cut off her organ. She did not like to have the lower part of her body admired, even her legs. On the contrary, she was very proud of her face, of her hair, and of her bust. She had a horror of hair on the body, but she was very proud of her own hair. When she was a little girl, the length of public hair seemed to her equivalent to phallic strength, but it was an ambivalent symbol which also brought to mind the absence of the phallus, from whence we get the displacement on to the hair.

Bousfield also recalls the history of a patient who had accepted her castration with respect to men, but who was unable to accept it with respect to women. The more a woman showed any superiority or the more she developed a masculine quality, the more the patient tried to show her superiority over these women, and forced herself to behave in the way she supposed a man would have behaved under the same circumstances.

Bousfield further comments that the castration complex does not always make the woman masculine. It sometimes happens, to the contrary, that this intensifies her femininity; she seeks to behave as differently as possibly from and to display character traits as much opposed to those of a man. One of these patients said, "I detest women who ape men." These women often seek to decentralize their libido and to diffuse it all over their bodies. They frequently sexualize their legs.

Bousfield then shows that it is difficult to know exactly what belongs to masculinity and what to femininity. Long hair can just as easily be a symbol of femininity as a castration reaction.

Beatrice Hinkle[32] has already insisted on this fact. In her article she recalls that the ancient Egyptians, like the Malays of the Philippines and other primitive peoples, did not believe that woman is inferior to man.

The articles of Abraham, Horney, and Bousfield present feminine psychology from the negative point of view of a sudden loss. In order to understand female homosexuality completely, we must also bear in mind the positive stage of femininity. No one has analyzed them better than Helen Deutsch; we shall now proceed to summarize her ideas.[33]

In the sexual development of the woman, two factors are important which do not exist in the sexual development of the man. First, the renunciation of considering the clitoris to be the equivalent of the penis; and second, the discovery of a new genital organ and the passing from the phallic phase to the vaginal phase.

The boy discovers the vagina in the exterior world, and his discovery brings in its train a certain sadism, in contrast to the woman who discovers it within her own body, with the masochistic pleasure of being conquered by the penis.

What achieves a normal development in the woman

is not the satisfaction of the infantile wish to have a penis, but the discovery of the vagina as an organ of pleasure and the renunciation of the penis for the realistic and equivalent pleasure of the vagina. This new organ has to become a sort of substitute for the ego in the same sense that Ferenczi speaks[33] of the penis as a miniature of the ego.

The development of the love object in the woman goes from the breast of the mother to the penis of the father, which, at the beginning, is an object of the oral phase. It is not until the anal phase that the penis loses its oral value and becomes an organ of strength, a sadistic organ, just as the sexual act is then understood sadistically. In this phase the anus represents the passive organ and the fecal column the active libidinal organ, in the same sense that the breast does in the oral phase. Therefore, by a displacement of the libidinal investment, the fecal column assumes the same narcissistic value as the breast does in the oral phase.

It seems natural that the displacement should turn toward the third opening of the woman, and that the penis should come to replace the breast or the fecal column, but here the woman is thrust up against the fact that a great part of the libidinal investment attaches to the clitoris; the difficulty becomes the passing from the phallic phase to the vaginal phase.

The compensation of the vagina is, moreover, less satisfying for the woman since this organ is neither seen nor felt. On the other hand, the clitoris is too small to be the object of an investment as powerful as that of the penis. Menstruation serves as the first indication of the vagina as an organ of eroticism.

In sexual intercourse with the partner, penetration is a reminder of the act of sucking at the maternal breast, a reminder that is reinforced by the trauma of the weaning process. In the penis-breast equation and the vaginal sucking, coitus accomplishes the fantasy of the paternal penis. In coitus, the woman, from the viewpoint of the unconscious, is at the same time the child (sucking of the penis-breast) and the mother (masochistic attitude of the infantile sadistic concept of coitus), something that will come to pass in actuality in the course of her being pregnant, when she is both mother and child.

By this we see that, as a last resort, for the woman, coitus represents the oral incorporation of the paternal penis which is then transformed into the infant (realization of the desire for a child by the father). The difference in the attitude between the man and the woman might be summed up this way: "The man actively appropriates to himself a part of reality and in this way attains the pleasure of the primitive state (coitus being a symbol of the return to the mother's breast). The woman, in accepting a passive role in the act of penetration, introjects a part of the external world that she incorporates in herself (pregnancy)."

In its role of suction and of incorporation, the vagina does not become what holds on to the penis but what holds on to the child; for this function the vagina does not take its strength from the clitoris, but from the libidinal investment of the entire body. The vagina is identified with the child and is invested with a narcissistic libido which, as a result of the act (pregnancy) will be transmitted onto the child. It becomes a second ego, a miniature of the ego, in imitation of the man's penis. If the woman succeeds in giving this maternal function to the vagina by renouncing the clitoris (substitute for the penis), she achieves her female development.

I shall not go on with Dr. Deutsch's work. It takes up the subject of maternity, which is far afield from our special interest.

III. The Choice of Object and the Homosexual Fixation

If the revolt against femininity and the castration complex has been relatively well studied in a whole series of works, one cannot say as much for the choice of the feminine object. We can track that back to various causes. First of all, in the majority of homosexual fixations without actual lesbian realization, the analysis primarily centers on the castration complex, and once this is resolved, the woman ipso facto renounces her homosexual attachment without its necessarily being analyzed. Also, these fixations are often unconscious and, in the mind of the patient, pass for simple friendships. The superego of all of these patients, by virtue of the repressed aggression against the male, is extremely demanding and guilt feelings are developed to an excessive degree. As a result, the fixations are often vague. Finally, up to the present, very few authentic analyses have been published.

Freud[35] has given us the fragment of an observation of a very pretty, eighteen-year-old girl, who was madly in love with a woman of the world ten years older than she. The young girl had assumed a masculine attitude toward her friend.

In her early childhood, she had transferred her oedipal desires on to her older brother. The analysis, which had been very short, brought up only one small bit of material on infantile sexuality. This woman was not neuropathic.

At age fourteen, she conceived a passion for a baby of three that she had seen in the park (desire to be a mother herself). That did not last long; very soon she brought all her interest to bear on women who were older than she. This change in the object fixation of her libido (age sixteen) had coincided with the birth of a third brother. Here the worldly woman was nothing but a substitute for her mother.

Just when the younger brother was born, the girl found herself at that state of puberty when the infantile oedipus complex is reawakened. The desire to have a child remains conscious, while the incestuous side of the desire remains unconscious. In place of her having the child, it was the unconsciously hated rival, her mother. Spurned, she turns away from her father and from men in general, repulses her own femininity, and seeks another path for expansion of her libido.

The homosexuality aimed at punishing her father who was all the more troubled by it as she engaged in it so flagrantly.

Sadger[36] provides us with two observations on homosexual women. The first is aged thirty-five. At age six she loved a boy with red hair who urinated on top of her. In her early childhood she had frequently surprised the coitus of her parents. Later, when she had become acquainted with sexual phenomena, she had at the same time a strong urge to have coitus with her father and an insurmountable disgust at the idea that her father's large organ should go into her. She reproached herself for her incestuous ideas and her disgust spread to all male organs. At age fourteen an anonymous letter informed her that her father had a mistress. From that moment on, she withdrew from her father in order to get closer to her mother. This succeeded in fixating her libido on the female sex.

The other case concerned a girl of seventeen who had also surprised her parents having intercourse. She had wanted to both act the father, and to play the role of father with respect to the mother. At this time she came to the sad realization that she did not have a penis, and she began to develop aggressive tendencies with regard to her father's organ, with the idea of appropriating it for herself. This explains why sadism is so often associated with female homosexuality.

Laforgue and Allendy[37] bring us an interesting observation of a psychic female homosexual.

She had acquired such an aptitude for identifying with other women that everywhere, in the street, in the subway, she sought to test out in herself the feelings of these others, becoming in turn mother, wife, mistress, prostitute, in her imagination exhausting every feminine possiblility, even the furthest removed from reality, for fear of the male. Having grown up with the idea that love is assoicated with bleeding and with grief and sorrow she imagined to herself women crushed in a train, drawn and quartered in an accident, and put herself in their place.

Jones[38] recently devoted a theoretical article to the first stages of female sexuality and the problem of homosexuality in women. We sincerely hope that he will publish the clinical material which served as the basis for the paper, to augment psychoanalytic observations of lesbians which are today so rare.

Jones thinks that the importance of the castration complex has been overestimated. It has often, mistakenly, been made a synonym for the extinction of sexual desires. It is important to distinguish the castration complex, which does not destroy all sexuality, from aphanisis, which represents a complete suppression of

desire; boys and girls have a far greater fear of
aphanisis than of the castration complex. Evidently,
among men, the suppression of desires is represented
primarily as a typical castration, while among women,
it is before everything else, a fear of being rejected. If
the child feels itself menaced by aphanisis, it is obliged
to choose between normal desires or oedipal desires.
These last lead the child to an identification with the
parent of the opposite sex.

These two types of reaction will give us two different
types of female homosexuals. First, those who keep
their interest in the male, but who at the same time
desire to be taken for a man. We find in this group
women who always complain of the fate of the weaker
sex. Second, those who do not attach any interest to
men and whose libido is wholly concentrated on
women.

In the homosexual solution, the individuals involved
become dependent on the imaginary possession of the
organ of the other sex; they may imagine they possess
it themselves (the second group), or they may identify
with a person of the other sex (first group). In
summary, the first group renounces the subject, while
the second renounces the object.

Jones remarks further that all homosexual women
have strong oral and sadistic tendencies. If the sadism
predominates they maintain interest in the male, but
with the desire that their own masculine qualities be
recognized. This type resents the male, and has castration fantasies with respect to him.[39] If the oral
eroticism predominates, the inversion takes the form
of a dependence on other women with no interest in the
male. The subject is masculine but also plays with her
femininity through identification with a feminine

woman who offers her satisfaction by way of a penis substitute, most often the tongue.

Jones remarks further that it is not possible to establish a fixed rule as to the conscious attitude of the homosexual toward the parents; one finds positive or negative reactions toward the father as well as toward the mother. On the other hand, in the unconscious, Jones has always found a strong ambivalence with respect to the two parents and an infantile fixation on the mother which goes back to the oral phase. This was later reduced by a fixation on the father.[40]

We have now summarized the history of the question and if along the way we have disclosed contradictions without taking sides, it is because we judge that we do not have enough experience to come to conclusions in such delicate matters. Besides, we are convinced that the processes which lead to homosexual fixations are numerous. All the ideas that have been presented we have been able to verify in this or in that patient, but they are not all true for every individual patient.

It has seemed surprising to us that in the works cited, the authors do not very often refer to the mechanisms of projection. Yet Freud[41] has shown the role that these mechanisms play in male homosexuality. It is clear that one group of the female inverts projects their femininity on to another woman, while another group projects their masculinity on to the partner. One woman can, alternately, project her masculinity and her femininity. Sadger has shown the same thing to be true for men. In summary, and this is an important point, the female homosexual fixation is, in our view, more a redoubling of narcissism than an object fixation. (I refer here to cases where the practices of lesbianism have not been realized.)

After the period of the reawakening of the castration complex (in Horney's sense), there is an unconscious ambivalence with respect to the two parents, and a phase of hermaphrodite narcissism. It is not unusual for these individuals to display mannerisms at once very masculine and very feminine; they show grace in their movements, they sharpen their sensitivity, they show themselves to be coquettish, but they also want to dominate through their intelligence, to show themselves as rivals to men in sport, and so on. These women project now their femininity, now their masculinity, and they attach themselves to types of women opposite to themselves. Besides, they seek to identify with their partner rather than to love the partner as an object. To them the object is a mirror which they invest with a masculine or a feminine narcissism, depending on the type of woman which is before them. These women, in very hermaphrodite fashion, have a very pronounced masochism (the aggressive tendencies having been repressed) and the result is that they voluntarily play a passive role toward other women who have had the opportunity to make men suffer. By doing this, they simultaneously act out their sadistic and their masochistic desires; this is the highest degree of love object relation that they are able to attain.

Much has been said about the homosexual fixation being a protection against the oedipus complex, but before being a protection, it has been an attempt to leave behind oedipal desires. This fixation, however, also runs up against opposition on the part of the superego. As a result, there often is a regression to the anal stage with a partial abandonment of the homosexual fixations and active and passive sadistic and masochistic fantasies with respect to the oedipal object. It seems that certain women, in the hope of escaping their neurosis, continually run the oedipal cycle: homosexuality, anal regression, reawakening of the oedipus complex on the anal plane, and so on.

For other women, the homosexual fixations are very different according to whether the patient has one or several brothers and according to whether or not she has sisters. But we do not want to take up these theoretical considerations without presenting some clinical material.

One would have to present a great many observations, but that would necessitate summarizing too many of the patients' associations. In this report we prefer not to give too many cases, but to put our emphasis on particular points.

IV. Clinical Observation

Yvonne was thirty-one, the daughter of a Swiss Romande intellectual father and a Swedish mother. Both parents are severely neurotic; the father especially has an authoritarian character. He is brutal and avaricious. All the children are severely neurotic: an older sister is married; she is frigid and obsessional. An older brother is married, impotent, and sexually perverse; then comes our patient, followed by two brothers and a sister whom I know less well. The father's brothers are also severely neurotic and avaricious.

Up to the age of twelve and a half, Yvonne was brought up in Belgium. Then she lived in various Swiss Romande villages, and in 1927 settled in Geneva in order to be analyzed. At age five and a half she had a severe inflammation of the ear, and spent some time in a hospital in Lausanne. When she was six and again at thirteen, she spent some time in Sweden. At age ten and again at twelve, she interrupted her schooling because of excessive fatigue. At age thirteen, while in Sweden, she had her first menstrual period. From that time on, she often remained in bed. At fifteen she had a short stay in Dr. deSalis's clinic in Berne. At seventeen she spent six months at Dr. Liegme's, and then went for a short time to the college of La Chauz-de-Fonds. At nineteen she was very thin and frequently ran a temperature. She was sent for six months to Leysin. At twenty-one she made another trip to Sweden; at twenty-three she spent four months in Germany, where she wept all the time. At twenty-five she was cared for, for several months, by Dr. Leschinski at Territet. Later, sent to the seashore to take care of children, she had to give up after a month because her health was too poor. She then went to social work school for two years, but did not get to practice social work.

Here are some important data from her childhood from the psychoanalytic point of view. She recalls that at five, during her hospital stay, she had been very impressed when her temperature was taken vaginally. From that time on, she had the notion that she was built abnormally. From the ages of five to twelve, she was madly in love with boys of her own age; she could stay quiet for hours looking at them, admiring them, and finding them big and strong. From ages six to ten, she engaged in clitoral masturbation, and during the same period she had girlfriends who, in her words, were "hers." They were her little slaves. She made them undress in front of her, and for long periods she used to look at their buttocks. "I never had the desire to beat them," she says, "but to make them cry." She also compelled her girlfriends to go marauding. She herself was always lying and stealing. She had no interest at all in little girls that she could not dominate. All these manifestations were probably compensations for her feelings of castration. At age seven, she came upon a coitus between a bull and a cow, and the boys in the street explained to her what it was all about. From then on, she has taken a great interest in slugs and especially in snails, which she breeds in great numbers "in order to see them reproduce."

From ages eight to ten, she would go to see her younger brother on the toilet so that he could exhibit himself to her. During this same period she took great pleasure in watching boys get whippings at school. At this time, she had various transitory hallucinations. She would often see a young faun; one was green and had a bantering air. She also believed that under her bed she could see a very tiny girl who had extremely long hands. When she was nine, her mother went away for a month; her father, instead of being gentle with his children, was very severe and nervous. He hit them and sent them off to bed no matter what they did. From this time on, she again became fixated on her mother.

The father and mother did not share a bedroom, and Yvonne, from the ages of five to ten, was in her father's room. When she was older, she occasionally got dressed there. At twelve she would stay in bed so as not to have to go to school. She read all sorts of books which were unsuitable for a girl her age, and in which there were even descriptions of coitus. "At this period, I had sexual obsessions. In my imagination I was always undressing boys. I found that there was no sense to school, and that I would have to begin my sexual life right away." At age eighteen, she had a further shock, hearing the sexual intercourse of her older sister and her brother-in-law in the adjoining room.

From the clinical point of view, once she had entered upon her analysis, she appeared strongly obsessional. She felt compelled to think of the sex organs of all the men she met, with the exception of those who were ugly or effeminate, and these disgusted her. She also had phobias, could not touch a man, and felt sick when she saw a woman in a low-necked dress, or even with bare arms (equating of breast, arms, and penis). She felt compelled to look at the feet of all the men she saw (equating of feet and penis). She could not walk next to a man without experiencing such fatigue that she had to give up the walk. She had feelings of fear, of repugnance, and of excessive hate toward her father. She felt that she was sexually abnormal. "I feel in myself a man's sexuality, a sensuality so strong that it seems abnormal to me not be be able to act like a man and go into a house of prostitution in order to satisfy myself sexually."

At certain times she appears to be so dissociated and so depersonalized that she almost gives the impression of being a schizophrenic. "I am frightfully agitated, I have an idea which bothers my brain, and I can't find it. I should like to move, to sit down, to throw myself back and start over again a hundred times. Wait—I have an idea—no, it's disappeared. If I were big enough, I would make the couch jump, but my other self is against my moving. I don't know which one it is that wants to move. I can't differentiate any longer between a Swede and a Vaudoise. In every case, there is a third. I am much more humble now."

But her obsessive state shows itself in a great difficulty in buying anything, and most particularly, clothes. "I just can't make up my mind to buy some material for a blouse for myself. I get to the point where I can't do what I've made up my mind to do. When I want to imagine myself in it, it's no longer what I want; I've looked at a whole mass of samples, and yet it's never there. If they would show it to me, I'd recognize it, but they never show it to me. I don't see it distinctly, every time I imagine it, I reach a different result. I don't reach the point of taking myself by surprise. There are the materials that I have chosen, and the next minute, they make me positively ill. This morning I spent three hours trying to make up my mind. I find one material too yellow; I go to play the piano; when I come back, I don't find it so yellow any longer; it has become pale and faded. That would make me look sick, about to die. And so it goes all day long, and finally, I am in despair."

Another example of the same obsessional difficulty follows. "Today I bought myself some shoes; they were a mistake. They are too big; they are meant for someone who is ten years younger than I. I don't want to return them, I can't always be returning what I have bought. I put them on thirty times, but I can't go out in them. It's devilish! I'm almost sure that I simply buy whatever it is. I know what I want, but I don't buy it, because I'm afraid of what I think of, and so on."

We cannot study all the problems raised by this analysis, but we will touch upon those which are in line with our subject.

1. THE CASTRATION COMPLEX

This complex manifests itself in Yvonne in various forms, primarily by a great fear of her own sex organs. "I have a terrible fear of feminine organs. They don't seem natural to me, much less natural than a man's.

When I was at the seashore, they gave me a little girl to take care of. I could not wash her between her legs. I could not look at this place; it made me ill....I don't like to take a bath because I don't like to see my organs. I don't like to be naked. I would have to love myself, then I'd also know how to dress myself. I don't like to look at myself because I have the impression of being spoiled or a failure. I find that I am pretty sad to look at. A man's body is less nasty. And yet I loved Annie's body (Annie was one of her friends with whom she had a homosexual episode), her body was very white, and at certain masculine periods, I have been obsessed by the need to look at women's organs."

These few associations already enable us to see that Yvonne has not succeeded in sublimating the narcissism of the phallic phase of the little girl into a narcissism which is directed onto the whole body. Like all obsessives, she preserves an ambivalent attitude with respect to her own body, which will drive her into further difficulties.

It is natural that in a young girl of this kind, menstrual periods revived the idea of castration and reinforced the thought that her vulva represents a wound or an injury.

Here are some typical remarks. "I was in Sweden when I had my period for the first time. Mama had told me about it, but I was terribly frightened. I didn't want to have my periods anywhere but at home, and the following months, they did not come. At this time, Annie brought me into her bunch of boys. I was very ill at ease. I had the feeling of having a body without a head [castration]. It is there that I had the impression, for the first time, that I was losing my hair. I had a feeling of inferiority, of nastiness. I had the impression that someone had beaten me.

"The blood reminded me of my periods and also of the male organ that I represent to myself as being red, and also the guillotine because when you cut the head off, an awful lot of blood flows [idea of castration]. Other times, I very much liked red, the color of wild poppies. [This was before her menstrual periods, in the sadistic phase and in the period of fixation on the penis of the bull which, for her, is associated with the idea of red.]

"When I am about to have my period, I hate to see men; that gives me very violent periods, that gives me cramps that makes me sick to my stomach. During two or three years, I was unable to go for a walk when I had my period. I thought of it all the time, I was afraid of showing red spots, I was afraid of losing my hair, I was afraid of people's eyes, even of my mother's. I didn't dare to look at anyone.

"One day when I was having my period, I was as stiff as a picket fence, whether I was lying in bed or standing up. I believed that there wasn't a single drop of blood that I could lose without having it noticed. When I was afraid like this, I would lose blood in quantity. It was terrible. During these days, I didn't dare to go to the toilet to evacuate. I absolutely perspired from fright. If I had to go to the toilet it was agony. I suffered terribly. I didn't dare go to sleep because I did not dare to relax. I would so much have liked to drop off to sleep so that I might forget, but I said to myself, 'How horrible, if it should begin to flow.' Then when it did flow, I was delighted."

Yvonne then reported that one day when she had her period, a nurse had come to beg her to help her mother. She had not gone, and had not dared to explain why. Her father came and beat her and accused her of being selfish. She had not been able to tell him what it was, but since then (a matter of fourteen years) she could no longer do anything while saying to herself, "That would help my parents." From that time on, she has nursed a need for vengeance that cannot be assuaged.

With a great many patients, where the castration complex has revivified the native bisexuality, one finds great ambivalence toward the breasts. Well-developed breasts are a compensation for the penis, but at the same time they are a feminine attribute. Yvonne said, "At fourteen I had well-developed breasts. I was proud of them. Some of my girlfriends made fun of me, and for a whole summer I would not eat. I believe that the more I repressed my sexuality, the smaller my breasts got."

Yvonne's castration complex became externalized in still another fashion, illustrated in a very significant fantasy of hers. "That night, you were sitting on a chair. I put my hand on your knees. You had become diabolical. You wanted to cut off my head with a kitchen knife. I had my hands behind my back and I kept saying, 'I will not budge, I will die.'" I join to this fantasy a remark made after quite a few months of analysis: "Today I am able to stretch my arms behind my head [symbol of erection]. Other times I always was afraid that you would cut them off....I am afraid that you will hit me if I budge. I have this idea and I ought to be punished. In my imagination I move about all the time. I see you getting ready to hit me. It is because, earlier, Papa used to hit me, and when he did not, it was just the same, because I was afraid that he would."[42]

I consider these three associations to be very important because they show us that the woman can suffer from a secondary castration complex very similar to that of a man. Following her disappointment at not possessing a penis, she eroticizes her legs, her arms, her bosom, and her head; she makes them into phallic symbols, but this usurpation does not pass without a sense of guilt which is translated into a fear of a new castration. It seems that, in her fantasy, Yvonne accepts her punishment. We find this ambivalence, created by the desire to give a phallic value to a member and the feeling of guilt which condemns this attribution, in the exhibitionist tendencies of these patients, as Bousfield has shown. Yvonne says about her legs: "There is the little girl who wants her skirts to be short. The girl next to her, a little older, finds that they are short enough. Another girl says, 'If you shorten them too much, you won't be able to make them longer again.' The other one says, 'So much the worse, let happen what may.' It goes on like this for hours, and at night I get up to cut the skirt short....I suffer because I have small feet; when anyone mentions it to me, it makes me ill."

The exhibitionistic ambivalence appears with respect to the color of stockings. If the stocking is not a dark color, the leg appears uncovered. "I can't bear light stockings with a skirt that is a bit darker. It is as if one were just getting up out of bed."

Just as Yvonne has displaced on to the choice of clothing the problem of her acceptance or refusal of her femininity, she has transferred this same matter to various problems relating to her teeth. To summarize this problem, which is the central core of her neurosis, is mixed up with all the other difficulties that Yvonne has met along her path.

Our patient was fifteen when she had the first left premolar extracted. A bridge had to be made, and from that time on, this tooth has leaned forward slightly. This failure of the tooth to lie parallel to her other teeth has annoyed Yvonne, who began hating her left premolar. By contrast, the right premolar has become her favorite tooth. "It was like a miniature of myself."

One day our patient dreams that her favorite tooth broke off. This dream arouses very great anxiety. Her disproportionate affect shows very clearly that there is a castration anxiety hidden behind it. But, as luck would have it, several weeks later Yvonne actually breaks this tooth while she is eating something hard. At this instant she becomes like a mad woman; she stops everything she is doing, runs to the dentist who tells her that he will have to put a crown on it, and appalled by this possibility, she takes to bed. She can no longer sleep. The next day she goes to another dentist who tells her that the matter could be fixed with a gold filling, but that eventually the other facet of the molar will or might break off, which would necessitate removing the tooth.

Her uncertainty and her hesitation became such that for more than two months Yvonne runs, alternately, to one or the other of her dentists, without being able to come to a decision. A crown, it seems to her, would cover up her personality, or it would still be a penis covered with a hood. To remove the tooth would be a castration, which would be worse than anything. The most agreeable solution for her would be the gold filling, but the danger of the castration frightens her. The tooth under the crown is the equivalent of the clitoris which is an organ that is covered up. That would mean an acceptance of her femininity, something that seems impossible for her. The solution of the crown seems to cost less than the other, but to decide on the matter of its being "a better bargain" would be to accept her poverty. Poverty is still equivalent to femininity. (See below. For Yvonne, money is an equivalent of male strength.)

This hesitation can be a defense against a repressed complex. Yvonne associates gold with the idea of the stool of a sick child. She does not want to have stool in her mouth.

2. PENIS ENVY

Such a feeling of castration does not appear unless there is penis envy. More than one association in the above section has already shown this. Here are some excerpts that are even more explicit. "When I represent a sexual act to myself, I am the man. That seems more interesting to me. There is also a woman in me, but she is more hidden. What has contributed to make me this way are the groanings of my sister that I used to hear from my room. She told me that she did not enjoy it."

Actually, the masculinity complex goes further back, and the memory concerning the sister is probably a screen memory of an act that she in former times came upon unexpectedly between her parents. Here is a very striking dream. "You were sitting with your legs apart. There were other people behind you. I was a man and I had intercourse with you. This coitus was repeated several times and gave me a great deal of pleasure. Suddenly I realized that I am only a woman and woke up in the greatest excitement."

In this dream there comes through, beside the desire to possess the male organ, the desire to dispossess the male of his organ. This idea will appear in a more sadistic fashion in the associations to the following dream.

"I am a Negress and I have before me a little girl of six. She holds up her nightgown. She has a male organ, but the glans is missing. In order for her to urinate, she has to put on a sort of thimble made of skin, which has to be pierced. I was terribly ashamed. I believe that it was for this that I was all black. When I was six, I was very envious of the male organ." (Yvonne that day cannot give any other associations.) The next day she said, "I have begun to understand that I was also the little girl of the dream. I always felt that I was about to take a man's organs out of his trousers, because that one (of my several personalities) who wanted to do that, does not understand why this would be forbidden. When I would look at my brother's organs, I did not touch them—I would not have been able to do that. I had a positive horror of it, but I could make gestures to that end, I could try to do it, but it would not be *sang froid*. It would be a strong impulse that I would contemplate with terror and anxiety. At the school for social work, I felt compelled all the time to look at the professor because I would have wanted to unbutton him and touch him."

If there is such anxiety about committing this act, it is because this is an ambivalent act, a kind of deference toward the organ of power and a sadistic tendency to destroy it. This shows clearly in the associations that the patient brought to this dream several days later. "I find that the masculine organ is too big.[43] One has to do some harm to it, to render it powerless, but not entirely, for then I would be sorry and then it could not be remedied (see above, the same idea expressed with regard to the skirt). It is a way of diminishing the man and of repulsing him. I don't insist on doing it myself, but I should like it to be done. When, in my imagination, I castrate my father, I am sad unto death. That is

what happens to me in my life every time I do not obey
him. But if I let him have all his authority, I have the
impression that it is I who am being destroyed. For me,
the idea of strength, of power, of the capacity to do evil,
domination, the idea of stamping with rage—these are
associated with this organ."

What a fine profession of faith concerning ambivalence!

In some of her fantasies she sucks the father's organ.
At other times she imagines that she has returned to
her mother's breast, and while she is there, her father
has coitus with her mother. Yvonne took advantage of
this moment to cut off her father's organ—to castrate
him. By that fantasied act she expressed the desire
never to have known the organ of her father, since she
destroys it before being born.

In Yvonne, the motif of the child received from the
father, and serving as a substitute for the penis, has
not been lacking. "I used to stay home from school
because I wanted to play house and be the mother of
my dolls and because I wanted to keep house (to replace
my mother). As it was not my own house, I was
annoyed. Mama understood it and said, 'You would not
like us to adopt a child; it is you who would want to
have it.' But I had already lost my taste for working
around the house. It was too late for me to be stirred up
again. Jacques (the brother eight years younger) did
not want to be my child, he objected to it, but I took
possession of him just the same. I just stuck to him."

3. AMBIVALENCE TOWARD THE FATHER

Such an ambivalence attached to the organ of the
father cannot exist without an equivalent ambivalence
for the father himself.[44]

I should like to bring up a dream from the fifth month

of the analysis which shows how much difficulty Yvonne has thinking of her father without thinking of his penis. "I see a large horse with a filly at its side. I would like to mount the filly, but each time the big horse prevents me. He also prevents me from making the filly run."

Fragments of her associations follow. "The figure of the horse reminds me of my father. It is certain that he has been an obstacle to what I see in other men, but I don't know why. When I used to see him getting dressed, I looked through his shirt at his organs. I would have had to have been afraid. It seemed to me that they were too big for me. When I think of it, it is the little girl of five who again comes up in me. I remember that at the age of thirteen I one day saw my father coming back from the garden, his trousers unbuttoned, holding his penis. There was something white and frothy on it.

"It was when I began to revolt against my father that I wanted to be Mama's husband. I was fifteen, and it was at this time that I began to fight him. My blows came impulsively. From the ages of fifteen to twenty-two, Papa beat me. It seemed to me that he was hitting me on my genitals [projection of her wish to beat the paternal organ]. In any case, it gave me the impression of being directly genital. Papa had given me some pocket money, but I gave it back to him. I could not owe him anything; I hated him too much. [There is still an actual difficulty in buying clothes. The money also represents the paternal power, and she does not wish to accept it, for that would be to accept her femininity.] It is my father who prevents me from loving normally, from thinking normally, from clothing myself normally. When I have a skirt that is a little short, he is furious. Papa loves me only when I am ill."

If we see in these associations a very strong revolt, conscious and unconscious, against the father, we will find in the following dream a return to her ambivalence. "We went bathing. I had an old, torn bathing suit. This bathing place was near to a railroad station. A steam engine came into the station; it was to leave in a few moments. I saved myself, and a child. Then I was alone on a road. Then a bear followed me. He was terribly big and almost blind [her father is myopic]. Then I find myself on a shady road. All around me are people picknicking, people who were a little like my family. The road led down into a gorge with a big brook. The bear kept following me. He walked on his hind legs and had a wild sort of air. Everybody at the picnic kept looking at me. At that moment I began to laugh. I put on a white gown and walked on tiptoe so that the bear would not hear me. I laughed because I was surely on a wrong road. The bear had crossed the water and then he was old. Then I saw a shadow in the water. It was a water sprite; she had on a fine white costume and a cape which swayed in the breeze. She had her eyes closed. She was like a sleep walker, and climbed up the hill. We were looking at her. All of a sudden, the bear saw her, ran after her and caught her. She fell to the ground, she was indeed more dead than before. She pretended to be dead [laughs]. The bear was old; he was a pervert. He wanted to have sex relations with her. She was lying down with her head up. She was dead, and it did not go well. No. At bottom I can very well say that, because it was nothing but a dream. He straddled her legs, but only a little because she did not want to. She made believe she had fainted. Never in my life have I had so much trouble to express myself. That went on all the time, in the front and in the back, because she did not put her legs far enough apart. It failed; his penis was too big. It kept growing bigger all the time. Then someone came and seized the bear, and chased him off because he was perverted."

Yvonne brings a childhood memory to the first part of the dream. The whole family had gone bathing. That day she had looked at the sex organs of a little red haired girl who lived in the same pension with them. "I had found that Papa's organ was too big. I am making a sacrifice when I say that. I do not want to speak of the bear. I do not understand him very well. I am afraid that you will hit me. I ought not to speak of it, because then I would be much more afraid. It would be better to ignore it. At first the bear just kept on walking, only then he followed me. He had a very big paw which was injured. What he had in mind to do with me with his paw when he had crushed me, I did not want to know, that is why I got out of the water like a sleep walker.... The bear does not always represent the same person; at first he was young, it was you in the beginning, then it was my father, but an imaginary father, thought of, I don't know when. The scene with the water sprite bothers me a lot. The bear had an organ like a stallion. It was as large as a big cudgel. I do not understand how Mother could have endured Papa."

At the next session, Yvonne announced that she had vomited after leaving my house. She says nothing and then says that she is afraid of me and did not want to take off her hat. It is impossible for her to get back to the dream. This dream probably hides a coitus that she had come upon unexpectedly between her parents. But it is without doubt the reflection of her ambivalent attitude toward her father. If this dream could have been analyzed completely, I am certain that Yvonne would also have identified herself with the bear with the enormous penis. It is because the dream represents very different layers of the unconscious that its symbolism appeared so obscure to Yvonne.

4. AMBIVALENT ATTITUDE TOWARD THE MOTHER AND TOWARD WOMEN IN GENERAL

Yvonne has a strongly accented sadistic phase. She had been nursed by her mother the first week of her life. Then her mother suddenly lost her milk. At this moment a terribly painful weaning crisis begins. For three months Yvonne lost weight, refused all nourishment, and cried to be taken back to the breast; they had to let her have a pacifier to suck the whole time. Later, when this was taken away from her, there was another dramatic situation.

It has not been possible for us to reestablish by the analysis the various phases of love and of aggression which succeeded each other in Yvonne's attitude toward her mother. It appears that at age seven, at the birth of Jacques, the youngest in the family, Yvonne's oedipus complex had already been reversed. She did not have any jealousy toward her mother, but toward her father. She wanted to be not the mother, but the father of Jacques, and the husband of her mother. This motif comes to light in the following dream: "While my father was shaving, I stood behind him and got dressed. I had just put on my shirt when I noticed that it did not have any buttons. It would have had to be hooked up to a waist, but I did not want to put it on. I decided to put on a second pair of drawers which would hold up the other one."

Father is shaving, a castration symbol. She does not want the blouse, that is, she does not want female attire. She puts on two pairs of drawers the way a man does.

This first part of the dream shows that Yvonne would like to castrate her father in order to put herself in his place. Here is the second scene in the dream: "I see Mama in a bed. Next to her there is a double bed in which Annie was. I was sad at the idea of Mama's sensuality." Annie is the friend who has played a male role toward Yvonne and with whom she identifies herself in this dream in order to play a male role toward her mother. Her mother's being too sensual is only a projection of her own sense of guilt.

Today the ambivalent sentiments with respect to the mother dominate. "When I see her, all my childhood rushes back into my mind. I love her so much and then she makes me terribly angry. She robs me of my strength like someone whom one loves very much and who dies under your fingers. That makes me crazy. When I reproach her, it is always to make her stand up against Papa. She has too many scruples."

I mentioned above that neurotic women, in their homosexual attractions, often hide a simple identification with another woman who makes men suffer. We see here that Yvonne cannot carry on this identification with her mother and that she holds herself aloof from an identification which would oblige her to recognize a part of her femininity. This ambivalent attitude toward the father and mother dictates her extremely diverse attitudes with respect to women. On one of the first days of her analysis she said, "I despise women; they sense that I don't like them. That's what makes me afraid of them. I only approach women who approach me. I don't love any type of woman; the young ones are rivals; the older ones and the nonmarried ones make me ill, so much do I pity them. Those who are married I am jealous of. I love men in such a way that it sometimes seems to me that I am a man. Then I have masculine fantasies. Everyone has always said that I was very feminine [indeed, that is so]. When Papa is not there, I become the husband of Mama. I feel that she needs a man and I adapt myself to the role."

At the moment when she externalized her castration complex, she expressed a different attitude: "At these times I find all men ugly, their faces are ugly. I find women quite pretty; they are very sweet. It is just the opposite of what it was before."

One sees that Yvonne, in spite of her castration complex and of her masculinity complex, has not completely renounced her role as a woman. In a great many dreams she bears witness to a normal femininity. But let us describe her attitude in some of the homosexual fixations that she has had.

The first incident of importance took place at eighteen with Annie, a very boyish girl. They went on a trip together and slept in the same bed. "She caressed me and she hugged me. That gave me infinite pleasure. We came back from the trip looking perfectly terrible. After that, I ate nothing for weeks. I slept badly. There was an unbelievable attraction between us. With her, I entered into another world."

This episode gave Yvonne a brief outlet for her formerly repressed libido. But this could not last for long. When she returned home, she displaced this affection on to her older sister. But here incest came into play and the two sisters never hugged and never caressed each other. Later, this sister got married, and with jealousy entering in, the feelings became ambivalent.

From this time on, Yvonne could never realize a homosexual relation with her friends, for she always projected on to them the ambivalent feelings that she had had toward her sister. But with two friends she had desires to press close to them, as if she were a man. She succeeded very badly in analyzing her impressions in this sphere. "When I am with Jeanne, I don't know whether I love her or whether I hate her, but I feel that I can no longer get married. I would have to get married to her."

All the rest of these manifestations are stamped with a tremendous sense of guilt, illustrated in the following dream: "Once I dreamed about Jeanne. Now, at this moment, the dream annoys me, but at the time I had it, I was not annoyed by it. She was in bed. I was beside the bed. I loved her very much ... but I do not like to tell you this, because she did not do anything like that. She had ... it is disgusting ... I can't say it ... she had taken off her shirt, she had undressed, she wanted ... no, it's terrible, that is. She wanted me to look at her sex organs. I understood. At bottom I would have loved to see it. I found that it was she who wanted to show them. I said to her 'I want very much to see them, if you love me.' I looked at them. It is very dirty; it is disgusting. I found that it was ugly, that the slit was longer than in other people's."

5. THE ANAL COMPLEX

We must not forget that Yvonne is an obsessive individual and it is because of this that her homosexuality takes on a special character. We must now return to the question of clothes. After a year of analysis, here is the conversation Yvonne and I had, which was the point of departure for a new phase of the analysis:

"When you said to me 'You must get to the point of buying this coat,' that gave me a feeling of pain between my legs."

"Why between your legs?"

"I should not like to say. It isn't necessary. I don't know ... I'm not sure ... yes, because if I bought it, I would wish for sexual relations, and then I have a feeling of being perverse. I say perverse, because I would wish to have these relations with the men of my family. I feel that it would be morally wrong, but it would not be truly a perversion. There was a long period in my life when I bought clothes to arouse the men in my family. And then, it made me terribly angry because they used to make remarks about it."

The following day, she goes into detail and tells me that when her brother gave her money, the money seemed to possess the virile strength and power of her brother and she did not wish to spend it, especially since she would use it to buy feminine clothes; to exchange his virility for her femininity.

The virility, symbolized by the money, clearly shows that it concerns an anal regression, for we know the fecal significance of money. We refer to the excellent article of Dr. Odier[45] for this complete argument.

This interpretation brought back two memories which very clearly show the role of anal eroticism in Yvonne. When, as a child, she slept in her father's room, her bed was set at right angles to that of her father's. At this age she was afraid, and it probably concerned a repressed desire that her father might commit an anal coitus with her. Connected with this fantasy was the idea of castrating her father and of retaining the paternal penis in her rectum.

Here is another memory which seems to confirm this attitude. At age eight she was seized with such terror at the idea of being given a remedy against worms that she made her mother stay by her side all morning. She describes her anxiety, "I was afraid of seeing the worms come out, and even more afraid that only half of them would come out." She herself associates the idea of a worm to the penis of her father. To preserve the worm was to preserve masculinity, as, later on, to preserve money (and not spend it) was to acquire her brother's masculinity.

After having left her childhood memories, she declares that she is more interested in the anus than in the vagina. She masturbates by way of the anus. A true regression has been made into this erogenous zone. Yvonne does not go to the toilet, but uses a vessel of her own. "It seemed to me to be too big a sacrifice to go directly to the toilet. I cannot give up my stool without seeing it. I often say to myself, 'It would be necessary to look at it to see if there are any pinworms in it.' However, I do not have any real distress about my stools. For me, fecal matter has the value of strength. Sometimes it is so strong that it prevents me from having my periods. The displacement is such that my periods seem to me like a game of skittles."

The analysis, which is not yet completed, did not succeed in clearing up this complex. Still later, Yvonne presented a dream followed by very characteristic associations. She reported the dream as follows: "I see a worm stretched out. I hit it, then I crush its back while I say to myself, 'Ah yes, it couldn't stand it.' I have a sadistic pleasure." In this dream she replaces the worm (masculine organ) by an anus (a blow on the back). She associated the following: "I am ill at ease. The analysis makes me afraid. That makes me feel weak in my back, and that is the worst of my fear. I feel you arriving in my back. I think that if I lie down on my back I do not run any risk, but then I would be obliged to laugh. I would have to blindfold my eyes, but behind the bandage I would be afraid that perhaps you might surprise me...." She then spoke of the difficulty she had in renouncing being in love with me. "And then, I would have to renounce Jacques' being my child. He is no longer a child...."

It is likely that hidden behind these associations there is an anal theory of birth, and following that, an anal theory of coitus which could have been set off by her seeing sex contact between the bull and the cow.

The problem of homosexuality is also involved with this anal complex. At the moment of buying the dress, the fear of spending (fear of losing her virility) obliges Yvonne to choose a dress that will preserve certain masculine attributes as a compensation for the expenditure. I say certain attributes because, from other material, we know that the dress is supposed to arouse the sexuality of the older brother and of the father, and, as a consequence, ought to be essentially feminine. There follows an anal regression where Yvonne, renouncing any purchase at all, takes pleasure in old dirty clothes.

This internal sexual complexity obliges Yvonne to project now her femininity, now her masculinity, on to other women, with a choice of object which responds now to a masculine type, now to a feminine type. If there were room, we would have a chance to show that in each patient there is an important individual factor and that we cannot give a single formula of homosexual fixations which applies to all neurotics.

Conclusions

At the bottom of homosexual fixations, there is always a warped bisexuality derived from the fact that the woman has not been able to accept her femininity. The idea of castration and penis envy condition this refusal.

There are two stages of penis envy: the first in early childhood, animated throughout with urethral eroticism and the desire for exhibitionism; and the second, which reawakens precisely at the moment when the little girl realizes that she will never have a penis and that all women are in the same situation. It is then that she revolts and looks for compensations for her inferiority (fecal matter, breasts, child, and so on). This revolt can take quite different paths, such as those we have studied in the course of this report.

The desire for a child can be the point of departure for an identification with the mother and a normal development. But if the desires for masculinity have been awakened in too strong a fashion, this identification with a woman becomes impossible and the girl, like our patient, identifies herself with her father in order to give a child to her mother.

Following the cases, one sees that the homosexual fixations correspond to the patient's projections. Most often, the neurotic projects her femininity onto her mother (see our patient and Mme. Dupont[46]), and then onto other women who continue to represent the mother. But almost as often the patient, thwarted at not being able to satisfy her masculine tendencies, exaggerates her feminine qualities, becomes excessively narcissistic, and sees herself mirrored in some way in other women who have a high degree of feminine narcissism. In these cases the patient, while remaining a woman, projects her femininity on to others. It is an identification with herself. Finally, in the homosexual fixations, we see certain women refusing themselves to men and giving themselves to other women who have known how to make men suffer. According to Odier, it is an identification with their ideal of aggressiveness, with their superego.

In my own experience, I have never met in homosexual fixations (with the exception of lesbians who act out their homosexuality) women who attach themselves to other women who represent the male. I think that if this proves to be true it would be due to the fact that these neurotics are still ambivalent and that, if they do present homosexual fixations, they present in addition and at the same time, heterosexual fixations.

We have dealt briefly with a very large subject. We are far from exhausting it, but we shall feel that we have attained our ends if we have led any of our colleagues to take an interest in the subject and thus to provoke the publication of new clinical observations.

NOTES

1. Rickman, J. (1927). *Index Psychanalyticus, 1893-1926*. London: Hogarth.

2. Westphal, K. (1870). Sexual inversion, symptom of a neuropathic state. *Arch. fur Psychiatrie* 2.

3. Charcot and Magnan (1882). Congenital inversion. *Arch. de Neurologie* 3:54; Zuccarelli (1888). *Congenital inversion of the sexual instinct in two women.* Naples; Havelock Ellis, etc.

4. Muller, O. (1882). A case of woman-hating. *Zeitschrift fur Psychiatrie*, p. 94.

5. Chevallier (1893). *Sexual Inversion*. Paris.

6. Moll (1893). *Sexual Inversion Based on Official Documents*. (Trans. by Pactet and Romme.)

7. Laurent (1904). *Hermaphroditic and Gynecomastia in Bisexuals*. Fere (1902). *The Sexual Instinct*. Paris: Alcan, pp. 257 and 362.

8. Krafft-Ebing (1901). *Psychopathia Sexualis*. 1st ed. Stuttgart: Enke.

9. Freud, S. (1905). Three contributions to the sexual theory. Leipzig, Vienna: Deuticke.

———(1908). Hysterical fancies and their relation to bisexuality. *Zeitschrift fur Sexualwissenschaft* 1:27–34.

———(1910). A psychoanalytic study of Leonardo da Vinci. Leipzig, Vienna: Deuticke.

———(1911). Psychoanalytic remarks on a case of paranoia.

10. Freud, S. (1920). On the psychogenesis of a case of feminine homosexuality. *Zeitschrift fur Psychoanalyse* 6:1–24.

11. Hirschfeld, M. (1914). *Homosexuality in Man and Woman*. 2nd ed. Berlin: Marcus.

12. Lowenfeld, L. (1907). *Homosexuality and the Penal Law*. Weisbaden; Stier, Ewald (1912). On the etiology of homosexuality. *Monatsschriften fur Psych. und Neurol*. 32:221; Block. *Sexual Love in Our Time;* Roemer. *Die Urnische Familie*. Amsterdam; Sadger, J. (1909). On the etiology of homosexuality. *Med. Klinik;* Ferenczi, Sandor (1914). On the nosology of male homosexuality. *Zeitschrift fur Psychoanalyse* 2:131.

13. Laforgue, R. (1928). The psychoanalytic practice. *Revue francaise de Psa*. 2:239–340.

14. Sadger, J. (1919). Various thoughts on psychopathia sexualis. *Neue Artsliche Zentralzeitung.* May 15:6.

15. Senf, M. R. (1919). Psychosexual intuition. *Zeitschrift fur Sexualwissenschaft* 6:81-98.

16. Sadger, J. (1920). New studies on homosexuality. *Fortschrf. Me.* 37:1-32.

17. Allendy (1928). A case of eczema. *Revue francaise de Psa.* 2:327-340.

18. Ferenczi, S. (1927). Gulliver fantasies. *Zeitschrift fur Psychoanalyse* 13:379-396.

19. Abraham, K. (1920). Manifestations of the female castration complex. *Zeitschrift fur Psychoanalyse* 7:422-452; See also Jones, Ernest (1922). Remarks on Dr. Abraham's manifestations, etc. in *Zeitschrift fur Psychoanalyse* 8:329, and Eissler, Kurt, same title, *ibid.* p. 330. Previous to Abraham's article, there must be cited the two important articles of Ophuijsen, J.H.W. Van. Contributions to the masculine complex in women (1917). *Zeitschrift fur Psychoanalyse* 4:241-251; and Starcke, August. The castration complex (1921). *Zeitschrift fur Psychoanalyse* 7:91-32.

20. There would have to be a long chapter written on this symbolism; we should like here, in passing, to report a theory of the sexual act of one of our patients who suffered from a severe castration complex. This young girl, although she had had exact information about the sexual act for several years, refused up until the age of eighteen to recognize the reality, and she imagined that the sexual act took place through the breast. Not having any penis, she could not accept this mode of coitus; the breast, on the contrary, gave her a superiority over her male partner.

21. Freud, S. (1906-13). The taboo of virginity.

Sammlung kleiner Schriften zur Neurosenlehre. Leipzig, Vienna: Deuticke 4.

22. Eissler, K. *op. cit.*

23. Sachs, H. (1920). The wish to be a man. *Zeitschrift fur Psychoanalyse* 6:252-257.

24. Lewis, N.D.C. (1927 and 1928). Psychology of the castration complex. *Psychoanalytic Review* 14 and 15.

25. Horney, K. (1923). On the genesis of the castration complex in women. *Zeitschrift fur Psychoanalyse* 9:12-26.

———(1926). "The Flight from Womanhood." *Ibid.* 7:324-339.

26. We apologize for repeating here at such length works that are familiar to those who read German and English, but we believe it is necessary to do so for our French colleagues, the more so as these papers serve as a basis for a considerable number of points of psychoanalytic theory.

27. Simmel, G. *Philosophic Culture.*

28. Freud, S. (1924). The infantile genital organization of the libido. *Ges. Schriften* 5:232-237 has shown that in both sexes there exists an age when the child does not know more than one genital organ, that of the boy. That is what he has called the phallic phase.

29. This is not always the case and the fear of castration can also lead to a homosexual disposition in the male. The opposite reaction in the boy and the girl has been envisaged a little differently by Freud, who writes, "While the Oedipus of the boy disappears through the castration complex, the Oedipus of the girl, on the contrary, is made possible and is introduced by this complex" (the envy for a penis evolving into an envy of having a child by the father). This difference is due to the anatomical difference between the sexes. See Freud, S. (1925). Some psychical consequences of the

anatomical distinction between the sexes. *Zeitschrift fur Psychoanalyse* 11:401-410.

30. Abraham, K. (1924). A short study of the development of the libido, viewed in the light of mental disorders. *International Psa. Verlag* 96 pp.

31. Bousfield, P. (1924). The castration complex in women. *Psa. Review* 11:121-143.

32. Hinckle, B. (1920). On the arbitrary use of the terms "masculine" and "feminine." *Psa. Review* 7:15-30.

33. Deutsch, H. (1925). On the psychoanalysis of the female sexual functions. *Zeitschrift fur Psychoanalyse* 11:388-394.

34. Ferenczi, S. (1924). "Thalassa: Theory of Genitality." *Intern. Psa. Verlag.* 128 pp.

35. Freud, S. (1920). The psychogenesis of a case of homosexuality in a woman. *Zeitschrift fur Psychoanalyse* 6:1-24.

36. Sadger, J. (1921). *The Theory of Sexual Aberrations (Psychopathia Sexualis) on a Psychoanalytic Basis.* Leipzig, Vienna: Deuticke, pp. 173-185.

37. Laforgue, R. and Allendy (1924). *Psychoanalysis and Neuroses.* Paris: Payot, 251 pp.

38. Jones, E. (1935). The first development of female sexuality. *Zeitschrift fur Psychoanalyse* 21:331-341.

39. Here we recognize the type of the false victim described by Laforgue (see Laforgue, "The Psychoanalytic Practice," above.)

40. Sachs, H. (1929). One of the motive factors in the formation of superego in women. *Zeitschrift fur Psychoanalyse* 14:2. Sachs has shown that oral eroticism with its sadistic tendencies directed against the mother's breast then turns, as the final stage of the Oedipus complex, against the father's penis. Then, not being able to give free rein to her fantasies, the girl

detaches herself from her real father and introjects the father into herself. From that moment on, her sadism turns back against herself. It is a mechanism that we can find in the very repressed female homosexual, and it ought not to be rare among those women whom, as Jones has shown, have a very pronounced sadistic phase.

41. Freud, S. (1911). Psychoanalytic notes on an autobiographical account of a case of paranoia (dementia paranoides). *Jahrbuch fur Psa. Forschungen* 3:9–68.

42. Freud, S. (1919). A child is being beaten. *Zeitschrift fur Psychoanalyse* 5:151–172.

———The Economic Problem of Masochism. *Revue francaise de Psa.* 2:211.

43. This impression of an organ that is too big, which has also been pointed out by Karen Horney, comes from what Yvonne has always had in mind, the organ of her father that she used to see when she was a very little girl of six. In this connection, it is interesting to recall a screen memory she told me about in one of the first sessions of the analysis. At age five, when she left the hospital, her father took care of her ear for over a year. "He used to take me between his legs," she reported, "and he introduced some cotton into my ear. But his fingers were very big, and they often hurt me." It is quite possible that already at this age, when she was engaging in masturbation and when she had already had a thermometer in her vulva which had provoked such great anxiety in her, she had had the desire for her father to come in somewhere beside the ear. In any event, she always speaks of hands with great fear and one day she admitted that, while she was in the same bedroom as her father, she would have

liked to feel her father's hands against her organs. She found her father's hands much too big.

On the subject of the symbolism of hands for Yvonne, I may add that she kept on her gloves during the first months of the analysis, which was a way of not exhibiting her masculinity to me. Later, it often happened that she kept her hands hidden behind her back.

44. The result of this ambivalence has been that for several sessions Yvonne has sought to transfer her positive feelings to her brothers; she has been, successively, in love with all three of them, but very quickly the aggression primarily directed against the father was also transferred to the brothers. Since the age of eighteen, the loving feelings that she was able to have for other young people had merely been substitutes for feelings for her brothers; they were accompanied by the most violent guilt feelings, and all of them failed.

45. Odier, C. Psychoanalysis and money. *Revue francaise de Psa.*

46. Odier, C. The obsessional neurosis. *Revue francaise de Psa.*

REFERENCES

Abelan, E.L. (1971). The role of the father in the separation-individuation process. In *Separation-Individuation: Essays in Honor of Margaret S. Mahler*, ed. J.V. McDevitt and C.F. Settlage, pp. 229-253. New York: International Universities Press.

Abraham, K. (1920). Manifestations of the female castration complex. In *Selected Papers on Psycho-Analysis*, pp. 338-369. London: Hogarth Press, 1948.

Alexander, F. (1927). The neurotic character. *International Journal of Psycho-Analysis* 11:292-311, 1930.

——— (1956). A note to the theory of perversions. In *Perversions: Psychodynamics and Therapy*, ed. S. Lorand and M. Balint. New York: Random House.

Arlow, J.A. (1952). Psychodynamics and treatment of perversions (panel report). *Bulletin of the American Psychoanalytic Association* 8:315-327.

——— (1954). Perversions: theoretical and therapeutic aspects (panel report). *Journal of the American Psychoanalytic Association* 2:336-345.

———(1963). Conflict, regression, and symptom formation. *International Journal of Psycho-Anysis* 44:12-22.

Atkin, S. (1975). Ego synthesis and cognition in a borderline case. *Psychoanalytic Quarterly* 44:29-61.

Atkins, N.B. (1967). Comments on severe and psychotic regressions in analysis. *Journal of the American Psychoanalytic Association* 15:606-626.

Bacon, C.L. (1956). A developmental theory of female homosexuality. In *Perversions: Psychodynamics and Therapy*, ed. S. Lorand and M. Balint. New York: Random House.

Bak, R. (1956). Aggression and perversion. In *Perversions: Psychodynamics and Therapy*, ed. S. Lorand and M. Balint. New York: Random House.

———(1968). The phallic woman: the ubiquitious fantasy in perversions. *Psychoanalytic Study of the Child* 23:15-36.

———(1971). Object-relationships in schizophrenia and perversion. *International Journal of Psycho-Analysis* 52:235-242.

Barahal, H.S. (1953). Female transvestism and homosexuality. *Psychiatric Quarterly* 27:390-438.

Barry, H., Jr., and Barry, H., III (1972). Homosexuality and testosterone. *New England Journal of Medicine* 286:380-381.

Benedek, T. (1952). *Psychosexual Functions in Women*. New York: Ronald Press.

Bergler, E. (1943). The respective importance of reality and fantasy in the genesis of female homosexuality. *Journal of Criminal Psychopathology* 5:27-48.

——— (1944). Eight prerequisites for psychoanalytic treatment of homosexuality. *Psychoanalytic Review* 31:253-286.

——— (1951). *Counterfeit Sex*. New York: Grune and Stratton.

────── (1956). *Homosexuality: Disease or Way of Life.* New York: Hill and Wang.

──────(1959). *1000 Homosexuals: Conspiracy of Silence on Curing and Deglamorizing Homosexuality.* Paterson: Pageant Books.

Bergler, E., and Eidelberg, L. (1933). The breast complex in men. *Internationale Zeitschrift fur Psychoanalyse* 19:547-583.

Bergler, E., and Kroger, W. (1954). *Kinsey's Myth of Female Sexuality: The Medical Facts.* New York: Grune and Stratton.

Berliner, B. (1957). Preoedipal factors in neurosogenesis (panel report). *Journal of the American Psychoanalytic Association* 5:146-157.

────── (1971). Book review of *The Overt Homosexual.* In *Psychoanalytic Quarterly* 40:148-151.

Bibring, G.L. (1940). On an oral component in masculine inversion. *Internationale Zeitschrift fur Psychoanalyse* 25:124-130.

Bieber, I. (1967). On treating male homosexuals. *Archives of General Psychiatry* 16:60-63.

Bieber, I., et al. (1962). *Homosexuality.* New York: Basic Books.

Birk, L., Williams, G.H., Chasin, M., and Rose, L.L. (1973). Serum testosterone levels in homosexual men. *New England Journal of Medicine* No. 23 (December 6, 1973), pp. 1236-1238.

Bleuler, E. (1911). Dementia praecox. In *Monograph Series on Schizophrenia* No. 1:410-411. New York: International Universities Press, 1950.

Blos, P. (1961). *On Adolescence.* New York: Free Press.

Boehm, F. (1926). Homosexuality and oedipus complex. *Internationale Zeitschrift fur Psychoanalyse* 12:66-79.

—— (1930). The femininity complex in men. *International Journal of Psycho-Analysis* 11:444–469.

——(1933). Uber zwei typen von mannlichen homosexuellen. *Internationale Zeitschrift fur Psychoanalyse* 19:499–506.

Bonaparte, M. (1953). *Female Sexuality.* New York: International Universities Press.

Bonaparte, M., Freud, A., and Kris, E. (1954). *The Origins of Psycho-Analysis: Letters of Wilhelm Fliess.* Trans. E. Mossbacher and J. Strachey. New York: Basic Books.

Brierley, M. (1932). Some problems of integration in women. *International Journal of Psycho-Analysis* 13:433–488.

——(1935). Specific determinants in feminine development. *International Journal of Psycho-Analysis* 17:163–180.

Brill, A.A. (1934). Homoerotism and paranoia. *American Journal of Psychiatry* 13:957–974.

Bychowski, G. (1945). The ego of homosexuals. *International Journal of Psycho-Analysis* 26:114–127.

—— (1954). The structure of homosexual acting out. *Psychoanalytic Quarterly* 23:48–61.

—— (1956a). The ego and the introjects. *Psychoanalytic Quarterly* 25:11–36.

——(1956b). Homosexuality and psychosis. In *Perversions: Psychodynamics and Therapy,* ed. S. Lorand and Balint. New York: Random House.

Calder, K.T. (1958). Technical aspects of regression during psychoanalysis (panel report). *Journal of the American Psychoanalytic Association* 6:552–559.

Deutsch, H. (1925). *Psychoanalyse der Weiblichen*

Sexualfunktionen. Vienna: Internationale Psychoanalyse Verlag.

———(1932a). Female sexuality (also: Homosexuality in women). *International Journal of Psycho-Analysis* 14:34–56.

——— (1932b). On female homosexuality. *Psychoanalytic Quarterly* 1:484–510.

——— (1933). Motherhood and sexuality. *Psychoanalytic Quarterly* 2:476–488.

——— (1944). *The Psychology of Women.* Vols. 1 and 2. New York: Grune and Stratton.

Dickes, R. (1967). Severe regressive disruptions of the therapeutic alliance. *Journal of the American Psychoanalytic Association* 15:508–534.

——— (1975). Technical considerations on the therapeutic and working alliances. *International Journal of Psychoanalytic Psychotherapy* 4:1–24.

Dorpat, T.L. (1974). Internalization of the patient-analyst relationship in patients with narcissistic disorders. *International Journal of Psycho-Analysis* 55:183–188.

——— (1976). Structural conflict and object relations conflict. *Journal of the American Psychoanalytic Association* 24:855–875.

Edgecumbe, R., and Bergner, M. (1975). The phallic-narcissistic phase: the differentiation between preoedipal and oedipal aspects of development. *Psychoanalytic Study of the Child* 30:161–180. New York: International Universities Press.

Eidelberg, L. (1956). Analysis of a case of a male homosexual. In *Perversions: Psychodynamics and Therapy,* ed. S. Lorand and M. Balint. New York: Random House.

Eissler, K.R. (1953). The effect of the structure of the ego on psychoanalytic technique. *Journal of the American Psychoanalytic Association* 1:104–143.

———— (1958). Notes on problems of technique in the psychoanalytic treatment of adolescence: with some remarks on perversions. *Psychoanalytic Study of the Child* 13:223–254.

Eisner, H., and Kolansky, H. (1974). Psychoanalytic concepts on the treatment of preoedipal developmental arrests. Paper presented at the American Psychoanalytic Association, December.

Ellis, A. (1945). The sexual psychology of human hermaphrodites. *Psychosomatic Medicine* 7:108–125.

Ellis, H. (1895). Sexual inversion in women. *Alienist and Neurologist* 16:141–158.

————(1905). *Studies in the Psychology of Sex.* Vols. 1 and 2. New York: Random House, 1940.

Fairbairn, W.R.D. (1954). *An Object Relations Theory of Personality.* New York: Basic Books.

———— (1964). A note on the origin of male homosexuality. *British Journal of Medical Psychology* 37:31–32.

Fenichel, O. (1930a). The pregenital antecedents of the oedipus complex. In *Collected Papers* 1:181–204. New York: Norton, 1953.

———— (1930b). The psychology of transvestism. In *Collected Papers* 1: 167–180. New York: Norton, 1953.

———— (1934). Further light on the preoedipal phase in girls. In *Collected Papers* 1:241–289. New York: Norton, 1953.

———— (1945). *The Psychoanalytic Theory of Neurosis.* New York: Norton.

Ferenczi, S. (1909). More about homosexuality. In *Final Contributions to the Problems and Methods of*

Psychoanalysis, pp. 168-174. New York: Basic Books.

—— (1914). The nosology of male homosexuality (homoerotism). In *Contributions to Psychoanalysis,* pp. 296-318. New York: Brunner-Mazel, 1950.

—— (1916). *Contributions to Psychoanalysis.* Boston: Badger.

—— (1926). *Further Contributions to the Theory and Technique of Psychoanalysis.* London: Hogarth Press, 1950.

—— (1955). *Final Contributions to the Theory and Techniques of Psychoanalysis.* London: Hogarth Press.

Fischer, S.H. (1965). A note on male homosexuality and the role of women in ancient Greece. In *Sexual Inversion: The Multiple Roots of Homosexuality,* ed. J. Marmor, pp. 165-174. New York: Basic Books.

Fleischmann, O. (1960). Comments on the "choice of homosexuality" in males. In theoretical and clinical aspects of overt male homosexuality (panel report). *Journal of the American Psychoanalytic Association* 8:552-566.

Fliess, R. (1950). *The Psychoanalytic Reader.* New York: International Universities Press.

Ford, C.S., and Beach, F.A. (1951). *Patterns of Sexual Behavior.* New York: Hoeber-Harper.

Freedman, A. (1969). Book review of *The Overt Homosexual. Bulletin of the Philadelphia Association for Psychoanalysis* 19:51-54.

Freeman, T. (1955). Clinical and theoretical observations on male homosexuality. *International Journal of Psycho-Analysis* 36:335-347.

Freiberg, S.H. (1962). Homosexual conflicts in adolescence. In *Adolescents: The Psychoanalytic Ap-*

proach to Problems in Therapy, ed. S. Lorand and H.I. Schneer, pp. 78–112. New York: Harper.

Freud, A. (1949). Some clinical remarks concerning the treatment of cases of male homosexuality. Summary of a presentation before the International Psychoanalytical Congress, Zurich. *International Journal of Psycho-Analysis* 30:195.

———(1951). Homosexuality. *Bulletin of the American Psychoanalytic Association* 7:117–118.

———(1952). Studies in passivity. In *The Writings of Anna Freud,* Vol. 4, pp. 245–259. New York: International Universities Press, 1968.

———(1954). Problems of technique in adult analysis. *Bulletin of the Philadelphia Association for Psychoanalysis* 4:44–70.

———(1958). Adolescence. *Psychoanalytic Study of the Child* 13:255–278.

———(1968). *The Writings of Anna Freud.* Vol. 5, pp. 384–390. New York: International Universities Press.

Freud, S. (1905a). Three essays on the theory of sexuality. *Standard Edition* 7:125–245.

———(1905b). Psychical (or mental) treatment. *Standard Edition* 7:283–305.

———(1908). Hysterical fantasies and their relation to bisexuality. *Standard Edition* 9:155–167.

———(1910). Leonardo da Vinci and a memory of his childhood. *Standard Edition* 11:59–137.

———(1911). Psychoanalytic notes on an autobiographical account of a case of paranoia (dementia paranoides). *Standard Edition* 12:3–82.

———(1913). The disposition to obsessional neurosis. *Standard Edition* 12:311–327.

——(1914). On narcissism: an introduction. *Standard Edition* 14:67-105.

——(1917). *A General Introduction to Psychoanalysis.* New York: Garden City Publishing, 1943.

——(1918a). The taboo of virginity (contributions to the psychology of love III). *Standard Edition* 11:191-209.

——(1918b): From the history of an infantile neurosis. *Standard Edition* 17:3-104.

——(1919a). Lines of advance in psychoanalytic therapy. *Standard Edition* 17:159-168.

——(1919b). A child is being beaten. *Standard Edition* 17:175-204.

——(1920a). Psychogenesis of a case of homosexuality in a woman. *Standard Edition* 18:145-175.

——(1920b). *General Introductory Lectures.* New York: Garden City Publishing, 1943.

——(1921). Group psychology and the analysis of the ego. *Standard Edition* 18:67-134.

——(1922). Some neurotic mechanisms in jealousy, paranoia, and homosexuality. *Standard Edition* 18:221-235.

——(1923a). The infantile genital organization: an interpolation into the theory of sexuality. *Standard Edition* 19:141-147.

——(1923b). The ego and the id. *Standard Edition* 19:3-63.

——(1923c). Two encyclopedia articles. *Standard Edition* 18:235-263.

——(1924a). The passing of the oedipus complex. In *Collected Papers* 2:269-277. London: Hogarth Press, 1946.

——(1924b). The economic problem of masochism. *Standard Edition* 19:157-173.

————(1925a). Negation. *Standard Edition* 19:235-243.

————(1925b). Some psychical consequences of the anatomical distinction between the sexes. *Standard Edition* 19:243-261.

————(1927). Fetishism. In *Collected Papers* 5:198-204. London: Hogarth Press, 1950.

————(1931). Female sexuality. *Standard Edition* 21:233-247.

————(1933). The psychology of women. In *New Introductory Lectures on Psychoanalysis,* New York: Norton.

————(1935). Letter to a grateful mother. *International Journal of Psycho-Analysis* 32:331, 1951.

————(1938a). An outline of psycho-analysis. *Standard Edition* 23:144-205.

————(1938b). Splitting of the ego in the process of defence. *Standard Edition* 23:271-279.

————(1951). *Sigmund Freud's Letters: The Origins of Psychoanalysis.* New York: Basic Books.

Frosch, J. (1967). Severe regressive states during analysis. *Journal of the American Psychoanalytic Association* 15:491-508.

Galenson, E. (1976a). Psychology of women: (1) infancy and early childhood, (2) latency and early adolescence (panel report). *Journal of the American Psychoanalytic Association* 24:141-161.

————(1976b). Psychology of women: late adolescence and early adulthood (panel report). *Journal of the American Psychoanalytic Association* 24:631-647.

Galenson, E., and Roiphe, H. (1973). Object loss in early sexual development. *Psychoanalytic Quarterly* 42:73-90.

Galenson, E., Vogel, S., Blau, S., and Roiphe, H. (1975). Disturbance in sexual identity beginning at 18 months of age. *International Review of Psycho-Analysis* 2:389–397.

Gedo, J.E., and Goldberg, A. (1973). *Models of the Mind.* Chicago and London: University of Chicago Press.

Geleerd, E.R. (1957). Some aspects of psychoanalytic technique in adolescence. *Psychoanalytic Study of the Child* 12:263–283.

Gershman, H. (1957). Psychopathology of compulsive homosexuality. *American Journal of Psycho-Analysis* 17:58–77.

Gillespie, W.H. (1952). Notes on the analysis of sexual perversions. *International Journal of Psycho-Analysis* 33:397–402.

———(1956a). The general theory of sexual perversion. *International Journal of Psycho-Analysis* 37:396–403.

———(1956b). The structure and aetiology of sexual perversion. In *Perversions: Psychodynamics and Therapy*, ed. S. Lorand and M. Balint. New York: Random House.

Glass, S.J., et al. (1940). Sex hormone studies in male homosexuality. *Endocrinology* 26:590–594.

Glauber, I.P. (1956). The rebirth motif in homosexuality and its teleological significance. *International Journal of Psycho-Analysis* 37:416–421.

Glover, E. (1925). Notes on oral character formation. *International Journal of Psycho-Analysis* 6:131–154.

———(1933). The relation of perversion formation to the development of reality sense. *International Journal of Psycho-Analysis* 14:486–504.

———(1939). *Psychoanalysis.* London: Staples Press.

————(1960). *The Roots of Crime: Selected Papers on Psychoanalysis*. Vol. 2. London: Imago Publishing, 1960.

Grauer, D. (1955). Homosexuality and the paranoid psychoses as related to the concept of narcissism. *Psychoanalytic Quarterly* 24:516–526.

Greenacre, P. (1952). Pregenital patterning. *International Journal of Psycho-Analysis* 33:410–415.

———— (1968). Perversions: general considerations regarding their genetic and dynamic background. *Psychoanalytic Study of the Child* 23:47–63.

Greenson, R.R. (1964). On homosexuality and gender identity. *International Journal of Psycho-Analysis* 45:217–219.

———— (1967). *The Technique and Practice of Psychoanalysis*. Vol. 1. New York: International Universities Press.

Group for the Advancement of Psychiatry (1965). *Sex and the College Student*. Report No. 60. New York: GAP Publications.

Handelsman, I. (1965). The effects of early object relationships on sexual development: autistic and symbiotic modes of adaptation. *Psychoanalytic Study of the Child* 20:367–383.

Harley, M. (1961). Some observations on the relationship between genitality and structural development at adolescence. *Journal of the American Psychoanalytic Association* 9:434–460.

Hartmann, H., Kris, E., and Loewenstein, R. (1949). Notes on the Theory of Aggression. *Psychoanalytic Study of the Child,* 3/4:9–36.

———— (1964). Comments on the formation of psychic structure. In *Papers on Psychoanalytic Psychology*. New York: International Universities Press.

Heimann, P. (1955). A contribution to the re-evaluation of the oedipus complex—the early stages. In *New Directions in Psychoanalysis,* ed. M. Klein, P. Heinmann, and J. Moneykyrle. New York: Basic Books.

Henry, G.W. (1934). Psychogenic and constitutional factors in homosexuality. *Psychiatric Quarterly* 8:243–264.

———(1937). Psychogenic factors in overt homosexuality. *American Journal of Psychiatry* 93:889–908.

———(1941a). The homosexual delinquent. *Mental Hygiene* 25:420–442.

———(1941b). *Sex Variants: A Study of Homosexual Patterns.* New York: Hoeber-Harper.

Hirschfeld, M. (1914). Forms of relationships of homosexual men and women. *Geschlect Gesund* 8:11–12.

———(1916–1921). *Sexual Pathology.* New York: Emerson Books, 1940.

———(1938). *Sexual Anomalies and Perversion. Revised ed.* London: Encyclopedia Press, 1953.

Hoffer, W. (1954). Defense process and defense organization: their place in psychoanalytic technique. *International Journal of Psycho-Analysis* 35:194–198.

Horney, K. (1925). The flight from womanhood. *International Journal of Psycho-Analysis* 7:324–339.

Jacobson, E. (1964). *The Self and Object World.* New York: International Universities Press.

Jones, E. (1912). *Papers on Psychoanalysis.* 5th ed. London: Balliere, Tindall and Cox, 1948.

———*(1923). Essays in Applied Psychoanalysis.* London, Vienna: International Psychoanalytic Press.

—— (1927). Early development of female homosexuality. *International Journal of Psycho-Analysis* 8:459–472.

—— (1933). The phallic phase. *International Journal of Psycho-Analysis* 14:1–33.

Joseph, E.D. (1965). *Beating Fantasies: Regressive Ego Phenomena in Psychoanalysis.* The Kris Study Group of the New York Psychoanalytic Institute, Monograph I. New York: International Universities Press.

Jucovy, M.E. (1976). Initiation fantasies and transvestism. *Journal of the American Psychoanalytic Association* 24:525–545.

Jung, C. (1916). *Psychology of the Unconscious.* New York: Moffet, Yard.

Kallman, F.S. (1952). Comparative twin studies of the genetic aspects of male homosexuality. *Journal of Nervous and Mental Diseases* 115:283–298.

Kardiner, A. (1939). *The Individual and His Society: The Psychodynamics of Primitive Social Organization.* New York: Columbia University Press.

—— (1954). *Sex and Morality.* Indianapolis: Bobbs-Merrill.

Karlin, A. (1971). *Sexuality and Homosexuality.* New York: Norton.

Kernberg, O.F. (1970). Factors in the psychoanalytic treatment of narcissistic personalities. *Journal of the American Psychoanalytic Association* 18:51–85.

—— (1974) Barriers to falling and remaining in love. *Journal of the American Psychoanalytic Association* 22:486–511.

—— (1975). *Borderline Conditions and Pathological Narcissism.* New York: Jason Aronson.

Khan, M. Masud R. (1965). The function of intimacy and acting out in perversions. In *Sexual Behavior and the Law,* ed. R. Slovenko. pp. 397–413. Springfield, Ill.: Charles C Thomas

Kinsey, A., et al. (1948). *Sexual Behavior in the Human Male.* Philadelphia: W.B. Saunders.

Klaif, F.S. (1961). Homosexuality and paranoid schizophrenia. *Archives of General Psychiatry* 4:84–90.

Klaif, F. S. and Davis, C. A. (1960). Homosexuality and paranoid schizophrenia. *American Journal of Psychiatry* 116:12.

Klein, H.R., and Horwitz, W.A. (1949). Psychosexual factors in the paranoid phenomena. *American Journal of Psychiatry* 105:9.

Klein, M. (1952). Notes on some schizoid mechanisms. In *Developments in Psycho-Analysis,* ed. M. Klein, P. Heimann, S. Isaacs, and J. Riviere. London: Hogarth Press.

———(1954). *The Psychoanalysis of Children.* London: Hogarth Press.

Klein, M., Heimann, P., Isaacs, S., and Riviere, J. (1952). *Developments in Psycho-Analysis.* London: Hogarth Press.

Kohut, H. (1974). *The Analysis of the Self: A Systematic Approach to the Psychoanalytic Treatment of Narcissistic Personality Disorders.* New York: International Universities Press.

Kolansky, H., and Eisner, H. (1974). The psychoanalytic concept of the preoedipal developmental arrest. Paper presented at the American Psychoanalytic Association, December.

Kolb, L.C., and Johnson, A.M. (1955). Etiology and therapy of overt homosexuality. *Psychoanalytic Quarterly* 24:506–515.

Kolodny, R.C., Masters, W.H., Hendrix, J., and Toro, G. (1971). Plasma testosterone and semen analysis in male homosexuals. *New England Journal of Medicine* 285:1170–1178.

Krafft-Ebing, R. von (1901). Neue studien auf dem gebiete der homosexualitat. *Jahrbuch fur Sex.*

———(1906). *Psychopathia Sexualis* with special reference to the antipathic sexual instinct. Brooklyn, N.Y.: Physicians and Surgeons Book Co., 1922.

———(1924). *Psychopathia Sexualis.* Stuttgart: Ferdinand Enke.

Krich, A. M. (1958). *The Homosexuals.* New York: Citadel Press.

Kris, E. (1955). Neutralization and sublimation: observations on young children. *Psychoanalytic Study of the Child* 10:30–47.

Lacey, W.K. (1968). *The Family in Ancient Greece.* Ithaca: Cornell University Press.

Lagache, D. (1950). Homosexuality and jealousy. *International Journal of Psycho-Analysis* 31:24–31.

Lampl–de Groot, J. (1933). Problems of femininity. *Psychoanalytic Quarterly* 2:489–518.

Lichtenstein, H. (1961). Identity and sexuality. *Journal of the American Psychoanalytic Association* 9:179–260.

Litin, E., Giffin, M., and Johnson, A. (1956). Parental influence in unusual sexual behavior in children. *Psychoanalytic Quarterly* 25:37–55.

Loewenstein, R. M. (1935). Phallic passivity in men. *International Journal of Psycho-Analysis* 16:334–340.

———(1957). A contribution to the psychoanalytic theory of masochism. *Journal of the American Psychoanalytic Association* 5:197–231.

Lorand, S. (1930). Fetishism in statu nascendi. *International Journal of Psycho-Analysis* 11:419–427.

————(1956). The theory of perversions. In *Perversions: Psychodynamics and Therapy,* ed. S. Lorand and M. Balint, pp. 290-307. New York: Random House.

Lorand, S., and Balint, M. (1956). *Perversions: Psychodynamics and Therapy.* New York: Random House.

Lorand, S., and Schneer, H.I. (1962). *Adolescents: The Psychoanalytic Approach to Problems in Therapy.* New York: Harper.

McDevitt, J.B., and Settlage, C.F. (1971). *Separation-Individuation; Essays in Honor of Margaret S. Mahler.* New York: International Universities Press.

Mahler, M.S. (1967). On human symbiosis and the vicissitudes of individuation. *Journal of the American Psychoanalytic Association* 15:740-763.

————(1968). *On Human Symbiosis and the Vicissitudes of Individuation, Vol. I: Infantile Psychosis.* New York: International Universities Press.

Mahler, M.S., and Gosliner, B.J. (1955). On symbiotic child psychosis: genetic, dynamic and restitutive aspects. *Psychoanalytic Study of the Child* 10:195-211.

Mahler, M.S., Pine, F., and Bergman, A. (1975). *The Psychological Birth of the Human Infant.* New York: Basic Books.

Mantegazza, P. (1932). *Sexual Relations of Mankind.* New York: Anthropological Press.

Marmor, J. (1965). *Sexual Inversion.* New York: Basic Books.

Menninger, K. (1954). In Arlow Panel Report 1954.

Miller, W.L. (1956). The relation between submission and agression in male homosexuality. In *Perversions: Psychodynamics and Therapy,* ed. S. Lorand and M. Balint, New York: Random House.

Modell, A.H. (1968). *Object Love and Reality.* New York: International Universities Press.

Money, J., and Ehrhardt, A.A. (1972). *Man and Woman, Boy and Girl.* Baltimore: Johns Hopkins Press.

Nacht, S., Diatkine, R., and Favreau, J. (1956). The ego in perverse relationships. *International Journal of Psycho-Analysis* 37:404–413.

Nagera, H. (1966). *Early Childhood Disturbances, The Infantile Neurosis, and The Adult Disturbances.* New York: International Universities Press.

Natterson, J.M. (1976). The self as a transitional object: its relationship to narcissism and homosexuality. *International Journal of Psychoanalytic Psychotherapy* 5:131–143.

Nunberg, H. (1938). Homosexuality, magic and aggression. *International Journal of Psycho-Analysis* 19:1–16.

———(1947). Circumcision and problems of bisexuality. *International Journal of Psycho-Analysis* 28:145–179.

Opler, M.K. (1965). Anthropological and cross-cultural aspects of homosexuality. *In Sexual Inversion: The Multiple Roots of Homosexuality,* ed. J. Marmor, pp. 108–123. New York: Basic Books.

Oraison, M. (1953). *Illusions and Anxiety.* New York: Macmillan.

Orgel, S.Z. (1968). The development of a perversion— homosexuality and associated transvestism. *Bulletin of the Hillside Hospital* 17(4):405–409.

Ostow, M., ed. (1974). *Sexual Deviation. Psychoanalytic Insights.* New York: Quadrangle.

Ovesey, L. (1969). *Homosexuality and Pseudohomosexuality.* New York: Science House.

————(1976). Pseudohomosexuality. In *Medical Aspects of Human Sexuality* 10:147.

Ovesey, L. and Person, E. (1976). Transvestism: a disorder of the sense of self. *International Journal of Psychoanalytic Psychotherapy* 5:219–235.

Payne, E.C. (1977). Psychoanalytic treatment of male homosexuality (panel report). *Journal of the American Psychoanalytic Association* 25:183–199.

Payne, S.M. (1939). Some observations on the ego development of the fetishist. *International Journal of Psycho-Analysis* 20:161–170.

Person, E., and Ovesey, L. (1974a). The transsexual syndrome in males: I primary transsexualism. *American Journal of Psychotherapy* 28:4–10.

————(1974b). The transsexual syndrome in males: II. secondary transsexualism. *American Journal of Psychotherapy* 28:174–195.

Peto, A. (1967). Dedifferentiations and fragmentations during analysis. *Journal of the American Psychoanalytic Association* 15:534–551.

Rado, S. (1933). The fear of castration in women. *Psychoanalytic Quarterly* 2:425–475.

————(1940). A critical examination of the concept of bisexuality. *Psychosomatic Medicine* 2:459–467.

————(1949). An adaptational view of sexual behavior. In *Psychosexual Development in Health and Disease,* ed. P.H. Hoch and J. Zubin. New York: Grune and Stratton.

————(1956). Schizotypal organization: preliminary report on a clinical study of schizophrenia. In *Psychoanalysis of Behavior: The Collected Papers of Sandor Rado,* vol. 2, pp. 1–11. New York: Grune and Stratton, 1962.

Rainer, J.D., Mesnikoff, A., Kolb, L.C., and Carr, A. (1960). Homosexuality and heterosexuality in identical twins. *Psychosomatic Medicine* 22:251-259.

Roiphe, H. (1968). On an early genital phase. *Psychoanalytic Study of the Child* 23:348-365.

Rosen, V.H. (1957). Preoedipal factors in neurosogenesis (panel report). *Journal of the American Psychoanalytic Association* 5:146-157.

Rosenfeld, H.A. (1949). Remarks on the relation of male homosexuality to paranoia, paranoid anxiety and narcissism. *International Journal of Psycho-Analysis* 30:36-47.

Ross, N. (1960). An examination of nosology according to psychoanalytic concepts (panel report). *Journal of the American Psychoanalytic Associaton* 8:535-551.

Rubinfine, D.L. (1959). Some theoretical aspects of early psychic functioning (panel report). *Journal of the American Psychoanalytic Association* 7:561-576.

Sachs, H. (1923). On the genesis of sexual perversions. *Internationale Zeitschrift fur Psychoanalyse* 9 (2):172-182. Trans. Hella Freud Bernays, 1964; New York Psychoanalytic Institute Library; this volume, Appendix B.

Sadger, J. (1909). Zur aetiologie der contraren sexualempfindungen. *Med. Klinik*

——(1914). Sexual perversions. *Jahrbuch fur Psychoanalyse* 6:296-313.

——(1915). Neue forschungen zur homosexualitat. *Berliner Klinik,* Fev.

Saussure, J. de (1971). Some complications in self-esteem regulation caused by using an archaic image of the self as an ideal. *International Journal of Psycho-Analysis* 52:87-97.

Saussure, R. de (1929). Homosexual fixations in neurotic women. *Revue française de Psychoanalyse* 3:50-91. Trans. Hella Freud Bernays, 1961; New York Psychoanalytic Institute Library; this volume, Appendix C.

Scharfman, M.A. (1976). Perverse development in a young boy. *Journal of the American Psychoanalytic Association* 24:499-524.

Segal, M.M. (1965). Transvestism as impulse and as a defense. *International Journal of Psycho-Analysis* 46:209-217.

Sherman, W., and Sherman, T. (1926). The factor of parental attachment in homosexuality. *Psychoanalytic Review* 13:32-37.

Silber, A. (1961). Object choice in a case of male homosexuality. *Psychoanalytic Quarterly* 3:497-504.

Socarides, C.W. (1958). The function of moral masochism: with special reference to the defense processes. *International Journal of Psycho-Analysis* 39:1-11.

——(1960a). The development of a fetishistic perversion: the contribution of preoedipal phase conflict. *Journal of the American Psychoanalytic Association* 8:281-311.

——(1960b). Theoretical and clinical aspects of overt male homosexuality (panel report). *Journal of the American Psychoanalytic Association* 8:552-556.

——(1962). Theoretical and clinical aspects of overt female homosexuality (panel report). *Journal of the American Psychoanalytic Association* 10:579-592.

——(1963). The historical development of theoretical and clinical concepts of overt female homosexuality. *Journal of the American Psychoanalytic Association* 11:386-414.

————(1965). Female homosexuality. In *Sexual Behavior and the Law,* ed. R. Slovenko. Springfield, Ill: Charles C Thomas.

————(1968). A provisional theory of etiology in male homosexuality: a case of preoedipal origin. *International Journal of Psycho-Analysis* 49:27–37.

————(1969). The psychoanalytic therapy of a male homosexual. *Psychoanalytic Quarterly* 38:173–190.

————(1970). A psychoanalytic study of the desire for sexual transformation: (transsexualism): the plaster of paris man. *International Journal of Psycho-Analysis* 51:341–349.

————(1973). Sexual perversion and the fear of engulfment. *International Journal of Psychoanalytic Psychotherapy* 2:432–448.

————(1974). Homosexuality. In *The American Handbook of Psychiatry,* vol. 3, ed. S. Arieti, 2nd ed., pp. 291–315. New York: Basic Books.

————(1975). Considerations on the psychoanalytic therapy of overt male homosexuality: I. general problems. Paper presented at the American Psychoanalytic Association, December.

————(1979—in press). A unitary theory of sexual perversions. In *Contemporary Sexuality: Contributions from Psychoanalysis,* ed. B.T. Karasu and C.W. Socarides. New York: International Universities Press.

Sperling, M. (1963). The analysis of a transvestite boy: a contribution to the genesis and dynamics of transvestism. *Psychoanalytic Quarterly* 32:470–471.

Sperling, O. (1956). Psychodynamics of group perversions. *Psychoanalytic Quarterly* 25:56–65.

Spitz, R.A. (1959). *A Genetic Field Theory of Ego Formation.* New York: International Universities Press.

Stoller, R.J. (1964). A contribution to the study of gender identity. *International Journal of Psycho-Analysis* 45:220–226.

———(1968). *Sex and Gender.* New York: Jason Aronson.

———(1975). *Sex and Gender. Vol. 2 The Transsexual Experiment.* New York: Jason Aronson.

Stolorow, R.D. (1975). The narcissistic function of masochism (and sadism). *International Journal of Psycho-Analysis* 56:441–448.

Stolorow, R.D., and Lachmann, F.M. (1978). The developmental prestages of defenses: diagnostic and therapeutic implications. *Psychoanalytic Quarterly* 47:73–102.

Stolorow, R.D. (1977). Psychosexuality and the representational world. Presented before National Psychological Association for psychoanalysis, November.

Storr, A. (1964). *Sexual Deviation.* Baltimore: Penguin Books.

Symposium: Acting Out (1968). *International Journal of Psycho-Analysis* 49:164–230.

Thorner, H.A. (1949). Notes on a case of male homosexuality. *International Journal of Psycho-Analysis* 30:31–35.

Tourney, G., Petrilli, A.J., and Hatfield, L.M. (1975). Hormonal relationships in homosexual men. *American Journal of Psychiatry* 132:288–290.

Van der Leeuw, P.J. (1958). The preoedipal phase of the male. In *The Psychoanalytic Study of the Child* 13:352–374. New York: International Universities Press.

Volkan, V.D. (1973). Transitional fantasies in the analysis of a narcissistic personality. *Journal of the American Psychoanalytic Association* 21: 351–376.

————(1974). Transsexuals: a different understanding. In *Marital and Sexual Counseling in Medical Practice,* ed. D.W. Abse, E. Nash, and L. Louden, pp. 383–404. New York: Harper.

————(1976). *Primitive Internalized Object Relations.* New York: International Universities Press.

Wallerstein, R.S. (1967). Reconstruction and mastery in the transference psychosis. *Journal of the American Psychoanalytic Association* 15:551–584.

Weinshel, E.M. (1966). Severe regressive states during analysis. *Journal of the American Psychoanalytic Association* 14:538–568.

Weiss, E. (1950). *The Principles of Psychodynamics.* New York: Grune and Stratton.

————(1960). *The Structure and Dynamics of the Human Mind.* New York: Grune and Stratton.

Weideman, G.H. (1962). Survey of psychoanalytic literature on overt male homosexuality. *Journal of the American Psychoanalytic Association* 10:386–409.

————(1974). Homosexuality, a survey. *Journal of the American Psychoanalytic Association* 22:651–696.

INDEX